Lord (Bernard) Donoughue is a British politician, academic, businessman and author. He created and headed the No. 10 Policy Unit under Harold Wilson and Jim Callaghan and was a key source for *Yes, Minister* and *Yes, Prime Minister*. He became a Labour peer in 1985 and served as Parliamentary Under-Secretary of State at the Ministry of Agriculture, Fisheries and Food under Blair. His books include *Herbert Morrison: Portrait of a Politician* (with G. W. Jones); *Prime Minister: Conduct of Policy Under Harold Wilson and James Callaghan, 1974–79; The Heat of the Kitchen: an autobiography; Downing Street Diary Volume 1: With Harold Wilson in No. 10* and *Downing Street Diary Volume 2: With James Callaghan in No. 10.*

Praise for Bernard Donoughue's previous Diaries

'fascinating' – *Financial Times*

'fresh and vivid' – *Literary Review*

'superb' – *Daily Mail*

'Donoughue offers fascinating insights' – *Times Literary Supplement*

BERNARD DONOUGHUE

WESTMINSTER DIARY

A RELUCTANT MINISTER UNDER TONY BLAIR

I.B. TAURIS
LONDON · NEW YORK

Published in 2016 by
I.B.Tauris & Co. Ltd
London • New York
www.ibtauris.com

ISBN: 978 1 78453 650 3
eISBN: 978 0 85772 861 6
ePDF: 978 0 85772 840 1

A full CIP record for this book is available from the British Library
A full CIP record is available from the Library of Congress

Library of Congress Catalog Card Number: available

Typeset by Riverside Publishing Solutions
Printed and bound in Sweden by ScandBook AB

Contents

Illustrations

All photographs are taken from the author's personal collection

1. Looking uncharacteristically optimistic before becoming a minister
2. Snooping in Northern Ireland with Minister Lord Dubs, 1997
3. The Labour government ministers in the House of Lords, 1998
4. Very slowly spin bowling for the Lords (aged 62) against the Commons at the Oval, author middle back row
5. Receiving the award for Best Horse Race Tipster by a seemingly unconvinced John Prescott
6. As minister of farming and food, 1997
7. As minister visiting a British Food (and apparently fancy dress) Fair
8. Sharing discreet Palace gossip with the Queen's former press secretary, Charles Anson
9. Celebrating the prospect of ever growing food subsidies in Central Europe, 1998
10. Beloved Honey in a terrier race on ministerial visit to an agricultural fair in Devon
11. With Tony Blair and comedian Stephen Fry (and partly obscured writer John Mortimer), 1998
12. Honey bravely attacks a stuffed fox at an agricultural fair, friend Lady Mallalieu and Lord Mason on left
13. In the garden at Fox's Walk with my two favourite ladies, Sarah and Honey
14. With Sarah on the beach in Ireland, 1997
15. Escaping from MAFF to Céret with close friend, publisher Graham Greene
16. In the Pyrenees with Sarah
17. On the terrace at Mas au Rocher reflecting on the Common Agriculture Policy
18. Relaxing in the Pyrenees with Sarah and her daughter Sasha

Preface

It is 36 years since I laid down my pen after finishing the last page of a weighty diary portraying the sad end of James Callaghan's Labour government. Exhausted and depressed after leaving 10 Downing Street on Friday 4 May 1979, and feeling my life henceforward might be of little interest, even to me, I ceased the nightly grind of filling those scores of handwritten notebooks. The latter were stored, to be unopened for many years, in the vaults of the NatWest Bank, hopefully safe from the prying eyes of MI5, possibly pursuing breaches of the Official Secrets Act.

However, for diarists, the itch and urge to record life's events, however trivial, can never be fully suppressed. That is especially true when we diarists can use the excuse that we are describing public life, in parliament and in government, claiming it is of 'public interest' and not just pruriently observing the private lives of others. So in late 1995, with the prospect of participating in another Labour government under the then charismatic leadership of Tony Blair, I resumed the disciplined routine of observing, remembering, taking detailed notes, and recording my daily life – though by then not in illegible longhand, but on a baffling computer word processor. The following book is a heavily edited version of that endeavour.

Any diarist should apologise in advance, as I do now, for any offence given to those appearing in his published work. The writer is of course aware that most readers enjoy sharp comments on the quirks of their fellows, but often object to their own portraits (unless full of well-earned praise). That is only human. But the writer should acknowledge that a diarist's trade is usually morally ambivalent. Much that is recorded is done so in possible breach of society's unwritten rules concerning the conventions or private friendship, where conversations and shared confidences are conducted on the assumption that they are not in the full public domain – which they become on publication.

This dilemma is particularly apparent when revealing detailed events inside government. There, ministers, and especially public servants, offer advice and criticisms on the assumption that they are not subject to embarrassing early revelation. Of course, that constraint of privacy is not normally assumed to operate forever, neither with public servants nor especially with private individuals. Otherwise, no serious factual account could ever be written of our national history. The price of achieving historical evidence is that documents such as diaries must reveal facts. But there needs to be some discretion and protection of individual participants over a reasonable time period.

That is one main reason why, with my diaries of the 1974–79 governments, I waited some 30 years before publication (there was then a so-called '30 year rule', although not all were aware of its implications). In the present case, I have waited around 20 years. Some fellow members of the Blair government have felt less constrained and published memoirs soon after leaving office. They may have been justified in the new social climate of instant reaction and revelation. My personal inclination now is not to have a precise timescale, but to wait for what seems to me a decent period. Individuals will vary in assessing that.

I am aware that the effects of critical diary comments on individual sensitivities are difficult to assess and probably have no universally accepted timescale. Broadly, I hope that I am not too intolerant or malicious a person – although I have observed that such characteristics have previously greatly pleased journalist reviewers and assisted the sales of some diaries. I – although perhaps not my publisher – will live happily with that personal failing.

I trust that this diary will offer an interesting picture of a slice of London's political and social life during the mid-1990s – or at least of one person's life at that time. I was then privileged to be, as I still am, a member of the House of Lords. Despite the many criticisms of the House by those who attack its undoubted failings, it was and is a remarkable institution. It has contained some of the most distinguished members of British public life, who have reached a mature stage at which they can reflect with some objectivity on how our political activities might be better conducted. It is admittedly also a privileged social club, with all the complacency that can go with that. But it is a gathering of human experience and quality that I have rarely encountered elsewhere. It was then, and is still, the only House of Parliament that seriously scrutinises, holds to public account, and frequently defeats in the division lobbies the over-powerful executive government of the United Kingdom. As such, as a non-elected body, ironically it does exercise a democratic function.

I do not expect that the House of Lords will survive much longer in its present form, especially now its membership is being, deliberately or unwittingly, inflated to a point of discredit. But I trust that these diaries, with their glimpses of daily life in the Upper Chamber, will convey to future generations its nature in the 1990s, exhibiting both its excellences and its curious frailties.

At the heart of the diaries, apart from my personal, political and social life, lies the progress towards a New Labour government under Tony Blair. When achieved, this brought to an end 18 years of controversial and often radical government under Margaret Thatcher and John Major, which itself had terminated the post-war cross-party consensus that ruled Britain with remarkable success until collapsing in the 1978–79 Winter of Discontent (described in my previous *Downing Street Diary: With James Callaghan in No. 10*, Jonathan Cape, 2008).

Personally, I never saw myself as New Labour or a 'Blairite', although I admired his work in making the Labour party electable again. I preferred the self-description 'Antique Labour'. But it is easy now, 20 years later, with the heavy criticisms facing him within his own party, to forget what a political phenomenon Blair seemed in the mid-1990s. He inspirationally revived his party to win three general elections and apparently disguised what now seems a process of long political decline. He also excited the broader British public for some years and was even admired by the rising generation of young Tory leaders, such as Cameron and Osborne, who governed us later.

Blair's subsequent stark decline from political favour (fully documented in my later unpublished diaries) should not be allowed to hide from history the remarkable impact that he and his New Labour colleagues made on British politics for a decade. Some of that impact is recorded (not always uncritically) in these diaries. Much of the policy detail described below concerns the fields of arts, sports, media and agriculture, where I was involved as a government minister or opposition frontbench spokesman. Blair's apparent obeisance to the modern media, and especially to Rupert Murdoch (not a particular hero of the author), gives repeated offence to the diarist. His perhaps most successful and historic project, launching a radical new peace settlement in Northern Ireland, is seen in its early stages here, with my personal if secret and unofficial involvement.

A few early readers of this diary have commented on the strong presence of horseracing in this 'political' book (much more lost in editing). I make no apology for that. Racehorses have always had an affectionate, if financially negative, role in my life. One in particular, the aptly named

'Peers Folly', runs through these pages, although too rarely on any racecourses. He was beautiful and important to me. Diarists should be allowed some self-indulgent weaknesses.

This diary volume concludes in mid-story, with me still a minister. Twenty further volumes of narrative stand on my bookshelves, reaching to the present day. I do not expect that future readers or publishers will be burdened with all of them. For the moment I trust that this book will give some pleasure in offering a contemporary picture of a particular political life in mid-1990s Britain.

I wish to offer my thanks to my daughter Kate for her love and her great editing and computer skills; to my loving wife Sarah for her kind tolerance at my frequent emotional absences absorbed in these earlier times; to my friends from most (not all) political parties who provide the fabric of life recorded in these diaries; and to my editor Joanna Godfrey for her great support.

THE DIARIES

Christmas Day, 25 December 1995

Christmas started at Sarah's house, in Shurlock Row, Berkshire, with a visit to Midnight Mass. En route I called, as local tradition requires, at the great Bell Inn at nearby Waltham St Lawrence. The village youths massed cheerfully round the blazing log fire, ready to tipple out into the 15th century Anglican church next door, its bells already peeling beautifully.

My nearest Catholic church at Twyford was packed for the lovely carols before mass. I do wish that I could sing in tune. I would exchange any other talents I have for the ability to sing properly and play an instrument. (In my forties I tried to master the clarinet but quickly capitulated.)

Christmas morning was bright and cold. The day followed its familiar rituals, with too much to eat, too many presents and too little exercise. Overall a lovely day, with no reminders of my bleak childhood Christmases.

Sitting here at my desk at the end of 1995, it is strange but nostalgic to be again writing my diary. It is 16 years since I left 10 Downing Street, exhausted and depressed, and stopped my nightly record of the Wilson and Callaghan governments. I then moved from public to private life and was unconvinced that what I did was any longer of interest – even to me. Hence I lack a record of those subsequent turbulent times, including working for Rupert Murdoch and Robert Maxwell, which might well have been of interest to others, if only because those two men, whom I came to view as monsters, had such an impact on British society.

Now I am back in public life, on the front bench in the House of Lords and facing the possibility of being back in government under the leadership of Tony Blair. It is time to start again the exhausting nightly slog of writing a diary (this time on my laptop, showing the passing of technological time). Now over 60, it will be a drain on my diminishing physical resources. But I feel it is worth describing the colourful roundabout – and sometimes dreary routine – of political and social life in the Britain of the 1990s.

Boxing Day, 26 December 1995

I head off to Kempton to watch the great One Man's expected win in the King George VI Chase. But it was abandoned because of the frozen going and I was trapped for hours in traffic chaos around the course. The English arrange these transport cockups impressively.

Wednesday 27 December 1995

Beginning of dark days and post-Christmas blues. Try to relieve my frustration on the magpies that murder our baby songbirds, but every time I push my shotgun through the bedroom window they scoot off. They must have access to special radar. One is clearly a feminist harridan from the way she bullies her long-suffering partner (she is possibly from Labour's committee on gender equality), so I will pursue her till the last cartridge.

Very satisfying afternoon with Eamon Duffy's magisterial 'The Stripping of the Altars', about early puritan hooliganism in the 16th century.

Thursday 28 December 1995

I finish off Duffy and turn to John Betjeman's Letters for a decent Anglican approach, celebrating beautiful churches, not desecrating them. Later sitting alone by the fire among the Christmas cards I reflect on times and people past and miss my brother Clem.

Friday 29 December 1995

My gang of four children arrived and we have a fantastic day. After they leave, I swap between Betjeman and Waugh's Letters, sharing literary lives and friends. Betjeman was more loveable and overtly vulnerable; Waugh superior, funnier, more perceptive – and nastier. I envy both their social networks.

My post arrives, forwarded from the Lords and scanned by Security since the Animal Rights Terrorists are trying to maim me because of my tolerance of country sports – although I participate in none. How odd that decent liberals align with these intolerant thugs who bleat about their concern for injured animals while trying to maim human beings.

Saturday 30 December 1995

The television from South Africa reminds me of recently playing there, aged 61, for the parliamentary cricket team, bowling eccentric leg breaks in Cape Town in September.

Another failed shotgun attempt on the lady magpie. She is beginning to strut like Madonna so I am even more determined to get her.

Sunday 31 December 1995

Even greyer and danker. Just books and champagne in bed at midnight to see off a very mixed 1995.

New Year's Day, Monday 1 January 1996

Politics intrudes at last. Labour's main hopes for a better 1996 lie in a general election. My own mind is beginning to face the challenges of the new Lords session as spokesman on culture, media and sports – all close personal interests. I've the BBC Charter on the first day back and then the Second Reading of the big Broadcasting Bill[1] a week later. There are piles of briefing papers on my bedroom window sill.

Racing at Towcester on Friday – the going will be testing but I'm hopeful. I've realised that when reading Towcester's announcements on the state of the going you have to allow for the Clerk of the Course's optimism: 'Good to Soft' actually means 'Bottomless'; 'Soft' means 'Course under Water'; and 'Heavy' means 'Horses under Water'.

Tuesday 2 January–Sunday 7 January 1996

Outside grey and cold. I read by the blazing wood stove and began work on the heavy parliamentary programme ahead.

Went briefly to London to collect mail from my little house in Ebury Mews, Belgravia, and to try to get my engines buzzing again, but not much happening.

Monday 8 January 1996

Back to the London treadmill.

Had lunch for the first time with David Montgomery, chief executive of the Mirror Group. This was a fascinating encounter. He is a great enemy of my friends Joe Haines and Richard Stott, whom he replaced at the *Mirror* amid acrimony and accusations. Montgomery is reputedly a hard-line Ulster Prod and to the right of Mrs Thatcher, so I was unsure we would find much common ground.

He must view me with suspicion, knowing the Labour and partly Irish Catholic camps I come from. So I opened by trying to build bridges. I told him the story of how Murdoch had sacked me from *The Times* (I was assistant editor) in 1982, for standing by the editor, Harry Evans, who Murdoch was

---

[1] The 1996 Broadcasting Act provided for the introduction of digital terrestrial television broadcasting and awarding digital multiplex licences. It also, among other provisions, amended the 1990 Broadcasting Act relating to the funding of Channel 4 and Welsh language TV and proposed to change the coverage of listed sporting events, making it possible for other broadcasters, such as Murdoch's Sky, to take them from the BBC.

also sacking. How Charlie Douglas-Home had knifed Harry to get his job and then, for Murdoch, subjected me to a kangaroo court and decided I shouldn't be paid my contractual redundancy, even though I had four small kids and no money. (I got the money when dear Bill Keys, print union leader, decided his members at *The Times* would 'need to discuss this interesting matter of principle – between 6 and 10 pm each evening next week'.) The cheque arrived promptly next morning.

Montgomery seemed to appreciate this, as he has also been sacked by Murdoch. He nodded and said, with his first expression of emotion, which I took to be admiration, 'Yes, Rupert can be mean.'

I then raised the question of Ireland, which he cares deeply about as a passionate Ulsterman, and told him of the IRA death threats I had suffered in the early 1980s. Carefully and cowardly steering clear of my work with Harold Wilson planning British withdrawal from Northern Ireland in 1974–76, I said how much better and more balanced Labour's Irish policy was now under Mo Mowlam: at last recognising that the Protestants are a majority with rights and that there can be no solution without them.

We then got down to business – the effect of the new Broadcasting Bill, which I handle in the Lords, on his *Mirror*. It shuts it out from the new multi-media broadcasting world, deliberately setting a ceiling of 20% of national newspaper sales to exclude it from purchasing an ITV company. Jack Cunningham, my shadow secretary of state in the Commons, has protested at this and asked me to try to correct it. On this, Montgomery warmed. He feels deeply that the *Mirror* is stuck in a print newspaper cul de sac and the government discriminates against it because it supports the Labour Party. (Murdoch breaches the ceiling too, but is exempt for supporting the Tories and is already massively in television with Sky.) I feel Montgomery would forgive even a Labour Catholic who corrects that injustice. We agreed to maintain contact and him getting me some legal advice in drafting amendments. He is more impressive than his reputation with *Guardian* liberals allows.

He graciously took me back to the Lords in his big car – driven by the same chauffeur who used to drive Maxwell. Chauffeurs, like butlers, House of Commons secretaries and 10 Downing Street doormen, see these great men come and go.

At the Lords I had a mountain of mail in the stuffy lower-ground room I share with four Labour peers. All my letters come sealed in brown envelopes, having been scanned for bombs. That is the downside of the Lords: hundreds of letters to answer every week without a secretary. Fortunately my writing is completely illegible so it doesn't usually generate any responses.

Tuesday 9 January 1996

Work on my big speech opening today's debate on the BBC's new Charter. The House was quite full and it felt like a serious occasion. Then sat on our front bench listening to all the speeches until 10 o'clock. We were delayed by the usual group of Tory Neanderthals – Orr-Ewing, Caldecote, Chalfont etc. – who bang on endlessly about how much sex, violence and bad language there is on TV. It is curious. They are all in their 80s, but they seem to think of nothing but sex and spend their lives watching it disapprovingly. It must be terrible spending their lives obsessively watching whatever offends them.

I look forward to tangling amicably across the Dispatch Box with the new Tory minister, Richard Inglewood. He said the government will listen to our criticisms and suggestions, but I know they won't change a thing in the BBC Charter – or in anything else. Under our electoral and Commons whipping system, whatever they decide happens, however disastrous, like the poll tax, and they always get re-elected. That is the reason why, in a parliamentary democracy, there must be a change of government every so often, regardless of whether the Opposition is any good.

The late finish delayed me going with Sarah to a ball at the Savoy given by Viscount William Astor and his wife Annabel for their 20th wedding anniversary. He was Inglewood's predecessor as minister at National Heritage and, though we had some robust exchanges across the despatch box, it was always good-humoured. Often at Question Time I would tell him beforehand what savage question I was going to fire at him. He would show me his book of replies suggested by his civil servants. Sometimes he recommended a better question! In this way, the Lords is much more civilised than the Commons: without its silly adversarial aggression and you more often get an informative reply. (Sarah is also a friend of Annabel's.)

It was a fabulous party, with terrific, though very loud, music (Jools somebody, who is apparently famous though new to me, playing piano) and it was lovely for me to dance with Sarah. We weren't in bed until three. Quite a day. By the end, the BBC Charter seemed a very distant and marginal document.

Wednesday 10 January 1996

Fragile and jagged this morning, but two Disprins got me off to the House in time for the weekly National Heritage team meeting at 9.30 am. All the MPs – Jack Cunningham, Lewis Moonie, Mark Fisher and Tom Pendry – were there. They were very interested in the BBC debate and my plans for the Broadcasting Bill. They know they are lucky, since I, as lone Lords minister, taking the Bill first in the Lords, have to do all the work and they can simply read *Hansard* [the official published record of proceedings in the House of Lords and Commons] for when these issues come to them. The public – and most MPs – have no idea how much legislative work we do in the Lords. Just me, one seventh of a researcher and no secretary. In the Commons, the team has four MPs, seven researchers and three secretaries, but the team spirit is good. Jack is very relaxed and runs it on a loose rein. I've known him since Downing Street 22 years ago and we always get on well. There is something about people from the North East that I find easy to empathise with. But, I feel that Jack didn't really want the Heritage portfolio (he was downgraded from Industry when losing the Shadow Cabinet elections). He hopes to move up next year.

Lunch with Greg Dyke of Pearson TV. He is said to be a solid Labour supporter (many emerge ahead of an expected Labour victory). He has a sharp vision of the way the future of digital television will go, so I ask him to fax me a few paragraphs to use to wind up my speech next Tuesday.

My views on the Broadcasting Bill are beginning to clarify – despite, rather than because of, the thousands of briefing notes and suggested amendments showering down on me and my excellent researcher Jessica. I spent the rest of the day shaping the structure of my speech.

Thursday 11 January 1996

First half of the morning at home reading briefings and then to my Broadcasting meeting in the Moses Room. About a hundred people from outside bodies and interests came along to suggest changes in the Bill. This is how our legislative process works. Because we do not have the resources to draft all the hundreds of complex amendments ourselves, we invite the whole world to do it for us. Then I've to go through it all and choose which to use at Committee or Report stages. It is a crazy, sloppy process. This legislation matters hugely, but the public won't grant us a penny to do the job of scrutinising and improving it. The government doesn't mind since it often gets off lightly with its bad ideas. The nation gets the lousy legislation it deserves.

At the end of the meeting I was approached by David Elstein and two other Murdoch heavies, worried at what I had said about trying to reduce Sky's privileges and introduce fair taxation into Broadcasting (Murdoch pays none).

I joined veteran Labour peer and old friend Denis Howell for lunch. We're hatching a plot to defeat the government and Murdoch over the televising of certain great sporting events. Murdoch is buying up the monopoly rights on nearly everything. We want to stop that and believe we have wide support. But it is a delicate question of how to draft and plot it, since the issue is nowhere in the Bill.

It is nice working with Denis again. We have been together in politics since 1960 when I joined him (and Bill Rodgers, Roy Jenkins, Tony Crosland etc.) in the Campaign for Democratic Socialism, fighting for Hugh Gaitskell against the Labour left (I became secretary when Bill went into Parliament in 1962). He put me on the Sports Council when he set it up in 1965. Denis is a shrewd Brummie Christian socialist. I remember consulting him when the Social Democratic Party was formed in 1981 and most of our Labour friends joined it in protest against the left-wing takeover of the Labour Party. He was very clear that it would fail because, as I also strongly felt, it had no roots. I trust his political judgement and am quite excited that we might pull this coup against Murdoch.

Then our first shadow front-bench meeting in our Leader Ivor Richards's room. All routine procedures and no serious discussion. Rest of the day working preparing the speech.

Saturday 13 January–Sunday 14 January 1996

A wonderful dinner party at Highclere Castle. Henry Carnarvon and Jeannie were celebrating their 40th wedding anniversary with family and a few close friends – David Pank from Newbury racecourse, Robert Fellowes (the Queen's private secretary) and his wife Jane (sister of Princess Diana), Chris Spence and a few others. The fun was that nobody had told the Carnarvons. We all arrived early, had some champagne and then hid upstairs in the gallery. Henry and Jeannie arrived with their children, Geordie, Harry and Caroline, and gathered around the fire drinking. At a pre-arranged signal, we all cheered and launched balloons from above. Henry, who loves all parties, games and celebrations providing that they involve only close friends, was delighted.

Supper in the great dining room was superb. I sat next to Jeannie and we gossiped about family and friends. Her marriage to Henry is a great love story, which sets an example to us all in how to care and remain close to one another and not let the years dull a relationship.

Monday 15 January 1996

Drove to London after lunch and had a meeting with Jack Cunningham in his room at 1 Parliament Street. I went through the issues I intended to raise in my speech tomorrow. They took notes – but neither has yet read the Bill. This is a Lords loner operation. The party doesn't yet have any policy in this area, so whatever I say tomorrow probably becomes party policy, unless vetoed by the Leader's office. Jack seemed relaxed about that. We trust one another so there is no tension. But I was careful to get him on board for the controversial issues like televising sport, opening up access to the decoding black boxes and bringing satellite into the tax net. Each involves conflict with Murdoch and I don't want to go out on a limb and find that if it goes wrong I am alone. All are justified on good policy grounds, but I shall have the extra pleasure of tweaking Murdoch. This could cost him tens of millions. It would have been cheaper for him to pay me my redundancy money on *The Times*.

Tuesday 16 January 1996

This was the great day of the second reading of the Broadcasting Bill. It is the biggest, most complex and most important Bill I've ever handled. The House was packed, as was the press gallery; there isn't anything that fascinates the media more than themselves.

I no longer feel nervous at the dispatch box and the speech seemed to go well. I trailed the issues I mean to pursue at Committee stage, especially sport, the black boxes, taxation, protecting the regional character of ITV, helping the *Mirror* and generally bringing Sky into the regulatory net. As always, I never mentioned Murdoch by name and stressed that these amendments were not aimed at any particular broadcaster. They are for the public good. It just so happens that it is him who has a monopoly stranglehold on parts of it.

I had to sit right through the debate till the end at after 10 o'clock. The usual list of Tory suspects banged on about sex and bias in TV. They think that ITV and the BBC are run by a biased bunch of Marxist lesbians (some undoubtedly are) – yet they read the *Mail* and the *Telegraph* every day without ever detecting a sliver of bias.

Wednesday 17 January 1996

The morning DNH [Department of National Heritage] team meeting was fairly quick and routine. I had a coffee with Mark Fisher from the Commons, alerting him to the problems we're having on the London Arts Board and with the Arts Council. He is too much on the side of the Arts Council, not spotting their bureaucratic tendencies and not minding their appalling political correctness. But I like him and we get on well. He isn't very political – in the sense that Jack is deeply political – and would make a good Arts minister.

A meeting of our team to plan the amendments for the Broadcasting Bill Committee stage. This was chaotic: the volume of paper is unmanageable and it is hard to get it into any order and allocate duties to the rest of the team. I cannot use my formal Lords deputies, Alma Birk and Joe Dean, as both are old and have spent much of the year in hospital. Our average age is certainly 77. So I've asked Brenda Dean, the former print union leader, and Margaret Jay, Jim Callaghan's daughter, to step in and take particular parts. Both are superb. Also my dear old friend Jack Ashley will do the disabled parts and Elizabeth Smith, John's widow, has agreed to help with the radio bits. She is very brave, having only recently come in to the House and done her maiden speech. I am very concerned to nurture her since I loved John.

In the evening I went to a Royal Television Society dinner. Sat on Labour peer and media mogul Clive Hollick's table. His people are excited by the prospects of opening up television. Home late and still buzzing about the television battles ahead. That is a modern world I would have enjoyed working in.

Thursday 18 January 1996

Another big meeting in the morning with the outside interests wanting to influence the Bill. I am now fairly clear about the dozen issues I want to pursue in Committee and press the relevant people to send in amendments. The one I discourage is the battle by Channel 4 to end its historic subsidy of the much bigger ITV companies. Channel 4's charismatic boss Michael Grade is fighting a very loud battle. He is basically right – but I suspect Labour won't want to upset its regional MPs who depend on the regional ITV companies for their constituency publicity. Curiously, I still don't have any views from the Commons on what line I should take. They are so uninterested in the Lords that they don't know what goes on there. In fact, the Lords is the only place where we can get amendments passed – and once in a Bill it isn't easy for the government to get them out. That is the irony of our system. The Lords, despite its antique hereditaries, is the only Chamber where we have open debates, a lot of free cross-party voting – and the executive government sometimes gets defeated. So ironically, it is the unelected chamber that secures democratic accountability of the executive.

Friday 19 January–Sunday 21 January 1996

I worked on the Bill throughout the weekend and began to tire. Don't have the stamina I had in No. 10, 20 years ago.

Monday 22 January 1996

In London after lunch and held another team meeting to plan the Committee stage. We have so many amendments and so much briefing paper that we sit in the chief whip's room (none of us has a room of our own to hold a meeting) surrounded by piles of paper and nobody can find the briefs for what we're supposed to be discussing. It is pretty chaotic, but I am grateful for the others for helping out.

Tuesday 23 January 1996

Worked at home in the morning and then to lunch at the Lords with Catholic priest Father McTiernan from North Kensington, who is assisting my erratic course into full Church membership. He is very forgiving about my spiritual failings and philosophical eccentricities. He doesn't worry too much about the Church's position on things like divorce or contraception or my support for married and women priests, where I am a deviant; just says keep your eye on the main faith thing. Afterwards did a radio interview on televising sport: that is hotting up.

Wednesday 24 January 1996

The team meeting was fairly quiet in the morning. I find 9.30 am a bit sharp for starting, though 10 years ago I was chairing my first stock market meeting at Kleinworts at 7.30 am.

Had a delightful lunch in the Lords Barry Room with Henry Carnarvon, his son Geordie, Robert Fellowes, the Queen's secretary, and my quasi-brother-in-law the great cavalier Colin Ingleby-Mackenzie, who used to captain Hampshire at cricket. Purpose was to hear Henry's brother-in-law, Malcolm Wallop, a Wyoming Senator, talk about his campaign management for the Republican Presidential candidate, Forbes. Millions of dollars being spent, but doesn't sound like a winner to me. I suspect that Clinton will be re-elected: he has all the political skills and the meretricious and sleazy qualities necessary, plus skill at managing the media. I would rather have John Major. He, with all his failings, may prove to be the last old-fashioned British prime minister, who occasionally looks at the policy and not just the presentation – though he does that too much as well.

Was interviewed for a TV programme on Harold Wilson. I am cautious at first, in case it is the usual journalist scandal-obsessed trash. But they seem to have some modicum of serious interest, so I opened up a little. But must handle the Marcia Falkender stuff carefully; don't want any headlines about earlier Labour horrors.

In the evening I went to a News International party. I am careful to be always accessible to the Murdoch gang as I don't want them to feel I am shutting them out. They used the party to make embarrassing propaganda speeches about the saintliness of Murdoch and how his newspapers and TV are solely concerned with the public interest – which they seem to define as getting a monopoly of all sports. Beneath this urbane surface there is a big war going on and I am told that Murdoch is spending millions, holding lots of PR conferences and taking peers out to lunch. Even so, I think we will screw him on televising sports.

As part of that noble objective, I've begun canvassing support among friendly Tories, Liberals and cross-benchers. Denis Howell is doing a magnificent job on the high profile media. I am doing the Lords networking. Before Christmas I spoke to John Peyton, the former Tory minister with whom I once worked closely to get the VAT on horse-breeding ameliorated. He promised he would sign our amendment. More importantly, I approached Marcus Kimball for support. He is vice-chairman of the Tory back-bench peers and one of the best operators I know. He will deliver several dozen Tories, especially the foxhunters from the West Country. He appreciates that I've been a rare voice on the Labour front bench defending country sports.

The cross-benchers are usually decisive in defeating the government in the Lords. So I pinned down Jack Weatherill, their leader, and the former Speaker of the Commons. He is closely connected with Wimbledon tennis, and two years ago I pushed through an amendment banning ticket touts from Wimbledon. He returned the compliment and agreed to sign our amendment. I also got the same commitment from George Thomson on the Liberal front bench (we have been chums since serving together on the Board of *Socialist Commentary* magazine 30 years ago) and in debate I always refer to him as my 'noble Friend', a phrase normally used to refer to only one's own party; I can't see any political difference between George and me.

So now we have a senior Tory, the leader of the cross-benchers, the official Liberal spokesman, Denis and myself. That covers the whole House. The image I've in mind for the debate is that the Tory minister will be like a cowboy beleaguered in his overturned wagon while the Indians encircle him showering arrows. Then Marcus will produce his Tory huntsmen in the lobbies. I am beginning to enjoy this. Just like the old days. It involves a bit of plotting and manoeuvring, but in a good cause. I hear that Murdoch is cranking up a massive campaign, with adverts in all his newspapers and his henchman appearing on all the media – especially Sky. That is why media dominance is such a threat: he can use every media channel to promote his financial interests. It could get tough.

Thursday 25 January 1996

Quiet morning working. In the afternoon I had a tense meeting with David Elstein and other Murdoch henchmen. In the stately and elegant Royal Gallery; I wanted to keep some space between and around us. David remains polite because we have known one another 25 years, since I worked as historical consultant to a documentary series he was making. But I can tell there is a lot at stake for him. He is less Hampstead and more Business now he is in charge of Sky. When I asked why he was unwilling to share the big sporting events with the terrestrial broadcasters, he stated that Sky was only interested in exclusive monopoly, and otherwise wouldn't bid. That was honest and reveals what it is all about. If Sky gets a monopoly then the BBC will be doomed because viewers will refuse to pay their licence fee if they cannot get any sport. The small ITV companies will fade anyway as the hundreds of digital channels overwhelm them. Then Murdoch will be the dominant player in British TV, and public service broadcasting will effectively be over. That – the continuance of public service broadcasting – is the real issue and principle for which I am fighting – apart from the pleasure of putting my finger in Murdoch's eye.

After the party, I spent an hour with David Montgomery planning my amendment to ease the restrictions on the *Mirror*. In a mutually cautious way, we get on quite well. It would be a grave mistake to underestimate him.

I stayed in London overnight to have lunch with my sisters Molly and Sheila, who, until my brother Clem was dying in late 1994, I hadn't seen for 30 years and 40 years respectively, following the separation of my parents. Very moving for me. Nice to have sisters again.

Sunday 28 January 1996

Terrific lunch with Bob and Jean Phyllis who live in the next village. Usefully present were Paul Fox, former head of BBC sports, and the chairman of the Independent Television Commission. We discussed the tele-sport issue and I showed Bob, who is deputy chief executive of the BBC, our proposed amendments. They don't wholly suit the BBC; I rejected their original amendment, which would have given the BBC a monopoly since I oppose monopolies on either side.

Monday 29 January 1996

Ward Thomas, the chairman of Yorkshire/TyneTees TV, came in with some complex amendments to secure fair tax in broadcasting – and also designed to help Yorkshire out of its financial hole. He is a clever operator. But I may need something simpler on the tax side.

Afterwards I went to dinner with Jack Cunningham who talked to me privately about the plan to 'promote' me from spokesman on Heritage to Education. But the more I reflect on it the less I want to do it. I love the arts, sport and the media, so I would be mad to move. Heritage may be technically the most junior post, but I enjoy it, and that matters. Jack has more political judgement and experience than all the children around Tony Blair put together.

Tuesday 30 January 1996

Took things quietly, working on broadcasting papers.

Had lunch at The Ivy with Melvyn Bragg. He is an old Hampstead friend and long ago we played football together. I always sense our common provincial working class background. I've always admired his output of novels and TV programmes. He wanted to brief me – like 99 others – on why the big ITV companies should continue to be subsidised by little Channel 4. I soon got him off that and we had a good gossip about the party. He is having dinner with Blair soon, which is something most party colleagues don't achieve. Media Matters Most. Melvyn would like to be chairman of the Arts Council, which he would do well. I would also like to see him in the Lords. He has also been invited to dine with the Mephistophelean Peter Mandelson – who is rumoured to be Blair's choice for National Heritage secretary. I look forward to hearing about that.

The afternoon was very exciting. Went back for a meeting with Inglewood, the able government minister handling the Broadcasting Bill. I was completely open: told him all the issues I would stress and warned him we would beat him on televising sport. He accepted my suggestions where to end each of the four Committee days' business and, in return, I promised to complete in four days. We already have an understanding not to have the Bill in the House while I am away skiing or racing at Cheltenham. That is typical of the Lords; civilised arrangements between gentlemen who keep their word, quite different from the yobbo Commons. I suggested he try to avoid defeat on sports by moving towards our position, but he made it clear that he was controlled from above. This confirms the impression I received when chatting to Heritage Secretary of State Virginia Bottomley. I then also suggested a compromise, but she rejected it, saying she didn't want to upset the sports (or clearly Murdoch) and anyway we would lose. After 17 years, these Tories have total faith in the whips and their authoritarian rule. And it usually works.

Then literally ran to Jack Cunningham's office for a meeting with Michael Grade on the Channel 4 funding problem. Jack wasn't there, because his wife is going into hospital. Quite right. I like to see politicians with the right personal priorities. But it meant that Lewis Moonie and I had to conduct the meeting. Grade was volcanic, claiming that Labour was betraying him; that Mo Mowlam, Chris Smith and particularly Tony Blair had promised to support him on ending the subsidy to other commercial TV companies. I said nothing. I didn't witness Blair make the promise, but Dickie Attenborough did. I was also phoned by a child from Blair's office last week saying that we must be careful on this and that 'the leader cannot remember saying this'. In my experience of two previous Labour leaders, they always remembered if they didn't promise something; and if they didn't remember, that meant they did promise. Michael was very impressive in his passion and I had a lot of sympathy for him. We will end with a compromise – getting the worst of both worlds, betraying Channel 4 without sufficiently pleasing Channel 3.

From there I sprinted until a taxi took me an hour late to the crucial meeting of the London Arts Board. There has been a lot of plotting among the Labour people not to renew the chairman, Clive Priestley. They want someone more media-fizzy and propose to announce that Clive will be out in eight weeks. This infuriates me. It is bad behaviour to boot him out overnight and then start looking for a rare star who will be available to work hard unpaid. It also opens the door for the Tories to place yet another party man into a top Heritage post (already there has been Chris Bland to the BBC, Grey Gowrie to the Arts Council and Peter Gummer to Covent Garden). My Labour colleagues – especially Nicky Gavron, David Powell and Trevor Phillips – don't see any of this and are steaming ahead. I've talked to Mark Fisher, but he supports them.

The meeting was tense and lasted three hours. I said little and waited to see how the straws blew. I was able to suggest 21 months. By then some of the booter-outers had left and we rustled up a majority. This way there will be a measured move towards change. Hopefully it won't take place until we're in government and then we can influence it.

Didn't get home till nearly 8.30 pm. Quite a day; but some things achieved.

Wednesday 31 January 1996

Went to the Reform Club library for a party given by the PR firm GWR. Plotted with William Astor how to defeat the government on Murdoch's monopoly of black boxes. Also nice to see George Jones, my oldest, close friend from the LSE [London School of Economics]. His views on some of his academic colleagues are as savage and accurate as always.

Thursday 1 February 1996

At our front-bench meeting and the subsequent party meeting I explained our plans, especially on defeating the government on televising sport. For the first time, I sense that the party is aware that we're on to something big.

After questions, Denis Howell and I met the horse racing representatives from the Jockey Club and discussed the Derby and Grand National, which are in the list of sporting jewels we will protect from Murdoch's monopoly in our amendment.

Afterwards, another meeting with George Thomson to keep the Liberals in line with us. He is a very decent man and with the two of us the Lib–Lab coalition is already fully operational.

Pre-dinner drinks with Labour MP Graham Allen and wife Alison at their flat. He was an excellent colleague in the Chris Smith Heritage team and it was a waste of good intellectual property to move him from our media side, which he had completely mastered, to Transport. Only in politics is there such a contempt for acquired knowledge.

Saturday 3 February 1996

I worked very hard but also watched some good racing and football.

Sunday 4 February 1996

All day writing an article on sports-TV for the *Telegraph*. The *Guardian* also asked me for one, but we already have the tiny *Guardian* vote in the Lords and need the numerous *Telegraph* regulars. I was quite pleased with it and faxed a copy to Denis Howell in Birmingham. He sent me yards of Bill amendments for Tuesday.

Monday 5 February 1996

This is the big week for the vote on the Broadcasting Bill. Spent morning revising papers for the Committee stage and then drove up for a tea meeting with Don Cruikshank, now the telephone Regulator. I worked with him on the *Sunday Times* in 1982 and he was in the consortium with Harry Evans, myself and the *Daily Mail,* which tried to buy the paper before Murdoch got his hands on it. He is a quiet and steely Scot. We ranged over the regulatory issues in broadcasting.

Before and after that I was busily striding the Lords corridors nobbling anyone I could on the vote tomorrow. I must have spoken to nearly 100 Tories and cross-benchers. There is a lot of support so I am beginning to get optimistic. But the government is trying to muddy the waters by announcing a last-minute nationwide consultation on the televising of sports. This is supposed to be completed before the third reading, which is ludicrous. It is a shabby device to persuade Tory backbenchers not to vote tomorrow but to await the outcome of the consultation. In fact, the weekend's opinion polls showed 90% of the public supporting our position – and 66% of Sky subscribers. It also showed a clear majority among MPs. So we're onto a hot political issue now. I issued a statement attacking Virginia Bottomley for this delaying tactic and calling on peers to not allow their House to be bypassed. That is the drift of my article in tomorrow's *Telegraph* specifically aimed at the Tory backbenchers by saying their House is being snubbed. The key to this is to get all-party support – which also has the advantage of not allowing Murdoch to see this is a Labour plot against him.

We had a peer's party in the Cholmondeley Room and Blair gave a good speech. I spent my time canvassing, making sure our vote will turn up tomorrow. Unless you remind them, they tend to go missing. Our chief whip was sceptical about having a three-line whip on this. Even worse was our leader, Ivor Richard, who said that the consultation gave us all we want and so we need not have a vote. In fact we're going to show them tomorrow. I've used all my credit with the Tories, appealing to the huntsmen because of my support for country sports, the racing and boxing men because of shared interests, and ashamedly promising to support Orr-Ewing and his right-wing moralists in their campaigns against sex and violence on every screen if they vote for us. And my friend Marcus Kimball has been doing a superb job whipping in the Tory backwoodsmen.

Tuesday 6 February 1996

The great day. I worked all morning on my speech and endless telephone calls with Denis Howell about our amendments. Denis is constantly appearing in the media putting our case. I do the undercover work. My article in the *Telegraph* is prominently featured on the op-ed page, and lots of Tories approached me and said they agreed with it.

The House was packed for the Bill and Denis began by moving our first amendment. It proposes a new part one to the Bill to get in first and have the vote early. Denis spoke strongly, stressing the social aspects. Then our supporters followed, Peyton from directly behind the minister, then Weatherill from the cross-benches and Thomson from the Liberals. We were firing arrows at the poor beleaguered Inglewood from all sides. Only cross-bencher Woodrow Wyatt spoke against our amendment, giving an embarrassing peon of praise for Murdoch (his paymaster for a weekly column of Thatcher sycophancy in the *News of the World*). At a key point, Willie Whitelaw rose, seeking as usual to arouse apathy, and said we should accept the government's kind offer of delay. I saw this coming and nipped across to Jim Callaghan on the Privy Counsellors front bench and we agreed he should intervene immediately. He was brilliant. To Whitelaw: 'We always know when the government is in deep trouble'; to Wyatt: 'I'm sure my old friend will, on reflection, agree it wasn't his most persuasive speech.' He then put the case for the House taking its decision now. When he had finished, I sensed we were home and dry, so I wound up briefly. The Minister was long and defensive, suggesting the national consultation. Denis pressed the button and we streamed to the lobbies. The atmosphere was electric. Our lobby was packed – with 77 Tories and 63 cross-benchers joining us and the Liberals. We smashed them by 223–106, the biggest defeat for a Tory government in the Lords since 1905. I was deliriously happy. (There were 70 hereditaries in our lobby – and Blair is about to abolish them!)

We decided not to push our next amendments, protecting sports highlights etc. Peyton was against humiliating his government further and I wanted to preserve our grand coalition intact, so we called it a day on sport. I then had to sit on the front bench till late at night handling all the technical stuff on multiplex digital broadcasting – while Denis went off to all the TV channels to celebrate. I don't expect much credit. Afterwards, went to join Sarah at dinner with a selection of local types including a bibulous Pakenham. Plenty of fine champagne to celebrate quite a day.

Wednesday 7 February 1996

Woke still on a high. Dashed to the Heritage team meeting where Jack led the team in applause when I entered. They appreciate this has been a big defeat for the government. Later I heard that Major had given Bottomley a rocket for leading them into this brick wall.

Had lunch with Robert Fellowes and his assistant Robin Janvrin from the Palace. Discussed Labour's attitude to the monarchy, in view of Blair's coming announcement of reforms to the Lords and removing the vote from hereditaries. I put forward my scheme for confining further the official royal family, so those inside do the work and get paid, and those outside are not really royals and do not involve the Queen when they do something terrible. Robert was pleased with our television victory, as Buckingham Palace loathes the Murdoch press.

I had arranged tea with Jane Reed and Les Hinton, chairman of Murdoch's News International, but as I waited for them at the Lords I received a message that 'due to unforeseen circumstances' they couldn't come. A telephone call from Murdoch no doubt.

Went in the evening to the John Smith memorial lecture. The whole of Labour's great and good was there and many hangers on. I sat with my two old friends Helen Liddell and Tessa Jowell. The Blair speech was good, though the piece on abolishing the hereditary vote seemed odd in the light of their massive vote in the Labour lobby yesterday. Went back to the Jubilee Room for drinks. Blair smiled thinly at me but said nothing about yesterday. I gather he is nervous about Murdoch's reaction. We then adjourned to the Pugin Room for more drinks with the Labour Scots Gordon Brown, George Robertson and Donald Dewar.

Thursday 8 February 1996

Home in the morning preparing for this afternoon's Broadcasting Bill committee stage. I received instructions from Blair's office not to push my amendment introducing fair taxation to broadcasting – which would mean including Murdoch's satellite in the tax net.

The attempts to placate Murdoch are desperate. Blair hopes to get the support of the *Sun* in the election. I doubt if Murdoch will deliver. I drove down to Berkshire very late. At least too late for much traffic to clog up the road works. Why they are called 'road works' I don't know, as no one is ever working there.

Friday 9 February–Sunday 11 February 1996

A quiet weekend recharging batteries. The newspapers are full of the victory on sports TV, but I don't get a mention. I am no good at doing the necessary briefing.

Monday 12 February 1996

A team meeting to prepare for the next committee stage on Broadcasting tomorrow. We discussed our policy approach on the rest of the Bill and stiffened resolve against Murdoch pressures on Blair.

Evening to Royal Society of Television dinner. Much discussion of our defeat of Murdoch. Earlier I had chatted with Michael Grade and tried to cool him down. He is furious with Blair and Labour for abandoning him in his fight to abolish the Channel 4 subsidy. Tomorrow I've to wriggle on this, on instructions from one of Blair's nursery, and not commit us either way.

Tuesday 13 February 1996

Spent the morning preparing for this afternoon's Committee stage, which has some big political issues. We have a three-line whip in case we vote, but I think I won't. Must not vote and lose or it dilutes the impact of winning.

Sat in the chamber from 3 till 11.30 pm, processing tedious clause after clause on the new multiplex digital era of broadcasting. Later the Welsh dragged on endlessly. It takes them two hours to say 'not moved'.

Wednesday 14 February 1996

Quiet day. Fortunately remembered to give Sarah a Valentine card. To team meeting in Jack Cunningham's room: Jack takes it very briskly and with great humour.

Thursday 15 February 1996

Dominated by last day of Broadcasting Committee stage. We were delayed two hours in the afternoon by the statement on the Scott Report on the sale of arms to Iraq. The government had done a scandalous job of news management. They had the report for eight days, but wouldn't let our people see it until an hour before the statement – and then only in a padded cell in the DTI [Department of Trade and Industry], with no telephone or notes and a guard outside to make sure they didn't see anyone. Ivor Richard, our Lords leader, and Roy Jenkins from the Lib Dems rightly refused to play this silly game.

Our Committee stage went slowly, with the morally righteous brigade spending hours talking about sex and violence. They must spend all night surfing the channels searching for something to disapprove of. We finished at 11.30 pm with a flood of amendments I didn't move.

Saturday 17 February–Sunday 18 February 1996

Felt very tired and mostly recharging batteries. Some golf practice and watched some terrific sport. Put £10 on Manchester United to win the league. They are 10 points behind, but looking good, while leaders Newcastle seem fragile.

Monday 19 February 1996

Drove to London at lunchtime, through the usual road works. Walked to the LSE for an emergency standing committee – the newly appointed Director (Sir John Bourn, Auditor General in Whitehall) has suddenly changed his mind and left us in the lurch. Odd because he was chosen as the elder candidate and a safe pair of hands. I preferred Professor Jeffrey Jowell.

People were pretty angry with Bourn, who only last week had dinner with our chairman Peter Parker and deputy Anthony Grabiner QC, with wives, to celebrate his appointment and prepare for the transition. Peter is abroad and apparently shattered. Now we have to go to the Court of Governors and start all over again (fortunately I shall be away racing at Cheltenham). If we had a committee with no academics on it we could solve it in a fortnight – with Jowell. I was on the selection committee and it was an excruciating experience. I don't want to go through it all again so may try to drop off the committee.

Afterwards I walked back past the wreck of the bombed bus in the Aldwych. Something eerie and almost artistic about the twisted metal. One consolation is that the IRA swine was blasted by his own bomb. These are animals, psychopaths who are only happy killing the innocent, like Sarah's poor husband Tony Berry, killed at Brighton. They hated the ceasefire and now are happy again slaughtering. But Major didn't handle it well. Missed the opportunity of the Mitchell Report on decommissioning arms and drifted apart from the Republic, which is politically fatal.

Tuesday 20 February 1996

Whole morning dealing with correspondence. I get 40 letters a day and without a secretary it is difficult to answer one pile before the next lot crowds my desk. Then to a fascinating meeting with the minister, Richard Inglewood. He revealed they are in a pickle over the televising sports issue. They have not yet agreed ministerially what to do about their defeat in the Lords: whether to accept our amendments or to produce their own. They are reluctant to give up their original position. I warned him that if they ignore the will of the House, we would inflict an even bigger defeat. He said he, personally, accepted that, but he couldn't speak for his secretary of state, Bottomley, or for the department. He said they might not have anything ready for Report stage. I said that would be ridiculous. But then we sat down together with the civil servants and began to try to draft some clauses that incorporated the spirit of what my side wanted but might also be acceptable to the government. This was bizarre. The Opposition shadow minister taking his coat off to sweat over drafting clauses for the government. Unthinkable in my days in 10 Downing Street. But the Tories have torn the heart out of the Civil Service. It is no longer a Rolls-Royce machine – just a demoralised rabble. But I like Inglewood, who is decent and deserves better.

Dashed home to change for a royal gala of Sleeping Beauty at Covent Garden. A mechanical production, though Darcy Bussell is captivating and it was lovely to see some of the original 1946 cast up on stage. In the interval we had drinks with our friends the Mosers, the Robin Butlers, and Elizabeth Smith and one of her daughters. The Queen looked old and lonely in the big royal box with just two young Armstrong-Joneses. Princess Margaret was going to be there, but she didn't show, allowing the atmosphere to be more relaxed.

Wednesday 21 February 1996

Usual 9.30 am meeting of the team. Then Lords for a team meeting to prepare for the Broadcasting Report stage. The briefs and suggested amendments are still flooding in. My files are 4 ft high.

Afterwards back to Jack's room for a fascinating meeting with Blair's senior (in their 30s!) henchmen. We were Jack, Moonie and myself. They were Jonathan Powell, Blair's chief of staff, which was a bit weird, as I've known his brother Charles for 20 years and he was Thatcher's willing hatchet man. Also Press Secretary Alastair Campbell, who was selected for lobby work on the *Mirror* by my friend Joe Haines – and who I like, though he seemed distant and tense. We went over the Broadcasting Bill, using a memo I had sent to Blair last week when oblique messages made it clear that our leader was worried about it and not too delighted by our victory.

They didn't say much, but finally revealed their worry about upsetting Murdoch. We pointed out that we were protecting the public interest and supporting public service broadcasting as Labour always had done. I pointed out that I had never mentioned Murdoch by name. They didn't seem convinced. It was a curious occasion, being forced to be defensive about defeating the Tory government and upsetting a media tycoon who is always trying to destroy the Labour Party. They looked uncomfortable as we took them through the issues. I don't feel they get on well together: Powell, the public school ex diplomat; Alastair, more streetwise and a natural Labour supporter. It must be hot in that kitchen cabinet, with Peter Mandelson cutting across all their lines advising Blair. Much more complex than in our day when it was just Joe and me solid on one side and Marcia being disruptive on the other, though often absent. Powell may not yet have much Labour feel, but he is clever and may prove to be an efficient office manager, which we lacked.

After an hour of mutual shiftiness I had had enough. As I rose to leave, I said to Alastair that I was happy to do anything the leader wished – as I had done by withdrawing our amendments supporting the fair taxation of satellite TV and supporting Channel 4. But I said that I would welcome getting the messages direct from him or the leader and not indirectly from some youngster in the nursery. He nodded.

Later things became clearer when Margaret Jay told me that Murdoch has flown in and visited Blair this week, partly to personally complain about my handling of the Broadcasting Bill and the attacks on him. Too bad. I am not willing to be a Murdoch marionette. Margaret also told me a funny story about Jonathan Powell. She went to see him about getting more money for the Lords under the Short Money scheme, which made some public funds available to the Opposition. This was arranged in 1974–76 by Ted Short (now Lord Glenamara), then deputy leader of the Labour Party and Lord President of the Council, partly because of concern over the slightly scandalous ways the Opposition had to raise money to pay for office expenses. So it is always referred to as 'Short Money'. In the conversation, Powell asked, 'Why is it called Short Money?', hence reconfirming our belief that, for this regime, history began in 1994.

Jim Callaghan also told me that before Christmas he'd received a letter, signed by a child in Blair's office, asking him to a meeting with the leader. Not from or signed by Tony – to Labour's last prime minister! Jim said to me: 'I didn't reply; that was the right way to handle it, wasn't it, Bernard?' Indeed. No history, nor manners.

Back to Inglewood's room for another friendly but curious meeting drafting amendments. He again said the government has no agreed policy yet.

In the evening, a dinner at the Claus Mosers. Present were Graham Greene, Camilla Panufnik (widow of the famous Polish composer), broadcaster Sue Lawley, a man who runs BBC World Service, and – intriguingly – Hayden Phillips, the permanent secretary at Heritage. The latter disclosed the pickle they are in over televising sports. Told me that Inglewood has still not been able to fix a meeting with his secretary of state to agree policy. I've known Hayden since he worked for Roy Jenkins in the Labour government and we thrashed out a policy approach. His wife told me that they were afraid to be seen out with Labour people because ministers disapproved. And that all his public appointment suggestions were scrutinised by No. 10 to ensure they were all Tory party hacks.

Thursday 22 February 1996

Rather tired and jaded. Wrote up the diary. Television people came in to film me for a programme on Harold Wilson. I said a little more about the Marcia business than usual and hope they don't use that out of context.

At the front-bench meeting at 1.30 pm I warned of my absence skiing in Switzerland next week and asked for a three-line whip for the Report stage the week after. Home in the late afternoon and hurriedly packed for tomorrow's departure to Geneva.

Friday 23 February 1996

Hard 2½ hours icy drive through the Swiss mountains, having as usual taken the wrong turn at Lausanne. We reached Gstaad at 7.00 pm, and by 8.30 pm we were up in Schönreid for a dinner party with a mass of cosmopolitan cafe society.

I sat all evening in the corner with my American friend Stanley Weiss, who filled me in on the US political scene; especially the primaries. The American middle class white collars are now being mass unemployed by the so-called 'downsizing' in the big utilities and conglomerates. New hard-nosed bosses are triumphal about redundancies and their stock options rocket while millions go on the dole. Stanley is an intriguing mixture: a mega-rich businessman with a strong intellect and a serious social conscience. He thinks the Clintons are shoddy.

Saturday 24 February 1996

Took my favourite 8 km walk up the valley to the pretty village of Lauenen. Sat quietly, as each year, for 20 minutes in its lovely wooden 17th century Protestant church. Sarah drove up at midday and we lunched outside the Alpenland Hotel in the sun with views across the snowfields. Ate too much sausage and rösti, so went for a walk beside the frozen lake, watching the langlaufers swoosh by and horse-drawn sledges with their bells ringing across the valley. Westminster began to slip away. Then I walked along the Tromweg, looking over Gstaad and down the valley beyond Saanen. Had walked about 16 km in all, not bad for a first day.

Sunday 25 February 1996

A terrific day. Walked through the snowfields down to Saanen and then back up beside the river. It was beautiful, quiet, with just the sound of running water and the sight of well-wrapped ladies walking their dogs and the range of snowy mountains behind. Went back for long bath and started to read a novel about Clinton and his primary elections by some anonymous writer. Harry Evans, its publisher, sent it to me. Full of awful people and horrible violent language, so is probably accurate about today's American politics. Perhaps New Labour as well.

In the evening to one of the best dinner parties ever. Each year we go to Vivian Duffield and Jocelyn Stevens's grand chalet and it is usually the social centrepiece of the week. There were about 24 guests in the huge sitting/dining room. I chatted with the Astors – a friendship founded when he was minister and I was supposed to attack him across the dispatch box. *Spectator* gossip journalist Taki was there extroverting loudly – I begged him not to write anything nice about me as that would ruin me politically. There was also Rocco Forte. He seems physically diminished since losing the takeover battle to Granada.

Lots of them intrigued by the prospect of a Labour government – especially by the Labour baronesses. They find Tessa Blackstone, Margaret Jay and Patricia Hollis a bit earnest. Perhaps they are. More humour would help. But they are formidable.

We drove back to the hotel at nearly 1.00 am. Taki had declined to leave and was being bedded down.

Monday 26 February 1996

Took another favourite walk, up the steep and snowy road to Turbach, a village at over 4000 ft with vast views. Each year Sarah drives up to join me for lunch after her gentle ski-ing. Before she arrived I walked kilometres up what I call Happy Valley, stretching far up into the mountains with just the sound of a rushing river and the birds. Afterwards, Sarah and I walked back up the Happy Valley together and sat holding hands in the sunshine on a wooden seat outside an old cowshed with 1764 carved on its side. London, Westminster, politics of yobboland all far away. That is why I love coming here each year. Sends me back refreshed for the challenges ahead – especially

Cheltenham, where this year's favourite horses and jockeys all seem to be already injured.

In the evening went for dinner at the Saanen station hotel with a strange crowd. I sat next to an American woman: aggressive, humourless and hating men in that dreary way that characterises these transatlantic feminist zealots. Sarah was more at home than me since she schooled here and has known most of them since childhood. My childhood is gone, long abandoned, and buried now that my brother Clem and dear friend Gerry Fowler are dead. I envy those who grow up in a consistent and continuing group of friends. This wasn't my gang at all. Anyway this is Gstaad. Cosmopolitan cafe society, from everywhere but often actually from nowhere.

Before dinner we had drinks with a delightful group at the Weiss chalet – Jung Chang who wrote *Wild Swans* and her man; Taki again, and Barry Humphries the Australian entertainer. I could have chatted with him all night. Clearly a special genius. A completely split personality, with Dame Edna his alter ego left upstairs. He was interested in my walks, because he likes to wander while he composes his books and scripts. His wife, Lizzie Spender, was there. I met her foppish poet father Stephen several times in the 1950s at Oxford when I was publishing some naive verse.

Tuesday 27 February 1996

Quiet morning reading on the balcony. Went for a terrific langlauf up the valley towards Gstaad. Super exercise. Much better than that downhill nonsense. Spent lovely quiet evening having a romantic dinner a deux at the Olden. This has been a wonderful holiday. I feel fit and restored, with Murdoch completely out of my system.

Wednesday 28 February 1996

We drove over the Diablerets pass to Martigny and then west again to France and Chamonix. Sarah's daughter Sasha and her boyfriend Rupert came to visit us and we had a sensational supper.

Thursday 29 February 1996

Sat outside for a long lunch, reading *The Times* about Major scraping through the big Scott arms vote by only one vote – mainly achieved by manipulating the Ulstermen. Reminds me of the humiliating manoeuvres we went through with Callaghan to survive in 1977–79. Major is now just hanging on, as we did in 1979. Just clocking up the days in No. 10.

Friday 1 March 1996

Home to grey England. George brought down a huge sack of letters from London and it took two hours to open them.

Saturday 2 March–Sunday 3 March 1996

Saturday afternoon watched England rugby ruthlessly but boringly grind out victory over the Scots. The forwards are awesome. Even the backs are as big as forwards were when I played briefly for Northampton and Oxford University second fifteens in the early 1950s.

Monday 4 March 1996

Still feeling great benefits from the snow holiday. Drove up on Sunday evening so I had a full Monday preparing for this week's Report stage. Spent most of the day answering the hundreds of letters which had accumulated while I was away.

At tea-time the government announced it was accepting our previous sports TV amendment, but would resist tomorrow's amendment to protect 'highlights' for national viewing. Denis Howell and I decide we won't divide tomorrow because there has not been time to assemble the troops, especially the dissident Tories.

Tuesday 5 March 1996

A pulsating day. After writing my speech in the morning I went to the Tote lunch – always the best lunch of the year, with everyone there from racing and politics. I sat on a good table with the magnificently anti-politically correct Jean Trumpington and opposite Cheltenham's nice Sam Vesty and an American man I've met before who works for Murdoch with a name like Alka Seltzer (as always we exchanged a bit of banter).

Woodrow Wyatt made his usual amusingly combative speech and Labour's Robin Cook followed: very funny and steeped in racing. I like and respect him; but he is very wary and difficult to get close to. A natural loner. I had to leave before the end to get to the Lords for our Broadcasting Report stage.

The House was very full again (and we might have won a vote). Denis made his usual good speech moving the amendment. It is signed by Weatherill, Thomson and a Tory hereditary Viscount Reading – no room for me, though, because we're trying to stress the non-partisan nature of it. The Minister asked to intervene after Denis and made his statement accepting the previous vote, which led to approval. The rest of us then made the case for protecting highlights, but I abandoned my full speech, saving it for next time, and briefly summed up. The House knows we won't press the vote so they like to get it over quickly.

We had a three-line whip on and the chief whip said we must vote on something or our troops will think we have called them in for nothing. So we divided on 'black boxes', the smart card access systems to pay TV, where Murdoch has a monopoly which could be abused. We lost by 20 but had a respectable vote. Brenda Dean did very well on the black boxes and Jack Ashley on the disability issues. I am lucky to have such a terrific team – though none of them are officially my team. I picked them as friends who can be relied on.

Wednesday 6 March 1996

Went to the WH Smith literary lunch, where they gave the award to the brilliant Simon Schama for his *Landscapes and Memory*. Afterwards I asked him to sign my copy – and he recalled my book on the American War of Independence published in 1964! Even I as the author have difficulty remembering that. Sat beside Lucy Hughes-Hallett a literary lady married to my publisher Dan Franklin. She was aware of my secret diary from the 1970s Labour government, still awaiting to be published by Dan.

Pottered the afternoon in the Lords, courting support for the amendment I am doing with William Astor tomorrow against Murdoch's monopoly control of the conditional access subscriber systems. This intrigues a lot of people because William was the Tory minister until last summer. We plotted all of this at Vivian's chalet in Gstaad last week. He is very fair minded and good fun. This seems to me the best way for us to handle the Lords. Labour has too few votes ever to win in a party confrontational way. We always need Tory and cross-bench support. That is why I spend most of my time courting the House of Lords while Denis is busy starring on TV.

Thursday 7 March 1996

The Broadcasting Bill Report stage. Very bad luck on our amendment. We lost by two – 103–101. Five Tories arrived at the last second. Several of my side were inexplicably absent. I was gutted and felt sad for the rest of the day. William and I had plotted this for weeks and it would have been lovely to win again.

Shortly before our Division I received a message to phone Anji Hunter, Tony Blair's personal assistant. She told me that Tony had received a letter from the Murdoch man, Selzer, at the Tote lunch – he writes for the *Sunday Times* – claiming that I had boasted to him that Labour's policy on the Bill was 'to bankrupt Murdoch so he wouldn't be able to afford to pay your wages'. Bizarre. I had indeed said precisely those words, in extravagant banter, during a very light-hearted conversation. He had laughed and then invited me to address his Washington research institution in the autumn. He knew I was just joking. But, two days later, he has decided that I was seriously describing Labour's policy (I wish it was that, but sadly it is mainly to appease Murdoch).

No doubt he has sent a copy to please Murdoch. I reassured Anji that I was joking. She was understanding, but, once again, the leader has jumped whenever a Murdoch creep pulls the string. I promised to write a reply and send Tony a copy. Pretty pathetic. But I should have remembered that Americans rarely understand irony and when we're joking. Next time silence.

We soldiered on till nearly midnight with another two hours on the right wing bid to put the broadcasters in chains on issues of taste, sex, violence and impartiality. The hilarious part of this was that earlier I had said – again jokingly – that if their right-wing troops supported me on the conditional access vote, I would speak for them on their morality crusade. Lo and behold, there they were – Orr-Ewing, Renton, Chalfont etc. – in our lobby helping us to nearly win. So at 11 at night, hoping nobody was awake and watching, I rose to give some comfort to them. I will need them next time on sports TV.

Friday 8 March 1996

The Lords had a big debate on protecting the integrity of the civil service against the depredations of this government. The whole Whitehall mafia supporting Ian Bancroft, including a permanent secretary who retired in 1962! Jim Callaghan used to tell me never to take on the Whitehall mafia when they are united and angry. They certainly were yesterday and the government was defeated by a hundred votes. Very satisfying.

Sat at lunch with Sarah's old friend Patricia Rawlings. She flatteringly said she was impressed because I always speak and answer questions at the dispatch box without notes. I decided long ago to do that where possible. But it isn't genius. I do a lot of homework beforehand. But I do think the House likes it better if you talk to them rather than read to them. That is why I did my maiden without notes in 1985. It is also a good thermometer of how far the Alzheimer's is making progress.

Saturday 9 March 1996

I took things quietly, walked, read and wrote up this diary. On Tuesday I go to my annual romp to the Cheltenham racing festival. Have excused myself from Wednesday's DNH team meeting, telling Jack I shall be officially inspecting equine sports facilities in Gloucestershire. Next year will miss this pleasure if we're in government. Hence my ambivalence on that prospect.

Monday 11 March 1996

This morning to Chancery Lane to talk to the Screen Advisory Council about the Broadcasting Bill. Dickie Attenborough in the chair. David Elstein was there and he spoke very fairly about me. Also John McGrath, the theatre writer and director who I knew as a promising fellow poet at Oxford. Marcia Falkender is on the Council – it was established in the last days of Harold Wilson and he told me it was his 'farewell present to Marcia', but she didn't turn up today. Our long stand-off clearly continues. We haven't exchanged a word during 11 years together in the Lords Labour party!

Spent the afternoon networking on our amendments to protect the broadcasting of sports highlights. Then to the Cavalry Club for a dinner of the Lincoln College Society. Saw old Oxford Lincoln friends but most of them were strangers from later generations. I am now very much an Old Member as well as Very Old Labour. It is hard to know where the years have gone, especially the 1980s, which were a waste.

Tuesday 12 March 1996

Off to Cheltenham first thing. I love it. Drove first to the Lygon Arms in Broadway, then off to the course. I love getting there early when the grass smells fresh, the bookies are opening their stands and there is still time and space to move around. The racing was excellent and I backed Collier Bay, the winner of the Triumph Hurdle.

Wednesday 13 March 1996

To the Ladbroke's box to lunch with their chief executive Chris Bell, who is very knowledgeable and serious on the whole racing scene. Several horses fell badly and were killed, which I find very upsetting.

Thursday 14 March 1996

Went to lunch with the Tote, which is always a splendid affair. Lots of friends at other tables. A terrific party, which disguised the recurring misfortune of my race selections.

We drove home. I was exhausted but elated.

Friday 15 March 1996

Totally exhausted and was deep asleep when Denis Howell phoned with the latest on next week's Broadcasting Bill. It all seems very mixed up with nobody knowing what the government will do. We have put down our amendments ahead of that, so may get out of sync.

Saturday 16 March 1996

One irritation today was a letter from Tony Blair complaining that my letter to Murdoch's henchman Alka Stelzer was insufficiently craven and had made his delicate relations with the Big M even worse than my original conversation. This could be treated as farce, and later I will do so. But for the moment I curse my lack of judgement in indulging my anger at this man. I may have lost my future as a minister – but am intrigued to find that thought doesn't worry me at all. But I shouldn't have wasted Tony Blair's time.

Sunday 17 March 1996

This afternoon I wrote up this diary and also drafted my letter to Tony Blair saying sorry I got it wrong. Never had to do that with Hugh Gaitskell, Harold Wilson, Jim Callaghan, Neil Kinnock, or John Smith. Sign my marbles may be going? But also evidence how terrified Blair is of Murdoch. Harold would have been delighted with my original tough letter to Stelzer. He encouraged Joe Haines to send lots like that. The difference is that Wilson loyally defended his troops, at least against the press rodents. Blair sacrifices his troops to them.

Monday 18 March 1996

Worked on papers and correspondence in the morning, including writing 14 letters. Went to the Lords for lunch and saw the team after Questions to plan next week's Third Reading of the Bill. Denis Howell is in Devon, so am still in the dark about his voting intentions on the Broadcasting Bill.

I went over to Jack Cunningham's room at 5.15 pm for a suddenly called meeting with Blair's office on the Broadcasting Bill. Jonathan Powell was supposed to arrive but didn't, leaving Geoff Norris to speak for them. To my astonishment their concern was to suggest that I should vote in support of Thomson's amendment for Channel 4 against ITV3, cutting off the cross subsidy. This is the very same issue on which at Committee stage they told me not to support C4. So another U-turn. Who has got at them now? They don't seem to have any consistent policy; just bending to the last media wind which blows. I was astonished. But Jack Cunningham was superb. Firmly he told Norris that whoever had nobbled the leader hadn't spoken to him, so he didn't intend to take any notice. Our position was to remain the same and we'd deal with it when in government.

I was very pleased with Jack. He has good judgement. It is ludicrous that the parliamentary party has voted him off the Shadow Cabinet. He has more experience and sense than most of them. But, of course, he's Old Labour so they write him off, dismissing the crucial quality of experience they all lack. He is also of course not a 101% admirer of T Blair.

Tuesday 19 March 1996

Talked early to Denis Howell about this afternoon's amendments to protect the televising of sports highlights from Murdoch's monopoly grip. I sense he is weakening. He has been in touch with the Sports Council. They are pushing a voluntary code backed by the government.

I talked twice to the Minister on the telephone. He said their position was to rely on the voluntary code. I said we didn't oppose a voluntary code if it really protected the highlights but I didn't trust it. I told the Minister that we would probably vote against but I was dependent on what Denis decided as the main signatory. When I went in before midday I saw some of the Labour girls in the coffee room – Nora David, Jenny Hilton, Betty Lockwood, average age over 70 – and they said we must have a vote. I agreed but said it depended on Denis. But I couldn't find Denis. I sat in his office chair until he arrived just before 1 pm with his family – his brother-in-law had just been to the Palace for his MBE and Denis was rightly entertaining them for lunch. I felt he was distracted. He said he didn't think we could have a vote in view of the voluntary code.

I went off to lunch with Virginia Bottomley at the Millennium Commission. Virginia was very emollient, agreeing with everything we said. But suddenly Patricia Hollis, a Labour frontbencher, sitting on Bottomley's left, delivered them a stern lecture on the iniquities of Tory policy towards local government.

I noticed Virginia stiffen and for the rest of the lunch sat showing Patricia only her back. Lovely body language between two ambitious ladies.

I walked back quickly to get in for the Bill, seeing the Tory chief whip, Tom Strathclyde, en route. I told him we would probably vote and he said we would probably win. Again I couldn't find Denis, and George Thomson told me he hadn't seen him either. So I hunted around and pulled them both out of the Chamber five minutes before our business came up. They hadn't co-ordinated how they would do it. It was a chaotic meeting. George said he wanted to vote; Denis said he didn't. When I pressed him, saying our troops were here expecting a vote, he snapped, 'We can't keep changing our bloody minds.' I hadn't changed mine. Denis then said he wanted to press the second of our two amendments. George said that was pointless since the second depended on the first and would fall without it. We were all waving our hands and copies of the Bill and the marshalled list of amendments. Our chief whip emerged to say we must go in, which we did in complete confusion. The Minister was already on his feet, admitting the defeat at Committee stage and proposing his official clauses to implement what we had voted for. That was very nice. But within minutes we came to our sports amendments.

Denis rose to speak, sounding very strained. After a vague introduction he said he was withdrawing the first key amendment. In a flash the Chairman was on his feet moving that and it was gone and the consequential amendment with it. Our side looked shattered and the House bewildered. Denis droned on, seemingly unaware what he had done. He should have moved the two amendments together, listened to the debate and the Minister's reply, and then withdrawn if the reply was satisfactory – and providing the other signatories agreed. He unilaterally withdrew it at the beginning and spoke to a consequential amendment that now had no meaning. George Thomson rose and was very angry for not having been consulted and saying that he would have pressed for a vote anyway. Others expressed bewilderment. Our troops and the Tory backbenchers were very angry because Denis had written to them only last Thursday telling them to come and vote. It hadn't helped that he and I were out of touch for a week, me in Cheltenham then him in Devon. But it was his amendment, he had talked privately to the Sports Council, and now unilaterally backed off.

I rose and spoke ad lib, saying we couldn't vote now, but that I didn't trust the voluntary code. The Minister was friendly in reply, relieved to have escaped from probable defeat. Afterwards I learned of the peers who had come from remote parts – including Harry Kissin from Nice – in order to vote. They hate Murdoch on all sides.

Very curious and very sad. Denis has been such a good friend for over 30 years. I felt miserable and that we had let down a lot of people. Murdoch's henchman will be laughing to the bank.

Actually it has been a huge job of work. I had two votes: we won one by over a hundred, lost the second by only two, and we would have won today but for the cock-up. Not bad in a House where Labour has only 20% of the active votes. The lesson is to work with the other parties and pick the issues for division. We never win on pure Labour issues and votes.

Wednesday 20 March 1996

Went to the Heritage team meeting to explain yesterday's debacle. Tom Pendry came along armed with newspaper clippings showing that Denis had buggered it up. I urged them not to snipe at Denis but to claim it as a big victory, since we only had the voluntary code because of our threatened vote. It is politically best to be positive – not that I personally felt very positive.

Afterwards I wrote thank you letters to all the team who had given me so much help on the Bill – Margaret Jay, Alf Dubbs, Elizabeth Smith, Nora David and especially Brenda Dean and Jack Ashley. They were marvellous, especially as none of them is actually officially in the DNH team.

I attended Lent mass in the Crypt at 5 pm, where dear Gerry Fitt, the brave Belfast peer, whose wife has just died, was distraught.

Thursday 21 March 1996

All morning ploughing through a pile of correspondence with my usual wodge of hand-written replies. After a late Lords lunch I took a PQ [Parliamentary Question] on the unprecedented 10 horse deaths at Cheltenham. It helped that I could say, 'I happened to be there.' Some on our side want to ban National Hunt racing (like hunting) and I was pleased to take the Question and give it a friendly twist. Several said afterwards that I got the balance between concern at the fatalities – which I genuinely feel – and defence of racing about right.

In the evening Sarah and I went to a splendid evening at Buckingham Palace to celebrate Yehudi Menuhin's 80th birthday party. We first had drinks in the long reception rooms, the walls covered in lovely paintings. There were lots of old friends there, including Robert Armstrong, Claus and Mary Moser, and Robert and Jane Fellowes, and some very new ones such as Barry Humphries and wife Lizzie Spender (we reminisced about Gstaad). Then we sat in the state room where they hold concerts (and knightings) and watched a film about Yehudi's remarkable life. He then conducted a concert by his youth music academy.

Yehudi made a remarkable and touching speech without a note, full of his own special serenity and philosophy. The front row was stuffed with royals: the Queen, Prince Phillip, Prince Charles, Edward, a Duke and Duchess and various European and Middle Eastern princes and princesses. Yehudi addressed them from a genuinely superior position, though with total humility. A great man – who is also our London neighbour.

We then all filed in to dinner – with Sarah and I at a huge central table. I sat four down from Prince Charles and between two beauties – Lady Palumbo and Carina Frost – with Tony Armstrong Jones on one side. Opposite, with Sarah, were Denis Thatcher, journalist Simon Jenkins and Peter Palumbo. The flowers were superb, the food reasonable and the wine erratic. It was a terrific evening, grand in style but very comfortable and relaxed. The royals should do musical evenings more often.

Friday 22 March 1996

Off early to Epsom to see Highclere Syndicate's two horses with Geoff Lewis. Our two-year-old, Referendum, looked good, but the three-year-old, Province, looks mediocre and moves like a dray horse.

I got very lost on the way looking for the A3, but there wasn't a single sign to it until I finally found myself on it. British road signposting is symptomatic of the management of the country as a whole. Very sloppy. The only drivers who can follow the signs are those who know the way anyway and don't need them. I remember that for decades there was no signpost at Dover pointing the way to London. They are probably still trying to confuse the German invaders.

Saturday 23 March–Sunday 24 March 1996

Quiet weekend.

Monday 25 March 1996

Lunch with my old fellow warrior from Wilson's Downing Street, Joe Haines, at the Lords. Don't see him often these days as he stays down in Kent. A bit depressing reflecting on our dire times with Maxwell, though we chose that. More irritating are the numbers of people who knew the monster better and supported him longer than us and yet get away scot free. All those bankers and lawyers who now behave as if they never knew him. There must be an art of disappearing from embarrassing associations, which I haven't acquired. Perhaps Labour people find it harder to disappear.

The government has clearly hoped that the BSE [bovine spongiform encephalopathy] problem would go away. But it hasn't. It didn't want to upset its farmer friends by slaughtering cattle, and saved money by reducing the inspectorate and loosening the regulations. So it risked the public health to help its economic interests. Now the public has decided it is a crisis and there is no point the government saying there isn't. Last week Hogg, the agriculture minister, said they would slaughter, today he said they won't. Hogg wears a big hat. As the lads in my village of Roade used to say, 'If you can't fight, wear a big hat.'

Tuesday 26 March 1996

Had a good meeting of our Heritage team on reforming the lottery. Chatted with my friend, the radical lawyer Helena Kennedy, over sandwiches. I discussed the obscene earnings of top lawyers, which she agreed, but said it is a minority who earn that much and she doesn't get much at her legal aid end. We both agree that James Mackay is a very decent Lord Chancellor, acting in the public rather than his profession's financial interest – which is why some lawyers want to get rid of him.

Had a nostalgic tea with Harry Kissin, who first introduced me into the Wilson political ménage in 1973. We reminisced a lot. He has contributed to a fund organised by Jim Callaghan to provide an income for Mary Wilson. All Harold's money seems to have gone. Harry also told me that as early as 1971 Harold and his doctor Joe Stone told Kissin that Harold had the beginnings of Alzheimer's. Wilson considered retiring because of it, but Harry persuaded him to do one more stint. (Marcia would have pushed for that as well and I don't suppose he needed much persuading). It explains why in 1974–76 he was always so obsessed with having everything written out for him and was afraid of going blank in a speech.

In the evening went to Vivien Duffield's 50th birthday. Jocelyn Stevens gave her a fabulous banquet and ball at Eltham Palace in south London. There were over 300 guests in the magnificent mediaeval banquet hall, with its high wooden ceiling and long tables. Entertainers dressed in ancient garb performed throughout the dinner. Eltham Palace was owned by the Defence Ministry for a long time but has just been bought by Jocelyn's English Heritage – which is presumably how he learned about it. I don't know if, as chairman, he rented it for the evening at a discount.

He made a charming speech about Vivien, she made a brief, characteristically punchy reply, and her son was hugely funny about both of them.

I sat between Tessa Kennedy and Barbara Amiel/Mrs Conrad Black. Barbara Amiel told me that she didn't want to go with Conrad to live in New York. We didn't discuss a curious time earlier, when she invited me to lunch at the Savoy and mainly talked about my divorced status and her three failed marriages. She told me how she wanted to get married again and was considering remarrying her third husband – though I wondered momentarily if perhaps I was under scrutiny.

Wednesday 27 March 1996

Woken early by Kate to tell me that she is going to get married.

I felt distinctly jaded. People at the Lords saw I looked pale and several asked how I was, but I always quoted the old Grieveson Grant phrase: 'great – seasonally adjusted'.

Watched *Newsnight*, which showed my farming interview. I was quite pleased with what I had to say, but not with the large bags under my eyes.

Thursday 28 March 1996

Today I've a debate on the film industry. So I wrote the speech in the morning, went to a tame front-bench meeting, and snatched a quick lunch sitting next to Ralf Dahrendorf. We discussed the terrible saga of the LSE directorship non-appointment (he was director 20 years ago). As a German-born social democrat who, as a child, was in a concentration camp, Ralf is always interesting. He agreed that a basic problem for the LSE is that the teaching staff are taking an ever bigger role in the governance of the School, but their competence for management is declining. Until recently there were professors who had fought in the war or worked in the real world. Now they are completely cloistered from cradle to classroom and get involved in practical decisions for which some have no sense or qualifications.

I gave tea to David Powell from the London Arts Board, where we discussed names for the next chairman.

My film debate came in the dinner break. Opened by Lord Drogheda, with a maiden speech. I recalled his father, who I often saw at the Royal Opera when I went regularly with Lionel Robbins and Claus Moser in the late 1960s and 1970s. I owe them a lot for my musical education as well as meeting some lovely people. My speech was quite short and knockabout and the Minister replied with fortunate brevity, so I was able to get away to Berkshire before 9.00 pm.

Friday 29 March 1996

Brought this diary up to date (I make daily notes along the way).

Saturday 30 March–Monday 1 April 1996

Diary not available.

Tuesday 2 April 1996

Incidentally, last Thursday Jim Callaghan told me that he had finally been for a chat with Blair. They mainly discussed members of the Shadow Cabinet and forming a Labour government – though Jim is always discreet and didn't reveal much. He told me that for tea they were served on a silver tray. Blair told him that he usually had great difficulty getting served at all, and certainly had never before been blessed with a silver tray. Everybody respects Jim. Tony should make more use of him. That kind of Old Labour has experience and wisdom that is in short supply among the New.

Lunch with Carlton TV. We mainly discussed the Broadcasting Bill and how Labour would handle the media. The three of them – Nigel Walmsley, Clive Jones and [future prime minster] David Cameron – all seemed on the ball. But Michael Green is the only boss who matters there.

Had dinner with Henry Carnarvon and Graham Greene. We had a fairly riotous time with three bottles of wine between us. He usually knows about royal things and has always told us the truth in the past, especially about Diana's waywardness.

Wednesday 3 April 1996

Another media lunch, this time with the newspaper publishers. They briefed me on how the newspapers should never suffer VAT because of their link with books and their alleged educational role. I made clear my belief that their honourable educational role had long since gone.

Saw my old pollster friend Bob Worcester of MORI. He had been to the last meeting of the LSE Court and said it was the worst meeting he had ever attended, totally chaotic. The School will have to be careful. It could get into a downward spiral. It is short of money, looking for a new director and a new chairman.

The House rose today so I will have a few days for pleasure and indulgence.

Thursday 4 April 1996

Spent the morning clearing off correspondence before the holiday. Also received a phone call from Graham Greene, who is about to take over as chairman of the British Museum, saying that our Arts spokesman, Mark Fisher, had given an interview with the *Telegraph* stating that a Labour government would return the Elgin Marbles to Greece. Bad politics. Typical *Guardian* guilt-ridden moralistic approach. To me there are no votes in it and it gives the wrong signals. People will think Labour never defends British interests. So I phoned Jack Cunningham and alerted him. I didn't say anything against Mark. Jack apparently moved quickly, phoning the BM to reassure them that this wasn't Labour policy, and alerting Blair's office. Graham later phoned me to say everything was OK.

Good Friday, 5 April–Monday 8 April 1996

In the evening I started Gitta Sereny's massive book on Albert Speer. Clearly a remarkable relationship and a tortuous Nazi personality, having lived under the skirts of evil yet not a fully evil man. Want to read more about that time and especially the Nuremberg trials, which I just remember.

Kept reading through quiet bank holiday weekend.

Incidentally, last week I received a brief but friendly letter from Tony Blair saying that he considered my dispute with the Murdoch man Stelzer closed. Don't suppose it has helped me in the stakes for high government office; but feel relaxed about that.

On Monday, Sarah and I set off early for Northamptonshire, mainly for racing at Towcester but first to visit my brother's and father's graves at Roade. That quiet cemetery, now full of my old footballing friends and my father's fellow pub drinkers, still moves me. I always inspect the new graves to see who else has passed on.

That part of Northants still looks fine, with rolling fields and small hills, though the building of new houses is extensive.

Tuesday 9 April 1996

Home all day reading about Albert Speer except for my usual two mile walk as exercise. Yesterday at Towcester, Alexander Hesketh, a former Tory chief whip, asked if I was going to be Labour leader in the Lords. I was astonished and said it was highly unlikely. He said it needs someone who 'can charm the Tories to get through the abolition of hereditary peers'. I said it would either still be Ivor Richard ('Doesn't understand the House', he said), or perhaps

Tessa Blackstone ('Even worse'), or somebody from the Commons like Hattersley ('Disaster'). He concluded 'You need somebody who can get the business done in the House by getting the support of the Tories. You could do that.' Flattering but seems highly unlikely. Blair will probably leave me out altogether, on Murdoch's orders.

Wednesday 10 April 1996

Daughter Rachel's birthday, so I phoned her early.

Thursday 11 April 1996

Important day. I finally plucked up courage, went to the local golf course and booked a round. Played all by myself. I don't have anyone to play with; like when a boy in my village carrying a tennis ball and looking everywhere for somebody to play football with me. They were all in their warm homes with their families. Now I don't know anyone of my age who is a beginner like me.

I completed my nine holes in 55 in two hours. It is sociological. In Northamptonshire, in my village and at my school, I had never heard of anybody who could play golf. In Hampstead I knew about it but our intellectual professional class didn't play, viewing it as a game for Tory buffers. Now it is almost too late. Pity. As with bridge, I've missed a lot.

Afterwards drove into London and went to a dinner with my old partners at the stockbrokers Grieveson Grant. They were the best bunch I've worked with. Nicer than the seedy journalists, more amusing than the politicians and more honest than the academics. Funny to say that about stockbrokers, who Labour people don't adore. We could do with a few more of their supportive team qualities.

Friday 12 April 1996

Spent a lot of the day reading about Albert Speer. Such a complex character. Streets more intelligence and quality than the Nazi gang of thugs around him. Yet still one of them. A moral dimension missing – though after the war, he invented one for himself. So he genuinely filled himself with retrospective guilt, though he didn't feel any opposition to the atrocities at the time. He just didn't want to know. Later he did much genuine penance. He obviously lied at Nuremberg when he denied knowing anything about the mass exterminations. He knew that if he admitted that he would hang. So he shrewdly chose the one central denial which would avoid the noose; and then admitted everything else. He was the only one to do the latter so the court spared him his life.

I thought of why people, including me, had put up with working for Maxwell – not an evil monster, but a monstrous villain. The real difference is that, although one suspected Maxwell was bad, we had little evidence. We thought he was reformed, or at least enough in the harness of his legal and accounting and banking advisers for it to stop him from following his worst instincts (possibly true until the recession forced him into the financial corner where his debts greatly exceeded his assets and he accelerated his longstanding fraudulent instincts). But we were wrong and many wiser people knew that.

The collapse of the Nazi Empire and the revelations about the camps in 1945 were the most influential political experiences of my life. It has affected my politics and my moral compass ever since, and especially my profound sympathy for the Jewish people and for Israel.

Sunday 14 April 1996

Jeremy Taylor arrived to collect me at 9.00 am and we set off for Lambourn to see Peers Folly, the seven-year-old that I share with (Lord) David Swaythling. The stable lads told me he is their favourite because of his lovely character. But to me he doesn't look strong or aggressive enough to be a successful jump racer.

I've felt this since we first bought Peers Folly, though trainer Kim Bailey denies this, saying he will be successful. On that basis we have paid Bailey to buy and feed him for the past 15 months, and for endless vets. Bailey always says, 'He will run in three weeks', but he has never been on a racecourse.

Tuesday 16 April 1996

Attended a tourism conference, which technically comes under me at Heritage. Blair spoke well to open it, including offering compromise on the minimum wage, which worries tourism since they often depend on slave labour. I went to the Commons for the broadcasting debate. It was lively and Jack was constantly interrupted by Tories quoting my earlier remarks in support of some ceiling limits on cross-media ownership. They were all pointing up at me in the gallery. When I said that, it was our policy to control media moguls. Now we have switched to courting them and the party policy has just become to have no limits at all; New Labour is way ahead of the Tories in our devotion to free market ideology.

Jack was magnificently robust in my defence, saying we were not only colleagues but friends for over 20 years.

In the evening went to a moderate LSO concert at the Barbican. Michael Tilson Thomas conducted as gracefully as always and he joined us at supper afterwards. I sat with Eve Arnold, the photographer in her 80s; she had spent a week with John Major for a big *Sunday Times* piece and concluded, 'He isn't as nice as is said.'

Everyone asks me about Blair. They all like the first appearance but are not sure what is down below. I always praise his skill in repositioning the Labour Party but point out that I know him less well than any Labour leader since and including Gaitskell. If he loses, all the resentments and jealousies will spew out and he might not survive defeat.

Wednesday 17 April 1996

My sister Sheila's 54th birthday. I've seen her only four times in the past 39 years.

Went to the PLP [Parliamentary Labour Party] meeting at 11.30 am where Jack Cunningham spoke on our Heritage work and again spoke generously in praise of my work. There was some applause, especially from my old boss Mo Mowlam. Tony B joined in with little taps on the desk with his fingertips.

Incidentally, Turner Broadcasting invited me to Atlanta to visit them and the Olympic Games in July. Under the new Nolan sleaze rules I feel I dare not take the risk and so turn them down.

Thursday 18 April 1996

Woke feeling I've a cold coming on. Cleared a mass of correspondence and prepared for the PQ on domestic quotas for European TV and film production. Angered by receiving a nasty letter from the Animal Rights Terrorists: just a sheet with a razor blade implanted. Fortunately I pulled the envelope open and saw the blade. Later, the police tell me that the animal rights lot have devised a way to place the blade so that it doesn't show up when scanned. They also address the letters to 'Mr X and family' in the hope of catching a child. Nice people. And oafish Labour MPs, like Elliot Morley and Tony Banks, give comfort to these monsters! I immediately send off more money to the country sports lobby.

Our weekly front-bench meeting was thin and dull.

Friday 19 April 1996

Woke with a streaming cold. Out of action.

Saturday 20 April 1996

Didn't wake till after midday, having feverish dreams.

Monday 22 April 1996

Felt really rotten. Drove groggily up to London in the evening where I was faced by the usual pile of mail.

Tuesday 23 April 1996

Went to Jack Cunningham's group discussing reform of the National Lottery. Today George Howarth, Labour spokesman at the Home Office, presented the paper he and I did on the reforms needed for the gambling industry. Quite good and economically very important. Gambling has never been looked at by politicians other than as a question of moral regulation by the Home Office. My main political point is that the Heritage Department needs to get involved in important economic matters or else it will always be marginal and never on the key economic committee in Whitehall.

We had a three-line whip on the Asylum Bill and won the first vote on an amendment from wonderful cricketer Bishop David Sheppard relating to torture. The Lords is still the only place that defeats the executive government – and usually on that kind of old liberal issue. Twenty Tories voted with us – mainly decent hereditaries who Blair proposes to abolish.

In the evening went to a party with the Parliament cricket club. England's batsman captain Mike Atherton was guest of honour. I had a brief chat and he seemed an intelligent and decent man.

Sat at dinner with three Labour MPs: Graham Allen, Parliament's last year's cricket captain when we toured South Africa, Roger Stott, who was Callaghan's parliamentary private secretary in 1977–79, and Clive Betts, a left winger from Sheffield. They spoke quietly and cautiously, but were very critical of the New Labour leadership. They all think the party has no principles and is wholly geared to presenting an image. They were prepared to go along with this until winning the election, but feel strongly that we cannot run a government on that basis. Both Graham and Roger are natural loyalists; the fact they are suppressing such discontent suggests the leadership is storing up trouble for the future.

Wednesday 24 April 1996

Had a speedy DNH team meeting with a very short agenda but Jack in excellent form. He is really getting on top of things. I hope he stays at the job after the election.

Lunch with David Montgomery. He was much more relaxed than previously.

Thursday 25 April 1996

Spent the whole morning replying to correspondence and telephoning people to decline invitations to parties, openings etc. I could fill every day three times over. Our front-bench meeting was as dull as ever.

Gordon Brown addressed our party meeting: very vigorous and well informed. He is over-optimistic about what we will achieve, but he has to be. He was very polite when Denis Healey, the old warrior who was Chancellor for five years, asked a shrewd question about how we can get unemployment down in an economy where all the pressures are for industry to 'downsize'.

Later I had a fascinating visit from Minister Richard Inglewood. Strictly private. He is afraid that the government is falling apart – and could fall before the Broadcasting Bill becomes law. He thinks that would be damaging to our industry, which would be in a black hole waiting for Labour to reveal its plans on digital. Nobody would invest. Murdoch would have a greater stranglehold. He asked if I would privately meet some from the industry to discuss this – and consider if we could have all-party support for getting the non-controversial digital bits of the Bill hurried through before the election. Very constructive, but politically significant. They must feel it is falling apart. He said the right-wing anti-Europe 'lunatics' in his party were uncontrollable. I will take up his generous offer.

Had dinner with Rupert Lee, our old neighbour in Pimlico. Gossipped about the collapse of his former bank Barings, and comparisons with the Maxwell experience. He said the ordinary staff are furious that the top management got away without punishment. He said they were milking the bank in huge salaries and bonuses without exercising proper management oversight.

Friday 26 April 1996

Went into the Lords, which had the Finance Bill, but still felt rotten and drifted off to the country at lunchtime.

Sunday 28 April 1996

Enjoyed mass, where Father Flanagan was in great form, supporting married priests and saying he had spent his whole life, 'fighting Punch and Judy – the demons drink and women'. He is very sweet and honest and will finally get me fully into the Church.

Depressed by a call from our trainer Kim Bailey saying that Peers Folly is yet again injured. But that is racing: only mad optimists buy racehorses.

Monday 29 April 1996

Today we Labour frontbenchers go to school to learn how to be ministers and handle Whitehall. I drove up to Templeton College, Oxford, where the consultants Arthur Andersen are organising two-day courses for the Shadow Cabinet teams.

All our team were present – Jack Cunningham, Lewis Moonie, Tom Pendry, Mark Fisher and myself. Also there were the transport team and the Scottish team under George Robertson. It was nice to see two of my oldest and closest, Tessa Jowell and Helen Liddell, who outshone most of the men.

We had a mixed bag of seminars: Gerald Kaufman was sharp and funny on how to be a successful minister, managing always to convey how brilliantly he had done the job – Gerald's decisiveness and authority as a minister have grown with the telling each day since he left office. He didn't mention to these putative ministers that his most successful technique was blatantly to flatter the Prime Minister's influential political secretary, Marcia! But he was very good value and his colleagues loved it.

But the sessions with the consultants were mediocre. It is ludicrous to pay consultants who have never been in Whitehall to teach people who have (like Jack and Jeff Rooker) been ministers, or, like me, worked for years in Whitehall, how to manage the machine. The evening session was apparently disastrous. I presciently boycotted it in order to watch Newcastle just beat Leeds 1–0. Jack is a passionate Newcastle fan and Tom is sports spokesman so we felt we were professionally justified in choosing the football.

I was very struck by the repeated comments of dislike for the Labour leadership style. It was the cricket dinner all over again, but with a different cast of critics. I cannot imagine that Blair is aware of the depth of discontent. Not with his policies, which a majority of the critics and most sensible people support. Not with his crucially important reforms to the party, sidelining the lunatic left wing. Not with his national popularity, which they all bathe in and realise will win them the election. But with the style: what they call 'the politics of sound bites'. At the root of it lies the fact that Tony makes no attempt to court them. He is quite different from Callaghan, Kinnock, Smith and Wilson, who nurtured the PLP and the trade unions, even if they loathed them as individuals. They each knew a party leader needs their help if things go wrong.

Blair's style is to ignore them, to have an inner core of apparatchiks, and to speak over the heads of the party to the national political middle ground and the media beyond. That is modern party leadership. It is working well now in electoral terms. But, when things go wrong, he may find that there is no cushion of support to fall back on. The media won't help him then; they are rodents who will try to kill him. And when he needs a supportive vote in the PLP or the union loyalists to get a helpful motion at party conference he will find that there are no union loyalists left.

The undertow of resentment at this meeting was disturbing. They won't criticise him openly because they want a facade of party loyalty to help win the election, especially when we're denouncing the Tories for being divided. But there is clearly a lot of paper over a lot of cracks.

We had an excellent late morning session with clever Andrew Adonis of the *Financial Times*, analysing the history of Thatcher's Poll Tax. There were a lot of lessons on how NOT to be a minister in that.

Sat at lunch with Helen and Tessa and then drove up to London taking Derek Foster, our former Commons chief whip, who is now shadowing the Duchy of Lancaster and preparing for the take-over in Whitehall. He is very nice – perhaps much too nice to be a successful chief whip. We delicately skirted round the leader/party issue, which he has seen from close to. He feels the problem lies with Tony's staff, who are inexperienced and often arrogant. They know nothing about the Labour Party, and appear contemptuous of it. We agree Tony needs a conference speech uniting the party by recognising the different strands in it and welcoming them all, including we veterans of earlier battles with the Left, for their various contributions. But to continue just writing off Old Labour will split the party and alienate the true loyalists.

Walked to the LSE for a dreadful meeting of the Standing Committee. We discussed the previous Court meeting, which had been chaotic, with many lay governors complaining. The academics on the Standing Committee responded by saying we should get rid of the lay governors – and 'good riddance to them', said arrogant political theorist Professor Barry. These academics want the unaccountable right to spend the public money on their pet intellectual hobby horses and then to use the lay governors – who are legally directors with all those financial responsibilities – as a fig leaf if things go wrong. And, of course, to raise funds for them.

I have had some sharp exchanges with them – they are not always fond of former colleagues who have become corrupted by the real world. The shrinking number of lay governors with experience of the adult world sit at the end of the table in silent dismay.

Wednesday 1 May 1996

Had an interesting talk with Derek Gladwyn, who ran the Labour conference and worked for Jim and for my GMB [General Municipal and Boilermakers] union, and is now with us in the Lords. He has a friend in the leader's office handling relations with the trade unions. Derek said these were appalling until a good recent meeting improved things. But he said that relations between Tony and his deputy leader, the irascible John Prescott, are terrible. John is shut out of everything and has nothing to do. He will become a loose cannon unless he is given some departmental work. We agree that the danger is now quite big. Prescott, Robin Cook and Clare Short have all been alienated. Together they are quite powerful in party terms. On Cook, Jack Cunningham told me that, when Blair moved him between Foreign Affairs and Industry, Tony told him it was so he could shunt Cook into the sidelines of Foreign Affairs. There is a limit to how many big-hitters a leader can marginalise.

I dropped into the all-party Media Committee to hear the new BBC chairman, Christopher Bland, give a sensible performance. I knew and liked him 13 years ago when we joined together in a consortium to bid unsuccessfully for the ITV Breakfast TV licence. But the gang of right-wing obsessives as usual went on endlessly about sex and violence so I left.

Then a meeting with our trainer Kim Bailey at David Swaythling's office. We had a friendly chat about Peers Folly's endless problems. Kim said they derived from his being still a weak baby. I pointed out that he was already a full seven-year-old and that the six-year-olds in yesterday's novice chase at Ascot all had an average of 14 runs each. When would he grow up? He might hobble from being too young and weak at 9 to being past it at 11, with very little action in between.

In the evening held a dinner party. The Bedfords – Michael is my favourite City man and now a close friend – and William and Annabel Astor. Invited them home first then to Mimmo d'Ischia, where we were joined by Graham Greene, in his first month as chairman of the British Museum and Patricia Rawlings the Tory peeress.

It became too noisy towards the end. Joan Collins came in with a party of toy boys and girls and then a huge gang of Spaniards or Italians brought in some music and began to dance around the tables. In the end the noise was intolerable and we debunked.

Thursday 2 May 1996

The letter arrived from the Maxwell/DTI inspectors with their comments on me. Nothing worrying or seriously critical. At least it is the final chapter in the Maxwell story for me. Still cannot comprehend how I went into that bog. Sarah says characteristic naiveté. More important at the time was that I sought a quick way out of my unhappiness at Kleinworts and liked the idea of rejoining Joe Haines. I also wanted to work at index tracking passive investment, which I thought had a great future, but when I proposed it to Kleinworts they dismissed it as a silly idea.

Went direct to the Lords and had my photograph taken in the chamber so a painter can use it for a painting of the current Lords (£150 each). Briefly into Questions.

Friday 3 May 1996

A quiet day. The DTI draft mildly suggests I might have asked some more questions about the Maxwell lending (which wasn't anything to do with me) but accept that I knew nothing about the wrongdoings. They have no idea how difficult, even impossible, it was to acquire information from people who were intent on hiding it and skilled at lying about it.

Saturday 4 May 1996

Off to Newmarket for a weekend's racing: the 1000 and 2000 Guineas. I always love to return to Suffolk, remembering 15 years of holidays with the children in a cottage at Wickhambrook. The sky is so big, unlike anywhere else in Britain. Stay with Mark and Gabriella Marlsford. Very nice house and grounds (900 acres) and views. I always enjoy discussing politics with him. I've a secret arrangement with him (and with William Astor) at the Lords whereby I encourage him to go home if I know we won't divide the House in the evening.

Back to Newmarket on Sunday morning and met my sister-in-law Agnes and her two little sons, Thomas and Joseph (my father's two names). I took them to William Haggas's stables.

In the evening watched replays of Manchester United's great 3–0 win at Middlesborough, which gives them the championship – and me a nice return on my March 2 bet at 9–2.

Monday 6 May 1996

Off to Towcester. I walked the course and met Dick Saunders, who once rode a Grand National winner. I discussed with him taking away our jumper from Kim Bailey for the summer and letting Dick look after him out to grass. Then we can get a separate assessment of whether poor Peers Folly might ever actually run.

We had lunch in the wrongly grandly named Empress of Russia Dining Suite. The food was absolutely filthy. Fortunately, Alexander [Hesketh], who owns the course, brought some magnificent claret and we mainly drank that and ignored the awful food. It was clear from the table conversation that all the ladies liked Blair and think he will win.

Tuesday 7 May 1996

Arranged to take Anne Heseltine to Towcester races next week. Phoned her last night and Michael answered. Funny to be phoning to take out the Tory Deputy PM's wife.

In the afternoon we had the Third Reading of the Defamation Bill. The government manoeuvred to get a last minute amendment to allow their MPs to sue newspapers while bypassing parliamentary privilege. This was effectively a major amendment to the Bill of Rights, but smuggled in on the Third Reading of a minor legal Bill. Lord Justice Hoffmann has been persuaded to introduce it, saying it was a mere technicality and would be on a free vote. In fact they secretly put on a heavy whip, with even Thatcher turning up. Lennie Hoffmann was aghast when he saw what had happened – and didn't himself even vote for his own amendment, which was passed with a massive Tory majority.

Our side was very angry with Lennie, who was clearly naive and taken for a ride just to allow Neil Hamilton to sue the *Guardian* and Rupert Allison to sue everybody.

I went to the Racing and Bloodstock committee to hear Woodrow Wyatt, chairman of the Tote, but in fact I couldn't hear him, as he muttered inaudibly into his cigar; nor could he answer our questions, as he is deaf and he couldn't hear us.

Wednesday 8 May 1996

I attended a meeting with Jacob Rothschild about his National Memorial Heritage fund, which now has huge funds from the lottery. He gave us several ideas for reforming the lottery procedures and Jack promised to include private heritage houses in the lottery. I committed us to this in the Lords long ago (without authority) and it is always a relief when each shadow minister confirms it.

I walked up to the Garrick for lunch with Harry Evans, visiting from New York (I am walking everywhere as I've suddenly put on 9 lbs). Less wine and food and more exercise are my plans as a diabetic from now on.

Harry was in great form. He is one of my closest old friends and we always immediately slip into gear together. We discussed all our past deeds and misdeeds. He was delighted I had defeated Murdoch on the Broadcasting Bill, sharing the sense of revenge for Murdoch's appalling treatment of us on *The Times*. We both agreed we made a mistake in 1982 in not joining Melvyn Bragg in taking over Tyne Tees television. We would all now be multimillionaires (Melvyn is anyway) and I would have avoided Maxwell.

Harry and his wife Tina Brown have done very well in America, an astonishing success story. I knew them when he first met her, an Oxford student, and she had sent him a brilliant article to apply for a job on the *Sunday Times*. He told me secretly he had fallen in love and he wanted to divorce his then wife and marry Tina. Today he still refers to lovely Enid as 'the wife' and to Tina as Tina.

Nobody can help loving Harry and he gets forgiven for everything. At lunch we discussed friendship and loyalty. He said there are no true friends in New York like some of us have here in Britain – who stick with you through thick and thin. He said, in New York, once you have failed at something nobody wants to know you.

Drinks in the evening with Melvyn Bragg, another true friend. He is very keen to take over the Arts Council when we're in government. I support that. He would do it very well. He also would quite like a peerage and I support that as well. Along with John Mortimer, he is one of the few top arts/media people who publicly supported Labour throughout our bad time in opposition. Most of the others kept their heads below the parapet until it began to look as if we might win. Some went over to the SDP [Social Democratic Party] but have still been honoured by us.

Thursday 9 May 1996

Rattled through a mass of correspondence and phone calls in the morning. I should get a secretary – but she would have to consult me on the nuances so it would still take as much time.

Our front-bench meeting was as tedious as ever. We never discuss politics or policies, just the legislative timetable. In the early evening I met up with Sarah at a fund-raising drinks party at the Ivy given by Tina Brown and the Royal Court Theatre. Talked with Dominic Lawson about how the *Spectator* has declined since he left, especially since Bruce Anderson has been brought in. He is turning it into a Tory party house magazine, losing all that fizz and unpredictability that made it so good.

I went back to the Lords for a 'surprise' ambush vote on the Asylum Bill. Our side hid in distant rooms and corridors so as not to alert the Tories. Not that they needed to. Somebody who gets our voting whip always warns the Tories and they were there in force to defeat us. We speculate on the traitor: presumably some Labour peer close to the whips' network, who gets rewarded with appointments by the government and who is bitter with Labour. There are not many candidates. I am sure I know who it is.

Friday 10 May 1996

Went to Lingfield for the racing. Lunched with George Ward who was the maligned boss of Grunwick when our unions besieged it in 1976–78. I am delighted that he saw the union hooligans off. How bizarre that decent liberal Labour politicians like Shirley Williams joined in that hooliganism to enforce the closed shop; taking away workers' rights as well as employers'. That is one thing Thatcher sorted out – and I supported her at the time. Ironically her trade union reforms made it possible for Labour to be elected again, because the union bogey was eliminated. We could never have done it otherwise.

Also saw Roger Easterby, now marketing manager there, who used to assist Albert Murray in Wilson's political office.

Sunday 12 May 1996

A very special day. I went to church in Twyford and after mass spoke to Father Flanagan, who is going in to hospital to have his hip replaced on Thursday. We have discussed my being fully received into the Church. I told him that I wanted him to do it, and was afraid that something might happen with his hip on Thursday to prevent that. He grinned and said, 'Well, let us do it today.' I went home very pleased and wrote him a letter of thanks. Curiously I mistakenly addressed it not to Father Flanagan but to Father Galvin, and only just spotted it before sealing the envelope. Father Galvin was the tall, magnificent Irish priest who used to visit my father and me when I was a child in Northamptonshire. I've not seen him for nearly 50 years. Yet I unconsciously wrote this letter of thanks to him.

Kate came for lunch and we discussed her July wedding at Highclere and the honeymoon in the west of Ireland. I begin to feel it is time I went there again. In 1956 I went on a wonderful walk from Mayo through Connemara to Galway with my Oxford friend Gordon Snell (now married to the mega-novelist Maeve Binchy). One of the greatest times of my life. My favourite

Irish cousin Marjorie tells me that we have relatives named Quinn in Mayo near Westport.

At 4.30 pm I turned up in my suit with Sarah at St Thomas Moore's church in Twyford and Father Flanagan was waiting to baptise and confirm me. It was a most moving moment. I felt that somehow I had come back home and that all kinds of loose ends were tied up. My father was born and buried a Catholic, my brother buried one. I shall be the same. It was a most important and private occasion for me.

In the evening I read some more Betjeman – who was clearly a much nicer and more talented man than the scornful trendies in Hampstead allowed.

Monday 13 May 1996

Went to see dear Peers Folly at Dick Saunders's lovely clean yard near Holdenby, in my familiar Northants. The horse had been taken from Kim Bailey's yard at Lambourn three days earlier and already looked improved. But the bad news is that the X-rays show arthritis. That is why he was always going lame. I cannot understand why the trainer didn't find it. We will try different shoes and TLC, but he may never run. A typical racing experience.

Drove on to the racing at Towcester, where I joined up with Anne Heseltine. She knows a lot about horses and hunts, but Michael isn't interested – he is interested only in politics and trees – so he doesn't mind anyone taking Anne racing so long as he doesn't have to go. Letting me take her is his only known cross-party concession.

Tuesday 14 May 1996

Our party group to reform the lottery met in the morning and made progress. Jack Cunningham talked to me privately about the rifts that are emerging at the top of the Shadow Cabinet. Gordon Brown is upsetting many colleagues – including the normally un-upsettable Chris Smith – by interfering in all their policy areas. Gordon also cannot stand Peter Mandelson, who is seen by many as Rasputin to Tsar Blair. Mandelson, who is a recent MP and with no formal seniority, though huge political ability, has privileged access to the leader.

Both Robin Cook and John Prescott feel excluded from the leader's counsels and are backbiting consequently. Many backbenchers are unhappy and attack Mandelson as a surrogate for attacking Tony himself. Jack says it is all very silly and derives from the fact that none has ever held responsible office. It is crazy if they now blow it so close to the election and after waiting for so long. Blair is quite tough and won't put up with nonsense; though his isolated style means he doesn't generate much loyalty. So he relies on authoritarian power. But in opposition, lacking patronage, there is a limit to that power. Jack is clearly much sounder and more experienced than any of them – but he has just been de-selected from the Shadow Cabinet and is politically weakened. The PLP must be mad to do that. They are short on his kind of wisdom and experience. I've sensed the discontent bubbling beneath the surface for some time.

Wednesday 15 May 1996

Went to a chirpy team meeting. Jack told us that the Greenwich Millennium Dome project was in total disarray and they cannot get the matching funds from the private sector. It would be funny if the exhibition missed the Millennium date. This government buggers up everything it touches. Jack and I had further words about the Shadow Cabinet rows. He said Blair must take hold of it and strangle it early or it will get out of control. 'Too many juvenile egos at work', he said. He isn't keen on Mandelson. Only Blair and the journalists are. I find him attractively different and very intelligent, though I don't really know him.

Jack also told me he is fed up with Mark Fisher. He still hasn't produced his Arts document and keeps missing meetings. Jack said: 'If I am secretary of state, he won't be the minister for the arts. He will just be a parliamentary secretary. He is very bright and nice but he simply cannot get his act together. He is all talk but doesn't deliver.' Jack has written Mark a formal letter of warning. I am sorry because I like Mark. But he has seemed a bit disorganised of late. And his Elgin marbles gaffe showed a lack of political judgement.

Went for lunch at the Hard Rock Café in Piccadilly to celebrate its 25th birthday. Nostalgic for me since I last went there at its opening with my pop artist friend Alan Aldridge, who wanted to put money in it and was rightly convinced it would succeed.

Later, was interviewed by a lady academic from Kingston University (of which I hadn't previously heard), who is writing on education policy and especially on Jim Callaghan's Ruskin speech in 1976, where I played a central role. We were interrupted twice by fire alarms when the new Lords café kitchen caught fire. It has just been built and clearly benefits from the particular skills of modern British builders and electricians.

In the evening I went to a reception given by the *Mail* and the *Guardian*, taking my son Stephen along. Walking there with Chris Smith, he confirmed that things were bad in the Shadow Cabinet and that Gordon Brown has been interfering with their social security policies without understanding them.

Thursday 16 May 1996

Usual Thursday morning clearing hundreds of letters and papers. Then the usual and equally boring front-bench meeting, enlivened only by news of our sick and dead (we have recently lost Douglas Jay and Douglas Houghton and are about to lose Evelyn Denington). The Lords is a permanent reminder of our earthly mortality, though it tends to delay that final ending because peers live much longer than the average populace. There was some discussion of how our planned secret voting ambushes always get out to the Tory whips. Some claimed to know from alleged Tory sources – and Michael Cox, ex chief whip and very sour, is the prime suspect.

Had a very good meeting with Denis Carter and Maurice Peston on reform of the Lords. We all feel the party is stupid if it thinks it will be simple to get through the abolition of the hereditaries vote in our first year of government. It could all get bogged down and hold up other more serious matters. We agreed to draw up a plan that we could secretly and informally discuss with the hereditaries, hoping to get agreement. My personal ideas are to let the hereditaries in each party elect a group of representatives. These would serve in the first parliament. If any died they wouldn't be replaced. In return, they would agree not to obstruct the Labour government's programme. If they did we would abolish them altogether. If they behaved they could stay on, slowly dying and tapering out. I like the prospect of the hereditaries holding a kind of mediaeval moot where they would gather to vote to agree or not agree. None of this has party approval.

Friday 17 May 1996

An overnight meeting of the London Arts Board. Very good debate on the problems with the lottery funding and especially on the plans for getting a new chairman. I had plotted it all beforehand and got the procedures and the selection committee we wanted.

Sunday 19 May 1996

I went to mass and took my FIRST communion. That was very satisfactory. An unintelligible Pole, with Father Flanagan recuperating, took the service, but that didn't matter. I felt very comfortable within myself and deeply pleased I've finally made the step to link both with my childhood and my father.

Monday 20 May 1996

It is the second phase of the Oxford course teaching us to be ministers. Jack and the rest of the team are busy in London so I decided not to go today.

Tuesday 21 May 1996

Off to Oxford in the morning and sat in on the final morning session, a paper on Labour's approach to civil service agencies (basically that we would accept them, but try to reinstall a public sector ethos, whatever that might mean) and Jeff Rooker quite brilliant on Scottish devolution. The best summary of the issue I've heard.

Had lunch with Jeff and with Tim Lankester, the former permanent secretary who was in Downing Street with me towards the end of Jim's time. He told me he thought the present group of Tory Cabinet ministers were the worst he has known. Tired and second rate.

The afternoon session was Tim and myself talking about the centre of Whitehall and Roy Hattersley on Cabinet committees. It seemed to go well, though only about a dozen MPs remained to the end. Tessa Jowell spoke very warmly of our talks. These sessions have been worthwhile and although tempting to laugh about going back to school several sessions were very good. The obvious defect was in the absentees. The top four in the future Labour Cabinet – Blair, Brown, Cook and Prescott – were all missing, yet they don't know any more about running a department than the most junior minister. Also Mandelson was missing. If any of them think they are so knowledgeable that they don't need to learn, they are wrong. The three people with the most knowledge of Whitehall – Stanley Clinton-Davis and Jack Cunningham as former ministers and myself from No. 10 – all attended.

I drove back to London with Graham Allen who was one of the original inspirers of these courses. He isn't happy in Clare Short's transport team, which he describes as 'shambolic'. He is very nostalgic for our happy, well-organised time at Heritage with Chris Smith and Mo Mowlam.

Then to the Degas exhibition at the National Gallery. Superb. I talked with Claus Moser, who complained he had sent his wonderful speech on education reform to Blair three months ago but had received no acknowledgement. The old story, I'm afraid: they don't understand about political courtesies.

Thursday 23 May 1996

Quite a dash in the morning clearing papers and then getting to the Lords before 11 am for the final session before the Whitsun break. I had a difficult

Question on deregistering charities, which was a bit too technical for the House, me and the Minister. Then I did my first ministerial order – on allowing gaming machines into betting offices. These often go through on the nod but I took the chance to say a few words on the Lottery threat to racing. Also not sure I will like these machines, turning friendly betting shops into gambling casinos.

Saturday 25 May 1996

Off from Gatwick to the Pyrenees. Before leaving I reflected a bit on the Lords. I don't often describe its membership in this Diary, though it is a big part of my life. I do enjoy it. Without it, I would get very reclusive. No wonder the peers live so much longer than the national average. The quality of debates is high and sometimes PQs come alive. It is also nice to see so many big political figures from the past, Tory and Labour ex-Cabinet ministers, though some of the Tory ones take little part, preferring to go off to earn from directorships. The Lords is a living museum of past British political history.

The best of the Tory front bench is Mackay, Lord Chancellor (wonderful dry sense of humour and a man of liberal principle). Tom Strathclyde is a sensible chief whip and my opposite number Richard Inglewood is both able and nice. Linda Chalker has surprisingly become a trifle pompous. Emily Blatch is perky and well briefed, but is blinkered in full Thatcher mode.

On our side there are a lot of very able people – too many for the jobs in hand and bound to be some disappointments in government. Ivor Richard, who I campaigned for as leader, is good in the Chamber, with experience and gravitas, but most of our side are disappointed with him because he isn't sufficiently proactive for their ambitious tastes, and allegedly doesn't speak up strongly enough for us with Blair. His deputy, Andrew McIntosh, is clever and experienced. His weakness is that he is locked into a time warp of *Guardian* liberal political correctness and all his Home Office responses are out of line with tougher modern Labour and national opinion. He still thinks only of rights and not responsibilities, and of delinquents as victims. Ted Graham as chief whip is genuine old fashioned Labour, which I like, and benefits from having been in the Commons. But he has a bit of a chip about intellectuals and long-haired academics and since our front bench is stuffed with the latter, including me, he has several problems. Tessa Blackstone, John Eatwell, Margaret Jay and Maurice Peston are keen to get rid of him this summer, when he will be 72. The problem is we will all be 72 soon – and then think it isn't too old for office after all.

The latter group are all very bright and do their jobs excellently. Tessa isn't too popular in the House, which sees her as strident, politically correct and short on humour. But she works hard and her judgement is pretty good. She has been a good friend of mine for over 20 years and I've always found her reliable. Patricia Hollis is bright, hard working and gets on top of her difficult subject. She will make a fine minister.

Margaret Jay is first class, tough and very professional. Probably our best – DNA matters as all horse racing people know. She tells me she would rather have a big job outside the House than sit every night late on the Lords front bench. With her family background, she knows how little Lords ministers matter in a Labour government. Maurice Peston is a good old friend who doesn't take the House or himself too seriously, but speaks very well and is always amusing, which pleases the House.

Stanley Clinton-Davis is our most experienced frontbencher, having been a senior minister and a European commissioner. Probably the most able of our side at the dispatch box is Charles Williams, but he isn't always popular with us or the Tories. He sometimes speaks unkindly (if perhaps accurately) of the failings of colleagues so he doesn't get the credit for the first class work he does. He always does his homework. His long Maxwell connection is held against him, but I'm in no position to be judgemental on that! Politics is tribal and you have to go through the motions of being a team player. I always enjoy having discussions with him on serious issues and he is a good writer.

Derry Irvine, shadow Lord Chancellor, suffers the usual jealousies of being a successful high earning lawyer and because he knows Blair well and was his head of Chambers. Gareth Williams – brilliant, charming and very Welsh – would make a more radical Labour Lord Chancellor. I think we're lucky to have them both.

Most of the others on the front bench are able – and chief whip Denis Carter is both able and very nice, becoming a good friend. Together, they are said to be the best opposition front bench team ever. But, in government, most of them have to be just dogsbody parliamentary under-secretaries, so there will be a lot of frustrated ability.

Saturday 25 May–Sunday 2 June 1996

A marvellous holiday at my house in Roussillon. The weather was perfect until the final 24 hours, very sunny and bright but fresh. I sat on the terrace reading, as I've done there every holiday day for the past 24 years, pausing to look over the lovely Reynes valley and up to mighty Mont Canigou. But our wonderful mulberry tree, which acts as a parasol on the terrace, was looking sickly and thin-leafed. If the mulberry dies, I will have to sell the house. It is all about sitting under the tree reading.

We had a lovely trip up into the Pyrennées, walking on the plateau over 5000 feet. Stayed overnight at a hotel in the tiny village of Llo. There were meadows of wild white narcissi, and other flowers stretching to the horizon. Next morning we drove to Valcebollere, a 19th century village frozen in a time warp close to Spain. Wonderful views.

One thing that struck us all was the high quality of French roads – no road works anywhere. Coming back to England and the nightmare of the M25 – rough concrete surfaces and miles of cones and traffic jams but virtually nobody doing any work – was a simple example of the inferiority of this area of life in Britain. The Thatcherite revolution has not touched our primitive physical infrastructure.

Monday 3 June 1996

A beautiful day to be back in England.

Tuesday 4 June 1996

Went up to London late last night to avoid the traffic and sat up very late reading my massive boring post.

Sat in on Questions and then attended the Twenty-First Century Foundation, which arranges good international seminars. Chairman Michael Palliser was an excellent Head of the Foreign Office in the early 1980s. He said he has never been so ashamed to be British as now, with the Government withdrawing all co-operation in the EU over the beef crisis. 'Major is like a small schoolboy in short trousers stamping his feet and saying he will take his football home if the other Europeans don't let him win.'

Went to the Racing and Bloodstock Committee. I sat with Tory peer Marcus Kimball, who is furious with the British Horseracing Board for secretly dropping the title 'national hunt' from our winter racing and simply just calling it 'jump' racing. This is a feeble capitulation to political correctness and the anti-hunting fascists.

Dashed home to change into black tie for a dinner given in honour of Stoker Hartington, who is retiring from the British Horse Board chairmanship (replaced by John Wakeham, who is very different, less straight but a shrewd political operator). Stoker has been a remarkable success, steering the Jockey Club out of the 18th century nearly into the 20th. At least racing has a chance of survival – though not a great chance, in my view, since the deregulation of other gambling opportunities and the growth of competing leisure pursuits means racing will shrink relatively unless it can offer customers better value. Why should young people pay £15 to enter a shabby racetrack that charges £2 for a glass of warm beer – and that is before they start losing to the bookies. Modern youth doesn't grow up in the country with horses over the fence, as I did.

David Swaythling told me that the latest prognosis on his leukaemia isn't good. Made me very sad.

Frank Judd told me that our foreign affairs spokesman, Robin Cook, wasn't consulted by the leadership over the line Blair took in not opposing the boycott of Brussels. Cook is furious and understandably so, as he has to pick up the pieces. We need a more collegiate style, or else the team will fall apart.

Wednesday 5 June 1996

This was a great and triumphal day. I played cricket at the famous Oval for the Lords against the Commons. We fielded first and they rattled up a quick hundred. I was brought on before lunch and felt nervous, having not bowled my leg breaks since last September, and only a dozen overs in the last 30 years. But I got Nick Scott with a big leg break in the first over and felt good. They continued after lunch and made nearly 300 – we had four weary players, including me, over 60 and only one, the Earl of Hardwick, under 40.

We responded quite well at first, with Charlie Fortescue hitting 50 and Mark Zetland doing well, but then we collapsed and I was suddenly in at no. 10 with 16 overs to go. With nearly an hour and 10 overs to go, our no. 11, my old friend and portly LSE economist Meghnad Desai, strode to the wicket and the Commons thought it was all over. But I said to Meghnad that we should take no runs but just defend our wickets. He did so magnificently. As time passed the Commons grew jumpy and brought their ace bowlers back on, but I took as much of the bowling as possible and we saw them off and saved the match.

I was very excited and we had celebratory drinks afterwards. Actually I was much helped by their captain Graham Allen fielding in the slips, who was quietly coaching me on how to play each of his own bowlers and reprimanding me whenever I yielded to my natural inclination to have a swipe at a loose ball. But it was a wonderful feeling.

Thursday 6 June 1996

Woke very stiff but still on top of the world. Cleared correspondence and then went to the front-bench meeting, where we had a rare and good discussion on policy. Drive to Shurlock Row and read till very late, still on Betjeman's Letters and still impressed by the generosity of his life. Pleased that I've finally made to work my brother's pretty old American clock on the bedroom wall. It ticked me calmly to sleep.

Friday 7 June 1996

Another sizzling day. Worked in the morning, all windows open and bird-song flooding in. Watched the Oaks from Epsom in the afternoon and get out my morning suit and topper for tomorrow's Derby.

Saturday 8 June 1996

DERBY day.
Terrific afternoon's racing after usual terrible journey. Finally to lunch with Michael Osborne, who runs the Irish Turf Club and Sheikh Mohammed's stud in Kildare. We had a good chat about the future of world racing, including their plans for Dubai. The race was won by William Haggas's Shamit. When I visited his Newmarket stable he told me it would win, but, typically, I didn't back it.

Sunday 9 June 1996

I read and walked. At night I finished off the Betjeman. Very touching at the end as Candida described him deciding that Cornwall was where he wanted to die and the moving funeral in the little church on the sands. I wept a little reading it and went downstairs to have a whisky. Sarah came down wondering what I was doing, so I told her we were going to Cornwall on Thursday morning to visit him; it is front-bench committee day but bugger that.

Monday 10 June 1996

Had my woolly grey curls cut and then went up for a lunch in the Lords with Jacob Rothschild, Jack Cunningham and a remarkable old Jewish fellow who is going to donate hundreds of millions of pounds worth of objets d'art to a new museum in Somerset House. Jacob has a wonderful scheme for reviving that wonderful building and returning it to the people of London. Jack said we would support that in government. The donor had grown up in the East End in the fur trade, and immigrated to California after the war where he made a fortune out of property. Now he is giving back much of what he made. Jacob handled him beautifully.

In the evening went to a magnificent William Morris exhibition at the V&A and then with Jamie Dugdale to supper with John Lewis (who is involved in the Tourist Board) to discuss problems in tourism – basically that the government doesn't understand and is unwilling to invest in our tourism assets. I knew John nearly 30 years ago when I worked with Clifford and Stephen Barclay, my introduction to high finance. Interestingly, Jacob Rothschild was also there with Clifford a little time, after returning from an unhappy sojourn on Wall Street (we were also contemporaries at Oxford, he at mighty Christ Church, me at modest Lincoln, both getting firsts in History in the same year, 1957). I now better understand the Anthony Powell books, with the same cast of people popping up in different contexts every decade or so; though my cast is sadly smaller. I didn't go to public school, so I don't meet anyone from my first 19 years, whereas Sarah and all her crowd are constantly meeting childhood friends. I envy that.

Wednesday 12 June 1996

Lunch with Carolyn Daly, an American from Turner broadcasting. I've declined her invitation to go to Atlanta for the Olympics in July. I thought it would be wrong to accept such a gift from an interested party – but then I've since learned that my Commons colleagues stepped in to fill the gap!

In the evening we gave dinner for various friends: Claus Moser and Mary, the Browne-Wilkinsons, Robin and Jill Butler and Graham Greene and Camilla Panufnik. Robin has grown more craggy than when we worked together in No. 10. Jill said he didn't enjoy working with John Major as much as he had for Thatcher because Major is 'a bit indecisive'. This is probably Jill's kind of diplomatic understatement.

Claus was in sparkling form and Sarah loves sitting next to him; she can understand why so many women have found him attractive. I've loved him for over 30 years since we met at the LSE, and we later saw a lot of one another in Whitehall. Together with Lionel Robbins, he was responsible for much of my love of opera, always inviting me to Covent Garden when he was chairman; I certainly passed the age of 45 almost without ever buying a ticket and virtually always seeing it from the royal box. Altogether it was a heart-warming evening and makes me feel I must make more effort to see old friends. As Betjeman said, in the end what matters most is being together with friends and close family.

Thursday 13 June 1996

Ducked out of the Fabian conference on the Lottery and headed off with Sarah down to Betjeman's Cornwall. The weather was brilliant. Stayed at Port Gaverne in a nice cliff-top hotel called the Headlands for £28. I immediately set off on the coastal walk over the cliffs for about six miles there and back. Haven't been to Cornwall for exactly 40 years.

Next morning we set off on our expedition to Betjeman. Drove to Trebetherick where he lived, walked on the beach and then to the little church where he is buried. Then drove to Padstow for a delicious fish and chip lunch. It was very pretty with the ferry trading across the estuary at very low water. We then drove to Trevose Head and walked around the cliffs, with stupendous views down to St Ives. A late lobster dinner on the quay in Port Isaac and a pint at a pub nearby. A tremendous day.

Saturday 15 June 1996

Woke rather stiff, but elated by the beauty of it all. When the weather is good and the crowds are not there, parts of Britain are so beautiful that there is no need to go abroad. The great change since when I was younger is in the quality and range of the food available, and in the service, which is no longer openly hostile and occasionally even helpful. I've had my French house for 25 years and am deeply attached to it, especially since the children spent their childhood holidays there; but for the first time I could contemplate withdrawing.

Went back into Port Isaac to the fishermen's co-operative to buy fresh lobsters and crab to take home. A lovely coffee and walk at a cove called Trebarwith Strand and then to lunch at Boscastle, which is a perfect gem. The journey back to Berkshire was fast.

Sunday 16 June 1996

What a lovely week. Not for John Major though, as his government falls apart around his ears; but here in Berkshire that all seems very marginal.

Monday 17 June 1996

Back to the Lords where we sprang a successful late ambush. We all went home in the early evening, then reassembled around 10 pm for a sudden vote in which we comfortably beat the government. But it is all a game really; just easing the general tedium of opposition.

Tuesday 18 June 1996

First day of Royal Ascot, always my favourite because it's so fresh. Dressed in a hurry; ancient morning suit and grubby topper. Reached Ascot and found I had left behind my vouchers for the royal enclosure so I had to visit the special office to prove my identity and that I wasn't an IRA bomber while Sarah, who was blown up by the IRA, was forced to drive up and down Ascot high street because they wouldn't let her park. But I finally got our badges.

Lunch with Tony Hall of the BBC. He has a good sense of public broadcasting values. But not everything went well. First I forget my topper and wasn't allowed into the enclosure. Then I lost Sarah and missed the St James's Palace Stakes, the great race of the day, where the Aga Khan's horse, carrying all our money was ahead but faltered on the line.

Then, worst of all, we met Sarah's sister Susan and husband Colin Ingleby-Mackenzie and consumed a bottle of champagne, which meant we failed to notice the passing of the fourth race – our moment to have tea with Her Majesty. When we got there it was too late for the introductions and Henry Carnarvon was waiting agitated on the steps. I squeezed in for tea sitting close to the Queen Mum (incredibly sharp at 94 and very anti-European Union) and the Duke and Duchess of Devonshire (he cleverly recalled me referring to him as a 'Whig' in the House many years ago and liked it). They were very nice and we discussed Betjeman, who of course had a long affair with his sister, which I managed not to refer to. Nice iced coffee and ice cream; and then HM strode swiftly to the box to watch the 4.55 handicap. I felt I should apologise to somebody, probably Henry, but couldn't focus on it. One of those days. May not be invited again.

Watched England footballers play beautifully in the evening, beating Holland 4–1. Have not seen them play better since 1966. So I decided I must watch them on Saturday against Spain and sent a fax to Washington withdrawing from an international media conference in Dublin due to 'unforeseen circumstances'.

Wednesday 19 June 1996

Off to Ascot again, starting with excellent Tote lunch. Sat next to the Countess of Bathurst and Jean Trumpington, who has long been my favourite opposite number in the Lords and we spar across the despatch box, but get on marvellously personally, which is widely known so we're often seated together.

Decided not to go to the Lords in my topper and tails, as some Labour colleagues view Ascot as certainly not socialist and even not New Labour.

Had dinner in the new Lords cafeteria. Sat with Robert Skidelsky, who I knew at Nuffield 35 years ago and has peregrinated from Labour through the SDP to the Lib Dems to the Tory peerage. He has written brilliant biographies of Moseley and Keynes and I always enjoy our conversations.

Thursday 20 June 1996

To the front-bench meeting, where we discussed the coming debate on constitutional reform. I told our leader Ivor Richard that I wanted to speak and he was very nervous, fearing I might, as often, stray from the party line. I won't do that today, however tempting, but I will float a few disruptive thoughts that the chip-on-the-shoulder brigade won't like.

Saturday 22 June 1996

Lunch near Theale with Michael Green, the media tycoon who owns Carlton TV. I sat near some interesting people, especially the two independent Tory Benyons, who own the odd 18,000 acres nearby. There was also a gaggle of extremely right-wing people. The pure selfishness of some of these, who care about only their tax levels and couldn't give a damn about the state of English society is breathtaking. It is when I meet people like them that I remember why I am still in the Labour party and why so many of us support Labour despite its many failings. One can be beguiled in the Lords where many of the Tories, especially the hereditaries, are responsible and caring people. But out in the Thatcherite bunkers are some pretty nasty rodents.

Watched the start of England's match against Spain then the rest at Shurlock Row. I hadn't the nerve to watch the penalty shoot-out, since English footballers usually cannot shoot straight from the spot, and hid in my bedroom until I heard the huge victory roar. Now the problem is that we have arranged a dinner party for when England play Germany in the semi-finals. I suggest a cancellation to Sarah but she is so far resisting. I suspect the guests will all drop out with BSE or some such excuse; Michael Heseltine already has, though Anne is coming. Michael Grade will be looking for an out, understandably.

I read the first 100 pages of Ken Tynan's Letters. When I met him in the early 1970s he was a bit frail and posturing.

Sunday 23 June 1996

Lovely day. Went to Jeremy Taylor in the village to play tennis – and beat people 10 years younger. Nice feeling. One of them a pretty young Asian girl friend of tycoon James Hanson.

Monday 24 June 1996

Worked on papers in the morning. And, surprise, surprise, Michael Grade dropped out of Wednesday's dinner because he wants to see England at Wembley. I completely understand. Wish I was there myself.

Drove to London after lunch for a three-line whip vote. Andrew McIntosh loses about three every day. It is a kind of machismo thing. I had only two votes on the whole of the Broadcasting Bill – we won one and lost the other by only two.

Tuesday 25 June 1996

Held a morning meeting of some of the Towcester racecourse board at my house. Mike Buswell and I are worried about our grandiose scheme for a new stand costing over a million – our annual profit is never more than £10,000 and last year was less. Owner Alexander Hesketh is very keen on it, and it is a fine scheme, but we have to make sure it doesn't sink us. We conclude that we can do it providing the Heskeths give us either a longer lease on the racecourse as collateral or a letter of comfort/guarantee. Sadly, I cannot go to Friday's board meeting.

Had lunch at the Café Royal with Jim Callaghan – he told me he is on the restaurant group council and gets a 30% discount. Callaghan's like that! We had a good chat. He said the thing he most regrets about the 1978–79 crisis was 'not being tougher with the unions and having a state of emergency'. He told me that Thatcher had assured him she would support him in a state of emergency. He has never published that. What swung him against was that Bill Rodgers argued against. He said Bill was normally 'a sensible toughie' and if he was against it might not be the right thing. He also knew he couldn't depend on the Tories, who might desert if he was in trouble.

Jim said he finds it impossible to identify with Blair: 'He is simply not one of us.' He said he liked Gordon Brown, Chris Smith and especially John Prescott. He thinks we have a very good front bench in the Lords and was particularly kind about me. But he thought our leader and chief whip were a bit below best. He thought it would be a mistake for Blair to send someone up from the Commons to lead us in government since they wouldn't understand the House; and that sadly Tessa Blackstone 'has no feel for the House and too humourless'. He said the most important thing for Blair to do is to identify one central issue to make succeed in the first parliament – and that shouldn't be devolution to the Scots or Lords reform (though he supports getting rid of the hereditaries). He would go for education and spend the money there.

Jim has been invited to give an education speech to celebrate 20 years since his Ruskin speech in October 1976 and he asked me to help him. I will. He was feeling a bit low and listless after his recent operation to remove a small growth but it was good to talk with him again. We agreed to do it again regularly.

Incidentally, he told me that his official biographer had found very few papers in Harold Wilson's collection donated to Oxford. That is curious. I remember seeing them with Joe Haines in a basement near Victoria and there were high rows of huge filing cabinets. I said to Jim: 'Who could have filtered them out?' 'I can think of one person, Bernard – and so can you', he said. How curious if, after all the fuss about not selling them to America, it should some day emerge that the donation to Oxford didn't contain the bulk of the collection anyway! Jim was going back to the House to see Henry Kissinger, so it really was an old times day.

Had a three-line whip and vote on Housing, where we came within six votes of winning. Patricia Hollis, who I admire for her hard work and professional approach, had done a good job of organisation.

A particularly tricky LSE Standing Committee. They bounced through us approval for the introduction of top-up fees for domestic students. This makes us the first college to break the Robbins principle of free higher education. It was done in a hurried way. When Kate Jenkins and I quizzed them on the reasons the answers were fuzzy – and mainly that we were under-funded because we didn't have science funding.

I went home troubled but feeling we had no alternative.

Wednesday 26 June 1996

Early on Tessa Blackstone phoned about top-up fees. I begin to get suspicious about last night's meeting and feel we were bounced. I asked Tessa about the alleged disadvantages of not having science, leading to under-funding. She said that is balls. I get more worried and telephone Peter Parker, LSE chairman, to say we may have been misled and to make sure it isn't peddled to Thursday's Court meeting. He phoned back later to say we had been misled, it wasn't true, and the Director wouldn't repeat it at the Court. It all sounds pretty sloppy to me.

The Treasure Bill became law this afternoon, restraining the looting of treasures by metal detectors. This gave me pleasure since I had given it great support from the beginning – indeed I announced Labour would support it in both houses before I had time to consult our Commons colleagues. Jean Trumpington also did sterling work from the government benches. But really it was a tribute to the Earl of Perth who has worked on this for years.

In the evening we had our much depleted dinner. It was really for Jocelyn Stevens and Vivien Duffield who are always so generous to us in Gstaad. But the two Michaels, Heseltine and Grade, dropped out so it was thin – but never too thin when Vivien is present. I was next to Vivien, who was dreading the Labour government, and Anne Heseltine. She said she considers herself quite non-political and constructs her life separately from Michael – who she says will retire from the Cabinet after the election. We will wait and see. Apart from his garden, only politics really interests him. But she says he will go back into publishing.

Before dinner we gathered in my house for drinks; but of course it coincided with England's game against Germany, so Jocelyn and I spent most of the time upstairs watching the game. It was still 1–1 when we set off for the restaurant, which didn't have a TV. So when they reported there was a penalty shoot-out, Jocelyn left to listen in his car (he had brought a small radio to my house, spent 10 minutes finding the station, and then forgot to bring it with us). When he returned with the news we had lost we were both devastated. He became emotional and began to denounce the absent Michael Grade as the 'greatest pornographer in Europe'. I felt he blamed Grade's presence at Wembley for our defeat. Max and Jane Rayne, who were not interested in football, seemed a little bemused.

One other familiar but boring aspect was a discussion on education where they all (except the Raynes) attacked the state education system and supported the restoration of grammar schools. Yet all, except Max and I, had been at and had sent their children to private schools. The products of our private system all speak with such authority and prejudice against the state system of which they have no personal experience. That is at the root of our national educational malaise. The top 10% denounces our state system but opt out of it and do nothing to improve it, just demoralise it.

Thursday 27 June 1996

In the Chamber I had two PQs. The one on the BBC World Service went well – I had tipped off the minister beforehand on what I would say – and I let the one on the hooliganism of our tabloid press roll before quietly intervening.

The LSE Court met at 5.00 pm and it was very uncomfortable. Both Kate Jenkins and I were troubled that the platform made the case for top-up fees on different figures from the ones put to us previously. I spoke putting the point that we had a fiduciary duty to eliminate the deficit. That was subsequently ignored by several academics who may not have the least idea what a fiduciary duty is. But I sympathised with Margaret Hodge and Frank Judd, who argued convincingly that the (now smaller) deficits didn't justify such a major break with principle on fees. The student representative also made a similar impressive plea. In the end the court defeated Peter Parker's Standing Committee motion and as usual passed one calling for delay. Now we must investigate every other way of saving money that avoids top-up fees – not excluding closing the odd department.

My real sadness is from the occasional thought that the present LSE is hardly worth fighting battles to save. Although it does have very many high quality staff, it is no longer the British centre of the social sciences educating British kids, many from the state sector, in radical social science. That is the LSE I loved. Around half of its present students are overseas high fee-payers, and most of the British are from the privileged private sector. Almost no undergraduates are ever taught by a full-time member of staff; that is now all done by graduates, many of whom don't have English as a first language. So the typical class is 16 (double that in my day), three-quarters foreign, being taught by a probably foreign graduate student. I am not sure that is what we all used to believe in or that future governments will be willing to subsidise it as a standard British university. It is probably time it went fully private and foreign fee-paying – and that I slipped away. I first joined the Standing Committee in 1968 and it is now a different show. I get very little satisfaction from it and cannot see what job we're doing for British education.

I drove sadly to the country. Sarah's Jack Russell Smudge is dying of cancer. I went to bed to read Ken Tynan's Letters. He was obviously a genius in a superficial way, but less creatively talented than Waugh and less engaging than Betjeman. Both of those left lasting cultural legacies. Tynan left little but fading vinegary review clippings.

Friday 28 June 1996

Most of the day spent writing my speech for next week's Racehorse Owners AGM. That will be tricky. Racing people always ask for a light speech but they don't laugh at jokes. I will try to provoke them on training costs.

Sunday 30 June 1996

The opinion polls are moving the Tory way – though still 20 points behind.

Monday 1 July 1996

We had our annual peers summer party on the terrace. I invited Anne Murray, widow of Harold Wilson's wonderful cockney aide Albert, who was in cracking form; she has just been Mayor of Greenwich. Blair made a rousing and funny speech, with several references to the rebellion against him on Scottish devolution.

I dashed from there to dinner with Andrew Graham (now Master of Balliol), who worked for me in Downing Street in 1974–76 and was a superb economic adviser.

Tuesday 2 July 1996

Rose at 6.00 am to write my speech for this morning's media conference at the Park Lane Hotel. I was standing in for Jack Cunningham at the last moment. It went quite well with an audience of lawyers who were all clearly rehearsing to be rich.

Dashed for lunch with Camelot, the lottery rip-off merchants, at the Reform. It was nice to go back there. I was a member for many years but resigned when joining the Lords because I didn't need another club. Went to the Lords to nod through a ministerial deregulation order. I didn't speak since the minister and I had agreed we didn't understand its technical details about wireless telegraphy so it was wisest if neither of us was drawn in.

Off to Holland Park with Sarah for a party with several old friends: John Gross, historian Asa Briggs and John Tooley from Covent Garden Opera.

Wednesday 3 July 1996

Up at 6.00 am again working at the computer on my big speech for today's AGM of the Racehorse Owners Association. Finished by 9.00 am and taxied in for our DNH team meeting. We went over plans for party Conference, which is at Blackpool and I would prefer to avoid. I also raised the question of the BBC and the new management changes – Stalinist centralism – whereby they absorb the World Service into their single empire. I press them to be aware that it might erode its distinct characteristics. Jack and Lewis [Moonie] go to the Atlanta Olympics in three weeks on the freebie I turned down. These MPs do get around. But I am not jealous. Airports and aeroplanes are the hell-pits of the modern era. My definition of a civilised life is never having to travel through an airport.

Went to the Lords for coffee with Denis Howell and a few other colleagues; worked trimming my speech as I drank. Some went off to hear Tony Blair see off the dissidents at the meeting of the Parliamentary Labour Party (which I rarely attend). I was later told he was very good and passionate. His handling is fairly autocratic. The attitude of the party to him is a mixture of serious respect, knowing he is right on most issues, but resentment that he doesn't bother to carry them with him. As one said to me, 'I wish sometimes he would be as nasty to the Tories as he is to us.' But he wants those Tory votes and assumes he has the Labour votes anyway.

To the Racehorse Owners Association AGM and lunch. My speech was devoted to exposing the high costs of training horses in the UK and suggesting that we needed a few Tescos and Sainsbury's as trainers as well as all the Harrods. The trainers didn't like it when I mentioned that they often had houses and holidays that the owners couldn't afford, but it was mainly done lightly and jokingly. I was relieved that was my week's speeches over.

Thursday 4 July 1996

Clear the huge pile of papers on my desk. Lunch alone and then to the dentists for three fillings – two without anaesthetic. Walked to the Lords to hear the opening speeches on Lords Reform and thought Cranborne, the Tory leader, was very poor: thin in content and pompously fluffy in style. As a hereditary he made no case at all for keeping the hereditary vote in the Lords.

The Tories are simply resisting all constitutional and Lords reforms and hoping they win the election. Then, if they lose, they will try to negotiate a compromise – but it will then be too late. I am disappointed because I support compromise and think the sooner the two sides start to speak the better for the future of the House. Ivor Richard gave a good speech for our side, quoting all the Tories who historically have admitted that reform is right – including Cranborne's grandfather.

Took train to Oxford and attended a farewell dinner for the maths don at my old college, Lincoln. It was a quintessential Oxford occasion. The Rector is Eric Anderson, from Eton, and he looked after us well, but the dons all hung shyly on the fringes. Dinner was splendid, lovely food and wine with terrific service, but the speech in honour of the departing one was excruciating. Given by a classicist contemporary of mine, it barely contained a reference to the guest of honour, and was full of obscure show-off classical references. You would never know that they had been colleagues for

35 years. As often at Oxford, the intellectual game serves to completely shut out human emotions.

Friday 5 July 1996

Went to Sandown where the syndicate had a horse, Navigate, trained by Richard Hannon, running; no luck as usual. It seems to run the same over any distance from 6–12 furlongs, and the same means not quite finishing.

Saturday 6 July 1996

Today the Big Day. My lovely Kate was married – at Highclere Castle, which made a wonderful setting as well as a touching link between loyal friend Henry Carnarvon and me. It was a brief civil ceremony on the main stairs of the castle but very touching. Altogether a terrific occasion. Driving back I felt both uplifted and sad that I had now lost both my girls. But they are both continuing to use the Donoughue name. That is one part of feminism I approve of!

Sunday 7 July 1996

Watched the Wimbledon final. Time is racing by and we shall soon be heading for France. I don't feel quite as excited as I used to when the children were small. That was a wonderful adventure. Maybe the time is approaching to close the Ceret chapter after 25 years. But it is very beautiful.

Monday 8 July 1996

To London after lunch, voted, and then set off for Newmarket to the Newmarket Jockey Club for dinner with the Thoroughbred Breeders Association. I was fascinated to see all the wonderful equine paintings on the walls.

Tuesday 9 July 1996

My sleep was disrupted by a horrible toothache and I went back up to London to the dentist. I must have been the only race lover leaving Newmarket on the day the July meeting started. The dentist was extremely painful as an infected wisdom tooth came out. And I had to be in the Chamber 30 minutes later taking a Question on animal welfare. My mouth was still frozen and my tongue felt thick as I spoke.

Received nice and friendly letter from Tony Blair today. May have repaired my fences. But he still hasn't acknowledged the one I sent him concerning the official position on a Roman Catholic becoming prime minister. Anticipating that he might get in this position I had asked the Clerk of Parliament for the official position. I sat on it till now waiting. Now it has emerged that Tony, although a formal Anglican, has been attending mass and taking Catholic communion. Lots of fusspots have complained and the press tried to whip it up. I sent him the clerk's favourable report, just so he wouldn't be deterred if he wanted to cross the bridge.

Wednesday 10 July 1996

Visit doctor to have diabetes tests. Some of my blood sugar and liver counts are bad. To the Lords for Question time. After voting I went to hear Cardinal Hume, Head of our Church, speak on spirituality. He spoke in a very ecumenical way. Then, for drinks with Cranborne, the Tory leader, standing on the balcony admiring the back of Westminster Abbey and St Margarets on a fine sunny evening. Finally, slipped across to the Abbey Gardens for the annual party of the university vice chancellors. A beautiful setting, where I chatted with a number of old university friends.

But a heavy end with the LSE pro-director, who pompously informed me how I was wrong on virtually everything and said it might be better if I left the School Standing Committee. Otherwise 'some senior professors might leave'. This suggested I must be right in the positions I've taken, but made me wonder even more why I spend so much time there. I still care about it as a great institution of the past; but the arrogance and pomposity of many of its staff are unbearable. Again decide to resign.

The newspapers are full of attacks on MPs for getting a big pay rise (we on the Lords front bench remain unpaid). I would like to pass a one-clause Bill that requires all journalists attacking public servants' pay to declare their own. There is probably not a single London journalist who doesn't earn more than his MP.

Thursday 11 July 1996

Great day's cricket. I played for the Houses of Parliament against Channel 4 at Vincent Square. I bowled six overs of spin and didn't get a wicket, but was quite tight even against Rory Bremner who was batting well and I enjoyed it. It was very hot and my gum was aching a lot.

In the interval I told Michael Grade, the boss of Channel 4, about my suffering, and he miraculously produced a whole pot of painkillers, so I was fairly doped when we batted. I went in last and was once again not out – I've not been out since 1953 – but Tremayne Rennell was bowled by Bremner in the last over so we lost. But a super game. I so wish I had played more, or indeed any cricket, in my middle decades. Heading for 62 is a bit late to find form and also puts my hamstrings at risk.

While waiting to bat I chatted with John Redwood, Tory right winger, who I've known since my City days when he was at Rothschilds and I was at Grievesons and we jointly managed the Cheshire county pension fund. He was quite sharp about John Major. Said he is a formidable politician, the best of his generation, but not at all as nice as his reputation. Recalled how, as Treasury minister, Major had set out to destroy his colleague John Moore's reputation when he was at Health and the main young political competitor to Major. He trapped him in Cabinet and then demolished him ruthlessly and with contempt before their colleagues, to the point where Moore was in tears afterwards. His career was finished and Major was then the only contender for the leadership. All in front of Thatcher, who was probably impressed by the ruthlessness. John said Major doesn't believe in anything in policy terms. Said in Cabinet he would never reveal a view of his own but would just go round the table until he established a majority and then join that side.

Dashed home to go to a great Labour gala dinner. This was exciting and the atmosphere heady. Gordon Brown and Richard Attenborough opened proceedings and later Tony Blair gave a most impressive speech. He started off funny, with self-deprecating remarks about himself, then moved into high moral gear about the basic principles of politics and public life. The audience was lifted and moved. Certainly moved to generosity – individuals bid £9000 for footballer Cantona's Cup Final shirt and £11,000 for a signed copy of Nelson Mandela's book. The party raised a clear £200,000 tonight. Yesterday a Lords colleague told me that a business man had just handed him a quarter of a million for the party. Apparently the funds are flooding in – and not from off-shore arms dealers as is the case with the Tories.

At the pre-dinner reception, Blair toured around. When talking to me, he complained that everyone says how small he looks on TV. In fact he is taller than me at over 6 feet. I also met his wife who seems to be over-intoxicated by the smell of power and the whole wave of success. She will learn the downside when they get into No. 10.

Afterwards I went for drinks with Stephen Fry the comedian – a strong Labour supporter. He said how sickened he had been to see at the great Mandela reception several Tories, especially John Carlisle, who had denounced Mandela as a criminal only a few years ago. Stephen had helped organise a Wembley rock concert to raise funds for him in jail and Carlisle and several

Tory MPs had gone to the High Court to have it banned as raising money for a terrorist. Thatcher had said that anybody who thought that Mandela and the ANC would ever govern South Africa 'lived in cloud cuckoo land'. Now they all sit sharing his glory and clapping his speeches. One has to be very Christian to forgive that degree of hypocrisy. Mandela does.

Friday 12 July 1996

Went into the Lords to collect mail and listen to a little of the debate on Northern Ireland – that is all going badly, with riots on the streets and the Irish prime minister denouncing Major for yielding to the Orange Men.

Then to Berkshire and go to Garsington for Mozart's *Idomeneo*. A magical setting, quite a good performance, and a good supper with Mr and Mrs Ingrams who own it all and have created it. It was lovely to see inside the house where Otteline Morrell presided. The local council is trying to have them banned for 'noise' (the average Brit's word for serious music) and I will try to help on that.

Saturday 13 July 1996

In pain with my gum so went to the doctor and was given loads more painkillers. These sent me to sleep so I spent most of the day in bed.

Sunday 14 July 1996

Even more miserable. Went to an emergency dentist in Maidenhead who dressed the wound, said it was still infected and the only thing I can do is keep taking the antibiotics and painkillers and wait for it to go.

Monday 15 July 1996

Bad day. Racked with pain. Didn't go to London so missed my PQ and vote on three-line whip.

Tuesday 16 July 1996

Went to the Lords to meet Christopher Bland, the new chairman of the BBC. I've publicly criticised his appointment as yet another Tory in the trough, but in fact he is better than that, with a good record in commercial TV and also a decent Tory of a liberal kind. When we met the other day and I warned him there were political troubles ahead over John Birt's new reorganisation, with everything centralised and bureaucratised, Bland seemed complacent and dismissive. Yesterday he phoned up to fix an urgent meeting and was now much more concerned. He realised it was all going wrong and admitted that Birt's lack of consultation of staff was a mistake. Bland said that Birt – an old friend and colleague of his – is 'a control freak'. Certainly a touch of the Stalinist centralist. Yet much of what he has done at the BBC is managerially right and he has grasped some necessary nettles.

In the evening went to the British Museum annual dinner. I was still down with pain and drugs, but it was very enjoyable. Sat next to a lady named Harrup I used to know at the Treasury. She has left now, finding Whitehall a much diminished place since the Tory onslaught on civil service numbers and morale. Sarah was across the table with my old friend Antony Lester, who left us for the SDP, but still does very well in law and in the House. He seems to have grown a bit self-righteously judgemental – though being in the Lib Dems now that should suit him and them.

Graham Greene made a fine speech as new chairman and Claus Moser followed up with his financial appeal. Princess Margaret was guest of honour and looked grumpy as usual. Virginia Bottomley made a headmistressy speech and then left for the Commons.

Wednesday 17 July 1996

Sarah's Jack Russell, Smudge, died in her arms en route to the vet this morning. She returned bereft, like losing a child with whom she has shared the last 14 years. This includes being buried together by the IRA bomb at the Grand Hotel when her husband was killed.

Attended our last DNH team meeting of the session preparing for party conference at the beginning of October. I hate them but suppose I will have to go. I asked why the Broadcasting Bill, the BBC and especially why culture was missing from the new party policy manifesto, which will rightly upset the arts lobby. Jack explained how he had submitted a 1000 word piece to the Leader's office, then was asked to cut it down to 250, which he did, and then, while he was away, it disappeared altogether.

One problem is that Mark Fisher has still not produced the Arts policy paper promised for April. So we didn't have a basic text to fight for. Second that the Leader's henchmen have no comprehension of the importance of our area, both culturally to society, and economically where it covers about 6% of GDP.

Had dinner with Henry and Jeannie Carnarvon. Henry told me that all the talk about Victor Rothschild being a double agent with the Russians was untrue and a code for the fact that his wife was very suspect and had a long affair with Anthony Blunt, the Soviet spy – and a homosexual; this was his only relationship with a woman. Victor was a most complex, difficult and devious man. Henry is related to the Rothschilds, one of whom married one of his Herbert grandparents and when Henry went to stay with them he found that his relative, the deviant Rothschild, had been expunged from the official Rothschild family list, although his marriage was to one of our oldest aristocratic families.

One irritation today is that I received a letter from Brian Morris of Castle Morris, our deputy chief whip and no. 2 in my DNH team, pompously admonishing me for being absent from a recent three-line whip. He even patronisingly said that if I had any personal problems I could talk them over with him. I sent it back saying fuck off and will reflect on a more measured reply. The fact is I was ill and did warn them I couldn't make it – and we lost by 70! They are boys playing a man's game and have no real experience of serious politics.

Thursday 18 July 1996

I left early to handle the Broadcasting Bill, which has been returned from the Commons with 300 amendments. I chatted with the minister, Inglewood, beforehand and we plotted how to handle it: I would say virtually nothing on nearly everything to get it through quickly and then we could concentrate on the two issues of the BBC World Service and the pensions of privatised staff. We did 200 amendments in the first hour. Incidentally Inglewood was very helpful and even gave me advance copies of the speeches and arguments he would give on various amendments. This civilised way of doing things demonstrates the great superiority of the Lords over the Commons, where that behaviour would be unthinkable.

Friday 19 July 1996

Reflecting on my clash with Morris and the whips over missing a vote, it actually results from a cleavage between the different ambitions and experience of frontbenchers. Some of us – Ivor Richard, Tessa Blackstone, Maurice Peston, Brenda Dean, Stanley Clinton-Davis, Frank Judd, Neil Carmichael, myself – have been in national government or high in national or trade union politics and are fairly relaxed about the future; though we would like to be ministers, we're not going to kill ourselves in pursuit of it. We have other lives outside Westminster and we don't take the House of Lords nor ourselves too seriously, knowing virtually nobody hears what we say there and that most of our great victories in the lobbies are quietly overturned next time in the Commons. Other academics such as Brian Morris have never operated on the national stage and are desperately keen to get there.

Patricia Hollis and Charles Williams have strong political ambitions so they take the Lords very seriously, working commendably hard, mastering their policy briefs and studying procedural devices to outwit the Tory hereditary enemy. That involves dragooning their more relaxed colleagues through their lobbies at all hours – Patricia has more divisions before tea on any one day of a Committee stage than I had on the whole Broadcasting Bill. Patricia deserves to and will surely become a minister, as should Charles. But for me a cricket match is as important as one of these votes – especially when we're going to lose by 70 anyway (which we all knew before last week's vote).

It is important to stop the nonsense of pretending we in the Lords are very important politicians.

Saturday 20 July 1996

A terrific time at Newbury races, but our horse Kings Witness played up terribly before its race, trying to eat Susan Haggas, the trainer's wife, as she saddled him. Really it is a question of character. I've never liked the look in his eye. A bit like Tony Benn, a look that suggests he isn't to be trusted.

Sunday 21 July 1996

Toothache still hurting and feeling low from being on a double dose of anti-biotics running into a second week. But went to mass which was lovely, with Father Flanagan back from his operation, reminiscing and saying how much he owed to both his mother, who was a deep believer, and his father, who didn't believe at all. 'You need to be able to disbelieve as well as to believe in this Church', he said. A lovely man who understands that faith is personal, that none of us is perfect and that our foibles and sins are universal.

Monday 22 July 1996

Fascinating lunch at Marcus Kimball's. Angus Ogilvy wanted to meet me to discuss joining the Prince of Wales Trust, which helps unemployed young people. I agreed on condition that he gets more Labour people, such as Brenda Dean, John Monks of the TUC, Melvyn Bragg and Bob Gavron.

Afterwards Marcus told me he was also considering having me as one of the Prince Charles Trust advisers. Not an easy job. Marcus said Charles loses his temper too easily and once did with him when Marcus, fishing with him, advised him on changing his fly. Resenting experienced advice isn't good for a future monarch. Maybe we should give my favourite Anne a chance – or even skip a generation.

Wednesday 24 July 1996

Lunch with Tory multi-millionaire industrialist (and famed asset stripper) James Hanson. Others present include an Anglican Bishop of unknown pedigree and probably wavering belief, a Tory peer and Sue Douglas, editor of the fast disappearing *Sunday Express*. Hanson was pleasant and concerned to rebuild the image of his company before the coming break-up. Its shares have fallen 30% against the market and, after years of Thatcherite idolatry from the press, he is now experiencing what we on the Labour side always suffer – denigration whatever he does. It has certainly humbled him. He will go out on a low note, as Harold Wilson is sadly doing now. It is hard to recover when you are down and old.

Called in at the Lords to collect my post and then set off for the country. Tomorrow morning fly off early to a long holiday in Ceret – my 23rd successive year. But 20 years ago I was travelling excitedly in a small crammed Ford Escort with Carol and four children, and joining up with Jean-Francois and Eliane and my late brother Clem. Now none are there. I will fly business class with Sarah, which is lovely, but nothing can recreate that sensation of adventure and the excitement of the kids. The sense of time past and people gone is quite gutting.

Thursday 25 July–Saturday 10 August 1996

The holiday in France.

The weather was worse than I've ever known, with storms and rain. So much less time in the pool and no visits to the beach in the first three weeks. Also my teeth went from bad to worse. I had to visit a French dentist in the village four times in the first fortnight. He discovered – at a cost of £12 including X-rays – what my posh Belgravia dentists failed to discover at costs running into hundreds – that the lower wisdom tooth below the extracted one was also dying and its roots infected. So he opened that up and left it to seep, dressing it every few days. Then, walking up the mountains, another tooth went wrong and I had to have further opening up.

All this drilling was done without anaesthetic: he explained that it was easier for him that way, as he could tell where the infected parts were by the way my leg shot up to hit the roof. But at least he was competent. He advised me to go back to London for root fillings as soon as possible, and so I did for the week 10–17 August.

Otherwise we had the usual Ceret routine: down to the village in the morning (I walked) to collect bread and yesterday's English newspapers; lunch on the terrace under the shade of the great mulberry tree; afternoons sleeping and reading and swimming; then dinner down in the village, where there are now several excellent restaurants.

My reading was very enjoyable. I started by devouring Evelyn Waugh's first four novels, almost like one work. But my greatest triumph was in shooting two cicadas with my rusty old pellet gun. They were disturbing our quiet reading. No bigger than a large grasshopper, nobody could believe I hit them. Nor me, since the shotgun is very old and inaccurate. I kept one corpse in a match box as evidence and souvenir.

The loveliest Ceret routine is the Saturday morning market. For me it never palls. Some of the traders I've known 20 years.

Saturday 10 August–Saturday 17 August 1996

We returned from Ceret on Saturday evening. Went to London on Monday for the dentist and had the latest baddie opened up. Then Friday for two hours having a root canal filling. After that to Newbury to see Snow Eagle make a pretty but insufficiently fast debut. I spent hours wading through 500 letters and also read more of a biography of Ottoline Morrell. A fascinating life story, especially the Bertie Russell part. But how petty and bitchy and self-obsessed all those Bloomsbury twits were.

During this holiday time, politics has ceased to be of any consequence. Tony Blair's long media honeymoon is over. The strains within the Labour Party are beginning to show. The Shadow Cabinet elections were OK, with Jack Cunningham getting back, but the Blair people fell and his critics rose. The latter claim that he doesn't have any principles, other than winning the election. So he is always concerned to appease the media. He seems to abandon any policies that upset the media. But he is very tough with the party. There is a feeling that he should be as tough with the Tory media as he is with his own supporters. But the final test will be success. So far he is keeping a good lead, though it is narrowing a little as the Tories fix the economy to be good in the election run-up. My view is that there is no practical alternative to his approach in the short-run, since if Labour lose for a fifth time it would destroy the party. But, in government, Blair will have to have some clear policy principles and guidelines or he will be blown off course by the inevitable storms.

Incidentally, Clive Hollick, Labour's only media tycoon, told me he had dinner with Murdoch who told him (a) that Blair was OK, but unproven as a party manager, that (b) neither Blair nor any political leader in the world dare stand up to him because of his great media power, and that (c) *The Sun* would probably come out for the Tories. That means that all Blair's work sucking up to *The Sun* is for nothing – but he may get the endorsement of *The Times*, which is for Labour electorally marginal.

Saturday 17 August–Thursday 29 August 1996 (France)

Flew back to Ceret on Saturday afternoon for a very busy and enjoyable time. My son Stephen stayed and Sarah and I drove up into the mountains at Llo and met my old Kentish Town friends Celia and Tom Read. Walked 7 km up the Llo valley to about 7000 feet. We had a splendid dinner and gossiped about old times.

Before dinner we drove to the next village of Eyne and joined up with Cabinet Secretary Robin and Jill Butler and a group of their friends who were on a walking holiday across our part of the Pyrenees. It was lovely to see them again: we soldiered together in No. 10 under Wilson and have kept in touch. He is a great public servant and a good friend.

We plotted a great walk together up to the Spanish border tomorrow. We had an elaborate plan to meet at a river bridge at 9.00 am, though Robin, knowing I am no early riser, was hinting mischievously at leaving at dawn. So, next morning we were up sharp and the Reads and I were on the path at 8.30 am. The Butlers et al. were not at the bridge at 9.00 am and I suspected they were ahead, having started trickily early since Robin is a very competitive Harrovian boy scout and wouldn't like the idea of a pirate like me beating him to it.

So we soldiered on for three hours. We reached 8500 feet in sight of the border pass into Spain and stretched on a patch of grass, spreading out our picnic lunch. Just as I was into the pâté I saw a bedraggled string struggling up from the valley below. It was them. Robin arrived nearly last, with a bad knee but honking with pleasure. We had a great lunch and chat together, with views for miles below. Then they parted to do the last lap to their Spanish lodging at Nuria. We saw them head around the col and then turned for home. It took three hours scrambling down to the car and we were all pretty shattered, though elated. We then drove the two hours home with a break in pretty Villefranche, one of Vauban's best walled fortresses. It had been a great adventure.

Apart from these mountain walks and the occasional trip to the sea at Le Racou I mainly stayed at home, with daily walks for a couple of miles down to the village to keep fit. I continued to eat up books, finishing the Ottoline Morrell and enjoying the gossip about the Kennedys in Gore Vidal's memoir *Palimpsest*. Quite incestuous. And shows how women like bonking power. Also nice vignettes on our Royals and the Windsors – the Duke seriously thick.

From the daily papers our politics is at a pretty low level and Blair is one of the few bright lights. Still France is worse. They still haven't had their Thatcherite revolution. Their economy is uncompetitive and their public services are bloated, yet they have 13% unemployed. Their socialist party is still naively Marxist. Something could explode soon, probably from their ever lurking fascist right. Living there, one sees how their national spirit has declined. They are tied to the Germans, restoring the European Reich that Hitler started to build in 1940–44, but this time willingly, peacefully and servilely, without the need of German military steel. The new Europe has cut off France's nationalist balls without replacing them with anything except stifling centralist state bureaucracy.

Friday 30 August 1996

Back home to a mass of boring post to open and answer, almost nothing hand-written, the usual indication of something interesting. Except a curious letter from an old school friend now in the north, who I've not seen in 44 years. He had watched me in the programme on Wilson and MI5 and the KGB. He offered to swap his 6th form history essay prize for my then captaincy of the school boxing team. I guessed who it was and wrote back to tell him that I was hanging on to the boxing honour and skill since ducking, weaving and counter punching were more useful in modern politics and media than any knowledge of history.

Sunday 1 September 1996

The newspapers have little in them. Still the campaign against Blair and Labour, but nothing of great interest. Labour has printed its list of financial backers, which puts the pressure on the Tories, though they won't want to reveal the names of various arms dealers and offshore tax-dodgers. One big Labour donor is a pro-animal man who may finance the animal terrorists.

Not good news, and may indicate bribes for a future ban on hunting, though I ignored newspaper calls to comment.

Monday 2 September 1996

Worked all morning on correspondence. Troubling rumours of military action in Iraq, where Saddam Hussein is attacking the Kurds and Clinton is anxious to do something machismo in the run up to the election.

Tuesday 3 September 1996

Woke up late to news that American missiles had punished southern Iraq. Rest of the morning finishing off the post. Sarah has gone to Childown (her father's old house) to arrange emergency decorating to make it worthy of the Pet Shop Boys pop group who are renting it.

I realise that I am 62 next Sunday. Quite unbelievable. I don't know where all those years have gone. Looking back to the 1960s seems no time ago at all. Dare not think what I've done with them. But I don't feel old. Physically just as strong as 10–20 years ago, despite the periodic diabetic sogginess. But I've to face the reality of the numbers. Must fit in as much as I can before real old age strikes.

Proms concert at the Albert Hall in the evening. The music was great with Simon Rattle and the Birmingham Symphony; Brendel doing the Beethoven 5th piano looking like Ken Dodd imitating a Viennese piano teacher.

Nice opportunity to have long chats with Alastair Campbell sitting close by, mainly about how to handle the move into No. 10 – though he seemed not too confident we would win. Shared views on the seediness of the British media. Amusing how all ex-journalists suddenly realise how appalling their own trade is once they move to being on the receiving end. Polly Toynbee was there from *The Independent,* a bit stridently self-righteous and as always suggesting that anyone who objected to the press's malice was 'paranoid'. I pointed out this was the wrong word since we did have real enemies in the media. John Birt and I agreed that, with current media coverage, the only people who could be sure to survive in public life are gelded monks.

Wednesday 4 September 1996

Nice walk over St James's Park for lunch with Nigel Kent-Lemon of Lingfield racecourse, who is trying to persuade me to head a worthy charity [Gamcare] he is setting up to help gambling addicts. Friends will laugh since they know how much I love the horses – but don't know how little and tinily I bet. I can watch a whole meeting without betting, just loving the scene and the beauty of the racehorses.

In the evening, went to a party at Harrods to launch the new *Punch* magazine. It was tremendous, with wonderful food and lots of interesting people – though almost no politicians, just Tory John Gummer, very arrogantly pleased with himself, and me. (Joe Haines, who has the magazine's lead article on Wilson's 1976 'lavender' honours list, arranged for me to go with some old *Mirror* friends). I talked a lot with Joe, Graham Greene, and later mainly with Terry Wogan (good fun as always) and ex Labour MP Robert Kilroy-Silk, who recalls being my pupil at the LSE and is very open and boastful about the huge sums of money he earns from TV journalism.

Joe and I concluded that our strange host Al-Fayed, the Egyptian owner of Harrods, should be given his much desired UK citizenship by Labour. He has revived Harrods and is now employing a lot of our old friends – perhaps too many very old ones for the commercial good of his magazine – and it's crazy to withhold citizenship from him when millions of yobs and crooks have it. How can we draw the line at him and not at some others who are not fit to polish his Egyptian sandals?

Thursday 5 September 1996

Had lunch at the Lords with son Paul. Afternoon on letters and in evening dinner with old friends William and Veronica Plowden. Known them since Veronica and I were at Oxford and William at Cambridge. Then he and I went in 1958 to America on graduate fellowships, he to Yale, me to Harvard. We worked together on *The Economist* when we returned and later at the LSE and again in government in the 1970s when I was in the Downing Street Policy Unit and he in the Central Policy Review staff next door in the Cabinet office, so our careers have weaved and interlocked, though I am not sure either of us has been completely satisfied anywhere. It is a while since we met so we celebrated with champagne and a good meal. Gossiped about our lives and how now, in our sixties, we have to get the last bit right.

Veronica still drives her Vespa motorbike as she did elegantly in the summer of 1958 when I sat on the back and we visited lovely Oxfordshire churches.

Friday 6 September 1996

Two hours of root canal filling at the dentist. Very uncomfortable.

Sunday 8 September 1996

Dreaded birthday. 62. Seventy ahead. Don't feel any different from 10 years ago, but knowing the years are flitting by makes me think differently. Less ambition to do things, accept invitations, agree to talks or writing articles and books. Have done all that. Don't feel anything can alter much the epitaph on the tombstone now. It could say 'Dabbler'. Increasingly feel that what matters are family and old friends. The power and political stuff is just an ephemeral game. On that, incidentally, Campbell told me a most encouraging thing about Blair: he spends little time reading the newspapers and doesn't even bother to watch himself on TV. If can build on that he should do well. Reminds me of the story about Clem Attlee told to me by one of his former secretaries. When prime minister in the 1940s, he was persuaded to have a Press Association news tickertape machine in No. 10 on the basis that it would carry the cricket scores. After a couple of weeks he sent for the official to reprimand him: 'You didn't tell me it would carry all this political rubbish as well.' It was still there tickering away outside the private secretaries' office when I was in No. 10 in the 1970s.

The birthday lunch was terrific, despite my misgivings about even acknowledging the anniversary. Lots of books as prezzies – Waugh's *Scoop* and Betjeman's poems from Kate together with the video of the film *Carrington*. Watched the *Carrington* later, with tremendous performance by Jonathan Price as Lytton Strachey. Made me sympathise a little more with that self obsessed crowd, but still a terrible mess: everybody bisexual, everyone in love with somebody else as well as their partner, of whatever sex. None of them ever had a proper job, which was part of their problem, since none was a truly great enough artist to be fulfilled that way. All very fascinating.

Kate looked lovely and we had a good talk planning my visit to Ireland. Her honeymoon is still vividly happy in her mind.

After lunch we visited Sonning church. The Anglican Church is in a mess – as this week's biography of ex-Archbishop Runcie shows. It's full of viperish queens, losing its congregation fast, but having all the beautiful churches which it cannot afford to maintain. We Catholics have the congregations, but not the churches. I do love the Anglican Church historically, for its tolerance, its dottiness and its Englishness; but it is presently going down the chute, ruined by the minority politically correct sects who blight everything they touch (including the Labour party and especially the BBC).

Monday 9 September 1996

Quiet day in Berkshire. I did letters all morning and start *Scoop* – Waugh writing as brilliantly as ever. For a stuffy, curmudgeonly unpleasant old buffer, he had a creative imagination, suitably tinged with acid.

The TUC is meeting at Blackpool and sounding very moderate and sensible. John Monks most impressive as secretary. Where have the dinosaurs gone? The Tories will try to raise scares about them but anyone must see they are now a responsible bunch. All lessons hopefully learned from the horrific lunacies of 1978–79.

Blair is shrewdly keeping an arm's length. He comes over well on TV.

[Diary for 10–18 September 1996 not recorded.]

Thursday 19 September 1996

Today and Friday in Berkshire dealing with correspondence, reading and plotting next week in Ireland. One development is that it is confirmed our horse Referendum will run in Ireland.

Saturday 21 September 1996

Great day. Set off for Heathrow, meet Jeremy Taylor and take the plane to Dublin. Probably six years since I was there. The suburbs of Dublin gruesome with bleak council housing estates, but we were soon on the fast road to Kildare and the Curragh. The rest of our syndicate party slowly arrived, led by Harry Herbert towering 9 ft high, and with tiny 5 ft Geoff Lewis, our crafty trainer, in tow. I enjoyed seeing the old military camp in the distance where the Army nearly revolted against Home Rule in 1913–14. The crowd looked much more prosperous than when I passed this way in the mid-1950s through the then austere and often unattractive De Valera's Ireland.

In the ring was the Aga Khan who was sponsoring the meeting. He is an old friend of Sarah's and I've stayed with him in Sardinia and Chantilly, so I went up for a chat.

Referendum was in front till the final yards – when he was pipped on the post in a photo finish. Later I felt disappointment that we just missed a fortune; but at the time I was elated at how well he ran in such a big race. Anyway, he got £40,000 for second place – and Jeremy won £1400 for his 65–1 forecast.

Sunday 22 September 1996

The judge has dismissed the Kevin Maxwell fraud case. The media, whose pre trial coverage probably made a fair trial impossible, are incensed, feeling deprived of headlines and blood. I was never called as a witness, not having witnessed the alleged wrongdoings. I never got on with Kevin.

Monday 23 September 1996

In London to prepare for this morning's briefing of Blair's private office. Excellent Peter Hennessy was running it for the Fabian Society. The speakers were Robert Armstrong, ex-principal private secretary in No. 10, and former Cabinet secretary; Ken Berrill, ex-head of the Central Office Review Staff and Treasury permanent secretary; Nick Monck, ex-Treasury and boss of Department of Employment, and myself. So quite heavy. Inevitably the politicos arrive very late – Donald Dewar, our chief whip who had come down especially from Scotland; Jonathan Powell, Blair's chief of staff, and David Miliband, putative head of the Policy Unit. Peter Mandelson phoned to say he would be late and never arrived at all. Alastair Campbell wasn't there; a pity, since he will be crucial in government.

But it went very well. I opened talking about occupying No. 10 on the first day, with practical things about getting the best rooms, recruiting staff, ensuring access to papers and key committees. And about establishing good relations with officials in No. 10 and the Cabinet office. Also stressed must maintain good relations with the Labour party. Robert followed with a clear description of No. 10 and all who worked there. We then had a good discussion. Jonathan asked the key question, which is how they keep an eye on the long term while being overwhelmed by the inevitable short-term crises. I suggested having a long term policy unit in the Cabinet office, like the CPRS [Central Policy Review Staff] but more political. Robert and Ken didn't like that, predictably, as mandarins, but Jonathan, David and Donald did. I also said they must set up ad hoc Cabinet committees on the key policy objectives, education and social security reform, to ensure we have achieved something in those areas by the next election. Several said they must have the central priorities clear at the beginning and not lose sight of them in the daily storms. We supported the Chequers special cabinets to take a longer deeper view.

It was very clear that the politicos didn't yet really know how government or No. 10 works, but their questions were excellent and they will clearly learn fast. At the end David and Jonathan said to me that it had been very helpful. I stressed to them that they must get Blair to sign a memo to the Principal

Private Secretary and the Cabinet Secretary BEFORE going in, authorising their access to papers and committees.

Donald Dewar walked down the stairs with me and said I was 'in cracking form' and asked to have tea soon to talk about the whips office. I told him to be ready with lots of suitable names to fill all the public appointments vacancies which will arise. When in there and overwhelmed with work, it is too easy to leave that to civil servants and then you get all the familiar Establishment luvvies in the jobs.

Tuesday 24 September–Saturday 28 September 1996

Fabulous visit to the beautiful west of Ireland. Sarah and I flew to Cork and from there drove direct to Dingle, pausing briefly in Killarney. Next day around the Ring of Kerry to Waterville where we stayed in a nice old inn, then right back across the mountains to Baltimore in west Cork. Finally a night in a lovely bed and breakfast overlooking Sandy Cove near Kinsale. The country and coastline were stunning, the loveliest in Europe.

We particularly enjoyed the erratic switch to kilometres, which affects some signposts but not all, and how the distances to your destination constantly vary. In the middle of Ballyspittal were three signposts showing 8, 7, and 6 km to Kinsale. But then they don't think that it matters how long it takes.

Sunday 29 September 1996

Went to Ascot for lunch with the Tote. Sat next to Petronella Wyatt. She told me that the *Spectator* wants to have a series of interviews and profiles but cannot find a journalist who will do a fair job. Reminds me of when the *Mail* did a series on the Monarchy and had to get a freelance to do it because, as Joe Haines told me, 'They don't have anyone on the staff who could do a fair job instead of a stream of snide nastiness.' The racing was good and I chatted to jockey Frankie Dettori who broke the record with seven winners yesterday. Only one today.

Monday 30 September 1996

Heading for our Blackpool conference. Not too excited. I first went to a Labour conference in 1960 at Blackpool to hear Gaitskell's great 'Fight and Fight Again' speech against the left-wing nuclear disarmers. Blair, though less rigid and prissy, has something in common with Gaitskell, being a moralist.

Certainly many of the policies that Blair claims for new Labour were being advocated by us in the pro-Gaitskell Campaign for Democratic Socialism (I was general secretary in 1962–64) 35 years ago: looser links with the unions, less commitment to nationalisation, pro-Europe (though not Gaitskell himself), anti-nuclear disarmament, anti the left in general. We were in some ways New Labour when Blair was in short trousers. So I support what he is doing with the party. It is just the shabby Blackpool hotels and the wet walks to the Winter Gardens that turn me off.

I drove to London, collected some post and then headed north by train from Euston. I barely had time to dump my luggage before dashing off to the Heritage team fringe meeting at the Clifton Hotel. It was packed, with a large overspill in the lobby outside. Jack Cunningham invited me to join him and Tom Pendry – Mark Fisher was late and joined us half way through, when his contributions were good. Jack seemed a bit irritable. There is a lot of muttering against him. But I find him refreshingly straight.

I did the usual round of evening receptions. I dropped into the Fabians, advertised to 'meet Peter Mandelson', but Peter wasn't there. It took half an hour to get into the Imperial, the security was so tight and laborious. Having finally got in, I had to leave again for a fish restaurant in the outskirts, eating with some media people. There was a bright young Labour MP, Ian Pearson, and we talked a lot. Labour's young ones today are very good, with few leftie nutters of the 1970s design. On return, I toured about five parties and networked with various old friends. Returned to the hotel at midnight and found Donald Dewar our chief whip watching the replay of Newcastle beating Aston Villa 4–3 in a magnificent match on the lobby TV. So I didn't get to bed till nearly 1.30 am. We discussed various of his flock: he is clearly disapproving of Marxist Alan Simpson – 'a wicked man', said with full Scots Presbyterian rigour. Actually I liked Simpson on our South African cricket tour.

Tuesday 1 October 1996

Linked up with Andrew Graham (who was my brilliant senior economist in the Policy Unit under Wilson) and we walked to the Imperial to attend the Channel 4 breakfast, which is always the social highlight of the year. Michael Grade entertained our front bench team and a few high fliers on his top table. He related how his uncle once told an audience of journalists that he defined 'gross ignorance' as 144 journalists. One of them asked, 'Why 144?'.

I went back through the gale force winds and walked with Margaret Jay and Brenda Dean to hear Blair's big speech.

The hall was already packed and they were turning everyone away except for ex-officio badges like us. We stood at the back. It was the most impressive leader's speech I've ever heard: well structured, starting in prime ministerial style with the big issues of the Middle East and Northern Ireland and then moving to Labour political party matters. It was full of sound bites and punchy jokes. None of the labyrinthine and tortuous paragraphs with which Harold used to send the party to sleep. Every paragraph was self-contained, punchy – often without verbs – and leading to a conclusion that provoked laughs or applause. Rather in the best *Daily Mirror* style, so I could see Alastair Campbell's clever hand there. Tony's voice was stronger than last year, on a lower register – I wonder if he has had elocution lessons à la Thatcher. The whole performance was an appeal to middle England, specifically rejecting Labour's old sectarianism and inviting the Tories and floaters to vote for us. It also had several personal passages – about his father suffering a stroke, about Sam McCluskie dying, about the Dunblane massacre, which made the hard media men cringe and mutter 'yucky'! But the women will like it. He was being human and like a sentimental scene in a popular film. The peroration went on too long and he couldn't sustain the high pitch, but people around me were wiping tears from their eyes and there was a deafening ovation at the end. I was unhappy with the final triumphalism, with loud music and Tony marching off, which had troubling echoes of both Kinnock's 1992 Sheffield disaster and Hitler's 1936 Nuremberg rally. But I'm sure it worked. The sense of joy and unity in the hall was almost tangible; they really want to win this time. Also the Tory journalists looked seriously miserable, which meant it must have been a success.

Afterwards I went for tea with Clive Hollick, Tessa Blackstone, Margaret Jay and various groupies. Clive is in great form, obviously enjoying carving up Express newspapers and running his TV stations. He is the best of the media moguls. I wish he would get the *Mirror*. We also plotted on our chief whip situation, where dear old Ted Graham is getting perhaps a bit old at 73 to lead us into the New Labour future. But it would break poor Ted's heart so I feel less gung ho than our hard faced ladies, who are a ruthless lot, suffering none of the warmth and sentiment that afflicts we soggy men – though Clive isn't too afflicted with sentiment, having sacked 80 *Express* journalists last week. A good start, but several thousands to go.

In the evening I did the usual tour of parties, where the best was the midnight craic with ITN. Had dinner with Yorkshire TV. It emerged in later conversations that they are considering me as chairman. I had mixed feelings. I would love the interesting job and the pay. But it would mean giving up the chance of being a minister. So I am not sure. Wish I had had the chance

10 years ago and not gone to Maxwell. Curiously it nearly happened. In 1982 I was linked with Harry Evans and Melvyn Bragg and we had the chance to take over Tyne Tees TV. In the end Harry said no, and the chance passed. I've always regretted that. I would have now been richer as well as more satisfied, with less career mistakes along the way.

Wednesday 2 October 1996

Two breakfasts this morning, both at the Imperial. First to the BBC World Service. I sat next to Labour colleague Chris Smith and we had a very friendly chat.

The *Guardian* has had a great week, with Neil Hamilton dropping his libel action case and admitting that their basic case against him on cash for questions was justified. This constant tide of Tory sleaze is a helpful background to Labour's conference – though we're bound to have one or two dodgy involvements. I pointed this out to Brian Wilson, who handles the media for the party, and warned him not to take too high a moral ground, since there is bound to be one of ours misbehaving somewhere.

My other breakfast was with English Heritage, where Chairman Jocelyn Stevens was in riotously good form – and attacking the Tories. Must have decided we will win. Afterwards I congratulated David Miliband for his excellent contributions to the Leader's speech. He said he is going to write to me about my Fabian talk on occupying No. 10; he wants more detail. He is very clever; perhaps not hard enough yet and still too academic for the hard battles ahead.

After lunch with the cable communications industry, I bought the newspapers and sat on the central pier reading them. Surrounded by Lancashire, Yorkshire and Birmingham accents, it reminded me of holidays in Blackpool with my father in the late 1940s, then both of us sleeping in a single room, he on the sofa, at a dingy bed and breakfast.

The evening roll of parties was heavier than ever: The *Mirror*, BT, Sky, British Airways, the Irish embassy (two pints of fine draft Guinness) and the Guinness party itself, with more draft Guinness.

Had good chats with Peter Kilfoyle, who is one of my favourite backbenchers, a tough Merseysider who sorted out the nasty Trot militants there and should one day make a fine chief whip. And with Gus Macdonald of Scottish TV – we planned to try to use Hollick to take over the *Mirror* and a big TV franchise so, together with the *Express* and Scottish TV and the *Daily Record*, we had a core media operation that would support the Labour government. Also thanked Alastair Campbell for putting in Blair's speech the piece thanking Old Labour for having fought to keep the Labour party intact through the civil wars of the 1980s so there was something of a party left for Blair and New Labour to lead. I know lots of people liked that. Recently they have felt forgotten.

That effectively was the end of this conference for me. I enjoyed it much more than I expected. The atmosphere is dramatically changed from the late 1970s and early 1980s, when it was poisonous, with the left-wing thugs intimidating anyone who admitted to a democratic tendency and I was often spat upon. It was such a pleasure to meet people who actually liked their fellow colleagues and could have a friendly discussion even when disagreeing – as I can do with leftie MPs Alan Simpson and Chris Mullins.

The other change is the recent massive expansion and dominance of the media at conference. They are there in their thousands; and the politicians give them priority. Yet nobody talks to them openly or in confidence or off the record as we used to, to some. Because we can now trust none of them. So they have lost knowledge while gaining power. The politicians now play games with them, ignoring their questions and offering boring replies of packaged sound bites. In return the journalists understandably get frustrated and abuse the politicians. There is no trust between them and everybody loses.

Thursday 3 October–Friday 4 October 1996

Had breakfast with Scots Labour MPs Donald Dewar, Helen Liddell and John Maxton and then took the cross Pennine train to York. My Parliament Hill Fields friend Tom Read, son of Herbert the anarchist and writer, met me and drove me to the moors near Helmsley. We walked high into gales and horizontal rain back to his lovely family house at Stonegrave. Dinner in a fine old pub then next morning up to Kirkdale and a wonderful hour walk up above the lovely old Minster there, where Tom's parents are buried.

We drove in the rain to Malton and I took the train to London. Sarah phoned me to say Humphrey Colnbrook had died in Maggie's arms that morning. He was a lovely man, remarkably sensitive for a politician, a gentleman and my best friend in the village. I will miss him. The fact that I am Labour and he was Tory chief whip never mattered. Now we must support Maggie.

Saturday 5 October 1996

Spent the day quietly catching up on sacks of correspondence.

Joe Haines phoned to hear about Blackpool. We have spoken on the phone on Saturday or Sunday at around 6.00 pm for most of the past 20 years, always covering the whole political scene, where he is still sharp as a button. It seems odd that he doesn't go to conference any more. He is disappointed with our old girlfriends in the party, Tessa Jowell and surprisingly Helen Liddell, who used to be constantly in touch and whose speeches Joe often wrote, but who he now finds distant, as if they have moved permanently on. People do move on as we oldies are no longer useful. I accept that, though Joe doesn't. Anyway it isn't true for me with Helen Liddell who is still a close friend and not driven by ambition, though she is far abler than most Labour colleagues. He is still very combative, but a completely loyal friend, one to go into the jungle with – not recommended as an enemy though.

I sat in the conservatory thinking and reading. If we don't win this coming election that is the end of serious politics for me and many younger Labour ones as well. But at that conference, amid such euphoria, it wasn't possible to contemplate that outcome. The Tories look rattled and I cannot imagine the electorate will give them another chance. But I do need a brief rest from all my travels before the session begins again.

Sunday 6 October 1996

Sat in the conservatory reading and watching life on the ponds. Went to lovely quiet mass in Wargrave. Father Flanagan on good form. His sermon stories are lovely. When he had read out the severe bible passage about 'If thy arm offendeth, cut it off, leg ditto', he paused, looked at us and said, 'I don't know if that inspires you, but it doesn't do much for me.' After reading out the Church's injunction against divorce, he said, 'But if any of you or your families are divorced, they are as welcome in my church as anybody else.' He said he was required by the Church to offer counselling if anyone had marriage difficulties, 'but I won't show too much knowledge, or you'll wonder what I've been doing on Monday evenings.' Then added 'To be honest, I've not much experience of living with anyone; if I got a canary, I'd have to take counselling myself on how to talk to it.' He said he was often asked why he had become a priest and had a clear answer to that: 'I can't for the life of me remember.' Another time he suddenly said, 'I woke up in the night and thought that we should have married priests.' He sat down and then rose again to add, 'and if I am not back here next week, you will know why.' He always says we shouldn't focus on the afterlife, but enjoy the beautiful things in life now, the birds, trees, sunshine and the sky. He is a truly wonderful man.

Monday 7 October 1996

Quiet day writing and reading and returning the scores of telephone calls awaiting me on my return at the weekend.

Tuesday 8 October 1996

Two important meetings. The first was at the London Arts Board where we're seeking a new chairman. They had done a good trawl and ended with three: Trevor Phillips from the Board (able and statutory coloured candidate) and two statutory women – civil rights lawyer Helena Kennedy and TV executive Liz Forgan. Predictably there is no white male, since the politically correct discriminate against them. Politically Correct Claptrap (PCC) prevails. So I fought to get a white male on the list and argued for Melvyn Bragg who, except for his racial, gender and colour disadvantages, is eminently qualified – almost over qualified.

I got some support and finally won. Actually Phillips, Helena and Melvyn are a formidable trio and I would be happy with any one of them. I argued just to make mischief against the PC Claptrappers.

Left before the end and walked to the LSE where we considered the appointment of a new Director and how to solve our financial problems. The financial figures were presented and quite different from before. But it does look as if we may have to have top-up fees to remedy the financial deficit. The atmosphere wasn't good.

After the LSE I realised that if I do take on the education portfolio I shall have problems, due to my lack of patience with the impracticality of some academics. But a good sign was to see my dear old friend George Jones at the Standing Committee. He is immensely knowledgeable and in government I should use him as an adviser if in the right area.

Wednesday 9 October 1996

Headed for Towcester races, but first I went to Dick Saunders's farm at Holdenby to see Peers Folly. The problem is his fore hoof, which is split from top to bottom, which we hadn't been told about until Dick drew our attention to it; the split has been there for years. It may never heal but we're trying a lot of linseed and will use lasers and much tender loving care. We decided to send him to Henrietta Knight at Wantage for full training.

Afterwards to Towcester for a terrific afternoon's racing, though most of the horses were second division.

Thursday 10 October 1996

Today much sadder. Funeral of Humphrey Colnbrook, former Tory chief whip and Northern Ireland secretary. He was always confident he would beat his cancer, but it had spread everywhere. Last Monday he went to see the specialist who told him he wouldn't get better. Humphrey said, 'Does that mean I will just get iller and iller?' 'Yes', said the specialist. Humphrey slumped, spent more and more time asleep and on Thursday morning died. He simply gave up.

The funeral was simple and moving in the old church across the road from his home. A few politicians came: Peter Carrington (they resigned together from the Foreign Office over the Falklands invasion); Michael Brougham and Vaux and Rodney Elton from the Lords; and Murdoch Maclean from the whips office. John Wakeham came for the service but not for the refreshments after, when we stood around quietly on the lawn.

Friday 11 October 1996

Spent the morning working on my memo for Tony Blair's staff on how to occupy and run No. 10.

In the evening to London for a magnificent dinner in the Painted Hall at the Royal Naval College, Greenwich. Robin Butler took me and we met for a drink in the Cabinet Secretary's office beforehand. It was strange to return there after 18 years. Much as I remember, though I thought John Hunt then had more porcelain on show in the casements on the wall.

Robin told a lovely story about Michael Heseltine. When the latter became deputy prime minister after last year's Tory leadership election, Michael had to have a room at the centre of government and came to see Robin about it. After a while he commented ominously on how nice Robin's room was and indicated he might take it. Robin smelled serious danger to his own position and pointed out that the room had always been the Cabinet Secretary's. 'But things are changing in Whitehall', said Michael, looking around covetously. Robin nervously saw himself as the first cabinet secretary to lose his splendid office and so (with shades of Sir Humphrey), he said 'But, Deputy Prime Minister, we have already allocated you a room BIGGER than this' – knowing that, for Michael, bigger meant better. However, there had in fact been no prior Whitehall discussion of which was to be the Deputy PM's room. Michael asked to see it and Robin astutely delayed him for three hours while he sorted it out. His staff informed him there was a big conference room upstairs, bigger even than Robin's room – but it currently had a huge table filling it, which would have to be dismantled to get through the door. This would normally take the civil service a week to accomplish. 'You have three hours', said Robin. 'Bring in the Royal Marine engineers if necessary.' Heseltine returned a few hours later to inspect his new room and when they went up to see it the great conference table was just disappearing down the corridor in the distance.

The room now looked so enormous that Michael was very impressed. 'I think you have entered into the proper spirit of things', he said, approvingly.

We were driven in Robin's official car through the ugliest parts of London to Greenwich and had a splendid evening. There was a marine band, drummers marching between the tables, and a chamber trio. Over 300 guests had come to celebrate Patrick O'Brian the great story teller of the Navy's battles against Napoleon. We had a menu from the period and Robert Hardy read brilliant extracts from the books. I've read the early ones in Ceret but must now get the rest. Most people there were aficionados. I realise that Patrick O'Brian lives only a few miles away from us in Ceret at Collioure. Decide to arrange a visit.

Opposite me were the American Ambassador, Christopher Bland (chairman of the BBC) and Max Hastings, editor of the *Evening Standard*, who had helped to arrange it. William Waldegrave gave a good speech. Saw William Plowden and Michael Grade. There were also lots of admirals. All very splendid and beautifully done.

Saturday 12 October 1996

Talked with Dick Saunders about Peers Folly. He had spoken to both trainers, Henrietta Knight and Kim Bailey, so that transfer has been arranged and smoothed out. Dick and his family are a lovely example of how to live a happy integrated life, with the farm and the horses in a beautiful quiet place and his daughter Caroline working with the horses there. We metropolitan whizzers know too little of that.

In the evening I drove to London to be ready for the early morning train to Paris. Referendum runs in the Grand Criterium, one of Europe's biggest two-year-old races, and the gang is going. There and back in a day. If Referendum wins, I shall remain in the clouds all week.

One story from last night in Greenwich. Robin told me a lot about the Neil Hamilton Cash-for-Questions affair. Robin had done the original questioning of Hamilton when he denied everything, and says he is 'a really shabby man' – adding there are quite a lot of junior ministers like that these days. He explained that Major had supported Hamilton in changing the law on Privilege because he was convinced that Hamilton was innocent and must be given the chance to clear his name. That was typical of Major: to want to be fair to a colleague but to be naive about some of the sleaze-balls around him in his party.

Lots of Tories generously gave Hamilton money to help him fight his case against the *Guardian* and the PM, Robin and Heseltine were all gearing up to go into the witness box on his behalf. But then Michael Heseltine came back from holiday and contacted him. Michael asked if anyone had asked Hamilton the 'killer' question – not just had he received money from Al-Fayed, but also from his PR man Greer? Robin said no, and suggested Heseltine do that himself. So Heseltine phoned Hamilton in Robin's presence and put the question. Hamilton said 'no'. RB made a note of this and the note was bundled in with the official papers sent to the court.

But Greer's papers contradicted this, declaring two payments totalling £10,000 to Hamilton. So the lawyer acting for both Greer and Hamilton resigned, now having conflicting evidence. Hamilton was exposed as a liar and their case against the *Guardian* collapsed.

Two points: how reassuringly honest British central government is to offer all documents however embarrassing; and that it was the shrewd old fox Heseltine who spotted the killer question. As Harold Wilson once said to me, 'Any fool can think of the right answers. The genius lies in asking the key question.'

Sunday 13 October 1996

Up very early to get the Eurostar train from Waterloo to Paris to watch Referendum in a big race at Longchamps. He ran well, leading for much of the race, but not quite lasting the mile and slipping into 4th place (though he won £14,000 for that, more than for winning many races in England). We were all delighted.

On the train back, I sat with fat journalist John McCririck for a while and heard his excessively loud views on the future of racing. He is very right wing and full of his own windy ego – all mouth and no trousers, as the Irish say.

Monday 14 October 1996

Took the fast train to Cambridge for the gathering of Catholic bishops and clergy I was due to address on the problems of gambling. Speaking first was the excellent John Kennedy, who is a Methodist, but with the style and humour of a Catholic Cavalier.

I prefaced with an admission of my own disreputable track record of supporting the high lifestyles of various bookmakers and that I hadn't always been a full practising member of the Church. I hinted that it was the annual convocation of the Irish Catholic clergy at Cheltenham races during Lent that had finally converted me. But I did express concern at the rocketing expansion of our gambling society with machines potentially coming in every betting shop and the social problems that grew with that. Father Frank McHugh of St Edmund College wound up placing the gambling issue in its catechism context, done in both a scholarly and a worldly way. I enjoyed it all and learned a lot. Apparently the Church will make some kind of statement of concern – not puritanical I hope – in the next few months.

Tuesday 15 October 1996

Spent the morning clearing the usual backlog of letters and phone calls. Ordered four more filing cabinets, such is the flow of paper. Snatched a quick lunch in the Lords sitting opposite Frank Longford, who was very entertaining. He said he had met many people who had done evil things, but never a truly evil man. That is his Christian spirit, moulded by a lifetime of visiting jails. I said I had met a couple of bad people, thinking of Maxwell and Rupert Murdoch. But evil is a strong word. There are distinctions between bad intentions, bad consequences, and bad personality traits. Maxwell had a touch of all three, though not much of the intentions. Murdoch has bad consequences but probably not the intentions and only some bad traits of personality.

We had our first front-bench meeting of this session. Mainly about procedural approaches to the Queen's Speech – where I am not required to perform because Heritage never rates as very important. I am still thinking about whether to move across to Education, which is much more important and where I might be a minister of state, but Sarah doesn't want it because it is more partisan and we won't be able to share much of it. I don't care too much what I do, and would just as soon leave the front bench and run the Tote if that were possible, or Yorkshire TV if it is still around.

Chatted with Jim Callaghan, who was off to give his 'revisiting the Ruskin speech on education', where I played a part. I had dug out the original document: my first green paper to him dated 15 April 1976, in which I suggested he should take a personal policy initiative and offered education as one of about four potential topics. He is kind to me in his speech tonight but won't want any suggestion that he didn't originate the Ruskin great education debate. He looks physically a lot shorter than when we worked together in No. 10. Age does that.

Took the train with Michael Bedford to Lewes. We went to nearby Glyndebourne opera to see the Marriage of Figaro. A rather ordinary production. Their house is lovely – starting fresh thoughts of buying what Sarah calls 'a proper country house'. Trouble is, that needs proper money, which we don't have, and may be a long way from London, which I don't want. So

I imagine it won't happen. Michael has just bought another beautiful house, which stresses their resources. Also stresses Deborah, since she appears not to have been fully consulted on the purchase.

Wednesday 16 October 1996

Next morning we woke to lovely sunshine on the Downs. Crawled up to London through the usual horrors on the M25 for our creative economy conference at the Royal Society of Arts. It is clear that Blair made a mistake in his Blackpool speech in not referring to the arts; the culture world rightly resent this and it is beginning to rub off against Jack. My advice to him would be to be more pro-active towards the arts. But that isn't his style.

Thursday 17 October 1996

Two hours at the dentist preparing for the caps on my two root-canalled teeth. Very uncomfortable. As is the bill. Afterwards drove to the country for a quiet afternoon.

Friday 18 October 1996

Finished writing up my brief for Tony Blair's office on occupying and running No. 10. In the end it was 10 pages. Don't know if he will ever read it but will send copies to Jonathan Powell, David Miliband, Alastair Campbell and Donald Dewar, our chief whip, so perhaps somebody will. Then finished off my paper on gambling for the Catholic bishops and sent that off to Father McHugh at St Edmund's College. Am more confident that will be read, but not sure any effect.

Monday 21 October 1996

Cleared more papers then up to London for a dinner party at Corinne Laurie's. Jonathan Miller was there in great verbal form. He is about to direct *A Midsummer Night's Dream* and did marvellous imitations of all the cast. He also told me that he would like to write an article attacking *Private Eye's* nastiness and especially its Waugh-style anti-Semitism. I will try to arrange it with Tina Brown and the *New Yorker*.

It is 43 years this week since I first met Jonathan Miller, but I remember it clearly. I had travelled by train from Oxford to Cambridge to visit the undergraduate from Northampton, Jill Booty, with whom I had been deeply and painfully in love for four years since I was 15. Jonathan came to her room in Newnham (where I stayed the night risking disciplinary disaster). She was already making a hit in the drama world there and I sensed I would soon lose her to that smarter and richer Cambridge crowd – which, within three months, I did to a smart young undergraduate and later as wife to author Robin Chapman, now a friend. But at the time it was devastating.

I remember Jonathan as willowy and droopy, just like now, and almost too clever for me to follow. He certainly viewed me then as a country bumpkin with my rough Northamptonshire accent and understandably now has no recollection of the meeting. But, unlike many of his Cambridge, public school, non-Jewish contemporaries I then met, he wasn't condescending and was very funny. Incidentally he told me that David Frost, who toured with them in Beyond the Fringe, was without real creative talent (a view later confirmed to me by their other acting colleague and my brilliant contemporary from Oxford, Alan Bennett). Frost apparently claimed that he wrote their scripts, when it was usually Peter Cook.

Tuesday 22 October 1996

Lunch at the Gay Hussar. Brought back many memories of the wonderful restaurant where I used to eat nearly every week in the 1970s when it was full of the old Fleet Street gang and lots of Labour politicians. Few journalists now come. The only person I recognised was Lord Frank Longford, who is still on top of everything at 92. It is fashionable to sneer at him but I am very fond of him. The Gay Hussar was very important in my life for nearly 20 years and I used to mention it in 'Who's Who' as one of my hobbies. Now it seems too far from Westminster and the Lords is a more convenient club for me.

Dinner was with Raine Spencer – now a French countess but I've never grasped her new long name and since the marriage is over almost before it began I shall not bother to learn it. I like her despite all the press snideness – probably the more because of that. She dresses very flamboyantly with magnificent hats, which always amuses me. But the main thing is that she is really a serious lady. Beneath all the flim-flammery and astonishing hair styles, her main love is English local government and she is dying to get back in there – she ran the Greater London Council for years. I suggested she take a more active role in the City of London Corporation.

She was excited that Labour might restore an elected government for London. She is much underestimated by the press. I can imagine that relations between her and her step daughter Princess Di had their tense moments.

Incidentally, Sarah used to go on charity work visits to the then impoverished Pimlico with her 40 years ago and says the ordinary folk loved her. She was never ill at ease in the slums.

Wednesday 23 October 1996

A glorious day for the State Opening of Parliament. After clearing my vast correspondence I walked to the Ivy restaurant for a lunch in honour of a mogul from the American film scene. A short mafia style Sicilian, he is a dynamo who walked up and down the table addressing us on the film and television industry. I was called to speak early and without warning but managed to flannel through. Walked back with John Whittingdale the Tory MP who used to work in No. 10 for Thatcher. Agreed we ought to write a book on the Policy Unit.

Lewis Moonie from our DNH team was there and told me Jack is still fed up with poor Mark Fisher – 'His bum is heading fast for the back-benches', said Lewis and suggested I might be a minister in the Lords. Nice, but will wait and see.

Thursday 24 October 1996

Had new filing cabinets delivered, since I mean to file my Downing Street papers properly and perhaps write that book on the Policy Unit. Also began sorting out the tons of Maxwell papers. Will keep the basic ones that will one day allow me to refute all the lies in *Private Eye*. But sort out the rest into five large sacks ready for disposal.

The debate on the Queen's Speech began and Ivor Richard opened very well for our side. He has a very good style for the chamber, dignified and sonorous, well trained as a barrister. Afterwards to a dinner of vets at the Animal Health Trust. Jean Trumpington gave a speech, saying she might have been Baroness Six Mile Bottom since she came from there in Cambridgeshire. I am pleased the Tories have reappointed her as a whip. I sat next to Christopher Foster, the chief executive of the Jockey Club, and we had a good talk about racing. He was curious to know how I got on so well for so long with Henry Carnarvon, implying that not everyone at the Jockey Club did. I answered that that was why I did get on with him; he is completely straight and doesn't convey that upper class thing of discomfort with Labour or working class people. In a curious way, aristocratic Henry is democratic and classless. If he likes someone he doesn't care what class they come from. Ditto if he doesn't like them – and he often doesn't!

Friday 25 October 1996

Dealt with my papers in the morning and walked and read in the afternoon. Joe phoned to say that a journalist named, I think, Hitchens had phoned him to say that he had been trying to phone Marcia to discuss a book he is writing on Jimmy Goldsmith. She wouldn't come to the phone and now he has received a letter from Goldsmith's solicitor warning him to lay off. This is presumably because they are afraid of something emerging on Goldsmith's knighthood and whether he paid for it.

Saturday 26 October 1996

Long drive to a dinner party in the Cotswolds, at lovely house of Lucinda Marchessini, Sarah's old school friend. There were about 24 guests, nearly all her old school friends. I envy that about the English upper middle classes. They went to school together, partied or college or the army together, and have socialised regularly ever since. Gives them all a comfortable social infrastructure, with loads of old friends they can trust and enjoy, or know not to trust, lots of cosy gossip about mutual friends. I lack that, having nobody from childhood or school, not even close family now my brother Clem has died. History begins at Oxford for me.

This group at dinner was incredibly socially interwoven. Lucinda had two ex-husbands there, still friends, and their wives as friends. Several others had married one another's ex-wives, all present. Lower down the social order, divorce usually produces such feelings of anger and rejection (usually about money) that ex-partners hate one another, or at least rarely meet after separation. With this group they continue to swap partners and houses with affection. It is a bit incestuous and makes it difficult for outsiders like me to follow the family trees. But it is in its way very civilised and leaves them all supported within the social group.

Demetri Marchessini, ex-husband but one to Lucinda, was in fine form and typically managed to pull the only single lady in the room, who had divorced two weeks ago and told him after only three minutes that she lived singly 'only two fields away'. Demetri may make it, providing his Bentley can get across the two muddy fields. At 62 he is still a consummate operator, knowing that English upper class women often enjoy being seduced by intelligent rich foreigners – perhaps lacking some of their attributes at home.

My Sarah looked the loveliest of all across the tables and I was quite content.

Sunday 27 October 1996

I am not happy about the current debate on politics and morality, with Blair and Major both trying to out-moralise the other. That is bound to go wrong. The behaviour of politicians is often so bad that they cannot maintain credibility in the preacher's box. I was talking to Richard Ryder, John Major's engaging and intelligent Tory ex-chief whip, on Thursday about this and he agrees. If politicians try to occupy the moral high ground, one of their colleagues will immediately fall off into the sexual or financial pit.

Monday 28 October 1996

Went to lunch with Bruce Grocott, Blair's PPS. He is a very good guy in an old fashioned way. I've always been interested in him because he followed my old friend Gerry Fowler into the Wrekin seat. He took me into the Commons dining room, which wasn't very crowded being a Monday (these days many members come up late Monday and return home late Wednesday or Thursday morning). We discussed his role as parliamentary private secretary to the leader and possibly to the future PM. He is 56 and knows he couldn't get far as a minister, so he is happy to sacrifice all that and stick as PPS or go to the back benches. He only wants to be PPS if he can do a proper job, and I pointed out how in my time most of Wilson's PPSs were redundant, never identifying a niche. He will be mainly in the Commons but I advised him to find a desk in No. 10 and to liaise closely with the political secretary there and with the chairman of the party in the Commons. Then he will be a linchpin in the leader's relations with the party at more than one level. He should also link with the Policy Unit so he can feed in a political dimension there.

Bruce is very modest and willing to learn, but in fact is intelligent, amusing and experienced. He is popular in the PLP and Blair is shrewd to have picked him. He said that Blair is very hands-on, taking an interest in everything and not delegating very much. He thought the leader's office team lacked experience and that there was no obvious political secretary playing the role done in my day in their very different ways by Marcia or Tom McNally. Anji Hunter is excellent as the administrative secretary but isn't politically experienced enough for more than that. Perhaps Bruce could do it himself? He seems good to me.

Afternoon in the Lords and then to a dinner with my media mogul friend Clive Hollick in the new *Daily Express* building. Very boisterous evening which was devoted to introducing our new Labour peer, Richard Rodgers the architect, to some Labour colleagues. Tessa Blackstone had to leave early for the close of the Queen's Speech debate on foreign affairs, but Margaret Jay was there in sensible form as ever; her doctor husband Michael Adler very graciously talked all the meal to Sarah, who was feeling poorly and anxious and had climbed nine floors because she hates lifts. She was the lone Tory but everyone was friendly and generous – 'more so than the Tories would have been to Labour', she admitted. Gareth Williams, our radical front-bench lawyer, was in great form, twigging all our tails delightfully. He is socially quite leftish and, as a Welsh puritan, wary of Cavaliers like me who like race horses and Covent Garden, but he is so bright and funny.

Richard Rodgers himself came over as very powerful, though his political guidelines are none too clear. Sarah sat next to him but he sadly never spoke to her. Too many successful men are like that. I am in the minority who like his Lloyd's building, having sat for two years at Kleinworts looking at it and finding it much more alive than the usual dead concrete blocks in the City.

Tuesday 29 October 1996

Visited the Wallace Collection in Manchester Square. Not been there for 30 years. Ros Saville the director showed me over and I was stunned. It is an absolute jewel – but how many Brits or tourists know that? Probably more of the latter than the former. My kind of exhibition: a real house with its contents, rather than acres of galleries.

I was a bit upset in the afternoon as various colleagues informed me (perhaps hopefully) that tonight's TV programme on Maxwell would probably do a terrible hatchet job on me. So I went to consult our party leader, Ivor Richard, who was fairly relaxed and recommended I talk to a libel lawyer at Lewis Silkin. I did so and agreed he would approach the BBC, saying that I was to be attacked, hadn't been approached or offered any chance to reply, and asking for sight of the text referring to me and offering to help with the information. He told me later that they had spurned all contact. This is modern tabloid television, avoiding the facts in case they spoil the pre-agenda story. The BBC is as bad as anyone else. The author is a tabloid hack called Bower. Margaret Jay told me they did not like him when she was at BBC Panorama because he was an obsessive who didn't ever seek a balanced view and whose concern was to expose target people he hated. The old *Private Eye* syndrome of Chippies United.

We went to Covent Garden to see a lovely production of 'Romeo and Juliet'. Curious I never look forward to ballet as much as opera, but am often disappointed by the latter and almost invariably pleased by the former. Tessa Blackstone, who is chairman of the Royal Ballet, invited us to the royal box and we had an interesting supper there.

The other guest was Jonathan Powell from Tony Blair's office (Tessa certainly knows how to work the influence network!). I really began to take to Jonathan. He bravely admitted to not having been to the ballet before. And that his boss and colleagues were short on political experience. That is a good and honest start.

He praised Helen Liddell, which always wins stars from me. He said she would be in the Cabinet in the first five years. I said it should be in the first five minutes; but he said there might be difficulties in that. He came over as a bright and loyal person, not pretending to know more than he did and I can see how Tony Blair took to him. He was also very funny about his brother Charles, laughing at the way he has changed his name pronunciation from Powell to the more historic and socially elevated Pole since his elevation into the heights of Thatcher's No. 10.

Charles's wife Carla is on the peak of a rainbow of media publicity about her hostessing qualities. Sadly she will learn that rainbows dip down and the press will slap her down just as they built her up. I note that while I was in No. 10 I invited her and Charles there for a state dinner, but in his seven years of running Mrs Thatcher as prime minister he never returned the invitation. Presumably he felt he had moved up and me down.

Saw the last bit of the Bower-Maxwell programme. My solicitor had again faxed the BBC asking that I be allowed to comment on – and help with – their allegations but was once again rebuffed. The programme was very bitty and in fact had only a passing flash about me. Said Maxwell had paid me to keep quiet about his crimes and then showed a picture of my contract with its confidentiality agreement. No understanding that virtually everybody in the City (and nearly every senior person in the public sector including the BBC) has a confidentiality clause. I was given no chance to refute the libellous imputation that I had known anything about his crimes, which I didn't. In fact I bought a lot of *Mirror* shares shortly after resigning, which I certainly wouldn't have done had I known he was stealing £400 million from the company! Nothing about the fact that on First Tokyo Investment Trust we directors secured for shareholders the return of the £50 million he had borrowed – or that no pensioner suffered the loss of a penny. That would all have muddled the indignation. It also missed out much inside information, which people like Joe and myself could have given them – but of course they didn't want any facts to spoil their story. Maxwell looked a sad, pathetic figure at the end, but I felt no sympathy for him. He was a monster who brought grief to many. Still it wasn't the expected turnover of me that was exciting some of my colleagues, so it will have been a severe disappointment for them.

I've to decide whether to write to the BBC to complain about their bad journalistic practices. But it wasn't much and I must be careful not to be seen to be throwing political weight.

Wednesday 30 October 1996

Had the first DNH team meeting of the new session – at 9.00 am, which is very testing for late-morning birds like me. Everybody was very chirpy and Jack Cunningham in particularly good form. I stayed after and we discussed next week's Heritage Bill, which comes to me in the Lords first. He was well on top of it and had some good suggestions. He was very supportive on the Maxwell thing and said he had learned long ago not to believe a word the media said.

Spent the rest of the morning in my room dealing with correspondence and then had lunch in the restaurant with Patsy Baker, a PR with Tory Tim Bell. We had a good gossip. She told me that the *Guardian*'s savage attack on Jack during party conference had been orchestrated by Mandelson and Mark Fisher. Nice. Now, if true, there is party loyalty from colleagues for you!

Conveniently, I had a Question on the growth of violence and pornography on TV and was able to put in a dig about the growth of tabloid television.

I generally buzzed around in the afternoon before, with Sarah, collecting Maggie Colnbrook to go to the Lords for dinner. It is only three weeks since Humphrey's funeral. She was very brave and tried so hard to be in good form.

Maggie told me about Humphrey's resignation from the foreign office over the Falklands fiasco. That it should have been John Nott who went, since he was centrally involved at Defence – and he went a few months later anyway. But Peter Carrington, as foreign secretary, had lived a gilded political career and had never been through the fire of political and media criticism. When they all attacked him that weekend for not knowing the invasion was coming, he couldn't take it, cracked and resigned. This left Humphrey exposed. He felt that if both Carrington and Nott went that would involve a big reshuffle; but if just the Foreign Office team went then it would be simpler. So he and Carrington both resigned. Presumably it would also be difficult to explain that the No. 1 had all the responsibility and the No. 2 had none.

Thursday 31 October 1996

Had to cancel my lunch with Harry Evans because of need to talk to the party meeting about next week's Heritage Bill. This went OK. The front-bench meeting was short and subdued and the rebellion to replace Ted Graham as chief whip thankfully subsided because people didn't want to rock the boat ahead of the election.

Home to change for the big Royal Court Theatre bash. The Court has received a large Lottery award to rebuild providing it raises another £6 million, which is pretty stiff. This was the fundraising dinner at the Porchester Hall (I went there decades ago to watch boxing). Harry Evans's wife, Tina Brown, has done much of the organising, which is incredible considering she was in New York and busy editing her magazine. There was chaos around the hall with all the celebrities arriving and hordes of cameramen – they all disdainfully lowered their lenses when I arrived, which certainly put one politician in his place. Tina welcomed everyone on the way in. We had to fight our way to our table, which was right beside Harry and Tina's. They had with them the Rusbridgers, playwright Tom Stoppard and wife Felicity Kendal (he is always very friendly to me) and Peter Mandelson – the Prince of Darkness always at the top table.

We had Denis Forman from TV and his wife. Sarah was very taken with Denis and couldn't understand how such a gentleman was Labour. She is biased and I hope out of date. Most of the gents are now Labour; since Thatcher, the Tories have all the second-hand car salesmen.

Harry came to sit at our table for the last course and we had a good gossip; he is still focused on Murdoch. Chatted with Melvyn Bragg – who I hope will be one of our future peers; former *Sunday Times* colleague Tony Holden, and top civil servant Hayden Phillips and his wife. Usual principle applies: Hayden cannot be all bad with a wife like that. Saw Robert Kissin, bright son of Wilson's former friend, whose wife said to me that she had enjoyed the Maxwell programme and was 'surprised you were not in it'. Very reassuring that.

Friday 1 November 1996

Woke late and drove down to Shurlock Row. Wrote up some of the diary from the voluminous notes I keep each week, and after lunch crawled into bed for a nap – and didn't wake until 6 o'clock!

Had a long chat on the phone with Graham Greene. He is deep into the financial battles at the British Museum. They have a serious financial crisis and some trustees want to bring in entrance charges. Graham is bravely opposed on principle and has been getting support from Jack Cunningham. Graham is doing a tremendous job at the Museum. We must get him a knighthood soon.

Am feeling quite harassed, with speeches to write for Monday and Tuesday, lots of letters to do and not much time.

Jonathan Powell and David Miliband each wrote very appreciative letters about my memo on No. 10 and Jonathan asked for a meeting. Nothing yet from Tony B or Donald Dewar.

Sunday 3 November 1996

Went to mass with Charles, who isn't Catholic but feels some spiritual need and told me he enjoyed it. Father Flanagan was great. Talking of Heaven, he told the story of the Dublin Bishop who went to the wild west of Connemara and visited an ancient crone in her cottage in the deserted countryside, where she sat smoking her pipe. He asked her if she believed in Heaven. 'Yes.' 'What do you think Heaven is like?' he asked. Taking out her clay pipe, she said confidently, 'Just like here in Connemara – but without so much of the sex.' He said he felt like Oscar Wilde, unsure if he preferred to go to Hell for the company or to Heaven for the climate. Charles thought he was really good.

Drove to lunch with Arnold Weinstock in Wiltshire. Arnold has been such a loyal friend through all my tribulations. Now he has just lost his lifelong job as chief executive at GEC, which he built, and has lost his adored son Simon to cancer. At 70 it isn't easy to recover from that. The house is superb with magnificent views. All quite grand, everything done with Arnold's perfectionism. I sat next to Netta Weinstock who I love. She agreed enthusiastically to come to the theatre with us since Arnold won't go. Apparently they went to a play 20 years ago and he didn't like it, saying, 'That's it, I don't want to go to the theatre again', and he hasn't. He loves opera but only at its best. He is a remarkable man.

On my other side was Verushka Lady Wyatt. Hitherto, sitting with her at the races, I've not been able to understand her quiet Hungarian – actually I was unsure if she was talking English or Hungarian. But today she was very good company. Told me she doesn't like racing, so the last 20 years accompanying Woodrow to Newmarket and Haydock has been a bit of an ordeal.

I am rather fond of the old rogue. Verushka said: 'Woodrow had all these wives before me. Did you know them, what were they like?' I do like her daughter Petronella. I'm told she prefers older men, which shows she has good judgement.

Monday 4 November 1996

My speech for this afternoon's debate on the new Heritage Bill went OK, including the jokes about hereditary peers in need of repair and facing demolition. Afterwards went to dinner at the Reads – just around the corner from where I lived when married for 25 years. Adrian Hamilton was there. I used to know him on the *Sunday Times* with Harold Evans. Told me how he had a similar experience to mine with the late much unlamented Charles Douglas-Home, who treated him badly and deceitfully. (Also that the appalling John Grant on *The Times* was one of 'the most malign' people he had met. I said that was generous.) Even worse was on the *Observer*, where the *Guardian* owners had sacked him and then tried to avoid paying his redundancy – just like me with Murdoch. Yet they write *Guardian* leaders sanctimoniously lecturing the nation on how to treat people.

Tuesday 5 November 1996

Chaired an all-day conference on Labour's policies. Very tiring and often boring. I had to make a 15-minute opening speech, which I wrote in the taxi going there. David Seymour of the *Mirror* came as the lunch speaker. He said to me that the one golden rule dealing with journalists is, 'Never speak to them on anything.'

Went back to the Racing and Bloodstock committee, where Tom Kelly of the bookmakers association gave us a depressing picture of the damage done to racing by the Lottery. Then home to collect Sarah and to two parties for the US presidential election. First at the English Speaking Union; handsome surroundings but we didn't know anybody. Then to Whitehall Court for a Turner Broadcasting party, full of MPs. Tory MP Robert Key told Sarah he thought I was OK, which doesn't often happen across parties.

On the stairs going out just ahead of us was a tall Tory MP. A young blonde bimbo dashed past and told him she was sorry he was going and said that she had a room in the hotel for the night. It was the most brazen proposition I had ever heard. Understandably he declined. But one can see how MPs get into trouble with such modern floozies around. No doubt she would have sold her story afterwards to the press.

Wednesday 6 November 1996

Went blearily to the DNH meeting. Not much of importance. Saw Ivor Richard afterwards who had seen last week's Maxwell programme and, as a lawyer, thought it was small though 'clearly libel'. The BBC Westminster man Michael Hastings told me that the Governors will consider my letter and I will get a reply 'soon'. No doubt they are all passing the buck.

Had tea with Brenda Phipps, who was my secretary in No. 10 with Wilson and then at *The Times* and now works for Tina Brown in New York. She was looking very chic and was very interested in all the children. Very loyal. She said that Harry is still as chaotic as ever and that Tina is very intense but incredibly able.

In the evening Sarah and I went to Harry's Bar, where Sarah is a life member. It was quite glitzy. Rupert Murdoch sat at the first table with his civilised young editor Peter Stothard. At a large table were the diminutive Lord Stevens of the *Express*, Princess Pushy and Prince Michael of Kent with celebrity Donatella Flick, recently divorced, getting £8 million and eyes already wandering everywhere as if hungry for another settlement. ('Don't get mad, get everything', is the latest feminist advice to wives. I was lucky in mine.)

Thursday 7 November 1996

Whole morning clearing papers. Then the usual routine Lords front-bench meeting. Late lunch with Frank Longford – peer with a name like Glentoran who is a Millennium commissioner – and very worried about the Greenwich shambles. He is trying to limit the costs to £200 million but he can see it running late and out of control.

Went for tea with Angus Ogilvy at St James's Palace to discuss the Prince Charles's Business Trust, where I am now a trustee or something. At my suggestion, he had brought along John Monks, general secretary of the TUC, who was very good, typical of the best of the unions: straight, practical and amusing, and Yorkshire. We discussed how to expand the scheme to give unemployed young a chance in business. Angus is sweet and modest, with no pretence to being a genius, but devoting himself to good causes. His wife Alexandra, who Sarah knows, is the best of the Princesses. The flat was very attractive. Those Grace and Favour royal residences are worth having.

I went straight on to meet daughter Kate to go to the film premiere of First Wives Club, a feminist tract which would lead any sensible man never to marry. In the cinema we sat next to film producer Michael Winner, who was partnered by a delectable if perhaps teenage blonde and always remembers that we first met in the Palace Hotel in Gstaad. Many of the film stars there were already over the top and I didn't realise they had ever been stars. But Goldie Hawn came on stage and she was stunning, deep into HRT, I imagine.

Friday 8 November 1996

Friend Jeremy Taylor came to collect me in his grand turbo Bentley to go to Highclere Castle to see this year's yearlings for our syndicate. At lunch, I sat with the young trainer Roger Charlton and tried to get advice on how to buy a jumper that might jump – Peers Folly still hasn't left the ground publicly after three years of expensive nourishment; hopefully Henrietta Knight will give him more lift-off. There were a hundred people there, a great occasion and tribute to the impresario qualities of Henry Carnarvon's son Harry Herbert who makes it all work.

Sunday 10 November 1996

Henrietta Knight phoned to say that Peers Folly has gone lame again – on the other fore leg. I felt crushed. Three years now. The end may be nigh. Henrietta said he is a lovely character. I would settle for worse character and better legs.

Monday 11 November 1996

Remembrance Day so I wore my poppies. To the Lords and then lunch with David Montgomery. While waiting, I saw Alexander Hesketh. Alexander agrees we need management changes at Towcester racecourse. We will get a professional chief executive to run it managerially as a leisure operation. David was in fine form. He is very concerned that Murdoch has already got away with a monopoly grip on the gateway black boxes. He is angry with the government for doing nothing about this.

We also discussed Northern Ireland and he said what the Unionists wanted was 'separate development within the union'. Told me he had gone to the same school as Ulster Unionist Leader David Trimble. That they both felt nervous and out of depth in sophisticated London. 'We Ulstermen are dark and dour and blunt, speaking what we think. It took me years to understand the language of the people in London. I couldn't work out what they were really saying.' Said Trimble was the first Ulster leader to attend a Labour conference and found it very stressful. On the first night David asked Trimble to join him for dinner with some top politicians, but he said he had to be on his own, feeling tired and stressed.

I find David increasingly open, though still wary, watching me closely over his rimless spectacles and occasionally giving a thin smile. I really enjoy it when we order lunch. He waits for me and inspects the price list closely to see what I order. I know it would offend his puritanism if I asked for expensive lobster or turbot so I order cheap carrot soup and grilled plaice, the cheapest item on the menu, with no dessert. He looks pleased and orders a salad followed by 'fish and chips'. I've one glass of house white wine and he has water. So each time it is the same ritual and I manage to avoid the stigma of being a cosmopolitan champagne socialist. Actually I don't much like champagne and disagree with Marxist socialism.

In the Lords I had a PQ on the Millennium scandal at Greenwich, which went very well. The minister admitted it would cost £750 million and leave little of lasting value after 2000. Meanwhile our schools and hospitals are screaming for money – and the British Museum may have to introduce charges because it is short of £5 million a year. This government is mad.

Had a nice family occasion when my long-lost sister Molly came for drinks with her two lovely daughters Tania and Nadia – whom she inexplicably deposited in Barnados and deserted for 30 years. That is all forgotten and Molly is great fun, now married to a Greek and (in the small business tradition of her mother, my impressive grandmother) running a little amusement arcade in Margate. We had a great gossip.

Tuesday 12 November 1996

Worked on papers and then went to Irish Charity Fund lunch at the Whitehall Banqueting Hall.

David Montgomery made a fine speech about being from Northern Ireland. He made a strong case for the Northern Ireland Prods, positive and funny and not defensive as they usually are. Hugo MacNeill, the former Ireland and British Lions rugby captain, came up to me afterwards and said it was the best statement of the Unionist case he had ever heard.

Walked to the Lords for Questions and then another film premiere in Leicester Square, this time with my son Paul. He enjoyed the razzmatazz, all the cameras flashing and the film stars preening. He especially enjoyed sitting in the best seats, immediately behind the Queen and Prince Philip (who conducted a running commentary, with hoots and throaty chuckles, throughout the film). We saw *True Blue*, the story of the 1987 boat race when there was a rebellion in the Oxford crew. It was amusing that I had the best seats and the Tory minister was stuck on the outside. They must think we're going to win the election.

Afterwards we went to the Café de Paris for supper, drinks and jazz. Good fun. I spoke to the Tory Paymaster General, David Willetts, who has just had two days grilling from the Select Committee over his attempts to fix the Privileges Committee on cash for questions. He seemed fairly shaken. I told him to relax since it would blow over. He is clever enough to survive.

Wednesday 13 November 1996

Heritage team first thing; me very bleary. We discussed the Millennium scandal at Greenwich and I advised Jack – not that he needed it, since his political nous is first class – to prepare for Labour to pull out. That three quarters of a billion pounds could go to better causes. He also told us that on Monday he had been summoned to a meeting in Blair's room with Murdoch and his henchman Sam Chisholm. Murdoch was worried about our position on the conditional access black boxes for digital TV, saying there was no need for us to regulate him. He also smirched the regulator, Don Cruikshank, saying he's out to have revenge for Murdoch having sacked him in 1982 (a familiar story; Murdoch's profligate sackings are finally catching up with him). Murdoch was trying to talk Blair and Jack into getting rid of Don. So his strategy has been: first, to stop the government Bill legislating to stop his monopoly activities; then, having succeeded at that, with the government arguing this issue would all go into the regulations under Oftel, he is now trying to blunt the regulations and neuter the regulator. He will probably succeed, since he is politically shrewd and neither side of politicians wants to upset him.

I pointed out what Murdoch was up to and I made a staunch defence of Cruikshank, saying he should be our overriding regulator. It demonstrates how Murdoch always operates: securing his commercial advantage through operating directly on the politicians, using the promise of support from his newspapers or threat of opposition as leverage. He can also rely on them not understanding the technology. He will still control the gateway and he will continue to have a monopoly control both of the programme suppliers trying to get through the gateway to the TV set, and of the viewers who won't have free and equal access to non-Murdoch programmes.

Jack quickly picked it up. But who knows what Blair will have promised Murdoch. With a PQ next Monday on this subject I may be heading for more tension with our leader's office. I had better not name Murdoch as the impressive monopolist he is, but I won't compromise the principle. Perhaps afterwards I will have more time to spend with the family!

Out again in the evening to a dinner at the National Gallery. Had a nice chat with Michael Quinlan, now running Ditchley, who was at Defence and in the Cabinet Office when I was in No. 10. I confessed that I had spotted early on that he and John Hunt were Jesuit trained. They had black arts beyond a simple fellow like me.

Thursday 14 November 1996

Set off for Towcester, having cleared the last of my pile of mail. On the way I began to think of revising my paper on running No. 10. What I did earlier was geared to telling the team how to manage their bits of No. 10. But it didn't say anything about how Blair should restructure No. 10. So I began to think out a new section on revamping the Political Office and having stronger Media, Political and Policy Units.

In the revision it became virtually a Prime Minister's Department, though without the hassle of bureaucracy and hierarchy in formally setting one up. I became so mentally involved with it that the next thing I saw was a sign saying 'M45 Coventry'. I had overrun 30 miles and gone virtually into Coventry. I was furious – and a bit scared, as I had no recollection of driving and don't know what would have happened had the car in front braked. So I was a bit late for the races, snatched a quick lunch in the stewards' room and missed the horses in the paddock for the first race.

Got back to Berkshire about 6.00 pm, having done nearly 200 miles round journey and feeling sleepy.

Friday 15 November 1996

Stayed in all day, my head full of restructuring No. 10. Sat at my word processor all day and wrote a new section, based on what I had dreamed up on the road to Coventry; and reconstructed the rest. It is now much clearer and more radical. If he wants a Prime Minister's Department he has effectively got it there – though without the formality of the title or the consequent bureaucracy and hierarchy. And there is a post for a 'senior politician' as Chief of Staff – it could be Mandelson if he wants it. (Jonathan Powell told me that Mandelson would start as a minister of state at the Foreign Office, since he wants eventually to be foreign secretary, like his grandfather Herbert Morrison, though that might be wishful thinking on the part of Blair's team, hoping to dispatch Peter abroad as much as possible.)

Saturday 16 November 1996

Didn't do much. Talked on the phone to Brenda Dean, my new excellent No. 2. She told me she had heard that Blair wants Tessa Blackstone to be Ambassador to Washington. That must explain why Tessa is suddenly looking so cheerful. She would do it well – though the Foreign Office will still oppose her, wanting to have revenge for her 1977 CPRS report exposing their extravagances. They will sabotage her if they can, as they did with Peter Jay as Washington Ambassador 20 years ago, and naturally want to give this plum job to one of their own.

In the evening we went to a black tie dinner down the road at Alan Godsal's stately house (his wife Lady Elizabeth is High Sheriff of Berkshire). I sat on the honoured right of Lady Elizabeth, who is part Scots Cameron and part Irish. On my right was Lady Blair Stewart-Wilson. Her husband served the Queen for 20 years as Deputy Master of the Household and she said there was a bit of jealousy over the Queen's favours between him and Henry Carnarvon. She thought the Queen, whom her husband adores, had always had a very soft spot for Henry.

Mary said, wistfully I thought, that she thought Sarah looked remarkably well and 'fulfilled'. Well, we do our best.

I find the (fortunately declining) practice of taking port, when the ladies leave the room, silly, since women are often more interesting than men. But the conversation turned to Europe, where all of them want Britain to pull out of the EU. They hate Brussels. Alan Godson said Major was 'hopeless and the sooner he is got rid of the better'. They mostly seemed to the right of Jimmy Goldsmith. Here was upper–middle class middle England – and they don't like Brussels. Alan – who owns Cobbler's Cove Hotel in Barbados – is a bit stuffy but I enjoy talking with him, since he is very straight and seriously interested in politics.

Sunday 17 November 1996

Realised I've to go up to London tonight to be there for the memorial service of my old friend and partner at Grieveson Grant, Tim Edwards. Another good man gone.

Monday 18 November 1996

Walked along Eaton Square to St Peter's church for Tim Edwards' memorial. It was full of old friends from the City, most of my former partners from Grieveson Grant there. Afterwards walked home with Michael Beaumont and we had a glass of wine and a gossip. I showed him the broker's bought note for my disastrous purchase of *Mirror* shares on October 23 1991 – just before Maxwell died – which shows I knew nothing was financially wrong. It was nice to see the Grieveson gang, who were the friendliest and straightest group I've worked with.

A letter was waiting for me from Christopher Bland, chairman of the BBC, saying he was putting the question of their mishandling the Maxwell programme to his complaints procedure. That will delay it. Ironically, he has just published with great fanfare some PR document with '250 promises' of good behaviour from the BBC. Included is a promise to give victims of their attacks the right to see and 'respond to the evidence'. Which is exactly what they refused to do in my case. Later Michael Cocks, deputy chairman of the BBC, said to me he had looked at the case and concluded 'it was an open and shut case of libel'. I told him I was keeping the libel option open, and would see what kind of an apology I got. In fact I don't want to get involved in that awful legal process again – and it would be difficult to reconcile with my position as official spokesman on the BBC.

Had lunch at the House and then had to speak on Brenda Dean's important question on conditional access in digital TV. It is basically a question about Murdoch's potential monopoly control of the 'gateway', which everybody attacked. I joined in but, as always, refrained from mentioning Murdoch by name.

Went home and did paper work for two solid hours. I never finish it. No sooner is one lot filed and letters posted than another pile comes through the letter box. It is like swimming against a tide that is eternally coming in.

Have an intriguing phone call from Angus Ogilvy. About honours – for him. Very discreet and deserved. He seems to trust me.

Tuesday 19 November 1996

In the country snow is settling, so I didn't go to the media conference. Three hours of paperwork instead.

Dinner with the Air Chief Marshal of the Royal Air Force, Sir Michael Graydon, in Admiralty House, which I don't remember visiting before. Terrific paintings. The air chiefs present were all in fine and formal uniforms covered with dazzling medals. I sat between Graydon and the Strike Force chief. I've always found the military chiefs our most impressive professional group and loved talking to them when they came to Cabinet when I was in No. 10. Talked about the 1939–45 war and the present mess in Zaire. I don't want us to get involved. They are obviously tempted, but say how the French play silly political games in these situations – and how Bosnia was a nightmare for our forces. Freddy Howe, deputising for Nicholas Soames as secretary of state, gave a nice speech of thanks. Afterwards chatted to Robert Ayling of British Airways, who astonishingly had read my Herbert Morrison biography; and to John Kemp Welch of the old Stock Exchange, reminding him that I am the only Labour frontbencher ever to have been a member of the old Stock Exchange (including passing its cursedly difficult exams).

Wednesday 20 November 1996

Slogged away all morning clearing letters – now get 50 a day at the Lords and have to bring them home.

Lunch at the House with John McGrath, a playwright and scriptwriter who I knew well at Oxford – and once boxed with in the gym there, regrettably cutting his eyebrow. He has directed some terrific films, including 'Carrington', and founded the remarkable 7:84 Group for political theatre, especially in Scotland. Told me he has just written and put on a play about our seedy press. Surprise, surprise, the journalist critics panned it. We had some good reminiscences and I hope to keep in touch. Nice to meet an actual practitioner of the arts instead of all these boring administrators, and such an impressive one.

I then dashed off to a dinner for the racing sponsors. Broadcaster and former Labour MP Brian Walden was guest of honour and spoke with his usual eloquence and force. Afterwards I chatted with him about old times – we both worked in the Gaitskell Campaign for Democratic Socialism (CDS) in the 1960s.

Thursday 21 November 1996

Home all morning clearing papers and reorganising my filing system, ready so that my new secretary might be able to find things. Also found a lot of touching old letters from my father. Am building up an archive ready for the memoirs!

Went to our front-bench meeting which was, as always, completely futile and could have been dealt with on paper. Had the Committee stage of the new Heritage Bill through the afternoon. Did very well with an amendment from the Tory side making sure it covers the Victoria County Histories and the Dictionary of National Biography. We were so strong that the Minister withdrew his amendments, which he wrongly believed covered the issue, and will come back at Report stage. Inglewood is always helpful.

Dinner with the 21st Century Trust. Sat next to Michael Palliser, former Head of the Foreign Office, who used to work in Wilson's private office 1966–69. He was very critical of Charles Powell's conduct under Thatcher, describing him as 'a courtier' rather than a proper civil servant. But admitted that Charles was able – he had recommended him for No. 10 in 1977 but Jim Callaghan didn't choose him and preferred boring old Brian Cartledge. So Charles came up again under Thatcher and then got it.

Michael said that Michael Hall was a very bad principal private secretary to Wilson, incompetent and under Marcia's thumb – she chose him for that purpose. Also that Harold never let her influence serious policy issues. At the beginning Michael had pointed out that he was a strong European and Wilson had said that presented no problems to him.

He found Jim Callaghan pretty impenetrable and said his process of decision-making – internalising everything, never showing his hand until he had made up his mind – 'worthy of psychological study'. He respected him but found him difficult. Also noticed Jim's 'long memory for old grudges'. Not alone in that, thinking not only of yours truly!

Michael never came to the Lords – unlike most of his FCO [Foreign and Commonwealth Office] predecessors and most successors – because he opposed Thatcher on Europe. Sad really, given his ability and the mediocrity of most of the peers the Tories have created, usually party hacks and funders. He could contribute a lot. We also discussed Ian Bancroft, whose death is in today's papers. He was a good permanent secretary who Jim respected. My old Whitehall contacts are dropping off the perch – and Jim told me today that he has two a week! Hope he doesn't go soon. Must fix another lunch with him.

Friday 22 November 1996

Stay in to do this diary and clear papers. Begin to prepare my big speech on gambling next week – my third in eight days. Wish I didn't agree to these things. Overall I feel very well at the moment. Healthy. I know I am doing a fair job in Parliament – Jack Cunningham told me last week that he wants me to be minister there. And life with Sarah and all our children is a delight. Also find my new personal life with the Church very satisfying. Very private, but

I do look forward to going to mass. As one ages, that inner peace becomes more important. I feel less of the anger, resentment and desire for revenge on enemies than I used to. The Church's teaching helps there; though I am not certain it has yet made me much of a better person.

Incidentally, my favourite Irish cousin Margery phoned to say there was a letter in the *Northampton Chronicle and Echo* from my mother's step-brother Roland. I just remember him. Also a photo of my grandmother, very entrepreneurial, who started the first tram service from Northampton to Duston and later ran a well-known sausage and mash shop in the town at 17 Marefair. I remember her as an able but very hard woman. Perhaps today I would appreciate her business achievements as an uneducated working class woman in the early 20th century.

Sunday 24 November 1996

I walked a couple of miles and plotted my speech on gambling for Wednesday. Son Stephen has done some of the briefs and sent me some very helpful faxes.

Monday 25 November 1996

Went to the Lords and dealt with much post. Then the British Museum to see the Mysteries of China exhibition. A world I don't know. Then home and collect Sarah for dinner with my Washington friend Stanley Weiss. I sat with Raine Spencer. We drove Raine back to Mayfair afterwards. I congratulated her on handling her divorce so discreetly. She said Princess Di has been very supportive. Raine is very excited about her new job marketing for Harrods and has already spent a day at the duty free shop at Heathrow learning the job and also how to work the till. She is 67 and full of life. When I let her out of the car in Mayfair she said 'Darling, please show me to the door, in case the footpads come to get me.' She has style.

Tuesday 26 November 1996

A new day in my life. Della came in to act as my secretary. Just in time as I was about to drown in paper and missed appointments. She opened at least 60 letters, I dictated a few replies, she telephoned answers to others and I was even able to get some work done on tomorrow's speech. I've known Della since Oxford and if she frees me from the paper tidal wave it will change my life.

To the Lords for questions and then to the Commons to hear Chancellor Ken Clarke's budget. He is very relaxed, amusing, decently liberal and pro-European – which is increasingly rare on the Tory benches.

I went straight to Jack Cunningham's room where we drew up our DNH response, attacking the lack of budget provision for the Arts, and especially for museums. From there straight to the Courtauld Institute to view the paintings. Have never been into Somerset House before and it is a treasure, with beautiful rooms, ceilings and stairs. A group of directors of university museums were there and made a good case for getting more help. They are isolated in the Education department, always suffering the biggest cuts.

Wednesday 27 November 1996

In early to the DNH team meeting where I had a lot of Lords activity to report about our Lords recent debates and PQs. Then dashed to a big conference on the Leisure Industry, where I was to speak on gambling, my latest specialism, greatly helped by a briefing from my son Stephen who also attended.

Then dashed to the Savoy for the great annual *Spectator* lunch to announce their Politicians of the Year. I sat on table 1 between Douglas Hurd – who said he is increasingly an admirer of Jim Callaghan (who was at the next table) – and Lib Dem Peer Conrad Russell, who was getting some award. Also at our table were John Prescott, Conrad Black and Petronella Wyatt. Hurd said that Heath interfered too much in everything as PM and Thatcher in everything except law and order, which she sensed was a minefield and left to blow up the Home Secretary.

Walked back to the Lords and caught only the last PQ then buzzed around seeing people. Called in at drinks for the Jewish Political Institute. Jacob Rothschild thanked me for my support over his Heritage Memorial Fund and also told me that the government line on the British Museum is that they have weak management and so shouldn't have more money. Typical black propaganda to switch the blame on someone else.

Dashed home to collect Sarah to go to a charity concert in St James Church, Piccadilly. Claus Moser played a Mozart concerto beautifully. Afterwards we walked to a buffet supper at the Museum of Mankind. Lots of friends there: Graham Greene, Max and Jane Rayne and economist John Fleming, who I knew at the Bank of England and has now replaced Claus running Wadham, Oxford.

Thursday 28 November 1996

Worked all morning clearing papers and beginning the long task of filing away my No. 10 papers, for which I've bought another eight filing cabinets. Start on the Callaghan material, which I had kept for 10 years in the garden shed. The case holding them was rotting and the documents all smelt very damp. Some were fascinating and I had completely forgotten some of the issues and incidents. I start to arrange them for inspection by Professor Ken Morgan who is coming in next week to use them for his Callaghan biography.

I had quite a noisy PQ on the Greenwich Millennium folly. The minister, Inglewood, didn't answer my direct question on how much money had been raised from the private sector. I asked it because I knew the answer was zero. Afterwards Inglewood sent for me to explain why he couldn't answer – it all depends on a meeting in 10 days. He is usually helpful. Then I saw Robin Glentoran who is a Tory Millennium commissioner and he told me a lot of the background. He doesn't want us to scupper the project, but sympathises with the aim of sorting out the financing, which could go badly wrong and leave the new Labour government to pick up the bill. He is very charming and gracious unlike most of the Ulster peers.

Blair's key aide Jonathan Powell was supposed to come to tea but called off for the second time. We will try again. I travelled with Frank Judd in a taxi to the LSE to announce the new Director – Giddens the sociologist from Cambridge, who sounds possibly OK, if a bit too trendy, populist and fash- ionista for my aging taste. They served champagne after but I declined, having another long night ahead.

Sprinted back to the Lords to collect my car and then the big Tate dinner for the Turner Prize. I got off to a dicey start by forgetting to put on a black tie, which Michael Grade clearly noticed in the receiving line. However, since he had sent the invitation to 'Lord and Lady Sarah Berry', I didn't feel too guilty. Lord Berry can get the blame. We went to see the 'art' of the four short-listed candidates, which was truly awful. The Turner Prize should be at the frontiers and isn't there to comfort the outraged readers of the *Mail* and *Telegraph* – but these were dreary, boring and showing little creative spark. Pity.

At dinner I sat between an arts journalist from *The Times* and Sue Robertson from Channel 4. She is now Grade's assistant and previously worked for David Owen, so she has been thoroughly tested through the fire. She has handled the press for years and said there were only two journalists today she would trust – and I guessed them: Peter Riddell and Don McIntyre. Both first class. Talked with George Walden on the way out, another Tory MP who is quitting while still young. I remember him as very able at the Foreign Office when I was in No. 10. He has quite independent views, especially on education, and that has not gone down well with the Tory whips and right-wing ideologues.

What a full week! I always love getting down to the country, but appreciate that the more because of the excitement of also being in London. The point is that I wouldn't like to be full time in either. Have to get the balance right.

Friday 29 November 1996

Spent the morning on more papers and filing my documents. My son Paul came round and we had an early lunch. Then down to the country.

In the afternoon I rescued another old case of damp documents from the shed and began sorting that. The Wilson papers are better filed than the Callaghan, since my great secretary Brenda did a splendid job there. Also there were the papers from 1961–64 when I was secretary of the Gaitskell support group CDS. And some old personal letters, which made me cry: letters from my father shortly after I was married, letters from my nieces Tania and Nadia when they were young children in Cyprus after their parents split up and my sister abandoned them; and from Françoise Elliet, the beautiful Parisian novelist who I loved at Oxford and she continued to return that feeling for 25 years until in 1983 she walked into the Seine to drown. I shall never forgive myself for not going to her funeral. Another selfish item where you cannot put it right later. You cannot rewind the film and show it again with yourself behaving better. Suffer from too many of those memories.

Saturday 30 November 1996

Jeremy Taylor came with me to Newbury. Didn't back the Hennessy winner but cheered it home, since it was an ex-point-to-pointer trained by a permit farmer in Cornwall who has only five horses. I like that. Only national hunt racing has that small scale personal touch.

Had quite an early night after reading more of Ken Tynan's Letters. There was something wild and adolescent in him, along with his genius. A lot about his 'Oh Calcutta' sex romp, which made millions (not for him) and which I thought juvenile and boring, just hoping to shock the bourgeoisie. Today it would seem worse.

Monday 2 December 1996

December has arrived without me noticing that another year is near its end. Our Lottery policy launch went quite well. Jack sat on the platform with David Blunkett from Education and dire Harriet Harman from social security. The rest of us sat in the front row. There was a slightly tense atmosphere since there have been more snide pieces about Jack in the press. The question now is whether this is a spontaneous burst of criticism or a well organised campaign by some malign party. Tom Pendry walked back along the Embankment with me to Parliament and he is in no doubt it is the latter – and to him the guilty party is Mark Fisher. Mark doesn't fit in with the rest of the team. He is a chippy Etonian gent; we're all jovial state system lads. He is said not to value Jack, telling his luvvie friends that Jack is a philistine (untrue, though Mark would view any football supporter as such).

He also has a 'lit set' girlfriend who is connected with the *Guardian*, where much of the bile appears. I've always got on well with Mark. But he is different, a round peg in a square Labour hole, and he failed to produce our arts policy document for about a year, for which Jack gets the blame. Ominously, most of the articles attacking Jack also include a sentence praising Mark. Insiders believe that is usually a footprint. If true, it won't work. Blair quite respects Jack – who in turn, like Jim Callaghan – has a long memory for enemies.

At noon had a meeting with the minister, Inglewood, and we agree the amendments to the National Heritage Bill, which ensure the Victoria County Histories and the Dictionary of National Biography will qualify for lottery grants. I will sign it. Then went to a lunch for the racing press awards. Was guest of the racecourses and sat with old TV friend Paul Fox. Discussed my complaint against the BBC with Paul and John Gau, both of whom have worked there. They say the Beeb is usually too obstinate and arrogant to apologise to anyone but they recommend I stick at it. One problem today is that management is afraid of its own journalists, such as Bower, who may attack them anonymously through *Private Eye*.

Tuesday 3 December 1996

Worked all morning at home, clearing letters and sorting files. The amount of material I've on 1974–79 is incredible. I could write a full history of those governments from those documents alone. One day I may.

Sat through a boring Questions and up came Michael Hastings, the BBC Westminster man. He told me he had had a meeting with Bland and advised him they were in the wrong on the Maxwell programme and should settle for libel. Later I saw Michael Cox, BBC deputy chairman, who told me the same but added that he wanted them to go for Bower, who he seems to have good reason to hate. I am not so sure of that. Don't want any witch hunts. I will be content with an apology.

To Soho with our Commons spokesman George Howarth to the Industry Forum seminar and dinner with the gambling industry. He was more cautious on gambling reform than I had been last week in my speech because he has had a warning message from the Leader's Office. A child advisor had phoned him to tell him to say nothing on our policies because we must not appear to be pro-gambling. This is bizarre given the whole tone of my speeches, which is against the gambling bonanza, and that I am advising the Catholic Church on controlling gambling. But the child brides and boys in short pants up in the office are permanently in a panic in case we say anything that might upset anyone – and especially Murdoch or the *Mail*. And George, of course, fears that Blair might be behind it. I trust he has more important things to do. But it is easier for me, since in the Lords I am not so tied to the leader's patronage – and don't care much whether I have his support. For MPs it is different, especially after waiting so long to get back into office.

Wednesday 4 December 1996

In early and bleary to the DNH team meeting – another nasty piece about Jack in the *Evening Standard* yesterday. I reported on all my doings in the Lords and then raised the question of the press hostility. Afterwards Jack took me to his room for coffee. He is still calm and taking it all on the chin unruffled. He said he has a contempt for the press and tries not to let them ruffle him. It will probably pass.

Had two Starred Questions. The first on the 2006 football World Cup went quite well, but the next on the British Museum, for which I had done a lot of work, was a shambles. Too many people tried to get in and suddenly the time was up and I couldn't get to the dispatch box. The first time that has happened to me. I could have been more assertive, but I don't want to upset our backbenchers, for whom PQs are the big moment.

Chaired a three-hour meeting at the LSE of the Investment Committee to select new managers for our investment funds. Foreign and Colonial have been very pleasant, but have under-performed, and Schroders, who were much the best. I complained about their high fees and will try to get them down but they will hopefully repay it in performance.

Thursday 5 December 1996

Woke early feeling fragile and a bit coldy. Nice Ken Morgan from Oxford, who is doing the official Callaghan biography, came; I am showing him my Policy Unit papers. He was quite overwhelmed by their richness and had nowhere near finished them by lunch so we arranged for him to come back next week.

Had a PQ on masthead programming for TV, which nobody, especially me, understood. Then the Report stage of the Heritage Bill, which went smoothly on the two agreed amendments. Had tea with Jean Trumpington who is trying to get me into running the Tote after Wyatt retires. I say that I cannot formally apply and be interviewed while on the front bench. She doesn't support William Astor and thinks Marcus Kimball good but too old.

I finally had my meeting with Jonathan Powell, discussing my paper on running No. 10 for nearly two hours. He said Blair had read the early draft and would have the final form in his weekend box. He described it as 'very, very helpful'. He said Blair has no experience of government and needs advice on how to do it. His experience is with words, both as a barrister and as an opposition politician. Now he will have to learn how to convert words into actions.

He was particularly interested in certain parts: what happens in detail on the first day, who travels with whom from the Palace, when they grab their rooms, what the PM usually does first etc. He didn't know who would run the Political Office, implying that Anji Hunter might not be of sufficient political stature and might be better as diary secretary. He didn't rise to my enquiry about using Grocott the PPS. I suggested Peter Mandelson but he said he had 'other ambitions, probably at the Foreign Office, and anyway Tony wouldn't want him that close. He isn't the most popular member of the parliamentary party.' True, definitely unpopular – but he is one of the cleverest politically. He took the idea of throwing the Church appointments out of No. 10 to create more room for policy advisers.

He said Tony agrees with me and doesn't want a formal Prime Minister's Department but does want his office strengthening, which is what I am recommending. He is thinking of making more use of the Cabinet Office to support him. He felt they might use civil servants in the Policy Unit 'at the beginning' but I argued against that, afraid that the civil servants might be able to exploit Tony's lack of experience in Whitehall. He said that Tony is very accessible and they all feel they can see him any time unless he has someone with him. They spend a huge amount of time preparing for Questions – sometimes all morning and over lunch as well. I said that was a waste of time and anyway they wouldn't be able to do that in government – Thursday morning is traditionally for Cabinet.

It was a good meeting and I can see his value to Tony. He is able and well organised and seems not to have his own personal agenda. I imagine his strength is that he has worked in the civil service and knows Whitehall – and his weakness is that he knows little of the inners of the Labour Party. He expressed thanks and said we would meet again soon.

Finally I gave him a copy of my first memo to Jim Callaghan in April 1976, on Themes and Initiatives for a New Prime Minister, with its lead to the Ruskin speech on education, and suggested he prepare a general one to give Tony when he gets in. Focusing on the policy priorities and how to achieve them in Whitehall. He was very interested and said they were intending to give an updated Ruskin speech. Incidentally, at the beginning, I raised the issue of Jack's bad press – to flush out if Tony or Mandelson were behind it. He was very aware but said it was frustrated arts luvvies and that Tony took no notice. 'Tony has a very high regard for Jack.'

I went home tired but pleased and drove to Shurlock Row, the media full of Major's problems.

Friday 6 December 1996

I cleared a lot of papers and also bid over the telephone for some jewellery for Sarah. It was exciting bidding hearing the auctioneer in the background. Secured her favourite, but told her mischievously that I had been outbid, hoping to surprise when she got it in her Christmas stocking.

Saturday 7 December 1996

Off early to Northamptonshire to see Peers Folly at Dick Saunders'. Met Kate and drove to the farm, in thick fog. The great horse looked terrific and has a sweet temperament. His injured foot seems better and he will be ridden next week. But whether he ever races is questionable. I think he prefers life recuperating at Dick's comfy stable and so whenever we get him ready to race he deliberately hurts a leg. Kate loved him. Then off to Towcester racing.

Sunday 8 December 1996

Telephone calls to Paul, Stephen, Kate, my French sister-in-law Agnes and Melvyn Bragg (who has decided not to go in for the London Arts Board chairmanship, wisely since they have stitched it up in advance for one of their own and anyway he is too good for them). And my weekly call to Joe Haines, who feels the government is finally falling apart.

Certainly Major looks in a mess with his Eurosceptics tearing the party apart. His problem is that he has no great vision of his own to lead them towards a better land, just twists in the wind of party divisions. He doesn't seem to care whether they stay in Europe or leave – a bit like Wilson in his final years. The Tories have about 70 MPs who are not standing again and don't care what happens. Most of the others think they are going to lose anyway so they might as well do their own thing. And Ken Clarke is a bit like Benn in 1974–79 – too big for the PM to dare to drop or discipline, so he follows his own agenda. The Tories are in the kind of mess that is familiar to old Labour hands.

Monday 9 December 1996

Dashed up to London and cleared hundreds of letters and lunched quietly by myself. Had Nigel Kent-Lemon in for tea and we discussed how to set up the new charity Gamcare to deal with problem gambling for which I am to be President.

To a meeting at the London Arts Board, where we discussed the short list for the new chairman. They have ended nine months later with a botch of three insiders. Really the selection committee started off wanting Trevor Phillips, who is nice, able, lively and above all black. So they have fixed the rest so Trevor must get it. This is bound to emerge. Especially since I made them include Melvyn Bragg on the list and since he is more qualified than anyone they had the problem of how not to select him. They did this effectively. The chairman of the committee waited till the last minute to phone Melvyn, who phoned me immediately afterwards. Melvyn said it was the oddest call he had ever had. Very oblique and making it clear they felt obliged to ask him but hoped he was too busy. Melvyn felt they were just doing it for the record. Certainly he, a big figure, didn't want to put his name forward and then be rejected. So he turned it down, as they hoped.

Even worse was an item discussing an appalling paper from the Arts Council on 'cultural diversity'. This was 36 pages of shoddy and incoherent Politically Correct Claptrap (PCC). It was basically asking for money for ethnic arts, which I certainly support. At least it honestly admitted that it defined cultural diversity as meaning Afro-Caribbean, Indian and Chinese arts. There were no numbers in it – such as that the Irish community in Britain is still greater than all these diverse ethnics put together. In fact it was a racist document because it defined out all white minority cultures as not qualifying to receive financial support. Had a white person written similarly arguing that no black cultures should receive support, these very same PC claptrappers would be trying to put him in jail under the Equal Opportunities Act (and I might support them).

I stated that I was genuinely all for supporting these minority ethnic arts, and even giving them disproportionately more support because of the social disadvantages under which many of them live and work. But providing we openly stated we were doing that, and why, and that they were currently less than 20% of the London population and barely 8% of the national population – and that white minority cultures such as the Irish could receive support as well. Clive was very strong in support. But our politically correct ninnies, especially the Labour and the Arts Council ones, were ducking and weaving.

Tuesday 10 December 1996

Up early and off to a Labour conference at the National Film Theatre, launching our proposed new University for Industry. It started as a typical Gordon Brown sound bite but has been turned into an interesting policy proposal by the Institute of Public Policy Research. I listened to Tessa Blackstone, Gordon Brown (a bit wall-paperish at times but commendably committed), and David Blunkett (excellent). I needed to get the feel for what it is all about because I was due to speak in the afternoon and hadn't written anything.

Had lunch with old friend Gordon Snell. We were mates at Oxford when he was at Balliol. We then walked the Cotswolds together and also in western Ireland for a riotous fortnight. He is now married to the super star novelist Maeve Binchy. We talked over old times. I had recovered from my archives a wonderful letter he wrote to me when I was at Harvard in 1958, full of jokes and including the original text of his 'pornographer's calypso', a monster work of cabaret. He was very touched to have it. It was so good to re-establish our friendship. He now spends his time writing excellent children's literature at their home in Dalkey, south of Dublin.

I had a PQ down on the need for more support for the theatre, which went quite well. Then I went back late to the conference, going straight onto the platform for my speech, which was quite brief and written in the taxi en route. The audience was still big and it had gone well.

Then dashed home, changed and drove back in traffic jams to the Middle Temple for a dinner in honour of Lord Scarman, a great figure in the fight for human rights. I had paid a £100 to go, which goes to the Human Rights charity, which may explain why there were absolutely no other politicians there. Disgraceful really, since he is a great man and many of the Left have based the rhetoric of their political careers on his fine achievements. Being humbugs, they are happy to claim the moral self-righteousness of supporting Rights but not to pay for it.

I saw a number of legal friends (surprised I still have any given my views on the rip-off nature of parts of our legal system, but I greatly admire their fine minds and anyway many of them share my views on the system – which we tried but failed to reform with our 1976 Royal Commission on Legal Services). Always pleases me to see Michael Zander – I was best man at his wedding 36 years ago – who told me he retires from the LSE next year and must be nearly irreplaceable as an inspiration to radical law students. Law Lord Nico Browne-Wilkinson had invited me and I sat on top table.

The main speech about Scarman was made by Anthony Lester. He too was a friend long ago and we worked together on the 1960s campaigns for reforms in race and homosexual legislation. His speech was excellent and moving. I circulated after. Talked to Lennie Hoffman, now a distinguished judge, a friend at Oxford when he first came from South Africa. He recalled our Oxford days, when I had long curls and wore a long cloak to match, saying I was 'very romantic and a poet'. Touching memories. Wish I had worn a shorter coat and been a better poet. More style than substance there!

I would have loved being a barrister, all that high level argument (and money and prestige) would have suited me, as well as the Oxbridge setting of the Temples and Inns. But when I was young in my village I had never heard of lawyers and didn't know how you became one till I got to Oxford and saw the students reading those boring law books late at night in the library. At that point I foolishly preferred Guinness.

The only lawyer I met before then was the one in the Northampton Family Court when I was 12, who asked each of us four Donoughue children in turn if we preferred to live henceforward with our separated mother or father. I alone said absolutely 'Dad'.

Wednesday 11 December 1996

Della came in to do valuable work diminishing the pile of letters; and Ken Morgan sat downstairs going through my Policy Unit papers for nuggets for his biography of Jim Callaghan. In between I went to the dentist to lance my infected gum. Have been to dentists more often in past five months than in previous 15 years.

To Jack Cunningham's Xmas party. Very good fun. Jim Callaghan came and was surrounded by young Labour MPs as he dispensed humour and political wisdom. He has shrunk and is now shorter than me, and walks very crookedly, but mentally is undiminished. Asked how he was, he quoted Attlee: 'quite well, compared to the alternative'. A big topic of conversation was today's resignation by the Paymaster General, David Willetts, following a Select Committee report accusing him of 'dissembling'. He was once in the Policy Unit so cannot be all bad. Really he is a sacrificial lamb trying to prove that the Commons can self-regulate. Willetts did no more than all whips offices do all the time and will rightly survive this.

I had a long talk with Jack about the shambolic Greenwich Millennium project, which I've been pursuing in the Lords. Now they are in the merde because business won't commit private money unless Labour promises our next government will continue to underwrite it. So far the government have shut us out and represented it as a Tory triumph. Now it is a shambles, they want Labour involved to rescue them.

I happily missed out on four other Xmas parties and went home to change for a charity dinner for victims of domestic violence. It cost us £200 each so this week I've put £500 to charity. I sat between two ladies I didn't know and opposite a sad man with dementia. I escaped after the main course and went over to sit with lawyer Helena Kennedy and TV writer Verity Lambert. Verity was furious that Channel 4 had just rejected her series of Vickram Seth's fine novel *Suitable Boy*.

Sarah and I slipped away early, but not before Helena, who was in such a hurry (she had a murder trial in Leeds next morning) that she mistakenly went into the men's lavatory. Modern feminists shouldn't mind that. She is very funny and attractive, which cannot be said for all of her harridan sisterhood.

Thursday 12 December 1996

Finally got out and went Xmas shopping for Sarah's presents – following Michael Bedford's insistence. Haven't actually been serious shopping for some years. I walked up and down Bond Street for some time, to no avail because I didn't know where the shops on Michael's list were. It was very cold and I felt a bit of a goon and thought about giving up.

A nice diversion was running into Michael Grade, the boss of Channel 4, who was clearly on a similar spree and equally clearly relieved to meet someone from the non-Bond Street society to discuss politics, the media etc. Anything but shopping. We went over the whole field. He feels the Tories have had it now and it is too late for them to recover. He told me about a visit to Virginia Bottomley earlier in the week when 'she was completely off the wall'. We must have gone on for at least 20 minutes delaying returning to the awful consumer expedition. But in the end we had exhausted it and bade reluctant farewells, he heading south towards the gridlock in Piccadilly, me north in the direction of the horrors of Oxford Street.

I felt I couldn't give up without having found or entered a single shop on the list, let alone buy a prezzie, so I pressed on, feeling rather like one of those

Victorians going exploring up the Zambesi among ever more alien people. Michael Bedford had suggested warm leather gloves, which I finally found in his recommended shop. They were nicely soft but priced hard at over £200 a pair so I decided to reflect on that. Seeking a shop on his list that sold 'lovely warm silk underwear', I finally went into Fenwick's department store and went up the escalator to the Personnel department on the top floor and there borrowed a telephone directory to look up the recommended shop. It was just around the corner. They did have some of the recommended silk thermal vests – £300, so I moved to the silk nighties. These were £700 so I spent a little time fondling them to test the quality and then announced the need for more time for reflection.

Deciding to be more generous, I set off down South Audley Street and into the last shop on the list, Thomas Goode, firmly intent on at least buying Sarah a jar of marmalade for her shrinking stocking (I had mentally decided to use one of my clean ankle socks on Christmas Eve, rather than a too capacious pillow case in which a marmalade jar might get lost). Sadly, they didn't sell marmalade and knew of nowhere that did. (My mistake arose because Michael's unfathomable writing seemed to say 'Thomas Foods', not Thomas Goode, and I expected to get jams there). Eventually feeling guilt-ridden and a bit ashamed of asking for even more time for reflection, I bought two of their best thick phallus candles in nice china pots. Cost £140. Outside I immediately took a cab to escape back to Parliament. It had been quite an education. I won't risk going shopping again. Clearly not for me. I certainly won't tell Sarah about the expedition. But I suppose at least it makes my racing seem better value.

Got back just in time to attend our weekly front-bench meeting. Not much achieved except announced two serious illnesses. Poor Alma Birk is dying (technically she is still in my team since Ivor, rightly as it turned out, didn't have the heart to sack her) and Bert Oram is poorly.

Incidentally the Tories today lost the Barnsley by-election, polling only 7% in third place and with it went their parliamentary majority. They are falling apart before our eyes.

Had tea with Tom Chandos, one of Labour's few hereditary peers, discussing the future shape of the media, and also the intention of the English National Opera, where he is a director, to move to the South Bank opposite St Pauls. He says Gowrie is only interested in the posh Covent Garden and is 'bitterly contemptuous of ENO'.

I walked to the Reform Club in Pall Mall for a Readers Digest party. The lovely library reminds me of my happy days at the Reform. We campaigned for women members and finally triumphed; our first female member was the blighted Sarah Keays, Cecil Parkinson's (pregnant) mistress! I chatted with Bob Worcester who told me his latest MORI opinion poll shows Europe rocketing up the 'important issues' table. He thinks this won't help the Tories since they are seen by the public as deeply divided on this. Labour is of course more shallowly divided – and kept by Blair more prudently silent since we want to win the election.

Took Elisabeth Smith to Claridges for the big annual ARCO dinner. Robin Butler chatted and Peter Middleton, who I knew well at the Treasury 20 years ago, now looks very prosperous in banking. Simon Jenkins at first complained of our attacks on Greenwich (he is a commissioner) and then admitted 'Jack is right and has handled it properly'.

At dinner in the splendid dining room at Claridges I sat between the journalist Anthony Howard and Reg Griffin of *Timeform* betting magazine (I am a devotee). Tony was interesting on politics as usual, having respect for Jack, though thinking he has lost some of his drive. He was at school with Charles Williams and dislikes him, saying he was always corroded with excessive ambition. I suggested he should write an article on the Anglican Church, pointing out that it has become like the Labour party in the early 1980s, a rainbow coalition of politically correct minority cults and therefore shouldn't be the Established Church of the nation, which should be broad, mainstream, middlebrow, tolerant, and reflecting the nation. He said he would think about it. His father was an Anglican dignitary, as was Charles Williams' (perhaps explaining some of the animosity), though he himself, as a modern British journalist, naturally believes in nothing.

I always go to this grand dinner because it has there everyone of political interest. Previously I've heard Margaret Thatcher and Ronald Reagan give the big speech. This time it was US General Colin Powell. He spoke magnificently, though for 50 minutes, which is too long for that audience late at night. But he was eloquent in a way that Americans rarely are, taking us through his career and beliefs. I could see how he sold so many books. He clearly wants to be President and would be better than any in a long time. He has a world view and also a heart. The best soldiers make good political leaders. America needs him badly to sweep up the Clinton meretricious sleaze and should grab him quick.

Friday 13 December 1996

Friday the 13th sounds dangerous so I decide not to risk going out. Spent the day very tired after a testing week. Wrote up the last part of this and watched the racing from Cheltenham.

Curiously these daily diaries grow longer. Is my life growing more full and exciting? Or am I just growing more garrulous with age? Bit of both probably, especially the latter.

Sunday 15 December 1996

Lunch at Sarah Palmer's, with Lord King, who privatised British Airways, and the Duke of Wellington as guests: the former now very deaf though still an effective operator and the latter a nice gentleman who invited me to his Apsley House, which I accepted, if only for its great address: Number 1, London.

Monday 16 December 1996

Had a bad night, sore throat and gunge flowing down my throat waking me repeatedly. Dismal day through the window – this is my childhood memory of Christmas time in England: grey outside and feeling rotten inside. Slept much of the day and Sarah kindly went to the chemists to get the usual bag of medicaments, which do no good. One consolation – I will miss all those Xmas parties in London.

Tuesday 17 December 1996

Went to sleep at 5.00 pm yesterday evening. Sarah woke me briefly with some soup, but then slept till she woke me at 10.00 next morning. Very groggy and temperature over 100. Pulled out of my PQ on the Greenwich Millennium; a pity since I would have exposed the mess they are in.

Wednesday 18 December 1996

Very wobbly but get up because want to go to dinner tonight in London with Henry and Jeannie Carnarvon. Talked on the phone to Brenda Dean who is taking my place leading in the debate on the Media and Democracy.

Went up to London in mid-afternoon and straight to sleep ready to enjoy the evening. Henry took us to Zafferano in Lowndes Street. We had a good chat and I forgot about my plague – anyway Henry had a cold with his eyes running and as always ignored it. Old class of the stiff upper lip. He is full of interest in all that is going on. Thinks that both Scottish devolution and the Lords reform will create problems for us in the next Parliament. He says that Tory Lords leader Robert Cranborne is 'a shit' and he wouldn't trust him. He finds Cranborne's arrogance insufferable.

They had both been upset by Vivien Duffield going shooting at Highclere and allegedly being terribly rude to the staff; dreadful bad language.

Thursday 19 December 1996

Hectic morning with Della clearing dozens of letters and Xmas cards. Every December I realise too late that I hate this time of year and should be in India. Instead went into the Lords for its final day.

Our side seems very confident politically. The government plunges from one disaster to another. The latest episode of it cheating over the pairings for divisions, pairing the same Tory MP with both a Labour and a Lib Dem, so they eliminate two opposition votes for every one of their own, simply adds to the feeling of sleaze and incompetence. I sense we will now win comfortably. On the polls it will be a big margin, but I don't believe the polls until the actual campaign begins.

A huge post faced me at the Lords and as I went through them I began to feel poorly again. So, after a bit of Xmas shopping, I went home to bed. Xmas for me is taking its historic path – in bed and grumpy.

Friday 20 December 1996

Groggy but rose to try to deal with the huge pile of cards which I had brought back from the Lords and more still flow through our front door. Tessa Blackstone told me yesterday that she ignores most of them and only sends cards to close family, friends abroad and old cleaning ladies (not everybody in the Labour Party has old cleaning ladies, but at least Tessa treats them well). That is sensible but requires courage, which Tessa has in spades but I lack. She was very sweet coming down to see me in my room and wish me a happy Xmas before we all broke up. She can be over-severe but she is a solid friend and has done a terrific job as Head of Birkbeck College. She has grandchildren, which makes me jealous.

Saturday 21 December 1996

Still feeling groggy with stuffed sinuses. Granite grey outside and getting colder. This is when I want to get abroad, but sadly Sarah can't travel far, so I am stuck.

However had a great family day with several of mine driving out for our Xmas lunch. Paul, Kate and her husband and my two lovely nieces, Tania and Nadia, came and we all went for lunch at the Bell in Waltham St Lawrence. Very nice atmosphere in the old pub.

Our Xmas tree was beautiful but it was too cold to join it in the conservatory. In the evening I sat by the sitting room fire meaning to read the Ted Morgan biography of Somerset Maugham but instead I slept for over two hours. Life slipping away in grumpy sleep.

Sunday 22 December 1996

No improvement in the sinuses. Ruins my sleep. Am into the sixth day of antibiotics.

Went to mass which as always improved my spirit. Father Flanagan asked us to pray for the nuns at the local nunnery, because at Xmas they had to look after him and a group of retired priests. He said the priests were particularly difficult because they had never had families and so had never learned to think of anyone human but themselves, ending up very self-centred. He is very sweet and humble. Afterwards I gave him a little bag with a Xmas card, two bottles of House of Lords claret and a cheque for the church – I was paid £250 for a lecture and had them make it out to the Twyford church (in fact I attend Wargrave but Twyford has more children and old people and could use the money over Xmas).

Out to a drinks party at Sonning. Met the new Tory candidate (and inevitable MP) for us and Maidenhead, Theresa May. Seemed bright, straight and strong though very unforthcoming and perhaps not very great on humour. Cautiously, though understandably in the presence of a Labour man, declined to give any views on their next leader after Major's inevitable defeat. Spent rest of the day inside clearing papers and reading Somerset Maugham in the evening. Spirits gloomy again.

{Christmas 1996 isn't recorded here. I flew to Gstaad in Switzerland on 28 December}

Wednesday 1 January 1997

Walked with Barry Humphries to beyond Turbach. We chatted all the way up that remote snowy valley. He told me that his father was a builder who was disappointed that his son didn't follow in the trade, or at least become an architect. But at Melbourne University he decided to become an entertainer and has done that all round the world for 40 years. His only flop was in New York, when that notorious negative theatre critic (name deservedly forgotten) killed his show stone dead. Dame Edna is based on any typical Melbourne suburban housewife, and surely his mother. 'They run Australia.

Despite appearances, it is a matriarchy.' Discussed the horrors of British journalism, from which both he and wife Lizzie have suffered. The *Mail* traced his
first brief wife from 40 years ago to persuade her to say what a rotten husband
he was. 'Their only interest is dirt', he said. The sewage men.

He knew and respected Betjeman and walked around London with him
admiring the old buildings and regretting the disappearance of ones, such
as the old Coal Exchange, vandalised by modern developers. He will never
forgive Harold Macmillan for allowing Euston arch to be destroyed. He is
remarkably literate, recalling the names, plots and authors of every novel
I mentioned. He collects books hungrily. He still loves going on stage and
performing. Told me how when a journalist visited him at his show in
Glasgow to write a profile, he offered her a ticket. She refused saying, 'You
can't bribe me.' He pointed out that, to understand him, one had to see
him on stage. She wasn't interested. Only interested in doing some pseudo-
psychological analysis. No facts.

I told him my story of the journalist who had written four defamatory
pages about a football manager without bothering to contact the victim.
When (my friend) the journalist's defence barrister, facing defeat in an
unanswerable libel action, asked why he didn't put the accusations to the
victim, the journalist said, 'I didn't want a negative quote.' Negative Quote!
Negative quote might mean the Truth. They never want that if it spoils their
vicious story. The barrister told me the libel cost the paper half a million but
the editor didn't mind since it made 'a good story', which boosted sales.

Thursday 2 January 1997

Home at midnight, 10 hours after leaving Gstaad delayed by snow at Geneva
airport. Good to be back, though England was freezing and all the turf racing
and much of the football cancelled. This isn't a civilised time of the year.
Makes more sense to go to the Orient in mid-December and not return till
February. If I lived alone, I would do that.

Friday 3 January 1997

Bleak day in the country. I stayed in bed and finished the Waugh/Nancy
Mitford letters. After that started her *Love in a Cold Climate* and flicked
through Madame Pompadour, just to get a feel for her writing. As I expected:
glittery and amusing, not very profound. They really were appallingly right
wing. Waugh admits to being anti-Semitic, which she claims she isn't, though
much of her family were, especially Oswald Mosley. At one point in 1959

Waugh reveals he still read Mosley's fascist publication *Searchlight*. He is also often on the edge of madness.

But I love the brilliant writing. And the eccentricity. Marvellous on Coronation evening in 1953 when at dinner in their scruffy, damp and freezing Somerset farmhouse he wore evening dress with medals at dinner, with his wife Laura wearing a tiara. Their sole guest, Susan Alsop, watched in astonishment – then he called on her to make an after dinner speech. It is worth it for that battiness. But I am glad that class was ousted from power after 1940. They would happily have settled for a soft fascism. Waugh liked the hierarchical and authoritarian side of the Catholic Church (not for me) and the traditional rejection of the modern world. It enabled him to live in a cocoon untouched by all he loathed in modern Britain. Also a touch of snobbery, linking him to the Catholic old aristocrats. He loathed the Irish immigrant Catholics, like my father's family.

Saturday 4 January 1997

Bleak House continues. Sarah feels terribly rotten, and barely rises from her sick bed. I coughed and read the papers.

Sunday 5 January–Thursday 9 January 1997

A dismal tale. I didn't once go out. Felt sick and weak, coughing and spluttering, with days slipping by in a sleepy haze of Disprin and no improvement. Mainly read. Sebastian Faulks's *Fatal Englishman* was a good read, but ultimately unsatisfactory – mainly because it was three long essays on homosexuals who died young. I was particularly interested in the essay on Jeremy Wolfenden, since I knew him quite well at Oxford and worked under him on the student magazine *Isis*. Faulks catches his destructive alcoholism and druggyness. Also his good side – that curiously, for an Etonian intellectual, he wasn't an intellectual snob nor a class snob. He was very friendly to me and I always looked forward to seeing him. Perhaps he wanted sex but that never showed. He seemed quite amused to keep company with a working class heterosexual and once came with me to where I did a bit of boxing training. What is never mentioned is his appalling complexion: it was pasty white, emphasised by his permanently wearing dark sun glasses, and dreadfully unhealthy, I suppose from sitting up all nights with drugs, drink and dissolute boys. I lost track of him later, though heard rumours of his spying pastimes, and wasn't surprised to hear when he died so young.

Also read two pop books. Singer Adam Faith's autobiography was a lively read and starts with a generous tribute to me – I stood by him as a friend when he was under attack for his unfortunate association with a crooked financier. I learned how if you lie down with pigs you catch fleas from my brief spell with Maxwell and know how he suffered from the nasty media. Also read jockey Frankie Dettori's life, much thinner than Adam's, but interesting incidental stuff on racing. He obviously is an instinctive genius and has no idea what makes him a better jockey than the others – apart of course from being given better horses to ride.

Thursday 9 January–Friday 10 January 1997

Went up to London Thursday afternoon. Faced by huge pile of letters, but fortunately Della came in to help and we got through them much more quickly – should have employed her years ago. Evening went to nice dinner with Colin Ingleby-Mackenzie (Sarah's brother-in-law) and her sister Susan. Colin is now President of the MCC. I advised him to get some Labour people in before we hit government. The MCC is notorious for favouring only the Tory side – unlike racing, which under Stoker Hartington and Tristram Ricketts has been very careful to keep on both sides.

Saturday 11 January 1997

Sarah insisted on sending for the doctor. He detected some infection in my right lung and put me back on antibiotics – the second time – and on an asthma spray. This is dragging on drearily. Watched a great rugger victory by Northampton over Leicester. From Franklin Gardens, where, in 1953, I played twice for the Northampton second fifteen. Regret giving it up soon after, though I did have a bad back. I retired from serious sport after my first year at Oxford mainly so I could devote more time to my studies, to my girlfriends and to other cavalier pastimes.

Monday 13 January 1997

Still feeling rotten – and Sarah worse – so stayed in and read half of Kipling's *Kim*. Brilliant evocation of Raj India. Also deeply anti-politically correct so I enjoy that.

Drove up to the Lords in the late afternoon and then home to open my mail. Out late to the BBC studio on Millbank to do a Midnight Hour discussion programme.

Tuesday 14 January 1997

To lunch with David Capel and Steve Coverdale from Northants county cricket club. We discussed their future and how to help them win a lottery award for an indoor centre at the county ground where the old Cobblers football stand was which I attended in my childhood and youth. Going to watch the Cobblers, we kids used to say that if you put down a pound note at the football entrance turn-style, the man selling tickets would say, 'Do you want a forward or a defender?'! And that the Northampton team, then lowly in the Third Division North, would do a lap of honour if they won the toss.

The cricketers were very lively and deserve support. David, who has played a few times for England, lives in my old village of Roade and we discussed mutual acquaintances and great Northants cricketers I saw before he was born, such as opener Dennis Brookes and the great fast left arm bowler E W Clarke. Nice.

Wednesday 15 January 1997

Off early to the DNH team meeting, everybody present. Jack reported to us on the Greenwich Millennium situation. It has virtually collapsed. They have overrun all their estimates, need private sector finance, but big business won't give support unless Labour underwrites it for the future. This means they are treating us as the future government. Jack's personal wish is to kill it; partly because it is a shambles, mainly because it absorbs all the money into London leaving too little for the provinces – where Labour's main support is.

Into the Lords for a meeting of the Arts and Heritage Committee discussing the Victoria County Histories, a project I greatly support. They were nice to me for having helped them during the Heritage Bill. It was clear that Northants is one of the best counties.

Incidentally, the *Evening Standard* has a vicious editorial blaming Jack for the whole Millennium mess! Where else but in the British press would an Opposition, which has barely and only recently been informed of this project, and has no executive control over it, be blamed for the fiasco? Nowhere did it point out that there is a Tory government in power which has two senior ministers on the Commission!

Thursday 16 January 1997

Cleared papers. Then into the front-bench meeting. One bit of progress is on the Police Bill, where we have forced our Commons spokesman Jack Straw to move from supporting the government on allowing unrestrained bugging of homes by police. There was a revolt by our front bench, many of whom said they would refuse to vote for our three-line whip with the government. Blair wants to appear tough on crime to the electorate.

Derry Irvine, an old friend of Blair, joined in the revolt. This seemed surprising, since he is normally sensibly conservative on these matters. (I share many of his instincts on social and legal issues, as also do most ordinary Labour voters. Derry and I, unlike the *Guardian* liberals, both come from working class backgrounds.) But in this case much of the legal establishment was on the liberal side, as was I. Confronted by the threat of a Lords front-bench revolt against a three-line whip, Straw capitulated. Of course had we revolted, each spokesman would have had to resign from the front bench – which is why I imagine not everyone would have delivered on the night. Still it was an interesting confrontation. There is a lot of talk among the Hampstead/*Guardian* set that Straw isn't up to the job. He is wrongly disliked by the radical chic gang because he is firm on the need to be tough on crime. They enjoy indulging in liberal principles and attacking the police, relying on the fact that criminals don't often come into their gated and privileged home territory.

In the evening to a fairly formal but excellent dinner with the Graydons. He is head of the Royal Air Force and she a painter. I sat opposite George Simpson, the new head of GEC, replacing Arnold Weinstock. Not as clever as Arnold – though few are – and we wait to see how he runs GEC.

Friday 17 January 1997

News headlines about Heseltine visiting Blair – the deputy prime minister visiting the leader of the Opposition!!! – to beg Labour to bail out the Greenwich Millennium fiasco. Tony was rightly tough and the talks continued today. In the end we gave way and agreed to underwrite it on condition that costs didn't rise further and that we could review it when in office (though it will be too late then, with all the contracts signed). So we didn't get the satisfaction of torpedoing and exposing their fiasco. But it is quite a good political victory. Nobody can fail to see that we were acting as the government and they cannot move without us. That applies in the Commons too since another Tory MP has died and they are now in a minority.

Sunday 19 January 1997

Did a 170-mile tour of training stables to choose a trainer for our horse in the new jumping syndicate. A nice group of old friends – David Lipsey from

The Economist; David Metcalf, professor at the LSE; Will Wyatt, head of BBC TV, and a couple of others. Saw Peers Folly who looks more handsome than ever and no injury problems so far. Fingers crossed he will run in four to five weeks, but must not mention it in his hearing or he will start limping again.

Monday 20 January 1997

Take my letters into the Lords where we had a three-line whip on the Police Bill against Howard's dubious suggestion that the police have the power to bug any citizen's house without permission from above. Our Lords rebellion against Jack Straw's acquiescence in this had forced him and Blair to change tack and allow us to oppose this. With broad support from Tory backbenchers, cross-benchers and most Law Lords we won by about 50. Usually I am for being tough on law and order, but this was a tough too far and our people feel pleased that at last they can vote on principle instead of just shadowing the Tories electorally.

Late in the evening saw Peter Savill of the Racehorse Owners Association to discuss reforms to racing. They were interested in my radical idea that racing should forget the Levy Board subsidy, get independence from the bookies, race when the courses want, and raise the money from the media. They are seen as troublemakers, but racing needs a shake – and the owners are badly treated.

Tuesday 21 January 1997

In the evening went to the Queen Elizabeth Hall for a concert in memory of pianist John Ogden, who Sarah knew. Except for the Festival Hall the whole of that concrete chunk of the South Bank should be knocked down and a marvellous light modern arts centre built, all covered in so people feel safe, dry and happy. I am irretrievably depressed by the time I get inside.

Wednesday 22 January 1997

Interesting lunch at St James's Palace for the Prince of Wales's Youth Business Trust. Angus Ogilvy had asked me to suggest suitable Labour people: there was Clive Hollick, Brenda Dean, Melvyn Bragg, Donald Dewar and Peter Kilfoyle. The conversation was constructive and businesslike. Donald was particularly sharp and Peter Kilfoyle very knowledgeable. Angus was pleased and will invite them on to the Trust; until I intervened it had no Labour people at all! Clearly the Prince of Wales isn't an easy boss. He doesn't want this scheme – which has an excellent record of getting young people started in business – to take the limelight away from his wider Prince's Trust. But it will because it is more successful. We decided to get in Thatcherite Tim Bell to do some PR. Melvyn took me back in his big chauffeured car (virtually all my old friends now have them – sign of my relative failure).

In the evening had supper with Henry and Jeannie Carnarvon celebrating Henry's 73rd birthday. You would never guess. He is as alert and wicked as ever. Told me that in the war Evelyn Waugh, who twice painfully married one of Henry's relatives, served under him in Egypt. Thought him a difficult and nasty man and that all the Waughs were a bit mad.

Thursday 23 January 1997

Spent the morning starting Martin Gilbert's massive book on World War I. Fascinating. His book output must equal the whole of the rest of the academic profession.

Our front-bench meeting as usual contained little of interest. We had some votes on health in the afternoon and I cleared my correspondence. Then to housewarming party at Michael Bedford's new Mayfair house.

Our poll lead is inevitably narrowing, and there are a lot of don't knows, but nobody has ever closed a gap of this width and length of time before. If we don't win this time we never will – and I will give up and spend my time reading, travelling and going racing.

Interestingly, Tessa Blackstone said I should be willing to do Education. That would be serious and satisfying – but exhausting and Sarah doesn't want me to do it because education is the kind of subject that divides people and leads to arguments. She prefers DNH where we can go to opera and the theatre. I would love DNH. But would ultimately find Education more satisfying. I owe so much to the state education system and all those marvellous teachers. It would be nice to try to give something back. But it is a bed of nails where most good intentions turn sour.

Friday 24 January 1997

In the country. Did little except read Richardson's fine biography of Picasso and take a short walk.

Sunday 26 January 1997

Nice mass. Drinks at the Bell with Jeremy Taylor and his son then home to finish fine Picasso book. Jeremy's son is becoming a journalist. But having first doubts. Told us that girl he knows works for the *News of the World*. He recently asked her what she precisely did there. She said 'entrapment'. He asked what that means. She gave him an example. Recently she arranged to meet a famous Merseyside footballer, got him drunk, then got him into bed with a tape recorder. The paper did a big spread exposing 'the Adulterer'. What a distinguished profession they are! Not even the police are allowed to entrap criminals.

Monday 27 January 1997

Read more of Martin Gilbert's World War I book. Interesting how even then the Germans had plans to integrate Belgium and control France had they won. Their drive to restore the Holy German Empire goes back a long way.

Tuesday 28 January 1997

Della came in the morning and it took three hours for the two of us to clear the correspondence. Thank God I've her.

A quiet afternoon with several votes, then home to take friends out to dinner. Tessa Blackstone sat next to Demetri Marchessini, Sarah's rich and very difficult Greek friend who strongly fancies her. She handled him superbly – and with luck will get a few thousands for Birkbeck. Graham Greene was sitting next to Camilla Panufnik, widow of the Polish composer, who would make a perfect wife for Graham. Quite expensive. Most people who invite me for a meal get it paid on expenses by their employers. I do it taxed out of my own pocket; but when it is nice like this I don't mind.

Wednesday 29 January 1997

Went to the DNH team meeting. I stressed how we must revive the BBC as a Public Broadcasting Service. That means getting somebody at the top who believes in PBS. Some say it means John Birt may have to go, though he believes in PBS and has done many necessary, unpopular things to control the dense BBC management. Must revive morale. Also discussed the Arts Council; Jack has definitely come down on my side against Mark Fisher in terms of cutting back the bureaucracy and pushing more money locally. Mark once said to me that 'Jack is just a philistine, supporting Newcastle United and all that sort of thing.' Terrible misjudgement. Makes me a philistine too. Also makes him a misfit in a team all keen on popular sports, as

Labour people should be. He looks unhappy and said to me that he feared Jack would drop him from the team.

Later David Miliband phoned me to say he liked my revised paper on reorganising No. 10 and that 'Tony will be taking decisions on all that this weekend.' He had double-checked on the geography of No. 10 so he would know where to go to grab my old rooms. He is very nice. In fact, except for its inevitable inexperience, I think the Blair team who I know are all pretty good. It is always a temptation and a mistake for us veterans to criticise the new young politicians as not as good as we were. They are also clearly not doing a bad job, since the latest *Times* MORI poll shows us up to a 25% lead. It won't be that on polling day but we should win comfortably. I try not to say that too often since I want to avoid complacency and I remember the disappointments of 1970 and 1992.

Evening to Strauss Rosenkavalier at ENO. Saw Jonathan Miller, playwright Michael Frayn and Princess Alexandra in the interval.

Thursday 30 January 1997

Lovely morning with Sarah, to the Royal Academy for a terrific exhibition of late Braque.

The front-bench meeting was uneventful as usual.

We lost a couple of Health votes in the afternoon and then I went to Buckingham Palace for the farewell party of Charles Anson, the Queen's Press Secretary, who I knew and liked in No. 10 under Callaghan and also at Kleinwort Benson. Prince Andrew was present looking even fatter than Fergie, and rafts of former press secretaries. I chatted with my old friend, historian Peter Hennessy, who pushed me to do a book on the Policy Unit. Antony Jay told me that Jonathan Linn will return from Hollywood in the summer to make a big film so we agreed to have a reunion of the old *Yes Minister* team. Robert Fellowes, private secretary to HMQ, made a funny speech and Charles a very long one. All very nostalgic for me.

Saw Jim Callaghan this afternoon and he told me that Ken Morgan, his excellent biographer, had sent him the chapter on his prime ministerial style. 'It appears you were more responsible for my style than I was', he said, perhaps at least a quarter joking.

Monday 3 February 1997

Drove up mid-morning to attend big film lunch at the Mansion House. Blair made the main speech – on our culture policy, which was pretty good considering that we haven't agreed one. Mark Fisher is now on his fifth draft, with all others rejected by Jack or by Blair's office.

I arrived there at the same time as Blair and had a brief chat with his aide Anji Hunter, who seemed friendlier than previously. I told her to tell him not to panic when the polls narrow as they inevitably will. Talked to Greg Dyke, who clearly fancies replacing Michael Grade at Channel 4. That would be OK. Grade was clearly demob-happy.

Afterwards I walked with Melvyn Bragg to Waterloo Bridge, where he branched off to the South Bank and I continued walking to Westminster. I asked him for his order of priorities for jobs under us if we win. He said BBC first and Arts Council second. He is very worried that the Tories will slip another Tory hack into Channel 4 so they will then control everything cultural – C4, Covent Garden, the Arts Council, the BBC – before we take over.

Tuesday 4 February 1997

Busy morning with Della clearing correspondence. Then the first meeting of Gamcare. We took a Lords committee room and got the charity set up and officers elected.

Joined at lunch in the dining room by David Owen. He told me he had never lunched there before and clearly still didn't know much about how the Lords operates. We had an interesting talk and I found him as clear and on the ball as ever. He is certain Labour will win the election – by about 60 – because he thinks the nation has decided it wants a change and won't alter that firm conviction – as Jim Callaghan said to me about the tide for Thatcher when driving around Parliament Square in 1979. He says he wants Labour to win, but will stay crossbench. He also says he likes Major and I sense he feels some obligation there. But he would move to Labour 'if Blair is in trouble'.

We chatted about the old Social Democratic Party. He said he could never have supported their move to merge with the Liberals 'both because it wasn't right and because I would have lost my seat in Plymouth, as there are no Liberals there'. He said that his former Labour colleagues Roy Jenkins, Bill Rodgers and Shirley Williams still don't talk to him because he rightly didn't join them going to the Lib Dems and they ostentatiously walked out of the Chamber when he was introduced as a peer: 'Didn't bother me, but pretty petty, I think.' I agree with that.

Reflecting on the previous Labour government he said that Callaghan's greatest mistake was not to have a state of emergency (Jim said the same thing to me at lunch recently). Owen argued for it in Cabinet, but Bill Rodgers took the opposite view and swung Jim. David would have sent in the troops to bury the dead and get the services going and if necessary have called an election on that. He said he was surprised that Jim kept me in running the Policy Unit because he was usually 'a bit anti-intellectual. That was to his credit.'

If he were Major, he would call an early election: because the worst option is to hang on and then be forced out. It was good to see him again. We always used to discuss tactics in government and kept in touch even when he separated from Labour to go to the SDP. I still respect him.

There were several votes on the Firearms Bill, where we were desperately trying – and twice failing – to help the government defeat its own backwoods rebels. So I couldn't get to the LSE for the Standing Committee.

Instead I went to the Racing and Bloodstock to hear the Channel 4 racing team. We then went for drinks to the peers guest room where I shocked them a bit by floating my idea of racing planning to do away with the Levy and becoming commercially independent.

Went out for dinner with Celia and Tom Read. Celia and I also discussed our old friend Tessa Jowell. Neither of us hears from her any more. But that is politics and I understand. The ambitious have to move on to more important people and leave yesterday's men behind in the constant scramble to climb the greasy pole.

Wednesday 5 February 1997

DNH meeting at nine with very little business. Jack seemed in good form. I walked with Mark Fisher and he took me to the Commons tea room for coffee. He is clearly depressed by his bad relations with Jack and his failure to get his arts policy drafts accepted. I tried to cheer him up. He now is convinced he won't be made Arts minister. But if Jack is moved to a different department, a new secretary of state might well keep him, as I would. I warned him to stay away from the Hampstead media and all those journalists who want to attack Jack by praising him. He clearly feels isolated and despondent. I sense his private life may, as often before, be in a bumpy phase. I feel sorry for him because he is a sweet man, but he lacks political judgement. I had to explain to him why we would need to replace the Tories' henchman in the key arts and media jobs with people more sympathetic to a new Labour government. He said 'You and Jack are more hard-nosed than me.' I replied that if we don't have sympathetic people down the line, then we would never get anything done. He still is unhappy with my policies to slim down the bloated Arts Council bureaucracy but accepts it will happen. 'Jack has clearly listened to you on that.' He had noted that on Monday Blair had referred to the Arts Council having 'a more strategic role' while more decisions would be 'pushed down to the regions'. That is code for eliminating the politically correct worms in the Arts Council woodwork. I hope we succeed.

Big vote on the funding of political parties. We lost. But the case was made when I arrived at the House and couldn't find a parking space because it was full of the Rolls-Royces of Tories who had bought their peerages by large con-tributions to Tory party funds.

We gave a dinner party in the Barry Room, sitting Raine Spencer (now Countess de Chambrun or something) next to my friend the pop singer Adam Faith. They got on like a house on fire. He is terrific fun and gently stroked her back throughout. She, in return, virtually sat on his lap. She makes a great effort with everyone, and beneath the glitter is a seriously effective operator.

Sarah sat between William Astor and Ian Stoutzker, who I've long known from the musical world. Annabel Jones Astor was on Adam's right. Everyone was in great form and seemed sorry we had to break up a little early so the Lords staff could get home. The one thing missing at Lords dining is some-where decent to sit before or after dinner so people can get to know those they are not sitting next to at dinner.

Thursday 6 February 1997

Worked at home in the morning and then to our front-bench meeting. On the way in I met Mo Mowlam and we discussed Northern Ireland, where she is spokesman. I said we ought to be persuading the Ulster Prods to pull the rug from under Major. She asked me to try to do something about it – which I will.

Front bench was as routine as usual. But there was one significant point. We discussed what we peers should do in the election campaign. Ivor Richard then told us, 'I've formally written a letter on this to Jonathan Powell to ask for Tony's views.' To Jonathan! He should write direct to Tony Blair. He has been a minister which Blair hasn't. Jonathan will be puzzled by that.

Had tea with Michael Conway, my old Catholic priest friend from Glasgow, who I liaised with when in No. 10 and he in Northern Ireland, keeping me in touch with Republican feeling on the ground. He is now aide to the wild Cardinal Archbishop Winning of Scotland, who recently denounced Blair as a hypocrite, leading me and others to write him severe letters. Michael said he won't do that again 'or he will end up in the Clyde'.

Also telephoned David Montgomery to have a long discussion of Northern Ireland. I want him to help push the Prods into pulling the rug from under

Major. He said he would do a *Mirror* editorial along the lines I suggested: that the Prods shouldn't go down with the Tory ship leaving Labour resenting them as having propped up Major; if they pulled the rug in cahoots with Labour, they could extract some concessions and carry forward goodwill.

He said he will talk to the Ulster Unionist leader Trimble and also to Blair when he sees him next week. He said the Unionists are very divided and unhappy with Trimble's leadership. Trimble knows that and needs some big action to show that he is a big leader. I said that throwing out Major would be a pretty big act. So we will see what happens there.

Drove to the country. Quite an interesting week.

Friday 7 February 1997

Lovely day at Towcester. The one sad side was dear Kisty Hesketh, whose son Bobby – probably closest to her, certainly in character and interests – was killed this week in Los Angeles by a drunk driver. Alexander is out there trying to sort things out, as wife and children are in hospital. Kisty came into the small directors' lunch tent, pale and hunched, and came into my arms and wept. She is a most lovely lady who has had a hard life despite coming from the privileged Tennant family – her drunken awful husband died young leaving her with three sons under five and little money. She didn't deserve this.

Saturday 8 February 1997

On Thursday, at tea I introduced Father Michael Conway to Frank Longford, who is always interested in and supportive of my Catholic activities. Frank was delighted Michael worked with Cardinal Winning and told the story of how the Duke of Norfolk brought in Winning to meet Frank. 'I went on my knees to the Cardinal to kiss his hand. "Stand up, you bloody convert", said Norfolk. I don't know if he was trying to lick the Cardinal's backside more than I was.' Frank is always terrific company.

Sunday 9 February 1997

Nice country lunch party today at home. I sat between Rosie Muir and Elizabeth Godsal. Rosie was full of the behaviour of Vivien Duffield at the Highclere shoot, allegedly upsetting the staff, swearing crudely and constantly criticising the shoot. Vivien said that at least they were going to a better shoot next time at Blenheim – and Rosie said 'that is a really lousy shoot' (she is

Marlborough's sister and grew up at Blenheim). Rosie also told me she had flu over Xmas and had to visit the doctor. When she phoned asking for doctor X they said sadly he was dead. So she asked for his successor. They said he was dead too. She hadn't been to the doctors for 20 years. She said some of her staff go every week. The new lady doctor offered her some 'new' antibiotics. She said she was quite happy with the old ones in so far as she could remember them. Tough breed those English county ladies. Henry Carnarvon says she is someone that he would go into the jungle with – and there are not many of those.

Monday 10 February 1997

Drove up to the Lords and attended a reception for victims of domestic violence organised by Jane Rayne and Cherie Blair. The latter spoke very well and I talked to her for the first time afterwards. She had read my No. 10 memo to Tony and was complimentary.

Talked to lawyer Hilary Browne-Wilkinson about the press increasingly using entrapment and telephone bugging to get stories, especially about celebrities and even, so I hear, the royals. She is on the Press Complaints Commission. I want to put this to it to get something in their code controlling it. The irony is that under the new Police Bill we have voted to stop the police using entrapment to catch criminals, because it is unacceptable – except for journalists!

Tuesday 11 February 1997

Della came in and we slogged away at the papers, though still didn't finish it and I was late for lunch with Sue Robertson from the London Arts Board. Discussed giving more support to Irish arts in London. This is my revenge on the Politically Correct Claptrappers at the Arts Council who discuss multicultural minority arts only in terms of black and Asian. In fact the Irish are our biggest minority and the Australians are a strong arts element – though each is white and so the claptrappers cannot bear to give them any support. We agree an exciting programme of theatre festivals, arts exhibitions and music.

Wednesday 12 February 1997

Went to the doctor for diabetic blood tests, which may explain why my infections persist. Thought a lot about Europe. Have adjusted my own position: still pro, a cultural European, but was always for a Common Market and never for a political union, towards which they are driving. I helped run the referendum in 1975 and I think we should go for a two-tiered Europe, with us in the second commercial tier with the Scandinavians and the east Europeans, leaving the inner core to the Rhineland countries, most of whom have been under German or French control most of their history anyway. Then we could be positive about Europe and not always whinge about it.

In the evening went to a lovely dinner at the Garrick given by Graham Greene. Many very old friends – most quit Labour for the SDP in 1982 – Claus Moser, Dick Taverne, John Mortimer, Hugo Young, Nico Browne-Wilkinson, Bill Rodgers. I am pleased I stayed with my Labour roots.

I sat between Penny Mortimer and Susan Crosland, widow of Tony. Discussed hunting with Penny and how to delay Labour banning it – I'm not optimistic. She was also taking a high liberal line on law and order and I pointed out that the folk in Poplar and Northampton disagreed and supported Jack Straw and Michael Howard in wanting something done about crime, which mainly affected them and not the posher communities. Susan and I agreed we were the only ones of those present who had stuck with Labour throughout and felt a bit isolated. We discussed what Tony Crosland would have made of New Labour. She said he would have been sympathetic towards dropping some of the old left baggage, but the big difference was on equality, which to him was central but has been marginalised by the New boys.

I also chatted with Allen Jones the pop art painter who I like very much. Went out with Ed Victor who told a horrifying story about Concorde nearly crashing with various pop stars, Elton John etc. on board. It will have a disaster one day.

Thursday 13 February 1997

Spent the morning at home clearing papers. Tea with Dennis Marks from the ENO and Tom Chandos, who is a director there. Discussed the site for their proposed new opera house. Agreed Paddington Basin was out and that Kings Cross was too crime risky, too far ahead of the proposed regeneration. Only two realistic sites, both on the South Bank: opposite Tower Bridge, where they have a site and money, or added on to the Festival site. I oppose the former – dreary, dead and bad transport. I've always supported an extension to the Festival site for a multi-purpose lyric arts centre. I agree to give them all possible support.

Then went to see Mo Mowlam about Ireland. David Montgomery had phoned me earlier with a response from the Ulster Unionists. Trimble said he was prepared to join Labour in bringing Major's government down providing

Blair would support his package: devolved power-sharing local government in the North and an amendment to the Anglo-Irish agreement to reduce the role of Dublin. I told Mo and we discussed it. She was interested because it was the most precise terms she had seen from the Ulster Prods.

Also she was very interested in defeating the Tories in Monday's debate of censure over Douglas Hogg and his mishandling of the BSE crisis – though apparently there isn't much chance of us winning and Trimble probably couldn't deliver all of his troops to us anyway. They are split. He will try because he needs a big gesture to shore up his crumbling leadership. John Taylor also supports him but I do not know who else. Mo said she would talk to Tony Blair and I said I would send him a memo.

I am not only concerned with Monday's vote, but mainly with the possible collapse of order in Ulster and I want Tony to get to grips with it before he gets into No. 10. I also know that the Unionists don't trust Mo (unfairly) and want to deal direct with Blair, so Montgomery and I provide that indirect opportunity. I really shouldn't get involved in Ireland after both my and Sarah's previous experiences with the IRA – me getting death threats from them and Sarah being injured and her husband murdered in the Brighton bomb. But if I can get Tony to build bridges with the Unionist majority, at least he will be in a better position to limit the disorder at marching time and to start moves towards a future Northern Irish peace settlement. Funny that it is a Catholic doing this.

We had a three-line whip in the Lords on the Police Bill and defeated the government on mandatory sentencing, but I couldn't get back from Mo in time to vote. They only give us six minutes and it's impossible to get down the stairs, through the security doors of No. 1 Parliament Street, across the long red lights of Parliament Square, through Westminster Hall and up the stairs to the Lords Chamber in time for that. I told our chief whip who promised to ask for eight minutes.

Drove to Berkshire and early to bed.

Friday 14 February 1997

Feeling worse and slept all morning. But the doctor phoned and said the blood tests showed nothing horrible, just a worsening of my blood glucose, and probably the diabetes makes it difficult to recover from the flu virus. He hopes giving up the drink for Lent will help. The day just drifted away. I did fax my memo on Ireland to Blair. Jonathan Powell was very helpful and appreciative.

Saturday 15 February 1997

Mo Mowlam phoned to say she had talked with Blair who is very interested and 'engaged' with the Irish issues I raised in my memo, but probably won't do anything for the confidence vote since it is too much too quickly – which is what I said in my memo. She will see Blair again and then talk to me after Monday's vote.

Sunday 16 February 1997

Read the newspapers, which always takes hours and I learned nothing from them. Montgomery phoned and I reported that Blair will probably do nothing for Monday's vote, but is now engaged on the longer term problem. We agreed we would keep working at this, hoping to avoid chaos in the summer. (David had arranged an editorial in Friday's *Mirror* saying that the Unionists should support Labour in Monday's vote. He also arranged a remarkable piece in a Belfast Prod journal saying the government should apologise over Bloody Sunday.) So will talk to him in the week. He said that Trimble appreciated having a route in to Blair and didn't want to use Mo.

Brenda Dean phoned from windy Cornwall about 'press entrapment' – she is on the Press Complaints Commission and will help. Told me horror stories about the BBC Panorama deceiving people in interviews to get the 'killer quotes' they seek rather than the truth.

Monday 17 February 1997

Went up to London at lunchtime to do my PQ – on lottery funding for churches and cathedrals. I used it to give support for a lyric arts centre, which is my code for the new ENO.

Sarah's daughter Sasha came in for tea. We went by taxi to Covent Garden to see *Lohengrin*. Mary Allen from the Arts Council arrived and took us to the ACE [Arts Council for England] box. Wonderful singing and conducting, well acted and a visually delightful production with no modern gimmicks.

In the intervals I had some serious chats with Mary, who I like very much, despite her occasional Stalinist tendencies. I suggested the Arts Council could operate without so much bureaucracy and political correctness. She liked Blair's arts speech the other Monday and grabbed his statement that they should be more strategic as if offering them an ever bigger role; in fact he meant more general and less bureaucratic interference with the regional boards. That battle lies ahead for us – so I arranged tea with her at the Lords so we can explore further.

Tuesday 18 February 1997

Della came and helped clear the correspondence while I wrote a piece for Richard Evans, *Times* racing correspondent, on my position on racing. Early to the Lords for a PQ on Sotheby's and art smuggling. I had agreed my question in advance with the minister, Richard Inglewood, pressing them to get the Treasure Trove Act operating and promising Labour support when the code of practice is tabled in Parliament. No point in playing party games.

Then coffee with Richard Evans, who will do a piece on me. We agree on the future of racing: that in the long term it must get away from the welfare dependency of the Levy and become a fully competitive leisure industry. But I muffle my views and mainly ask for an independent enquiry into that question. I don't want the headline 'Donoughue will abolish the Levy', since at the weekend there was total chaos over the floating of the intention for us to privatise the Tote by Gordon Brown's nasty, inept adviser Charlie Whelan. This made front page headlines in yesterday's *Times* and had to be killed by a public torpedo into Brown's midriff by Robin Cook. Apparently, later, Whelan told *The Times* that instead he would investigate the idea of having a levy on betting to help racing – not knowing we have had one for 34 years!

We had a three-line whip and several votes on the Police Bill, but nothing exciting.

Wednesday 19 February 1997

A brief DNH meeting, with nothing except fun at Gordon Brown's expense over Whelan's Tote fiasco, then back home for more papers and phoning. Lovely letter from Dubai inviting me there for the World Cup racing at end of March. Spirits lift dramatically.

Dinner with Camilla Panufnik. Beautiful old riverside house, full of mementos of her composer husband. With Max and Jane Rayne and playwright Ronnie Harwood and his wife. Ronnie, who used to write the jokes for Thatcher's speeches, was in very amusing form.

Thursday 20 February 1997

Home in the morning, dealing with papers and phone calls – including David Montgomery and Jonathan Powell both on Northern Ireland – and the time slipped away. In the end failed to get to a Channel 5 lunch and late for the front-bench meeting. There we planned an ambush on the Education Bill for late next Monday night. Afterwards I saw Jim Callaghan who asked me to come to tea with him and Audrey.

Supper with Claus and Mary Moser. Mary was very brave giving the party, having bad shingles but in great form. The others were very legal. Lord Lloyd, a distinguished Law Lord who savagely denounced Michael Howard as the worst home secretary ever. A South African barrister shared that view as did their delightful wives. Howard may be that – though his redeeming feature is that he upsets the legal establishment.

After midnight drove down to the country in order to wake up there in the morning, which I always love.

Sunday 23 February 1997

I struggled to mass where Father Flanagan made an attack on his Bishop Crispin Hollis. 'The Bishop is a Christian enthusiast and I've never got on with that sort of thing.' He apologised that his sermons were 'boring' and said 'The bishop's sermons are not boring but uplifting and designed to get you into heaven; mine are designed to keep you out of jail.' He is a great man.

David Montgomery phoned to say that the Ulster Unionists were moving quickly on plans for a Northern Ireland settlement. Trimble, Taylor and Molyneaux had met and formed a plan for fast track elections after our coming general election and a power sharing executive. Hoped this progress would head off the summer marches. He said if Blair agreed in principle then they would all vote for us in a confidence motion. David would send me a fax from Trimble setting out their position tomorrow morning. I suggested we might use Senator Mitchell to persuade the Irish and USA to go along with it since at least it offered real power sharing, with all parties taking their share of the committee chairmanships. I will send it on to Blair.

Monday 24 February 1997

David Montgomery phoned mid-morning and then sent the fax – a single page summarising their proposals. There were two versions, the later, following my comments, being softer on nationalist participation in the election, not requiring prior commitment to the Mitchell principles of rejection of violent methods.

I went into the Lords in the afternoon for a three-line whip, with a couple of votes which we lost – to lull the Tories into not suspecting our planned ambush late that night. In fact, as always, the Tories knew well in advance of our secret plot and had actually stated on their whip last Thursday that we planned an ambush tonight, summoning their troops to repel it.

I went over to Blair's Commons office and handed the Trimble fax over to Jonathan Powell. Very odd to go down that corridor behind the Speaker's chair after all these years. It is different, no longer having the entrance to the Prime Minister's room, the entrance is now only from the floor below. Blair's office is where I first went to visit Harold Wilson in early February 1974, with Bob Worcester of MORI, taking our opinion polls to him. As we entered then, Ted Heath dissolved for the general election and Wilson sent me off to lunch with Albert Murray and we met later to plan the election campaign. That was the start of so much exciting life for me.

Jonathan has a room down the stairs below Blair. We discussed the fax. He said, 'We cannot do all this. It conflicts with what we support on the Anglo-Irish agreement and the peace talks.' I agreed but pointed out again the benefit of starting the process with Trimble and trying to head off trouble in Ulster in the summer. He asked if they would really support us on the confidence motion. I said that my information was possibly – but pointed out that my prime concern had always been getting the loyalists on board longer term for when we're in government and trying to move towards a new Northern Ireland settlement. He said that Blair is now fully engaged and keen on achieving something – but was aware that the loyalists could be treacherous and currently were also trading with Major.

I returned to the Commons and arranged with Patricia Hollis to pick her up later for supper. Then we could go back for the great ambush vote on the Education Bill.

Went home and opened my mass of post and also began to prepare some notes for Montgomery to give to Trimble tomorrow. I collected Patricia and went out for a quick supper and a political gossip. She now feels that Ivor Richard will keep the leadership in government, faux de mieux. I say that I think that Tessa Blackstone is qualified for the leadership. She silently dissented, meaning that Tessa is too rigid and strident. None of the women support one another. I am very fond of Patricia, despite her excessive reaction to anyone being absent from one of her own votes, and greatly respect her hard work and mastery of a difficult social security subject.

We drove back to the Lords and, as we walked through the lobby, there were groups of Tories, Maurice Saatchi, Peter Gummer and Sarah Hogg, waiting for the vote, and James Hanson, usually absent unless it was critical, in the background. So we concluded we couldn't win. If they had left their grand dinners to come in then the Tories must have their whole army out. The division bell finally went at about 10.30 pm and we marched in not too optimistically. We had a pretty full turn out and they were not as crowded as we expected. To our delight we won by 8 on an amendment to do with grant-aid schools. The Tory minister, Oliver Henley, who is very unpopular with our side, looked black, which added to our pleasure. Apparently, although the London glitterati had turned up to vote, like Saatchi and Hanson, the county shooting set had stayed away to punish the government for its unpopular bill banning handguns. So even though they knew of our secret plot and put it on the whip, they failed. So we won, but not because of the virtues of our arguments but due to the abstentions of those we usually disagree with.

Tuesday 25 February 1997

Della came in to help with the post. Tom Kelly arrived from the betting office association to brief me ahead of my lunch speech to them at the National Liberal Club. When he left I had to sit down and rapidly write it on the word processor.

I sat between Tom Kelly and Tristram Ricketts of the Horseracing Board, with Chris Bell of Ladbrokes at the table. My interview with Richard Evans on the bleak future of racing and my idea to set up an enquiry into whether to scrap the Levy Board was headlined over a quarter of a page in today's *Times*, so there was a lot of interest. My son Stephen was also there, advising me and beginning to make an impact as a young guru on the racing and betting world.

My speech went down reasonably well – especially the light bits about Labour's fantasy plans to privatise the Home Office and nationalise the Tote. I also told them about Peers Folly running at Newbury on Friday, about how he always got a crafty limp in the past when due to run, so I had instructed Henrietta Knight not to let him read the racecard entries in the racing press so he wouldn't be alerted. The prospect of him finally running has lifted my spirits and I am really looking forward to seeing him on Friday.

Back at the Lords I phoned David Montgomery and briefed him for his meeting with Blair to discuss our Ulster plans and prepare Blair for his meeting with Trimble on Thursday. We arranged to meet afterwards and he collected me from the central lobby. We avoided the guest bar since it was full of gossips so I took David to the Royal Gallery where we sat in private splendour, beneath the wall hangings of Waterloo and Trafalgar, and discussed what to do next. He said Blair had been very engaged and keen to make progress on Ulster – also keen to win a confidence vote with their help.

I suggested that David gets the Unionists to produce a blueprint of what their power-sharing executive would look like, with names of the SDLP and moderate republicans in place as chairman. He will ask them for that. He said, 'Tony was engaged, intrigued, but nervous. He wants to do something, but is afraid it will blow up in his face: that the Loyalists will betray him and the Republicans will denounce him. He worries how to follow our scheme at the same time as supporting the Anglo-Irish agreement and the peace process.' I said he is now on the Anglo-Irish runway, which many people think is going in the right direction, and is waiting for take-off. For us he needs to move to another runway to a big new peace agreement, and that is difficult.

Blair had agreed to concede a Grand Committee for Ulster, but that isn't enough and they are about to get that from Major anyway. He is also attracted to a fast track to early elections in the North, but is afraid of a violent IRA reaction and bombs on the mainland. David had told him he will get them anyway. Blair had referred to the paper I had sent on Monday; David said he was aware of it, without revealing our partnership in writing it.

We agreed we would draw up a memo showing how the new power-sharing executive would look, with moderate nationalists in place, so they could be attracted away from the IRA. I will pass it to Blair.

Leaving through the central lobby we met George Robertson and Helen Liddell and had a chat. It was a bit tense since David sacked Helen when he took over the *Mirror*. Afterwards I criticised him for that and he said it was because she was 'tainted' with Maxwell. I told him to rebuild bridges with her. He said he hoped he had by supporting her so strongly in her by-election campaign.

Also saw Labour MP Dick Caborn, just back from campaigning in the Wirral by-election. He says there is a remarkable feeling on the streets there, with passionate support for us and the Tory campaign collapsing. He thinks we'll win by around 8000, which would be a tremendous turnaround for a safe Tory stronghold. Yesterday Peter Snape, a very experienced old hand, told me the same and we agreed it was only possible because of what Blair has done to the party. He has made it possible for some normally Tory supporters to make the complete switch to us. He has virtually eliminated the fear factor associated with Labour.

Wednesday 26 February 1997

Early to the DNH meeting, little going on, and after with Mark Fisher for coffee in the Commons tea room. He was very helpful for my speech in today's film debate – on which I've only just focused. He was also critical of Jack for not fighting hard enough with our Treasury team to get more funds for our Arts budget. Perhaps Jack doesn't expect to be there when we spend it.

Went home and worked on this evening's film speech, working in most of Mark's ideas. Also a long phone call with David Montgomery. He reported that Trimble cannot deliver all his votes to Blair on the confidence vote since four of them are out and out Tories. So there can be no deal for next week. But he is still very interested in a long term deal, to reach a new settlement on power sharing with the moderate nationalists which will marginalise Paisley and the IRA. He says he wants to achieve something for Ulster in the long term or would rather get out. We agree that Blair must get briefing from the security services on the likely violent reaction to any initiative towards a settlement. He must be made aware that the Northern Ireland civil service is hopeless.

Then back for a late lunch in the Lords canteen. Sat opposite the Duke of Norfolk, our senior lay Catholic. Discussed the Bishops in the Lords. I said there should be two Anglicans, two Catholics and the chief Rabbi. He said 'and the Muslims'. He criticised Cardinal Hume for not accepting a peerage, saying he was a Benedictine, too saintly, but also shrewd since it meant he didn't have to speak there on tricky subjects like embryos. Has a point there. Of course the Anglican bishops resolve that problem by simply not turning up for tricky subjects – or speaking solely about 'on the one hand, on the other'.

I sat in the chamber to hear Henry Carnarvon open his debate on London government with a very good speech, balanced and even-handed. Henry is deeply knowledgeable on local government and commands the House. I slipped away and took Jeannie Carnarvon and Jane Fellowes to tea. They had come to support Henry but were glad to escape from the debate. William Huntingdon also joined us. They were all very sharp about Andrew Lloyd Webber who was introduced as a peer today. Somehow he isn't popular with anyone who knows him in Hampshire. Last week he threatened to leave Britain if Labour was elected and raised his taxes. Jeannie said that clinched it for a Labour victory. There is an early day motion in the Commons welcoming his promise to depart.

Our film debate started at 7.45 pm and Sarah and Kate were due in for supper at 8.30 pm so I was in the chamber when they arrived, but they went straight to the Barry Room to wait. Our debate was worthy, but fairly boring, with only five speakers. I was glad to get away and had a nice dinner with the girls.

Thursday 27 February 1997

I woke in good form, buoyed by prospect of Peers Folly running tomorrow, even though the ground is a bit soft for him. After all these years feeding him this means a lot to me.

I phoned David Montgomery to discuss Blair's meeting with Trimble today. He said that now the vote of confidence wasn't on, he'd told Trimble to stress the long-term vision. Trimble wanted to trust Blair. I set out some points he might put to Blair when he talks to him this morning (realised afterwards I should have sent them to Blair myself):

(1) TB wants to build long-term trust with Trimble.
(2) Interested in long term more than any confidence vote.
(3) Explain Blair's general position on Ulster, stressing has moved Labour away from republicanism:
  • consent must be basis for a new constitutional settlement, and consent of Protestant majority critical;
  • wants peace and to revive local government with power-sharing.
(4) On specifics:
  • grateful for paper setting out Ulster Unionist position – helpful;
  • now accepts Grand Committee for Northern Ireland;
  • interested in achieving fast-track early elections, providing doesn't destabilise peace process.
(5) Obstacles:
  • must not provoke more violence;
  • must explore UU view on cross border relationship;
  • must not alienate USA and Republic (Senator Mitchell help?).
(6) Taking these talks forward:
  • Has Trimble anything to suggest on summer marches? Could he set out in more detail how his power-sharing executive would look in practice? How are moderate nationalists involved? What does cross-border consultation really mean – is it worth anything? Where would they meet?

The final point could be on the agenda for the next meeting between Blair and Trimble.

I was just preparing to leave for the country when Henrietta Knight phoned. Unbelievable! Peers Folly had woken with an infection. He is already in all the newspapers for tomorrow. He must have read them. Will have to be withdrawn. Yet again. What a saga. I was shattered and nearly broke my Lenten vows by opening a bottle. Henrietta said the consolation was at least we didn't run him and do him harm. On that basis we should never run him to avoid harming him. The little people are clearly against me. The old Donoughue luck. My father would have said you cannot fight them so you might as well give up. I drove to the country angrily and went to my bedroom for the night.

Friday 28 February 1997

Woke still very grumpy. Couldn't bear to read the racing page of *The Times*. Worse, dear Dick Saunders phoned early to wish me luck. I had arranged tickets for us at Newbury but didn't go.

Not even cheered up by the Wirral by-election where Labour had a stunning victory, with a 17% swing and nearly an 8000 majority as Dick Caborn had said. On this basis we would have a Commons majority of around 200 – but that won't happen.

Spoke to Jonathan Powell about the Trimble talks with Blair. He opened dismissively by saying, 'Well, that project has gone down the drain.' He said Trimble was pathetic in saying he had to go on holiday over Easter so couldn't have an early election (not mentioning that he couldn't deliver his troops). I pointed out that what mattered was the medium term and we discussed that. I mentioned Blair getting an official security briefing and he was pleased with that. I realised I should have contacted them before the Trimble meeting reporting the vote wasn't on. Thinking too much of Peers Folly. Jonathan also said that the talk was good but ended with no suggestion of a repeat. So I contacted David and said we must get a paper out of Trimble as the basis for the next meeting.

In the evening Woodrow Wyatt phoned in a quite manic way. Just returned from Marrakech, he had heard that Michael Howard is going to appoint Will Astor to chair the Tote. He went bananas. Read out the letter he has written to Howard saying that Astor is 'lazy and lightweight', that Peter Jones is 'mendacious and self-promoting' and that only his General Rous will do. He said Howard is 'a terrible man', has handled it badly and should have decided before. Howard has told him he is consulting the Opposition (he thought that meant Robin Cook but I said more likely Jack Straw) so Woodrow said he would do the same and so is phoning me and will phone Cook – he wants me to talk to Straw. My problem is that I am a referee for Astor, though I never thought he would get it. But I will try to get Jack Straw on Monday, just to make sure he has been consulted. Really it is quite wrong for the Tories to make an appointment only a few weeks before an election. Woodrow really cares about these things and doesn't want his beloved Tote to go into the wrong hands. Above all he was hilariously funny and indiscreet, reading out to me all the Home Secretary's private letters to him.

Saturday 1 March 1997

Still gloomy about the horse. But then enjoyed watching France beat England at Twickenham in a remarkable rugby game.

Sunday 2 March 1997

Still so depressed about the horse that I didn't go to mass, blaming even my maker who ultimately controls these things and so must carry some responsibility. The papers now all assume a Labour landslide after the stunning by-election result. It does look as if the electorate has decided it wants a change (as it did in 1979). If that continues then the campaign will be irrelevant – as it was in 1979. And all the current scandals and headlines are irrelevant too. But of course something big might change that.

Monday 3 March 1997

Delayed going up to London by a flat tyre – my first since getting the old Toyota 12 years ago I think. So missed the education vote, but since we lost by 60, my absence doesn't matter.

Tuesday 4 March 1997

Into the Lords for tea with Mary Allen from the Arts Council. I was in a bit of a hectoring mood, lecturing her about the intolerable political correctness at the Arts Council, but she put up with it quite well. Then Sarah collected me and we went to the National Film Theatre for a preview of the *English Patient*, the much-hyped new film with a lovely Juliette Binoche lead. It has won many Oscar nominations and the audience cheered afterwards, but I had reservations, not always following the plot and finding Fiennes a bit wooden.

Wednesday 5 March 1997

To the Tote lunch at the Hyde Park Hotel. Everyone was there, with the Prime Minister as guest of honour. I sat at the next table, with the Dukes of Devonshire and Marlborough, Lady Wyatt and Petronella, Andrew Parker Bowles and Lord Hollick. Woodrow made a terrific speech, very funny with some good side swipes at the Home Secretary, who was at his table. (Rumour says Howard has delayed his announcement of the new Tote chairman because of fear Woodrow would attack it today – which he told me he would have done). Major also made a good light speech and seemed very relaxed considering how all is falling down about him. He has just announced a brave reform of pensions, but almost before it hit the headlines the wretched Douglas Hogg is in another food hygiene scandal, suppressing evidence and reports. Hogg also broke his ankle at the weekend and everyone believes it was slipping on a banana skin. Major only keeps him because of misplaced loyalty to his wife Sarah who ran his Policy Unit.

At the reception beforehand it was a great racing buzz and I circulated talking with Stan Clarke, who runs Uttoxeter, the fat self-publicist John McCririck, clearly dressed for light opera, and Peter Jones, who hopes to get the Tote (though Andrew P-B says he isn't up to it). Lord Vestey, the fine boss of Cheltenham, told me his sister-in-law (Henrietta Knight) thinks highly of our Peers Folly, but David Swaythling says that is no consolation if it never runs – and mumbled worryingly about 'the bullet'. I was supposed to leave early to answer a Question, but checked by phone and found Joe Dean wouldn't raise it – a relief since it wouldn't have looked good to walk out in the middle of Major's speech.

Jean Trumpington gave me a lift back in her ministerial car, a symbol of House of Lords graciousness, which impressed MP Patrick Cormack who also hitched a lift. Jean told me she worked in the Bletchley code-breaking squad in the war, which is quite a badge of honour.

Thursday 6 March 1997

All morning with the belly-wobbles and slept the rest of the day. So no Towcester or Lords front bench. Couldn't drive to the country so in London overnight.

Friday 7 March 1997

Still very queasy and rocky but managed to drive up to Shurlock Row. Slept most of the time. This has been a rotten year. I've felt ill for more than half of it. Will have some more tests before going to Dubai. The diabetes doesn't help.

Saturday 8 March 1997

Still very wobbly but drove early to Sandown. Went up to the royal box and Andrew Parker Bowles and his wife Rose made me welcome. The usual racing set there, I recognise all their faces but not always their names.

When the Queen Mother arrived, Andrew hiked me up for an early chat. She is very tiny now and I had to bend right over to speak. But she was very bright and alert. At lunch I sat next to her and we discussed our horses which never run. She said, 'It is very hard for families like mine, which don't have any money of our own.' I wasn't sure about that. Like me, she much prefers chasing; said she doesn't like hurdling because it 'isn't natural' for the horses; they should either run on the flat or jump properly.

Sandown is her favourite course because of the atmosphere. She remembered the names of her horses and jockeys from over the years, which is remarkable for someone of 96. I cannot remember my selections for Cheltenham next week. Her face is quite large for such a small body and is lightly lined like cobweb tracery on a piece of Portland stone. Her eyes are fiercely bright. It added interest to an anyway good day.

Sunday 9 March 1997

Sarah's birthday and had failed to get her a present, so I felt grumpy, not her. Nice family party, with her brother Charles and sister Susan. Nothing in the papers. The *Sunday Times* is now a wadge of fudge. Just vacuous text commissioned to fill the space beside the adverts. Sad decline since Harry Evans edited it so brilliantly.

Monday 10 March 1997

Feeling still low. No energy. Got up in the afternoon for an evening vote, but hoping Cheltenham makes me feel better. I've been so looking forward to it and have done quite a lot of research into form – this usually helps me to identify the favourites rather than the winners!

Yesterday I chatted to my French sister-in-law, Agnes, who has been feeling low ever since my brother Clem died. I've been missing him deeply. Sarah found a letter from him with lovely photo of him and son Thomas and tears streamed from my eyes. Funny how I took him for granted and made the usual niggly criticisms, but always assumed, as the younger one, that he would be there. Now it is very painful. He was my only remaining close link to my childhood.

Tuesday 11 March 1997

Feeling much better and reached Cheltenham a bit after ten. It was so exciting to see the course opening up on a beautiful morning. I phoned Sarah and settled in the car for a while finishing my analysis of the racing form. Then wandered around, visiting the shops and meeting several old friends. I like watching bookmakers handling their books and changing their prices. I might have enjoyed that as a career more than all this political nonsense.

Went to lunch with Ladbrokes who had a nice box overlooking the finishing post. The top Ladbroke team did a jackpot based on Ladbroke's inside information but as usual it went down on the second race. I wandered around and enjoyed mixing with the excited crowds of Irish men and priests who were in great form even though their horses were not.

At supper enjoyed my wine because Father Flanagan has clearly pronounced that Cheltenham is exempt from Lenten pledges against alcohol. This is very prudent of the Church since there were at least 2000 priests at Cheltenham drinking Irish whiskey by the gallon.

Wednesday 12 March 1997

Just remembered Father Flanagan's sermon last Sunday. It was really about tolerance, of which he is a good example. Told us that when he was in Africa, in small village near a great river, he was approached by the girls from the local brothel. He said he wouldn't call them prostitutes and never liked the way the Bible referred to Mary Magdalene as such. He preferred the way the African girls were called 'daughters of joy'. Any way the daughters of joy came to him and said there was a new head chief in the area and he had decided to make an impact by closing the brothel and sending the girls down river. They didn't want to go: they liked the village, liked the school for their children, and coming to Father Flanagan's mass because the sermons were so short. So they asked him to intercede with the Head Chief. He persuaded him to reverse his decision – but on condition that the girls would do penance and that the priest would drive all the seven devils out of each. Father Flanagan arranged to do that. But as he was about to exorcise the prettiest girl, she said she had to ask him something privately first. They went into a corner of the church and she said: 'Father, please would you settle for six?'

Went up for lunch in the grand Hatton Grace suite with Coral's who are sponsoring today's big race. Son Stephen was already there. I had a terrific time with Stephen, dashing everywhere, and visited Ladbroke's for tea and also saw Colin and Susan who were there for the day. Charles told me that they were clearing about £2000 a day on their bookmaking venture. I might try it if we lose the election.

Thursday 13 March 1997

Went through the usual delightful agenda. Sarah loved the shopping malls and thought it was hilarious to see her distinguished brother standing on his wooden bookies box calling 4–1 the field.

Lunch was with the Tote who sponsor the Gold Cup today – so I've lunched with the three top bookmakers, presumably on the basis that they owe me a meal given my contributions to their annual turnover (though I am a small and mean punter). Labour's Robin Cook was at the next table and we had a couple of quick chats. But he is never easy to get close to, always polite and smiling but keeping one at a distance and quickly returning to his form card.

The peak moment was the Gold Cup, put on with great style. I had backed ante post Mr Mulligan at 20–1. He jumped wonderfully and we won. That more than recovered all the recent losses so we felt great and left immediately and I headed for London.

Dinner intriguingly was at the grand Kensington home of Conrad Black, Canadian proprietor of the *Daily Telegraph*. It was an impressive but for me curious occasion. When I arrived, I was greeted by various uniformed staff who asked if I had come for 'the meeting' or just for dinner. Apparently the board of the *Spectator* was also meeting to approve its figures. I don't qualify for that so I was ushered upstairs to champagne in a huge sitting room. I read the *Financial Times* alone for a while.

Then a group of rampant Tories poured into the room: Norman Tebbit (whom I always like and with whom I feel some ex-working class identity), clever Algy Cluff (chairman of the *Spectator*), editor Frank Johnson, ex-editor Dominic Lawson with Rosa his wife, Robert Cranborne the over-grand Tory leader in the Lords, toughie Bruce Anderson the Tory journalist, a Fraser lady, towering Conrad Black with his hooded menacing eyes, and Petronella Wyatt. Norman talked to me about the election and the dire tactics he would use to un-ship Tony Blair. He still hankers after his heady days with Mrs Thatcher and doesn't mention Major.

Around the huge table, with several feet between each chair, I sat next to Petronella and the company secretary. Looking around the group I felt more than a little uncomfortable and politically lonely and couldn't see why I was there among two Tory ex-Cabinet ministers and several very right-wing Tory journalists. I could see some of the latter viewing me with puzzlement, so at least we had that in common. I realised that Petronella must have kindly arranged it, perhaps in the remote hope of converting me.

Chatted with Conrad, who gets more right wing by the day – I first met him in Canada in 1980 when I worked for *The Economist* and was struck by his phenomenal memory. Also by his deeply hooded eyes. His *Sunday Telegraph* is doing very well, with 900,000 circulation, nearly double what it was when I worked there in the early 1960s. Apparently the *Sunday Times*, where the editorial content is now flatulent, is getting very worried and is spending millions a month on promotion to try to retain its circulation lead. Typical of a Murdoch paper to take that advertising response rather than trying to improve its editorial content.

On the way home I considered how most there were not my sort of people, except Frank Johnson, Dominic Lawson and Petronella. I am probably still most comfortable with those of common origins with me – such as Joe Haines, Albert Murray, Gerry Fowler, Jeff Rooker and Jack Cunningham. In the Lords, I am always happy to chat with the old style trade unionists, though they are dying off. I am Old Labour to my roots and toes. But have always been interested in and tolerant of a wide range of different people; to see how those with privilege enjoy – and sometimes abuse – it. Oxford first opened that door to me. Racing has always given me this wider entrée to other classes, sharing a common love of beautiful horses – and the wicked excitement of a small bet. In that sense racing is classless, though it is structured otherwise. The Lords has entrenched this opportunity, with access to the most talented of the upper and the professional classes, together with some amiable buffers and bores. I've some marvellous friends among the Tories there. Grieveson Grant gave me access to middle-class stockbrokers, straight and decent colleagues. And, of course, Sarah introduced me to a much wider social milieu. The glitzy parties I attend in these diaries are mostly from her school friends and I float through them as a complete odd bod. I certainly could never join the Tories politically. My Labour roots are too deep, though that does not stop me from disagreeing with the party on many matters.

I've never sought the narrow comfort zone of the tight tribal communities that are prevalent in our still class-ridden society. Such as the Labour people refusing to mix closely with any Conservatives, seen in Parliament when they avoid common dinner tables and cluster in little gangs who are united by Clause Four nostalgia and the highly visible chips on their shoulders. And as equally seen in the Conservative clubbies, who mix only with other public school (usually lesser public school) types at the golf club lamenting the alleged decline in social standards and the existence of reds under every bed. They are seriously boring as well as deeply prejudiced. I've never been comfortable with either tribe.

I am least comfortable, however, with the high-minded, sanctimonious, morally superior, progressive liberal breed, often found in Hampstead and Islington and the older universities, usually reading the *Guardian*, and infecting the newer Lib Dems and the academic ranks of my Labour party. Some of these include dear friends who stand for decent liberal values which I respect and which make our British society so tolerable. But I find their self righteous tone difficult to bear and that is why I currently dread the proposed deal with the Lib Dems contemplated by Blair. The coalition of the self-righteous, which that would involve, daunts me. It is probably the only thing that could provoke my departure to the cross benches. I trust that our likely large election majority will make that unnecessary.

Tonight's strange gathering made me realise that I do enjoy a wide range of acquaintances and friends. I am not a Ramsay MacDonald who has abandoned my Labour roots in pursuit of duchesses. I enjoy different types and classes of people, providing they are interesting, decent, and even sometimes wicked. Hence, my friendship with Henry Carnarvon, who started at the top, appreciates decent people from all classes – and is impressively intolerant of irresponsible types from the privileged. So I was fascinated tonight to watch those right-wing Tories at work and at play, although some stretched my eclectic and elastic tastes to the limit.

Friday 14 March 1997

Very busy morning. Drove to the Lords to collect post, and came back in time to meet Kate who was coming for a birthday lunch with me. It was nearly 3.00 pm when I kissed her goodbye and set off for Shurlock Row. Really enjoyed this week and worried that going into government might spoil this life of pleasure.

Saturday 15 March 1997

The election is getting closer. Major is fighting hard, but the rest of his gang have clearly given up and are fighting one another for the leadership afterwards. It is all a bit seedy and the sooner it is over the better.

Monday 17 March 1997

Read in the morning and up to London after lunch. Had some votes in the Lords where everything is buzzing about the coming election. Major announced that it will be on 1 May as expected – a six week campaign, which is as long as in 1979 and will get boring. But I understand his position. He is over 20% behind in all the polls and his only hope is to have a long campaign and hope Labour makes a big mistake. In my day you could have relied on

Labour to do that; but under Blair it is tightly disciplined and very profession-ally managed.

Went in the evening to a meeting of Jack Cunningham's industry forum in Soho. My son Stephen presented a paper on the gambling industry, demon-strating its massive financial scale and taxable potential. He did very well. Most of the top gambling people were there, all apparently assuming that we will win the election.

Tuesday 18 March 1997

I went into our Lords bar and chatted with some Labour colleagues. All very excited at the prospect of being in government. Had lunch with the Casino Association, then back to Millbank for our arts policy launch. In the end it wasn't too bad. The press conference was pretty thin with no questions of substance.

Wednesday 19 March 1997

Off early (for me early) to our last team meeting before the election. Just chat, nothing serious to discuss. Afterwards, went to Jack's room to discuss a possible new name for our department. Some advertising people had done a presentation to Jack, recommending Department of National Affairs. I didn't like that, pointing out that it could include everything including adultery and the armed services. They chose it because of the acronym, DNA. Lewis Moonie had said yesterday this reminded him of 'semen on a sheet'. Jack said that was 'a doctor's view'. After a lot of dithering, someone suggested Department for the Creative Economy, and we all liked that. Jack seemed to agree, but generally was very preoccupied. Afterwards Tom Pendry said Jack is troubled about which ministers to choose for the department. We're too many. Tom said I was safe, Mark wasn't but nobody else knew. Tom was unsure of his own position. Actually Tom knows the sports world inside out – as Mark knows the arts – and it would be safer to start with them as safe pairs of hands. But Jack is clearly anguishing over who to drop.

Had lunch with Len Murray, discussing old times at the TUC. He said what a poor lot of TUC leaders existed in the late 1970s Winter of Discontent – Moss Evans was terrible and the NUPE man worse, and David Basnett not up to it. They couldn't deliver their members, most of whom didn't care if they destroyed the Labour government anyway. He thought that In Place of Strife in 1969 would have made a difference but 'it was handled badly'. Didn't mention that his TUC bitterly opposed it.

Just before Question time, which I wasn't proposing to attend, the minister told me we had a last minute PQ on digital TV, so I went in and obliquely attacked the Murdoch monopoly. But it was luck I was there at all. It was my last exchange with Richard Inglewood as minister. He has been very good and straight to deal with. He told me he needed a job if they lose and hoped I would look out for something. I will. He seemed to have no doubt about the likely result.

Thursday 20 March 1997

To the Lords to speak at a special party meeting to prepare for government. A warm atmosphere of high excitement. All week in fact the air has been electric even in the Lords as people anticipate that we might at last be back in government. The Tories look glum and I noticed when I went into the government whips office that they had a blackboard with a sweepstake on the result: almost everyone was betting on a Labour victory, often of over 100.

Major has suffered a tactical setback. He had hoped to launch the election on the good employment figures yesterday. Instead Labour has run on the suppression of the Downey report into cash for questions sleaze and Major is again on the back foot. Ten Tory MPs are still in the frame and some have admitted taking money and not declaring it for tax, which is a criminal offence. I am not happy with us running sleaze, since we should be talking about the policy issues on which the Tories have failed. But so far this has worked. Our central campaign operations are impressive.

Had another Question, about making a museum of Bletchley Park codebreaking. Went very well. I paid a tribute to Jean Trumpington, who was having her final performance at the dispatch box. As usual we had a talk beforehand and agreed what we would say.

Then to the Commons to hear the last Question Time exchange between Blair and Major. Very febrile and noisy. Major has a more powerful voice than Blair and is always on top of his facts. But he is better when he is calm. Blair seemed nervous to me. And I don't like his constant implication that he lives on high moral ground and others are moral backsliders. The trouble with taking the high moral ground is that someone from our side is bound to fall over the cliff one day. But he did look like a winner.

The Commons lobby was full of people from my political past about to become ghosts – Alf Morris, Stan Orme, Paul Channon, John Biffen, David Steele, Peter Shore, all about to retire, some presumably to the Lords. Sad chime of passing time for me too. Odd to recall that I was offered a very safe Commons seat in the North East by the mighty boss of the GMW union back in 1962 and I might have been there for over 30 years. But I don't regret not taking it. I suspect I might not have survived the leftie lunacies in the party in the 1980s. Not going to the SDP, but getting out.

Friday 21 March 1997

To Wantage to see Peers Folly exercise. Henrietta Knight schooled him over hurdles and jumps. He went well – and beautiful as ever.

Then visited William Astor at his house in Betjeman country, where I would love to live. We mainly discussed the Tote where he is very jumpy, having got into the final three and now being opposed by the outgoing chairman and waiting on tenterhooks while the Home Secretary Michael Howard dithers.

The other two on the short list are Peter Jones, said to be a Labour sympathiser, though I question it, and General Rous, who is Woodrow's creation. William is against 'another bloody general'.

Back to Shurlock Row. In the afternoon I dreamed of Peers Folly tomorrow, praying he will start and then finish in one piece.

Saturday 22 March 1997

Woke very early very excited. Strange to see my name as owner next to a racehorse in the *Racing Post* and *The Times* (David Swaythling having kindly let me be the registered sole owner, which may explain our problems with the horse, since mine never win). Read all the press – cash for questions still dominating the election headlines and Major clearly disoriented by it – then off to Newbury. I became quite tense over lunch and went out early to wait for him in the pre-parade ring. He looked very beautiful and bigger than any other of the 19 horses.

Henrietta told jockey Titley to keep him wide with plenty of space and settle him down before bringing him late when he had found out what it is all about. That is exactly what happened. He was last but one for three quarters of the race, but jumping OK and with a nice action. Around the final bend Titley eased him forward a bit and I lost him in my binoculars. Then the announcer said 'Peers Folly has been pulled up at the rear'. My stomach turned cold. I desperately swung my binoculars over the field, but couldn't find him. I lowered my binoculars sadly as they announced the finish – and then saw the flash of yellow as he finished strongly, passing half a dozen horses in the last furlong.

The announcer had got the wrong horse pulling up. I should sue for my aggravated heart condition. Afterwards, Titley said he had run very well and would 'make up into a fine chaser'. Henrietta was delighted, having been so afraid he would break down again in front of us that she had gone off to watch alone. I was ecstatic. Henrietta said he might be a Grand National horse. That would be really something.

What a great day. At last!

Sunday 23 March 1997

Incidentally last week in the *Guardian* or the *Independent* (I read neither), Hugo Young attacked Margaret Jay and me for having voted with the government on last week's Criminal Justice Bill. Said we were 'once of repute' but no longer. Typical high-minded Hampstead crap. Fancy watching politics for 30 years and not understanding that as a frontbencher one votes with the three-line whip. If not, you resign. The idea that we would split and vote against our party and then half the front bench would resign on the eve of an election, giving the Tories great headlines, is ludicrous. Especially since our vote was the result of a deal in which the Tories had abandoned some of their Bill as a concession to us. But must remember that Labour has always had an excess of the sanctimonious tendency and, along with envy, that is one of our least attractive characteristics. The Lib Dems, like Young himself, now compete with us impressively for that sanctimonious territory.

I always imagine that Hampstead is full of nightly judgemental dinner parties devoted entirely to self-righteous disapproval of everyone else except themselves. All others (especially Margaret and me), in their view, fall short of the lofty moral standards, which the sanctimonious, having never had responsibility, are able to maintain because they've never been tested. (Like Young, they also usually have private incomes to bolster life on the high moral ground.)

Monday 24 March–Tuesday 25 March 1997

The day drifted away packing for Dubai. Having more time meant I packed more. Sarah took me to Heathrow and we took off around 8.30 pm. We were met by representatives of the Dubai Racing Club, whisked through customs and driven in a large Mercedes to the Hilton Beach Club hotel. This was terrific, overlooking the beach, and I sat and ate breakfast on the terrace in the blazing sunshine. Then slept till mid-day and then had a nice lunch again looking over the sea. Afterwards I joined a bunch of racing journalists – Colin

MacKenzie from the *Mail*, Julian Muscat from *The Times*, Jonathan Powell from Radio 5 and Geoff Lester from the *Sporting Life* – and we had a good gossip. They are a good lot. Very interested in the Tote and all agreed that Michael Howard made a complete fuck up. Sat on the terrace for hours drinking lime sodas and felt this was an enjoyable life.

Phoned sad Sarah, whose Jack Russell, Lucky, died this morning at the vets. She is very sad. That is both dogs gone now and she is bereft. Her husband Tony took both the dogs for a walk on Brighton promenade before returning to bed shortly before the explosion that killed him and buried Sarah and the dogs in the ruins of the Grand Hotel all night. Now they have gone and only Sarah remains.

Wednesday 26 March 1997

Collected by Mike Dillon to drive to the Al Quoz Godolphin stables on the edge of the desert. We were looked after by Sheikh Mohammed's impressive man Simon Crisford. There are over 100 horses there and they looked superb. I noted a list of the best dozen. The whole place was remarkably clean and relaxed, with very airy boxes and scientific testing of feed. Makes some of our trainers look a bit shabby – though, backed by a few oil wells, they also might do better.

Back to lunch on the terrace with the same bunch of racing journalists. The place is coming alive now as the top racing personalities poured in.

In the evening we went to the Forte hotel for an official reception and supper on the lawns. I chatted with charming Johnny Weatherby and sat at dinner on the lawn beside the beach with Brough Scott and discussed merging the *Racing Post* with the *Sporting Life*, which he, from the *Post*, would like to do.

Thursday 27 March 1997

In the evening we went to a fabulous Arabian Nights evening way out in the desert. Sheikh Mohammed had built a large compound for it, which was blown over in a storm on Tuesday night, but hundreds of men had worked non-stop to rebuild it. I was wearing Arab robes, which had been left on my bed for the purpose. I thought everybody would comply since their host Sheikh Mohammed wanted it and the robes were left on our beds, but most shrewdly feeped out. Nigel Dempster, the snake gossip columnist for the *Mail*, came up and photographed me in the strange desert gear, saying, 'It is very game of you to wear that.' I don't suppose his comment in the paper when he prints it will be as appreciative.

The fort was like a village with dozens of food bars and large tents where we sat on the floor at low tables to eat our supper. In the middle was a large stage on which was a large Arab band making very strange noises and Arab ladies wobbling their tummies and shaking their heads. Strings of camels paraded around giving rides, including to Rod Stewart the rock star, who seemed very friendly to all. Late on Sheikh Mohammed arrived in full procession with dozens of black robed relations and court hangers-on (known collectively by malicious racing insiders as 'The Oil Slick'). Everyone kow-towed and queued for two minutes conversation and to be blessed, like a mediaeval court. The show finished with a glorious fireworks display.

Back at the hotel joined Andrew Lloyd Webber and wife with his new gold Oscar from Hollywood for *Evita*. His wife boasted to Mike Dillon that her husband is now 'a multibillionaire'. A bit vulgar. Dempster was lurking sinisterly close. His gossip-columnist friend Charles Benson said with rare perception that he had recently given an after-dinner speech where he claimed to have won the 'sponger of the decade' award. Commendably honest.

Went to bed at 2.00 am, leaving them all quaffing (at the Sheikh's expense).

Friday 28 March 1997

Blearily in the car early to collect Mike Dillon and off to the course. He is quite astonishing. Has a mind like a computer and can remember where every horse ran when and at what price.

The track was already alive. All the trainers there and the horses came out in pairs from each country and exercised separately because of quarantine reasons. There is no local betting because it is forbidden by Islam. Every few minutes someone, even the locals, mutters in Mike's ear and he writes a little note. One American owner's bet was for £6000.

Breakfast in the stand with Mike and the great Irish jockey Mick Kinane who was studying the form for the races he will ride in. At other tables were Irish, French, Japanese and Americans all very excited. I cannot wait.

Saturday 29 March 1997

This is the great race day. I wake excited – but worried by grey clouds and a dodgy weather forecast. Went to the souk with a posse of lady jewellery advisers and finally picked a bracelet and a necklace; that will see me through Christmas with Sarah. I hate having to think about presents and missed her birthday a couple of weeks ago.

Had lunch with John Wakeham and the Ricketts on the terrace, under increasingly threatening skies. Discussed the press where Wakeham, as chairman of the Press Complaints Commission, is still very protective of journalists and their malpractices. To me he seems to see his role at the Commission as protecting the press proprietors from injured and complaining citizens, rather than protecting the public from the intrusive, offending press. I am pushing him (certainly over-optimistically) to do something about entrapment and phone bugging.

The election campaign is still dominated by alleged sleaze. This has been the only issue in the media for two weeks. I dislike corruption and wouldn't object if they were also raising prominently the serious issues of, say, economic and social policy which affect the nation. But most of these stories are just trifles of individual behaviour. The chairman of the Scots Tories has today resigned over a homosexual incident, which is of no consequence. So Major's 'long campaign' is dripping in petty scandal and none of the main issues has been seriously discussed. Not his fault. It is all tabloid media led.

Labour is still 20% ahead in the polls and the spread betting now points to a 90-seat majority. But there is a month to go. It will be intolerably boring.

I went back to my room to change for the races – and then the skies opened. I went to the course in a small bus and the road was awash and the surrounding desert a brown lake. At the entrance to the course the police were turning back the ordinary public, but let me in.

Everything at the course was under water and it washed over my desert boots so my socks were soaked, my suit as well and I could squeeze water out of my shirt. I had taken an umbrella from the hotel but the wind blew it inside out and the metal ribs buckled. This was bizarre. It rarely rains in Dubai – and heavily only once every five years. Yet it did it to coincide with the great race. It was so sad for Mohammed who had put so much into it and brought in the racing great from all over the world. On television he looked suicidal.

The tents and restaurant chalets were flooded and nearly collapsing under the weight of rain. I went to the Hilton chalet and they undressed me, gave me towels and hot coffee. Some were isolated there all afternoon and a nice Irishman slowly sank forward drunk. To escape, they laid out beer crates in a line and I walked over them just above the flood. The course was like a muddy river and everything was called off. So I slopped back to the clubhouse to have an elegant if deeply depressed supper. I felt bereft, as if I had come to my wedding but my bride had failed to show up. Went home quietly in the bus.

In the hotel a vast party was in progress. All those who hadn't even bothered to try to go racing – the Bensons, Dempster and various other Raffia – were celebrating, dining at Sheikh Mohammed's expense and as far as I could see not giving a bugger for the tragedy he had suffered. The spongers and poncers were celebrating, race or no race. They have postponed the races till it has dried out. I would love to stay – as many are – but have to return to Westminster.

Sunday 30 March 1997

Sat by sea reading until time to go to airport. Feeling very sad. Chatted with England player Alan Lamb about Northants cricket and with trainer Michael Stoute about (Sarah's father) Raymond Clifford-Turner's horses – Raymond first set him up in training. Sarah met me at Heathrow and nice to be home despite deep sense of deprivation. Now back to the election and all that dreariness.

Monday 31 March 1997

Woke early in Fox's Walk on stunningly beautiful day and the land is very dry and short of rain. Perhaps we can import some from the Dubai desert.

First went to visit Paul Webber's stable near Banbury. He showed me the horse he has chosen for our syndicate. Pedigree for a Derby winner but too big for the flat and may make a fast chaser.

Wednesday 2 April 1997

Nasty piece by Nigel Dempster in the *Mail* today accusing me of being a spoilsport for not staying on in Dubai. No doubt he and fellow sponger Benson are unable to understand how anyone could turn down more days of freebies, which is all their lives contain, in order to go back to work. Also criticises my working for Maxwell. This is a cheek from Dempster, since I was there when he tried to get a job with Maxwell on the *Mirror*, but failed because he demanded 50% more money than was paid to the *Mirror* editor! His sanctimoniousness about not working for Maxwell is based on his being too greedy to get there. Everyone in Dubai was saying how much they loathe him.

Read John Hale's last book on Renaissance Europe. Brilliant. He was my tutor on the Italian Renaissance at Oxford. I persuaded Callaghan to appoint him to the National Gallery, where he ended as chairman.

Thursday 3 April 1997

Answered my post and shopped before going back to Fox's Walk for late lunch and then watched first day at Aintree. After Aintree, they showed the postponed races from Dubai, which made me feel very envious and wanting to be there.

Friday 4 April 1997

Finally finished Hale (600 pages). His knowledge of that Renaissance period is stunning. At night started Graham Greene's *It's a Battlefield*. I shall pursue him chronologically through all his novels, as I did with Waugh; the best way to understand them is to follow an author as he develops.

Saturday 5 April 1997

Great excitement about the Grand National. I wake at 7.00 am and do the form, choosing two, one a favourite and one an outsider. After lunch settled down to watch the TV – but the race was abandoned because of an IRA bomb threat. Couldn't believe it. First the rain in Dubai and now this. I was very angry with Aintree for giving in to the IRA. Should have cleared the stands and then run the race, 99% were watching on TV anyway. And that would have said get stuffed to the terrorists. But nobody seems to have done any preplanning for this possibility. Tonight, if the SAS went in and disposed of a few terrorists, there would be little complaint here – or in the Irish Republic, who all love the National. Two thirds of the jockeys are Irish.

Sunday 6 April 1997

Set off with Sarah driving to Lynmouth in Somerset, but decided this isn't our country. Prefer it further west. So drove to Instow, and stayed at a nice hotel with a room looking over the estuary.

The election campaign rumbles on in the background. Major is getting very defensive and irritable as the polls still show Labour 20% ahead and the sleaze issue continues depressingly.

Monday 7 April 1997

Drove to Clovelly, which is very pretty with no tat even on the edge of the village. Then on to Bude for lunch at a seashore pub and sleep on the low cliff afterwards. We both like this more, being back in Cornwall. After lunch, drove south towards Salcombe. At rescheduled Grand National start off time, I spotted a pub and we parked and dashed in to see the race start (30 years ago that would have been inconceivable, as no pub would have been open!). My choice Lord Gyllene won and I had a couple of hundred pounds waiting to be collected. There was a small group of locals, so I bought a round of drinks for them.

Tuesday 8 April 1997

Woke early and watched the election coverage on TV. The Tories have been able to open up some of Labour's flanks, showing Blair changing policy as he goes along. They accuse him of U-turns, but of course it isn't. He never believed in the original old policies anyway. As each policy issue arises he puts his stamp on it. This does look like making policy on the hoof, but since the public agrees with the direction in which he is going, it shouldn't do him much harm.

For lunch drove down the coast to Lyme Regis, which I knew only from Jane Austin and John Fowles.

Then back to London on the A303. What a typical British main road. Long stretches of dual carriageway, with frequent small stretches of single carriageway, sometimes only for a couple of miles. Each sudden narrowing produces terrible jams, braking and near accidents. What explains it? Lack of money? Lack of systematic planning more likely. The incompetence of our road network will prove the ultimate historic proof of why we didn't have the competence to remain a serious major power.

The TV headlines were full of Neil Hamilton disrupting Martin Bell's 'clean politics' campaign and getting himself nominated. Now sleaze can continue to run. Labour is still looking wobbly on a lot of policy issues, where the party position seems to be whatever Tony Blair happens to think today. But the Tories are not getting much chance to exploit it as sleaze dominates the news.

Wednesday 9 April 1997

Had a long chat with Michael Hastings of the BBC. He said that Gerald Kaufman is angling for a peerage, willing to give up his seat at the last moment to let a Blair favourite in as the deal. Then he hopes to get my Heritage job in the Lords. That could happen. Agent of Marcia's revenge! I don't mind. Then I could go to Education – or more racing. I am easy either way.

Read *Alice through the Looking Glass*, which I bought, along with *Lorna Doone*, in Devon. Due to my curious childhood, I never read any of the children's classics. My mother never read any books to us and I believe never read any book in her life. So I've a blank period, deprived of all those books which are part of the upbringing of nearly everyone I know. I did start reading at school but then read older books, mainly school histories of battles, knights, kings and the British Empire. And to my children I read more recent children's books, but not the real old classics. So now I propose to fill in a gap in my cultural upbringing. I particularly look forward to enjoying any that the Politically Correct Claptrappers try to ban, about golliwogs and red Indians etc.

I am really excited about this, though I must say I thought *Through the Looking Glass* wasn't very childish, but subtle and needed vivid imagination. It tested me, though I enjoyed it greatly and thought it just right for my age. Incidentally the election is still very boring and cannot compete for my attention with Alice.

In the evening go up to London to go out to dinner with David Montgomery.

The dinner was excellent, with guests from the Princes Youth Business Trust and from Reuters. The conversation was very lively, focusing mainly on the election and the media. They accepted my view that this campaign is boring because for Labour this time, unlike in 1992, everything is tightly controlled by Alastair Campbell: no detailed policies like poor John Smith's shadow budget, no jokes and nothing off the record, just boring sound bites which cannot be taken apart by the Tory media. Consequently the campaign is boring.

After dinner, David and I adjourned to discuss Ireland, where we agree to continue our campaign to ease Blair into achieving a dramatic new Ulster settlement. David is convinced the people of the North are now at last ready to compromise to achieve that. He recently had a meeting with Gerry Adams and was impressed by him – saying he wished 'my Protestant side had a leader as good'. He feels Adams is like Arafat or Mandela, a former terrorist now ready to do a deal to get away from the gun and into government. I said Blair should appoint a young secretary of state for Northern Ireland who is dedicated to achieving the peace settlement, someone who will obey Blair and doesn't have his or her own agenda. We both like Mo Mowlam immensely, but she might find it difficult to do the deal with the Unionists, which must be done. Blair must take this and have it as his secret objective for government success.

We agree that the North is only now ready for it; and that Callaghan was quite right to close it down with Roy Mason in 1976 (though I wrongly disagreed at the time) since the time was then not yet ripe. I suggest David writes to Blair on this for his first weekend box after winning.

Friday 11 April 1997

Wrote obituary of dear old Alma Birk. A very sparky lady.

The campaign drags on, with polls showing Labour's lead well back up above 20%. The Tories have started to squabble about Europe, with ministers putting anti statements in their constituency manifestos, contrary to Major's instructions. They have a death wish. Whenever Labour starts to unravel, the Tories step in and shoot themselves in the foot again.

Joe Haines said many on our side are irritated by Blair's policy-making on the hoof – which Joe defined as 'Here are my polices – and if you don't like them, I will change them.' Blair is trying to please everyone and seeming afraid to take any firm position which might offend anybody. He is dedicated just to winning. I see the point. If Labour lost again it would be finished. It is time for a change. But there must be change for some purpose. He has not defined what that purpose is, other than to get the Tories out. Really he is offering Tory policies but with Labour. The electorate seem to want that. But it is hardly a crusade to get excited about. He is copying Clinton, who won the last US election by adopting the Republican platform.

Saturday 12 April 1997

With Sarah to Ascot to watch Peers Folly; linked up with my sons Stephen and Paul. We went up into the owners stand with trainer Henrietta Knight and Terry Biddlecombe to watch. At first he was going easily, but then was suddenly pulled up. I was desolated, so was Henrietta. Bleeding again, profusely from the nose, all over jockey Jason Titley's silks. We were gutted, and quietly parted ways and went home.

Sunday 13 April 1997

The election is still dreary, with the Tories totally negative, just personal attacks on Blair. Tomorrow Blair will try to be more positive with Labour's education policy, but I doubt if anything can infuse some interest in the campaign. For the first time in my adult life, I am not watching the election coverage on the evening TV news. Joe and Lennie Hoffman tell me that it is the same with them.

Monday 14 April 1997

Went on a nice long walk to get some exercise and then start the next Graham Greene – *Brighton Rock*. The book is much better than the film, with a vivid picture of Brighton 60 years ago. I read late into the night.

Tuesday 15 April 1997

This afternoon to Slough to canvass. Cannot forget Betjeman's 1939 poem starting 'Come, friendly bombs, and fall on Slough'. Too few did.

I can see what Betjeman meant. A truly dreary place. Went to the head-quarters and met our candidate, Fiona Mactaggart. Everyone tells me that the party organisation is vastly improved compared to the shambles of Transport House in the 1970s. Andrew Smith, our shadow Transport spokesman, arrived and we set off for a middle class housing estate, tradi-tionally Tory.

The absence of local support and total absence of Labour posters anywhere reflects what I got on the doorstep. The atmosphere is very flat. But no hos-tility. Several told me that they had previously been Tory but were now going to vote Labour. So we will win here, but no fizz. I think partly due to the Tory negative campaigning, which has turned people off (their strategy is clearly to abandon hope of winning but limit the loss by getting the turnout down). And our move to the middle ground, matching Tory policies, has removed all trace of a Labour crusade.

Wednesday 16 April 1997

Tories in shambles over the European Monetary System.

Thursday 17 April 1997

Spent morning clearing up papers and then to the country to resume my fascinated tussle with Graham Greene – now exploiting the election break to read a novel a day in chronological order.

Saturday 19 April 1997

Still spend more time with Graham Greene than on the election. The polls show slight narrowing of Labour's lead. The campaign is becoming testy with the Tories ill-tempered and desperate. Major seems very defensive. Labour is still well disciplined. But, in fact, Major is more powerful on TV than Blair,

Looking uncharacteristically optimistic before becoming a minister

Snooping in Northern Ireland with Minister Lord Dubs, 1997

The Labour government ministers in the House of Lords, 1998

Very slowly spin bowling for the Lords (aged 62) against the Commons at the Oval, author middle back row

Receiving the award for Best Horse Race Tipster by a seemingly unconvinced John Prescott

As minister of farming and food, 1997

As minister visiting a British Food (and apparently fancy dress) Fair

Sharing discreet Palace gossip with the Queen's former press secretary, Charles Anson

Celebrating the prospect of ever growing food subsidies in Central Europe, 1998

Beloved Honey in a terrier race on ministerial visit to an agricultural fair in Devon

With Tony Blair and comedian Stephen Fry (and partly obscured writer
John Mortimer), 1998

Honey bravely attacks a stuffed fox at an agricultural fair, friend Lady Mallalieu and
Lord Mason on left

In the garden at Fox's Walk with my two favourite ladies, Sarah and Honey

With Sarah on the beach in Ireland, 1997

Escaping from MAFF to Céret with close friend, publisher Graham Greene

In the Pyrenees with Sarah

On the terrace at Mas au Rocher reflecting on the Common Agriculture Policy

Relaxing in the Pyrenees with Sarah and her daughter Sasha

Lunch with friends on the terrace at Mas au Rocher. L to R: Margaret Jay, Tom Read, author, Sarah, Mike Adler, 1996

Military-style planning for a testing Pyrenees walk with Cabinet Secretary Robin Butler, 1996

Walking in the Pyrenees, author standing between Robin Butler and friend
Celia Read, 1996

Skiing cautiously with close friend Dr Nori Graham

The author, when younger, plotting with close friend Joe Haines, Harold Wilson's press secretary

With former Prime Minister James Callaghan and Lady Williams

With friends, Baroness Margaret Jay and Lord and Lady Clive Hollick

A tactile meeting with actress Joan Collins in Gstaad, Switzerland

With Sarah and Princess Diana at a London Symphony Orchestra concert

Equine hypochondriac Peers Folly on a rare race appearance

With Lord Weinstock and Lord Stoker Hartington at a horse racing occasion

With the Princess Royal at a serious racing lunch

who suffers from a light tenor voice, which gives an impression of being light-weight.

Sunday 20 April 1997

First to mass, where Father Flanagan gave a powerful sermon calling for Catholic priests to be allowed to marry. I agree with that.

Finished *The Heart of the Matter*, which is Greene's most powerful so far. Have now read eight. His erratic but obsessive Catholicism gives a framework to an underlying current of moral debate. His weaknesses for me are the prevailing bleakness, and that all his characters are dark and virtually all incapable of profound and self-sacrificing loving relationships. Like Waugh, he was a Catholic convert and the comparisons are fascinating. Ultimately I suspect more of Waugh's novels will survive the test of time because they were 'perfectly' written. But Greene explores wider and deeper issues and is a more interesting man. Both were nasty and created a lot of unhappiness and seemed incapable of fostering truly loving relationships.

Monday 21 April 1997

Drove into north Northampton to canvass for Sally Keeble. The Tory Tony Marlow, a serious far right winger, had a majority of over 3000 last time, so it is a marginal we might win, though his anti-European views will probably give him an edge.

Our local party organisation was much more impressive than Slough, with a lot of local supporters at headquarters and on the ground in the constituency. She is an impressive, if slightly humourless, candidate and has been working hard there for two years. Her workers obviously have great respect for her.

We went to some outer estates, which were still green field farmland when I was at school here in Northampton. They seemed to have little social spirit and lack facilities or good pubs. But on the doorstep we got a lot of positive response. There wasn't a single Tory poster. Our canvassing team were a delightful lot and made me feel very much at home. The fact that I still followed the Cobblers football team and the Saints at rugby went down well.

Tuesday 22 April 1997

Left at dawn for Gatwick to go to Ireland. Sudden decision yesterday after talking to Peter Savill, who lives nearby and kindly offered me a bed out in Kildare for Punchestown races. The Ryanair cheap flight was packed like sardines with appalling service almost approaching hostility. Then a taxi to the Kildare Country Club.

Peter welcomed me to a lovely little house in a courtyard and I took my time settling in before driving to the races in the little old sports car he loaned me. It was a great occasion, some 20,000 people and just like Cheltenham except more relaxed, more room and more fun. At dinner we discuss the problems of English racing. He is a tough Yorkshire multimillionaire who went to Ampleforth with Alex Hesketh. I like him instinctively but imagine he could be quite ruthless.

Wednesday 23 April 1997

Set off for the Punchestown course and great racing. The local town of Naas was in festive spirit with flags and music. Met Peter for a last chat before leaving for the airport. Curious how I always end up going to these places on my own. Partly because Sarah won't travel – and my main political friends don't go racing. I suppose I am a misfit. A North London academic expatriate in horsey territory.

Thursday 24 April 1997

Spent the morning clearing letters in London. Then again read the *Quiet American*. Less dramatic than the film. Beautifully told story.

Election getting very aggressive. Major accused Blair of being a liar. Their attack is now wholly on Blair, so it is bound to become personal and nasty. It may work, though I doubt it. What it does do is make Major out to be a less pleasant man than he usually seems. In 1979, when Callaghan was losing the election, some advisers suggested he tear into Thatcher personally and he refused, saying to me that isn't how a British prime minister behaves towards someone who may be the next prime minister.

Friday 25 April 1997

I answer letters and write this diary. Also sent a memo to Tony Blair on how to conduct the critical last week of the campaign. And start *Our Man in Havana*. Still enjoying it, but feel am near the end of this Greene odyssey.

Sunday 27 April 1997

Polls still show Labour averaging 16% lead, pointing to landslide victory of over 150 seats. I think it will narrow, but then I've never counted chickens because, since childhood, have been afraid of disappointments. The Tories seem to have given up; except for Major who deserves a medal for dogged courage. He also deserves fewer rats around him.

I spent ages revising David Montgomery's Ulster Unionist document for a new settlement, proposing a new elected Administrative Assembly in Northern Ireland, making it more acceptable to Blair. Funny if it goes through, having been redrafted by a Labour Catholic.

Monday 28 April 1997

Off to Falmouth in Cornwall canvassing. We were about 20 MPs and peers taking part in a last week blitz of marginal seats. We gathered at RAF Northolt by 9.30 am for a 10 o'clock take-off. We were delayed half an hour because Harriet Harman, being very important, was very late arriving. Then there were head winds which nearly blew the old plane backwards.

My old West Country friend Jean Corston, our party agent down there, met us at Falmouth and we filled two buses and went off on mass canvasses. In safe Labour council house areas and the reception was much warmer than in Slough or Northampton. There were posters everywhere and people very friendly. Some of the housing was brutally ugly. It must be grim to be unemployed down there – as 12% are. Privatised water was a big issue, with charges up 100% and the service terrible. That will cost the Tories seats in many areas. Only saw one Tory (Seb Coe) poster. I now finally begin to believe the polls and that we will have a good majority.

Flew back with the wind behind, so a bit quicker – I commented that the plane was clearly based on an early basic version of the ancient Wellington bomber.

Reflected on my attitude to the election. Sarah keeps commenting that I am not very excited. True. I always suppress that anyway, afraid of disappointment. I am apprehensive, remembering how Labour led until the last couple of days in 1970, October 1974 and then 1992, and each time blew it. So I've been tense and nervous about the result. But also about afterwards even if we win. If I am not in the government, that will be a public snub. If I am in, that will be a dramatic change of my lifestyle for the worse. Travelling to boring meetings, up in London five days a week, sitting up half the night in the Lords waiting for a vote, which usually doesn't come. No time for reading or racing. It won't be easy. But I would like to do it. To complete my political journey. Like tying up a loose shoelace. But I will soon be 63 and won't want to keep at it for more than two years.

Incidentally, Blair clearly reacted to my memo and sent a letter to all our people on Monday saying, in my words, they must campaign till the last minute on Thursday. So some marginal influence. Quite pleasing when I saw that announced on TV.

Tuesday 29 April 1997

The long election drag nearly over. Polls still steady. Tories seem to be falling apart, with squabbling over the conduct of the campaign, seeking scapegoats for failure. Major actually has fought a strong and brave campaign, often seeming almost alone. He is a bigger political figure than I had allowed. But not big enough as a prime minister. He is one of those middling, well meaning, wanting-to-be-nice people who are fatal as leaders because they have no decisiveness, no ruthlessness and no real leadership qualities (as Thatcher did have). The German military expert Clausewitz said that when you had that kind among your army generals you must take them out and shoot them straight away.

Phoned David Montgomery and we planned the next move on Ulster. I suggested the *Mirror* on Friday should urge Blair to drop his mediocrities from the Shadow Cabinet – Tom Clarke, Michael Meacher, Clare Short, Ron Davies, and more – and bring on some of the bright young ones like Bryan Wilson, Tessa Jowell, John Denham and Helen Liddell. I hope Blair follows the advice and appoints his best possible team.

Joe told me that Alastair Campbell has asked him for a brief on how to run the press office in No. 10, so obviously they are beginning to focus on going in there. Also Blair now looks much better on TV, more relaxed. It is easier to play well and win when you are winning, footballers know that.

Wednesday 30 April 1997

Polls still look good and hard to see how we can lose. Just a question of by how many. Went to Kleinworts (really Dresdnerbank now since the German takeover) to have usual pre-election lunch with old friends. Michael Bedford organised it. All accepted defeat for Tories. I gave my explanations. Very nice to see some of the old City team. I always look back on brokers Grieveson Grant as a happy time in my life with a lot of decent people.

Dinner with Max and Jane Rayne. Max, though very rich, is content for the Tories to go out. He says any prime minister who uses Jeffrey Archer as a confidant deserves to lose. Max has had dealings with Archer and says 'He should be in jail.'

Jane was also interesting on Marcia Falkender. Jane is sister-in-law to Jimmy Goldsmith. Discussing Jimmy's knighthood, she says he had expected a peerage, had been promised one by Marcia and has always been bitter at not getting one; just a knighthood on her 'lavender' honours list.

There were some £100 million of assets at the table supporting Labour. That is a tribute to Blair's skill in getting business and the City to accept and even support Labour. Sadly few of those assets were mine.

Thursday 1 May 1997

This is the great and beautiful day when the British people and Tony Blair will get rid of this clapped out Tory government. Sarah drove down to Berkshire to vote. She feels she must vote Tory and could never switch, though she is deeply unhappy with the government and like many of her Tory friends is quite content that Blair should win.

Son Stephen came in mid-morning and we worked on the finances of the gambling industry. It is quite clear that they are massively under-taxed and offer scope for Labour Treasury revenues. But I will wait before I talk to Gordon Brown and Alistair Darling. Had lunch with Peter Savill. Discussed how to revolutionise racing. Peter has just got on to the British Horseracing Board – by just one vote after a tie first time round. He will shake them up.

I wandered round to the Westminster polling booth to vote in the local elections where at least I've a vote – peers don't vote in the General Election. But hadn't noticed no local elections in London. So much for being a political pro. Still, I learned that the turnout wasn't anything special.

Graham Greene and Camilla Panufnik came round for our election eve. I decided not to go to the grand BBC party since they refused my request to invite Graham – even though he is chairman of the British Museum and son of a former distinguished Director General of the BBC. We went to Mimmo d'Ischia in Elizabeth Street for supper. But I was very jumpy and left early. Not just because of the impending result, with all that might imply for me (devastation of my private life if I get a job, and public rejection if I don't) but because of an alarming development at Towcester racecourse.

At 7.00 pm I had been phoned by Mike Buswell from Towcester. He said that Alexander Hesketh so far had not paid the £800,000, which he (as owner of the racecourse) was committed to pay for the new stand – which he had proposed and is now finished, with the builder asking for his £250,000. As directors, Mike and I had refused to authorise starting the new stand until the financing was firmly in place. Some came from the bank and some from the Levy Board, but we insisted that Alexander give an unequivocal guarantee for his share. He did that in writing, together with professional assurances that the money was there and ready.

We're furious. We agree we may have to put the racecourse company into liquidation on Monday, because without that cash it has nothing to pay the builder and will be trading while insolvent. This will create a most tremendous row, destroying a fine old racecourse, making staff unemployed and busting the poor builder. I would hate that, but we have to meet our obligations as directors. We should convince Alexander that the publicity would damage his career in business. Apparently he already owes the banks, but he has massive assets in land.

During dinner I couldn't focus on the conversation and my mind raced over tactics. I decided Mike and I would go to the British Horseracing Board before liquidation, and the Levy Board, and put the whole situation to them. They could try to buy the course to protect it and their loans. If not then we will have to put it into liquidation. I would hate to close a course, especially one I love like Towcester.

Returning home I phoned Mike and put my proposals, with which he agreed. He reported that Alexander Hesketh had begun to soften a little when confronted by our ultimatum and is talking about selling some land. That was a bit more encouraging, but it left a cloud over the evening's celebrations.

Sarah and Graham and Camilla came back and we settled down to watch the results. There were only three before midnight, indicating a good Labour victory but nothing astonishing. Graham fell asleep and had to be up at dawn to go to the board meeting of brewers Greene King in Suffolk, so they went off. Sarah went to bed also, so I watched for a while and the results got better – with the best swings in the marginal constituencies, showing that our improved organisation had paid off. Whatever the reservations some have about Peter Mandelson, he certainly did an incredibly good job in modernising our ludicrously bad party machine. I can see why Blair is said to find him indispensable.

Took a taxi to the Festival Hall beside the Thames, where the great party celebration was in full swing. I had a great time with masses of friends. From the Lords were Tessa Blackstone, Alf Dubbs, Clive Hollick, Margaret Jay etc. Best for me was celebrating with my old No. 10 team – Andrew Graham, Gavyn Davies and David Lipsey. The atmosphere was euphoric, with people singing and dancing and cheering every result, which showed the endless list of Tory defeats. Best for the party was the defeat of Michael Portillo in Sarah's late husband Tony's old seat of Enfield (I didn't join in that, liking and respecting Michael), but I did cheer the defeat of that awful man Shaw at Dover.

The hours passed happily. It was the happiest political night of my life. I can remember 1945, which as a young lad I followed on the BBC radio, but then I knew little and took Labour's victory for granted, assuming that as the party of the working people they would be in power for ever. Since then there has been nothing like this, the greatest victory this century and Labour's greatest victory ever. The New Labour team has been fully justified. Blair's party reforms made it possible for the country to vote for him. That is why the South had the biggest swing. All those middle classes wanted to vote the Tories out before, but couldn't vote for us until we threw out the old Left and became electable in their eyes. Nice for me since I've supported much of the broad New Labour approach – moderate, modernising and anti-left – since working with Gaitskell. In each of the seats in which I canvassed – Northampton, Falmouth and Slough – we won. Not that my contribution was much. In fact we won all the marginal seats and many non-marginal.

Around 5.00 am we all poured out on to the Embankment beside the Thames. The sun was about to rise behind St Paul's and the atmosphere had all the symbolism of a new dawn. We waited nearly an hour for Blair to arrive, with the crowd singing and waving to the tune of the campaign song, 'Things can only get better' (a theme which conflicted with my whole life's political experience). The encouraging thing was the large number of young people. They were climbing up on the Queen Elizabeth Hall, waving Labour banners. I recalled well Wilson's sombre election campaigns in 1974, when the crowds were quiet and sullen, and the party workers elderly and subdued. Wilson himself was admired, but had none of Blair's capacity to generate warm enthusiasm. It was a wonderful atmosphere and I didn't feel tired at all as it grew to full daylight. The adrenaline and joy at final success eliminated all tiredness.

Tony Blair finally arrived around 6.00 am and made a good and moving speech, full of talk of unity and healing and governing for the many and not the few. His voice was stronger than early in the campaign. Success is a great regenerator.

After he finished, I slipped away home, though many young people were still celebrating and dancing. I walked towards Westminster Bridge; several cars saw my red rosette and flashed their headlights and hooted their horns. It was a great feeling. I couldn't bring myself to go to bed, but watched the break-fast news. Still more Tory seats had fallen, the last by two votes at Winchester to the Lib Dems and seven members of the Cabinet were out. The nation had spoken emphatically. Tony Blair has a total mandate for his reforms. At least there is no question of the country's will – they want the Tories out, com-pletely out. We have 419 seats, the greatest for us ever, more even than in 1945, and the Tories are down to 165, a mere rump, leaderless and divided. Blair has it all made now and must not let it slip.

I slept for an hour and then was woken by a string of telephone calls. My Irish friend from Trinity College, Dublin, Trevor West, phoned with congratulations and begging me to use our new power and make sure that Ireland doesn't win the Eurovision song contest again this weekend since they cannot afford to keep putting it on. My old French friend Jacques Pomonti, who had been an advisor to President Mitterand, phoned with congratulations from Paris. Children and friends came on the phone. So I got up and went to the ITN studio, where they interviewed me as they filmed Blair travelling from Islington to No. 10, with me recalling what it was like last time with me travelling with Harold Wilson 23 years ago. I met Ken Livingstone at the studio, where he was already beginning to earn a rich living being the left winger the media could rely on to attack the new Labour government.

Afterwards back home – Major had announced his coming resignation, having had enough of those bastards in his party – and then drove down to Berkshire, where I lay in the garden in the hot sunshine, read the papers and dozed. But not really tired. The adrenalin still rushed. Great times, to be savoured. Blair handled his entry to, and Major his departure from, Downing Street very well and each with dignity.

Saturday 3 May 1997

Still on a cloud and read every result. Watched the 2000 Guineas from Newmarket, won by Michael Stoute's very good Entrepreneur and then took a long walk. Two of my neighbours, wealthy and previously voting Tory, told me they hadn't this time because of their arrogance.

The first Cabinet posts announced nearly as expected. Only surprise Donald Dewar goes to Scottish Office instead of George Robertson, who gets Defence. And Harriet Harman gets Social Security but has Frank Field as Deputy to keep her up to the mark. Both good moves. Then sad that Jack doesn't get Heritage – he would have made me a minister of state. He goes to Agriculture, which underuses his considerable political skills. Chris Smith comes back to Heritage. That is nice for me personally since I get on so well with him. But it means he has been demoted from Health (blustery Frank Dobson gets that) and will lack clout in the Cabinet. Michael Meacher and Tom Clarke from the Shadow Cabinet are not included in the Cabinet, which is understandable. David Clark survives as Duchy of Lancaster. Mo Mowlam keeps Northern Ireland, which is good, though she looks very tired (or ill?). Jack would have done that well.

Sunday 4 May 1997

Went to mass then read papers. Tom Clarke is deputy at Heritage as consolation for not being in the Cabinet. I know him but don't know if he has any interest in the arts and am certain he knows nothing of sport.

Watched Sleepytime win the 1000 Guineas and then wrote this diary. Also my resignation from Towcester, which I will take with me to tomorrow morning's critical meeting with Alexander Hesketh at Easton Neston. That could prove very messy.

Good late news was that Helen Liddell has been made minister of state at the Treasury. She is very good and a good friend.

Begin to feel tired and flat.

Later on Tessa Blackstone phoned. She knew nothing of her own position. A bit critical of the new Cabinet as too cautious – Dobson not up to it and no need to include Tom Clarke. Then Chris Smith phoned to say he knew nothing about who would be his minister for heritage in the Lords, but he hoped it would be me. He is a good friend.

Monday 5 May 1997

Heavy day. Set off early for Towcester to have our emergency board meeting. Started very tense. Kisty complained that as chairman she had been excluded from the crisis. Then Alexander's representative from the Trustees complained that Mike [Buswell] and I had made too much of it, 'gone over the top'. Mike explained our concerns and I came in to support him, pointing out that as directors we had a responsibility to ensure we were not trading insolvent. Those assurances were given by Stuart Richie the lawyer from Dixons. He said the difficulties were only technical and the money was there. Kisty said the family didn't want to give a longer lease but Mike and I insisted and we agreed 50 years. The lawyer gave repeated assurance that there was no problem and I felt relieved when we broke up. I warned them I would have to resign if I got a government job, but assured Mike that I would take a continuing interest if things went wrong.

I had taken my resignation along, but didn't hand it in because I will have to rewrite it now the financial thing is sorted. They said that Alexander knew nothing of the problem. Had we liquidated the racecourse that would have been a terrible blow to Alexander's business career. I didn't want that as he has been a good friend to me.

I drove rapidly from Towcester to Kempton and there saw our syndicate horse Memorial run moderately in the opening race. Then lovely fish lunch with Sarah's sister Susan and Colin. We were preparing to watch his horse run, when my portable rang. It was Sarah warning me that Downing Street was on the phone. I quickly moved away from the racehorse parade ring to sit in my car in the car park so that the new Prime Minister wouldn't phone and hear the course loudspeakers giving the names of the runners in the next race and so guess how I was wasting my time at the races at this great and serious moment in the nation's history.

They rang me, but then the switchboard said he wasn't ready. That was 4.00 pm. It happened again every 20 minutes till nearly six. I was stuck. I couldn't go to watch the racing. Dare not drive home in case he phoned when I was on the M3. So I sat in the car park for nearly two hours, until the racing was over.

Then Blair came through. I congratulated him on winning the election and he said, 'Thank you. You haven't been able to say that for a long time.' Then he said, 'I want you to have a position in the government.' I was excited.

Then he said, 'I want you to go to Agriculture. It is an important area in the Lords. The BSE question is very difficult and it needs someone who is experienced at handling the Lords.' My heart sank. I knew quite a bit about most policy areas, but agriculture is the one I know least about. It is also bottom of the Whitehall pile in departmental seniority. He said, 'You will want to get in touch with the department to arrange to go in – but then you know more than I do about those kind of things.' I thanked him and we cut off.

I told Sarah, who was very disappointed. All my years of mastering the arts and sports and broadcasting fields were wasted. So I drove home feeling very down.

I tried to understand why Agriculture? Then realised that Jack Cunningham was made the new minister and had presumably asked for me. It will be nice to work for him, but it is no favour to have this department. And one of the other ministers is anti-hunting fanatic Elliot Morley. We shall clash on country sports.

I started phoning. Tessa Blackstone was out. Henry Carnarvon was disappointed for me but said the farmers would be pleased. Joe Haines was very disappointed – as was Graham Greene who wanted me as his arts and museums minister. But I was cheered when I spoke to my putative private secretary, who was very pleased – saying they didn't usually have a minister in the Lords, just a spokesman. We discussed the department and he said my car and driver would arrive tomorrow morning at 9.15 am for ministerial discussions. I decided I have to be positive. Either turn the job down or be positive about it. No point in taking it but whingeing. Then Woodrow Wyatt phoned saying he wanted me to take the Tote. Everyone says that.

I think I would be relieved if it happened, but cannot see how to manoeuvre it. That has been the problem throughout. Cannot see how to apply for it from the front bench.

Sarah and I had a subdued supper, then I went up to London to be ready for tomorrow as my first day as a minister. Am certainly pleased to be a minister. It seems to complete my career. But I cannot imagine I will be there more than 18 months. Either up or out.

I still wonder why Blair has done this. Apart from Jack Cunningham asking for me, it must be an unfriendly act and he must know that. I wonder if he wants to get me away from broadcasting? Is that a deal he has done with Murdoch? Anything is possible.

Once I got to London my mood changed and I realised I was above all pleased to be in the government as a minister. This mood was confirmed further when I phoned Alf Dubbs and he revealed to me the full horror of the blood-bath on the Lords front bench. I realised I was lucky to have survived. Among the casualties are Andrew McIntosh (our deputy leader who is probably being punished for opposing Jack Straw's hard line on the Police Bill but on the front bench for 13 years and took eight bills very skilfully in the past parliament); our chief whip Ted Graham (aged 72 but served nobly for 10 years); Charles Williams, our former deputy leader and very good at the dispatch box; Neil Carmichael, former Commons minister; Muriel Turner; Frank Judd, former Commons minister and lovely man; Tom Chandos, though he didn't expect anything, being established in the City; Peter Archer, former Commons minister; and Maurice Peston, our industry spokesman for many years and adviser in the last Labour government. There will be much weeping and gnashing of teeth from these people who have served unpaid for years long into the night. We may have difficulty in getting them out to vote.

The winners are Tessa Blackstone, who goes back to Education as minister of state; Margaret Jay, who is minister of state at Health; and Stanley Clinton-Davis, minister of state at Environment. Gareth Williams goes to parliamentary secretary at the Home Office, where he will be superb, but sadly knows nothing of racing; and Liz Symons, who is very able but goes straight from the back benches with no experience of the Foreign Office. There will be some misplaced resentment at the latter, which will be seen by some of the older generation as typical of Blair's trendy political correctness, promoting women right, left and centre (Margaret Jay is rightly made deputy leader). Patricia Hollis keeps Social Security as a parliamentary secretary, John Gilbert will come up from the Commons to take Defence from Charles Williams (John traded it for his safe seat so Blair can parachute some friend in there); and a businessman will come to Industry. There is no minister at Heritage, which makes it a little easier for me to leave it – but not much.

Then I phoned Tessa again for a talk into the early hours of the morning. She is delighted for herself. But very critical of the Liz Symons appointment. Few modern ladies enjoy the success of their sisters. We agree to keep close in touch – have known one another for 30 years and good friends for over 20. I think in time she or Margaret Jay should succeed Ivor as leader and ask her to promise to give me Education, which she does.

Feel much better as I go to sleep. Realise I couldn't have been a minister at Heritage, since there isn't one in the Lords. Also realise on reflection that this afternoon was hilarious. Me being phoned at the paddock at Kempton Park and then running to the car so Blair wouldn't hear the race commentary when he offered me the job! Then waiting all that time for the final word (someone today said he was delayed when the No. 10 switchboard had phoned the wrong Donoughue, Brian in the Commons). And backing the winner of the previous race and not having time to collect the winnings from the Tote. Quite proper order of priorities! People in racing will be pleased that I had stuck with them till the end.

Tuesday 6 May 1997

The Ministry of Agriculture and Fisheries (MAFF) driver, Maggie, came to collect me shortly after nine.

Ahead lies being in government office, though one outside my usual interests. Hope I enjoy it. If not, I will quickly get out. To me, private life still matters most.

It was a strange feeling driving up to the Ministry of Farming, Fisheries and Food in Whitehall Place – the original site of Scotland Yard. My private secretary, Peter Grimley, met me and ushered me in and up in the lift to the second, ministerial floor. My office was not very grand – only half the size of my No. 10 place in 1974, but, it will do. Ugly; I will get Sarah in to spruce it up. Went on a tour of the other offices – none of the other ministers were in yet: Jack; Jeff Rooker, who is minister of state dealing with animal health (BSE); and my old adversary Elliot Morley, the hunt-hater, with whom I nearly had a fight when with Mo Mowlam at DNH. He has animal welfare, so hunting will soon come up.

I began to read the trays of papers waiting for decisions and a vast file of briefings for new ministers. Lunch at the Lords. Only a few there, but sat opposite Charles Williams who was clearly devastated at being dropped and complaining that it would all end in tears. He said it was simply because he didn't wear a skirt – and there is truth in that. Had there been a woman with his impressive experience on the front bench she would certainly have been minister of state. But the way he took it revealed his sensitivity.

Went back in the car – strange feeling to have a driver waiting outside and must make sure I don't give up my walking exercise. Then met the Permanent Secretary, Richard Packer. He is shrewd and knowledgeable, but quite different from the permanent secretaries in my day. Not smooth or supremely confident; seemed nervous and unsure, and shell-shocked from the attacks on the department over the past two years. No Sir Humphrey this. Not sure he'll survive, or that he wants to. Also met Jack's private secretary, whose morale was much higher – because, I later learned, he's bailing out and going to the Forestry Commission. I know how Churchill felt 50 years ago when he took over the bunch of generals who'd suffered Dunkirk – demoralised and defeated. This will be a real problem for Jack.

Had dinner with Henry and Jeannie Carnarvon. Appropriate since he is a good friend from way back before I was in Downing Street and knows 10 times more about farming than I ever could. He's pleased I'm a minister but sad not in a ministry where my knowledge and experience could be better used. I tell him I want him as my unpaid special adviser on farming. I was exhausted and we left early to collapse into bed. Endless nice messages of congratulation on the answering machine.

Wednesday 7 May 1997

First proper day as a minister. Collected at 8.20 am to go into the 'prayers' meeting of the ministers plus the Permanent Secretary. No agenda, so a bit messy and we order that next week is better prepared. Jeff Rooker very concerned that BSE (Mad Cow Disease) is about to blow up in sheep. He has papers I haven't seen (afterwards I tell my secretary that mustn't happen again). Jack didn't look happy. I said we must have a timetable of future events and possible crises before us at each week's meeting so we get ahead of events, not behind as the Tories always were. It's clear the department is demoralised.

We discussed the James Report on setting up a new independent food safety agency outside the department. Needs legislation and not clear if we we'll get it in the first session. Will lead to a battle with Department of Health, as they want to take the initiative from us. On present experience, my money would be on them winning. That will be my old friend Tessa Jowell, who is minister of health.

Then first of a series of meetings with the senior officers in charge of relevant divisions. Much more encouraging. Kate Timms seems very able and on top of the issues and I can work with her.

Incidentally, I am to be called Minister for Farming and the Food Industry. That accurately describes the areas of life of which I am seriously ignorant. But it's 15% of the British economy, so it's very important.

At 10.30 am, we ministers walked down Whitehall to attend the first meeting of the new Parliamentary Labour Party – in Church House because there is nowhere in Parliament big enough to take our 419 MPs.

Jack and I walked together. I advised him to shake up and revitalise the department. He has decided to change its name and I suggested changing senior officials so we can have a new start uncontaminated by past defeats. He also told me he was 'gobsmacked' when offered Agriculture. A curious chain of events. Gordon Brown apparently vetoed Chris Smith for Health because he is too soft and cannot say no to big spenders. So Chris had to be found another job; the obvious was Heritage since he was popular there before. That meant moving Jack and the only Cabinet post available was Agriculture, as the incumbent in Opposition Gavin Strang was young and expendable (to Transport). When offered, Jack gasped and said he must have a minister in the Lords, because of BSE and all the Tory farming experts are in the Lords. So he asked for me.

And that is how I become minister of farming and food. No plot or hostility from the PM. Nobody else stealing my beloved DNH. Just a political chain starting with the veto on Chris Smith at Health.

I tell Jack he must take it seriously and do it well, because you never know what happens in politics and another better vacancy might arise. But he's depressed by the fact that it's a bad news ministry. Nothing cheerful. Everything going wrong. I thanked him for giving me the Common Agricultural Policy (CAP) renegotiations and farming, trade and the food industry – all the policy and economic aspects, which I'll enjoy.

The PLP was an incredible gathering. Atmosphere electric. All the excited new MPs congratulating one another. All the new ministers delighted. Lots of waving, cheering and kissing. The new chief whip Nick Brown opened proceedings and introduced John Prescott, who looked happier than he'd ever done before, though some of his sentences were still incomprehensible. He then introduced Blair, who made a dramatic entrance from off-stage. He spoke well and pulled no punches. Told the MPs they were there only because of the Labour Party and so they'd better toe the line. He had obviously gained in confidence from the landslide and means to run things dictatorially. No harm in that, till things go wrong.

I sat with Patricia Hollis and Bruce Grocott, who told me things were going well for him as parliamentary secretary to Blair. Earlier I had chatted with Jack Straw, Frank Field and Helen Liddell (agreeing to fix lunch), and congratulated Mark Fisher on having the Arts job I wanted. He was very warm.

From the floor, left wingers Dennis Skinner and Ken Livingstone made their predictable whinges about Gordon Brown's brilliant move in making the Bank of England independent. They complained he was giving way to the centre of capitalism the power to raise interest rates. They don't understand that this will create the trust in the City that may give us lower interest rates. But those kind of people are full of posturing clichés and will never understand economic realities.

Afterwards I chatted with Alastair Campbell, who thanked me for my paper on No. 10, which he said was very useful. I told him of the tradition of the PM calling all junior ministers to No. 10 to hear the Queen's speech and have drinks and he said he'd arrange that.

Talked with Gordon Brown who was very friendly and I alerted him to the potential of taxing the gambling industry and he said I should come in for a meeting with him and Helen. I walked back with George Howarth and discussed racing and the need for an overview of the gambling industry.

Had lunch in the cafe downstairs with Derek Gladwin, who told me that Andrew McIntosh has at least been compensated with deputy chief whip. Quite right. I supported him for chief whip, though I'm happy with Denis Carter. Also commiserated with Ted Graham, who told me he is 'very sore' at being dropped.

Afterwards went into the Lords Chamber for prayers and to swear in. Very strange feeling to be on the opposite side of the House for the first time in 12 years. The Tories were there in our seats in full force; all their front bench looking smaller when out of a job. I exchanged kisses with Jean Trumpington, who had sent me a warm letter. Our front bench was empty and I didn't dare go and sit there alone in case that looked triumphal. Finally our lot trooped in. But Charles Williams and Maurice Peston were missing, having been dropped, and Andrew McIntosh looked as if on the edge of a heart attack. Rejection in politics is like in love: very traumatic, and these are all too old to recover and achieve something else.

One thing is clear. There is a world of difference between being a minister and not being one. I am lucky.

Back to the department for an intense briefing from Mr Thornton, our officer on the BSE side, and asked for a series of seminars to educate me on all these technical problems, especially CAP and BSE. Later hear that Jack thinks that is a good idea and he asks to join in. Worked till 7.00 pm trying to catch up on the endless flow of papers. Haven't been able to write replies to any of the dozens of letters of congratulation. The outgoing Tory ministers came in for a farewell party and I arranged to have lunch with Tim Boswell, who may alert me of any land mines.

Going home, the lady driver told me that the previous Tory ministers had been exhausted and Hogg had made it clear he was praying for the election defeat to come so he could get out. She also said she'd heard from the No. 10 drivers that John Major had had a nervous breakdown on Black Wednesday. All day vomiting in the lavatory. She drove Stephen Dorrell from studio to studio to deal with the media because the PM was unfit to talk.

A battle is developing over the James Report recommendation of an independent food safety agency. We hear that it's not in the Queen's speech, which is a setback, and that Health will lead on it. Jack will fight for it at Cabinet tomorrow.

Thursday 8 May 1997

Another meeting with Kate Timms when we got down to the nitty-gritty of CAP. So much to master. Hanker after DNH where I was on top of every detail. Now aged 62, I (and Jack) have to begin at square one on a subject of which I have no knowledge or experience. It's a terrible waste of intellectual property. But also, as they say, challenging. Afterwards meet a Mr Saunderson, officer in charge of the regional network, and we arrange for me to take the South, Wessex and the South West. Nice to get back to Cornwall. They want me to close the Truro office, but I'll consult our Falmouth MP on the politics of that.

Off to my first official lunch at the Savoy for the Academie Culinaire de France awards to chefs. I spotted a land mine, as Grimley and I had both (wrongly in my case) been declared as vegetarians. No beef. I told him afterwards that in future, at food occasions, I would happily eat British beef. Don't want nasty paragraphs about me betraying British farmers.

Back for meeting with Mr Hunter, in charge of beef and BSE. Alarming story. Landscape full of land mines. As Jack says, there are no good news stories at MAFF [Ministry of Agriculture, Fisheries and Food]. Have to kill more cattle, cannot afford to compensate for them, huge disposal problem, and no hope of a better CAP deal. I felt like Hogg; time to get out, when am barely in.

Then worse. To a meeting on BSE, scheduled just for ministers, but a dozen staff turned up, all the vets. Jack nearly called it off, not least as none of us ministers had the right briefing (civil servants black marks). Jack loaned me his big portfolio and I found some relevant papers. The story was alarming.

We might face immediately a BSE crisis for sheep. No clear scientific evidence but we can't afford to be caught napping. Jack seemed very jumpy and not his usual laid back self. Rooker was also alarmed. And I will have to take this in the Lords even though I don't understand half the scientific terms. The crisis will erupt in two weeks, associated first with an EU meeting in Brussels and then a meeting of our scientific advisory committee, which wants crisis measures to remove the spinal cords from all sheep before sale. That will set the media off with another scare headline about not eating sheep meat. Then our farming will collapse if there is a ban on exports of sheep as well as beef – and the Treasury won't want to pay any compensation. Agriculture may be a backwater, but it's certainly politically not a quiet one. No wonder it's known as a political graveyard.

The Queen's speech situation still unclear. Rumours that the new food health agency will now be included. But Jack not leading on it. He spoke to the PM about it and Tony was getting irritated and wants it settled one way or another. Interestingly, the Minister of Health (Tessa Jowell) declined to attend this meeting. I suppose they're fighting territorial games and won't come to our ministry in case that concedes we are leading. The politics of it are to show that the farmers are no longer in control.

Had a brief meeting with the President of the National Farmers Union, which has historically run MAFF as a sub-office. That won't happen under us. But they are very powerful and can destroy the reputations of ministers who oppose them. Jack will need the PM's support if we are to resist their demands for ever growing compensation.

I read papers until after 7.00 pm and then went back home, and took my huge red box in my car to the country. I was exhausted and went to bed early.

Friday 9 May 1997

All day reading papers from the red box. Hundreds of pages of briefing. It was after 6.00 pm when my eyes collapsed and I went for a walk to freshen up. Two drinkers came out of The Plough to congratulate me. Bad news is that The Plough may close in a fortnight. Another sign of the decline of rural life! I wish the CAP paid to preserve rural pubs.

Saturday 10 May 1997

Not my usual lovely Saturday. Had to drop out of lunch at Lingfield races. More papers – and writing some of this up, which takes hours. Very tired, but too excited to sleep when I try to nap.

So the end of my first week. Exhausting. All so new. Also feel a little marginal at Agriculture compared to going into No. 10, 23 years ago. Slightly shabby surroundings and some of them unimpressive people – though my two private secretaries seem good.

Blair has made a stunning start. Very decisive leadership. Abolishing one of PM's Question Times, which is quite right because it absorbs too much time and energy in Downing Street. But is upsetting colleagues by centralising power. Everything has to be cleared through No. 10. Blair is exercising more power than any previous PM. Can see why he admires Thatcher. Has gone beyond her in exercising central power. Providing he doesn't make any big mistakes, that is fine. If he does, he will get the blame. But Blair at his beginning must be much more exciting to work for than Wilson at his end. I shall watch it with interest.

Sunday 11 May 1997

Had a good walk, which cleared my brain, and drove up to London to be ready for tomorrow's meetings.

Monday 12 May 1997

Felt impatient to start so ordered my car an hour early. Find I cannot sit around and relax.

Straight to the Lords for a meeting with Denis Carter. He is Labour's only farmer and was previously agricultural spokesman; he gives me some good steers. He is clearly enjoying being at the centre of things as chief whip, dealing with No. 10 etc. I feel very much at the margin.

I moved into my new Lords ministerial office, alongside Patricia Hollis and Helene Hayman. Certainly lighter and less cramped than the previous one. Had lunch at the Lords, hoping to gossip with a few colleagues, but nobody was there. They are all down their ministerial rabbit holes. In the afternoon had introduction meetings with three more departmental officials. From the diary it seems these meetings stretch on forever.

My MAFF office is not very impressive: narrow and pokey, with dreary modern furniture and a big table filling most of the centre. Painted off-white, with off-white curtains and shabby doors, one into my private office and one direct into the outside corridor. Certainly no trappings of power here.

The outer office is small, with three people crammed into it – a secretary who cannot take shorthand, so I never use her; Barbara, who handles my diary; and Peter Grimley, my private secretary. The last has a PhD and until recently was working in a MAFF agency at Tolworth. He is quite cheerful and positive, probably because he was away from Whitehall during the recent BSE storms, which clearly demoralised the central department. Once I heard him say over the phone: 'He {me} clearly finds being a PUS {Parliamentary Under Secretary} here a lot different from running the Policy Unit in No. 10.' Quite true. It's like shopping at Tesco after a lifetime at Harrods.

Also interesting to see from the Cabinet minutes the degree of central control from Downing Street. Ministers have to clear most initiatives and all speeches. Jack resents this but no minister (except Gordon Brown) is independent enough to resist it.

Tuesday 13 May 1997

Another string of introductions to grade 3 and grade 5 officials, so they all begin to merge. In between I hand write dozens of letters in reply to congratulations. Nobody has dared to say condolences outright, but it's often between the lines. I still feel bereft of arts and sports, and find it difficult to read all the papers on animal diseases or grain support prices with enthusiasm. Privately decide to give it a year and then to pull out quietly. At least I don't disagree with any of the main New Labour policies. Never in the past 40 years have I agreed with so many of the party policies.

I took Helen Liddell to lunch at the Lords. Collected her from the Treasury and visited her room. Have always loved the Treasury with its long curving corridors and all those quality officials. Helen has two stunning rooms. Her office is four times as big as mine with an imposing desk. Next door she has an ante-room, which had been tarted up by her predecessor, Anthony Nelson, like a brothel boudoir. Helen, who is Scottish Cromwellian, will soon eliminate that. We had great difficulty finding our way out, but it took me back 20 years walking along those Treasury corridors and down the great staircase. Terrible they are thinking of selling it off.

She was in good form. Joe Haines had written congratulating her, which was a relief, as they had fallen out and I am keen to get them together again. I spent much of lunch telling her of my schemes to raise more revenue from gambling and especially gaming machines, and we agreed to take that forward.

I returned for a meeting with the British Retail Consortium. Jack was looking much better after his visit to Brussels. He did well and this gave him confidence. He seems to have come through a barrier of doubt. Afterwards I saw the Permanent Secretary, Richard Packer, to discuss my investment portfolio, which has three food or horticulture shares and I don't want any sleaze questions. Packer sounds South London rather than Whitehall Mandarin, but he is sharp.

At 6.30 pm I walked down Whitehall and into Downing Street for the No. 10 eve of Queen's speech party for junior ministers. They set this up after I reminded Alastair Campbell and Donald Dewar, but I imagine others reminded them as well. It was a lovely feeling going back in through the big black front door. Only the second time since leaving with Jim Callaghan 18 years ago.

I deliberately walked slowly through the lobby and along the corridor. As I turned to go upstairs, Tony Blair emerged and walked up with me. He apologised for what he called 'my cock-up' over offering the job first to Brian Donohoe rather than me. He said he simply asked for B Donoughue and forgot about Brian. He clearly doesn't know Labour MPs very well, as Harold Wilson always did. I decided not to ask whether it was true that he first offered to Brian the higher status of minister of state originally intended for me; and that when he finally got round to me all the limited number of offices of ministers of state had gone. But I did address him as Prime Minister, ignoring his trendy appeal that ministers 'call me Tony'. I said, 'I've used the formal approach too long and too often to adjust now.' I told him about our party's tradition of slamming the doors shut and the PM reading the speech, but he said he didn't want to read it. 'I have seen enough of it already', he said.

Inside the crowded White Sitting Room it was bubbling with excitement and I circulated, having chats with lots of people. Had a long talk with Jonathan Powell about Ireland. Explained our plans for an administrative assembly and confirmed that I could send him papers direct from the Unionist side. He was very interested and indicated that Tony was keen to take an Irish initiative. I said that if he could make a success of the present peace talks, fine, but if they ran into the sand then our more radical approach to a new peace settlement gave the PM a fresh initiative. That it was most important not to let the IRA regain the initiative. I spoke similarly with Mo Mowlam, who encouraged me to keep involved. She thanked me for my flowers in the campaign and gave me a kiss. But she didn't look well and sat on a settee in the corner most of the time.

Discussed racing and the Tote with George Howarth at the Home Office. He told me that racing people had pressed for me as chairman, but that Jack Straw felt it wasn't possible to start off by appointing a Labour minister to a top job. He indicated they were favouring Guy Watkins or Maurice Lindsay. Had nice chat with Derek Scott, who was in the Treasury with Healey in the 1970s, drifted into the wilderness with the SDP and is now back in No. 10 as

Blair's economic adviser. Promised Peter Mandelson to send him a signed copy of my biography of his grandfather, Herbert Morrison.

Had a long chat with Chris Smith who was idyllically happy at DNH. I reminded him about honours and spoke up for Melvyn Bragg, Graham Greene and Clive Priestley, all of whom would have been honoured if Jack and I were still there. I told him straight that I was suffering withdrawal symptoms and was not enjoying Agriculture too much. He is sympathetic. He will do the job well and the arts world is delighted that it has him and not (unfairly) Jack. I wish I were with him.

Also a long talk with Cabinet Secretary Robin Butler. He has invited me to a dinner with him 'so we can chat privately', but it clashes with the Aga Khan wedding party. We discussed the plight of the Agriculture department. I told him we must have a revamp including changes at the top. He agreed, saying that Packer had a bunker mentality and had cut off from the rest of Whitehall. He said he would move him out and put someone fresh in the moment he could arrange 'a Whitehall reshuffle'.

David Miliband seemed a bit sad not to be fully running the Policy Unit; Jonathan Powell told me they were going to get an outside heavyweight to run it, with David below him.

So it was a really fascinating evening. Blair made a brief and good speech. For the rest we all chatted and networked. The years slipped away and I felt renewed vigour.

Wednesday 14 May 1997

Very bleary into the office for the ministerial meeting, where we had a long agenda. I saw through my disbanding of the regional advisory councils. Then the other ministers went down to the Palace of Westminster for the State Opening. Curiously I, who had the right to be in there in my ermine drag, hadn't arranged anything. So I watched it on my office TV while clearing a mass of papers. At noon I walked down Whitehall. The Queen was just returning in her splendid coach to the Palace. It was a lovely sight in the brilliant sunshine.

Sarah was waiting for me at the Lords and we went to Derry Irvine's Opening of Parliament party in his Lord Chancellor's grand apartment. I would settle for one of his several bathrooms in place of my dingy office. It was a good party. Traditionally, only the judges are invited, but Derry had opened it to his Lords colleagues, which was a good starting move. I talked a lot to Tessa Blackstone about the Covent Garden crisis and to Alf Dubbs about Northern Ireland, where he is parliamentary secretary. Agree to work closely.

In particular, the Europeans have indicated they will lift the beef BSE ban for Northern Ireland, because the situation is much better there. But the Scots – Dewar, Cook and Brown – have all intervened to stop it because it would upset the Scots not to be included. The Scottish mafia is clearly very powerful and very insular. We desperately need to get the ban breached.

Had a terrific lunch on the terrace. The marquee was full of friends and colleagues – some, like Maurice Peston, rightly sad at being excluded from office. My sons Stephen and Paul came together with Sarah's brother Charles. Terrific atmosphere of exhilaration and feeling that Blair and the team have made a brilliant transition into power. Even Tories like Sarah say there is a new atmosphere in the country.

Sit in the chamber for the opening speeches after hearing the Queen's speech then at 5.30 pm attended a reception by Ivor Richard for his new front bench. Not everyone seemed to be there and a low-key atmosphere. People are focusing on their jobs – and not sure Ivor will be there much longer. Had a slight altercation with Andrew McIntosh who told me that *Private Eye* was the best source for advice on agricultural matters. It might be on sewage, but I said it lied too much for my taste and I hadn't read it since Harry Evans and I successfully sued it on 14 counts of libellous lying.

Thursday 15 May 1997

Had another string of introductions with officials and then went to the DTI for a ministerial meeting on competitiveness in Europe. I was irritated at not receiving my briefing until just before the meeting but managed to make my points. I said that agriculture was an area where the common policy was complete but with zero concern for competitiveness, and that was why I had the job of renegotiating the CAP, but I didn't expect to achieve that in the first two weeks.

The first meeting of our front bench ministers. Quite different attendance from the front bench compared to before the election, with all the casualties absent. In Ivor's magnificent Leader's room. Quite muted since we all have a light programme for the next three weeks. Then the Bills will start arriving. Not to me fortunately, but I will have to sit there late at night. Sarah won't like that. Nor will I. So I begin to focus on a 12-month departure target.

Big ministerial meeting, being briefed ahead of the Agricultural Council. Very interesting and well done. Afterwards, I was irritated to learn of a vile piece in *Private Eye* attacking my appointment and describing me as a 'flea-ridden fat cat'. Par for the course from the gutter sewage men there. This may be by the abominable Porkie Bower. I don't bother to read it.

Apparently there have been no follow-up phone calls. People know that much of the *Eye* is malicious lies.

More meetings with faceless officials, cleared masses of paper and wrote lots of letters, then staggered out to drive down late to the country.

Friday 16 May 1997

Worked all morning on the red boxes. Then to Newbury races for a lovely relaxed afternoon. Our horse Referendum came second. Back home to find another red box had arrived.

Saturday 17 May 1997

Finished off the red boxes just before dinner. Am feeling a bit stronger and more on top of the subject.

Sunday 18 May 1997

Finish reading the papers. In general feel better than last week. Especially since I have decided not to stick this too long. I miss my freedom.

Monday 19 May 1997

Driver Maggie arrived to collect me and take me to London. Quite a luxury being able to read the newspapers in the car. But not as comfortable as my dear old Toyota Supra: a small clapped out Vauxhall, no air conditioning and I cannot listen to classical music. These are the 'chauffered ministerial limousines' the journalists bleat about. Still, mustn't complain.

A big seminar briefing for all ministers on CAP reform. Well done (I had originally suggested this to officials), but not encouraging. The fact is that our farming interests and the continental farming interest almost never coincide. The protective, inefficient status quo of subsidising over-production suits them fine. Some countries see the rationale of our arguments for a more efficient market-oriented agriculture, but they have no incentive to fight the French vested interests in seeking it. The farmers across the channel have too many votes. Also the continental mentality is not interested in providing a competitive service or product, as we see on the airlines. They prefer high price, cosy monopolies. Also the main victim paymaster is Germany, which is content to suffer it as part of the original deal with France: leave the CAP untouched and France will follow Germany in everything else. The old 1940–44 alliance between Vichy France and the Nazi New Order effectively remains in place. While Germany blocks reform (its coalition with the agrarian SDP also makes it difficult for Chancellor Kohl to act even if he wanted to), then there is little hope of us achieving reform. Our only hope is that external forces – especially European enlargement and the World Trade and GATT negotiations – will force them to reform. The nightmare scenario is that the EU will enlarge with the east European countries without reforming the CAP. Then the cost to us would be horrendous and we might have to consider pulling out. Still I remain basically a cultural European, providing we pursue our interests in Brussels positively and without the whinging of the previous government, who always threatened and then capitulated.

Straight to a meeting with the Meat and Livestock Commission, which was very lively but basically fighting the case of more subsidies for our stricken beef industry. BSE has already cost us nearly £2 billion. There is a tough time ahead. The Treasury has written saying we must cut the payments to farmers. Jack and I agree. But that means unhappy constituents for us in MAFF. Under the Tories the ministers were all farmers and they made sure the farmers were paid well regardless.

Interesting episode with the Chelsea flower show. At the last moment they reluctantly invited me as minister for horticulture to go there on Thursday evening, a second division occasion. The important people get invited today on the Monday opening day. But I cannot go on Thursday, so I declined and suggested today. They rushed me a ticket for the gala charity tonight, saying how unprecedented it was for anyone to have a free ticket to that (I didn't ask for that, just the Monday preview). So I quickly declined, saying I didn't want any special privileges and sent them £50 for the charity. Now as horticulture minister I don't get there! Have gone privately for years. (Later in the week there was a typical snide piece in the *Telegraph* criticising me for not bothering to attend the show.) Worked in the office till after 8.00 pm trying to clear papers.

Tuesday 20 May 1997

Went early to the government art collection in Soho to pick some pictures for my walls. I was offered a poor lot. No flowers at all or nice landscapes. Emphasised my decline in status. In No. 10 I had Constable and Gainsborough.

Spent rest of morning preparing for tomorrow's Lords question on BSE. Did a video link with officials outside London. Struck by how defensive they are. A lot of advice not to 'attack the previous government' because our policies are 'the same'. In fact they are not. We are accelerating the cull of endangered cattle. They really mean don't attack them.

Had lunch at Lords with Ralph Lucas, the previous spokesman (not minister) in the Lords. He is very knowledgeable and helpful. Said the department is demoralised and Permanent Secretary Packer must be moved. Also said they have covered up a lot. We must publish all our research and scrutinise the vast expenditures administered locally. I went straight back and wrote memos to Jack on this.

An interesting Cabinet committee on devolution, mainly establishing the basis for Scottish devolution. Dominated by Derry Irvine from the chair and Donald Dewar as Scottish secretary. At the end of the meeting Jack Straw took me on one side and spoke about hunting. He is trying to slow down or avoid the ban. Said I must tell Jack to 'corral Elliot Morley'. Actually Jack is doing very well so far; much more impressive than expected. Donald Dewar also spoke to me about the appalling relations between MAFF and the Scottish office. Apparently at one point Packer instructed MAFF officials not even to talk to the Scots officials over fishing. Ludicrous. We agree to try to put that right.

Stayed late at the office clearing huge piles of papers and getting even more tired. But had to be in the Lords for a good wind-up by Helene Hayman, nearly falling asleep on the front bench.

Wednesday 21 May 1997

Early to weekly team meeting in Jeff Rooker's room. Jeff is terrific. Strong Brummie accent, and very quick, funny and energetic. He has cleverly been exploring the other MAFF buildings and found some desirable ones in Smith Square – been hidden from us because excellent and now occupied in great comfort by officials. Real *Yes Minister* stuff. Jeff, inexperienced, asked the officials to explore this possible move. I told him this simply alerted them to block the move. Should have agreed it among us ministers first and then instructed them to execute it. After many years the officials have managed to manoeuvre the ministers into miserable small rooms and to grab all the best rooms for themselves. Unstitching this will be straight Sir Humphrey/Hacker stuff. As previously the senior adviser to Jonathan Lynn and Antony Jay on *Yes, Prime Minister*, my money must be on them defeating us.

Had a briefing meeting with David Naish of the National Farmers Union and his team on why the farmers must be given even more compensation. The NFU come in here every week as if they own MAFF. Which in the past they have done. Some farmers are receiving over a million pounds a year in compensation (the biggest is embarrassingly Labour's ally the COOP, with over £2 million). Yet they always want more. When sterling strengthens they want compensation. When it falls there is no question of clawback. But Naish is quite impressive and I watch them with exhausted amusement.

Lunch at the Lords and then my Question. Asked by Woodrow Wyatt, with kind references to me, about BSE being hidden on the Continent and imported here. Some truth in that. Several countries have it but bury the cattle without reporting it. I can see all those Tory farmers opposite sitting waiting to pounce if I flounder in these unfamiliar waters. So having done a lot of homework on it, I decide to answer without referring to my thick folder (anyway I don't know how you speedily find the right page and answer in the two seconds available for answer). So without notes I responded to a number of very shrewd questions and tried to make them laugh. I said our policy was to get closer to our European allies and referred to this morning's newspaper photo of Jack with his arm around Italian Commissioner Bonino.

My one difficulty was a question from Radnor, who I couldn't quite hear asking something about the number of cases of proven CJD [Creutzfeldt Jakob disease]. I said I had the number 16 in my mind but would write to him. My officials were agitated afterwards because the 16 referred to new strain CJD and nothing was proven. I suggested to my private secretary a clarification to Hansard, which he was unhappy with but did. Afterwards I felt it was risky to tamper with Hansard and won't do that again, even though they do often do clarifications. When I reported it to Jack, he said they do it all the time in the Commons. Still I felt pleased to have survived my first questions and several Tory peers congratulated me on having done it without notes. Jim Callaghan was more perceptive. He passed me a note on the front bench saying, 'Bernard. Congratulations! Never has such a thin veneer of knowledge been deployed with such panache and conviction!' Spot on. I will keep that note for the memoirs. But he is right. Even worse, I have no feel for it. Reinforces my feeling that I should get out as soon as possible. Some day the veneer will crack and my ignorance will be exposed.

After that swam against the ever incoming tide of paper. Then went into the Lords again to support Margaret Jay doing an excellent wind up to the whole Queen's speech – note how the ladies are being given the prime roles in the Chamber. I admire all of them.

Also depressed because friends have phoned to say that shoddy Tom Bower of *Private Eye* has been in touch with them about a profile he is doing of me. His broad approach apparently is to ask why on earth am I in the government and what corrupt hold do I have over Blair. Both Tom Macnally and George Jones said that when they started to say something in my defence he lost interest and put the phone down. He is also quizzing old colleagues at Grieveson Grant. Wants to do a hatchet job. Could do without this. Is like having a sewage rat chewing at one's ankles. Perhaps can get him dealt with under MAFF's pesticide regulations or the arrangements to dispose of infested sewage.

Thursday 22 May 1997

Highlight an excellent ministerial meeting on 'alcopops', the alcohol drinks cynically marketed towards children, the market for which has boomed by 500% in the past three years. At the Home Office where George Howarth is in the chair. He and Jack Straw are proposing draconian action. Strongly supported by Tessa Jowell from Health – nice to sit next to her in a Cabinet committee after 20 years of friendship. I am asked by officials to say something in defence of the drinks industry because MAFF sponsor it. I made it clear I supported the Home Office in their actions. George looked very pleased. After the meeting he asked me to stay behind and we discussed appointments. On the Levy Board he asked me to think of a new director, since everybody put up by the department was ex-Eton and Army. I suggest my LSE friend David Metcalf.

To Heathrow to join Sarah and fly to Barcelona. It was nearly 2.00 in the morning before we got into France and to Ceret. Quite a relief. Am tired and tense and ever more committed to a quiet exit – perhaps as early as August. No satisfaction in doing something about which one is ignorant.

Additionally, I had woken at 5.00 this morning very worried about the job and my press coverage. I walked early through St James's Park to the office and immediately saw Jack and discussed it with him. He was very good, quite relaxed. 'Don't worry. Ignore the press. I never read them. They're all reptiles. I won't take any notice of anything they say about you because I've experienced enough lies from them myself. It's now like water off a duck's back to me.' I asked him how he was enjoying the job, admitting my doubts. He agreed, saying, 'I wake up in the morning saying, "Is this how it all ends?"'

Jeff Rooker told me yesterday he had a private meeting with Elliot Morley to discuss the badger problem. Two hours later his private secretary produced eight officials to hold an unscheduled meeting with him telling him why what he and Elliot had privately agreed was wrong. He is deep into Sir Humphrey country. But these are not as clever as Humphrey and we can outwit them sometimes. Not too often though.

Friday 23 June–Thursday 29 June 1997 (France)

I spent too much time dealing with architects, builders and insurers about the Mas au Rocher swimming pool. The whole huge platform is cracked, has slipped several inches down the mountain side and is poised to fall on my neighbours far below. In Catalonia nobody takes the blame and nobody pays – except me.

When possible I read, finishing the Angus Calder collection of essays on World War II.

Returned Thursday via Barcelona. Maggie collected me, handing over a huge box stuffed to the brim. I read the papers in the car and in the office till after 8.00 in the evening. Had quick supper then opened vast pile of letters. There is no end to this tidal wave of paper. But, curiously, I begin to feel better about the job, more interested and more on top.

Friday 30 May 1997

Wake early and kill off some more from the red box. Clive Hollick phoned me yesterday for a chat and was very encouraging. Must see him regularly. He is special adviser to Margaret Beckett at DTI, which he'll do well. We both agree that Margaret is a very safe pair of hands.

Off to a lovely nostalgic lunch with Harold Evans. He's been helping Labour by raising money with the ex-pats in the USA. Personally spent $15,000 on entertaining and hosted parties for Prescott and Brown. He has been giving lectures on the press. Says it has become appalling in the USA. He acknowledges that what he proudly personally started as fine investigative journalism with Insight at the *Sunday Times* has been hijacked and distorted by a bunch of yobbos who use it to exorcise their dark obsessions and attack anyone who is successful. It's very sad for him as probably the greatest post-war British editor. I was sad to say goodbye and hope he finds a way to return.

Maggie picked me up and we drove in the heat to the country. I sat on the grass and finished my latest red box, also the pile of letters waiting for me here. I'm much happier about the job. Curious how that's changed. Just feel more positive. But endless work ahead.

Saturday 31 May 1997

Jeremy Taylor collected me and we drove to Lingfield to watch Referendum in a big race and our Cherry Blossom in a smaller one. Lovely day and many friends from the syndicate there including Joe Haines and wife Rene.

Everything was going well. Chose the first winner. Then disaster. Cherry Blossom had led for most of her race, then she stumbled and staggered with a broken shoulder. Had to be put down on the course. I couldn't watch. Finally Referendum ran appallingly and came last. Joe Haines, Rene, Jeremy and I were so gloomy we all went home before the next race.

Sunday 1 June 1997

Lunch party. Jeanie Carnarvon sat on my right and Terry Wogan's wife Helen on the left. In the middle were William Huntingdon, the Queen's trainer, and Jeremy Deedes from the *Telegraph* and the Tote. Terry Wogan held court funnily. We sat outside looking over the garden and the ponds.

Monday 2 June 1997

Another meeting with Naish, President of the NFU. These threaten to become daily and I wonder if he gives MAFF as his office address. Also sent a letter to *The Times* correcting its inaccurate statement today that the Policy Unit always had half career civil servants – I never had any. (Cleared it with No. 10. New Centralised Labour!) Then faxed David Montgomery with my suggested changes to David Trimble's policy document; focusing it more as a positive response to Blair's recent excellent Belfast speech on Ulster. I've now written about a third of the Unionist statement and amended some of the rest. The Jesuits would approve!

The meeting with Naish went well. He's always pressing the farmers' vested interests, but that is his job. He wants more compensation for the beef farmers hit by BSE and also for the rise in sterling (they are silent when it goes down). Afterwards, worked on papers, clearing another huge pile. I sent another note enquiring about the unemployment consequences of banning hunting. Also pressed for some movement on changing rabies quarantine, particularly for dogs returning from abroad. Hope changing that will be my main legacy. Certainly will give Sarah the greatest pleasure.

Tuesday 3 June 1997

Maggie collected me at 7.20 am to drive me to Kings Cross to take a train to visit the Harrogate Food Exhibition. Before lunch I gave the prize for the winning national sausage of the year. At lunch I was photographed eating the winning sample – and by late afternoon was feeling very queasy and burping impressively. But that is the price ministers pay. I dare not turn down the offer of any British meat or they will accuse me of betrayal.

On the train back I worked on tonight's speech at the Savoy and also grabbed half an hour's sleep. Dashed into the office to sign some emergency orders and letters, then home to change and take some stomach medicine to avoid emergencies in that department. Then driven to a Savoy working dinner with the food industry. A good discussion and I learned a lot.

Wednesday 4 June 1997

Excellent ministerial prayers meeting. I had put several items on the agenda and also asked for minutes to be kept so we could follow up decisions. (Officials don't want that since they believe they, not ministers, take decisions.) Jack was in fine form moving business along. He is really doing the job well, much better than at DNH. This has more politics and that suits him. On dog rabies, Jeff Rooker was reluctant to look at reforms but I pushed him, pointing out that in the election Labour had been sympathetic (as they had been to everything raised by every single issue interest group). Also agreement to my proposal to publish all MAFF research.

But most important was the report from our advisory group SEAC saying that we must take BSE measures on sheep, cutting out the spinal cord and spleen, killing all showing signs of disease (more compensation) and discussing applying our beef controls to imports. This is not quite the 'beef ban' on our EU partners that the media present it as; but it may work out like that. We cannot 'ban' them under EU law. But if we apply strict controls it will cost them a lot and end up similar.

Also discussed important question whether to hold a formal, even judicial enquiry into the BSE crisis. All us ministers want to do it, since nobody understands the history. But officials don't want us to know that. Their one good argument is that a big enquiry would hold everything up. The EU will say it won't lift the beef ban until the enquiry reports. Obviously, officials don't want past failings to be exposed. We want it all out in public, including the disastrous Tory handling, but we don't want another Scott Arms to Iraq Report chaos. So it's difficult. A Commons Select Committee might be the best answer.

Afterwards Jack went to visit our prospective new rooms in Smith Square. He is slowly realising that this present building and the ministers' rooms are quite unsuitable for receiving visiting ministers during our imminent EU presidency. Jeff Rooker has discovered civil servants working in great splendour in Smith Square. The department predictably feels it would be unnecessarily disruptive and expensive to move the officials into less palatial accommodation!

I went to a meeting of the presidential task force in the Foreign Office's great Locarno Room. It's 150 feet long and 60 feet high. The table was 40 feet. Foreign Secretary Robin Cook looked even more than usually small and elfish in the chair. He gave a good introduction, but when he said that Britain mustn't use the presidency to over-press our British interests, Mandelson rightly intervened to say we mustn't under-play them either.

I said that MAFF was deeply involved, with over 80% of its work EU-related. Cook ticked me off gently for calling him Foreign Secretary, saying, 'You've known me long enough, Bernard, to call me Robin.' He said that MAFF must be more food and consumer orientated. I replied we were changing MAFF accordingly.

Mandelson then gave an excellent presentation on how we as a government should 'sell' our presidency. He said we must celebrate it, not be timid. Must seek a 'Labour vision for Europe'. Must recreate popular support for Europe and boost UK's standing in Europe, changing the perceptions of the British people of EU and EU of Britain. For this immense task he had a 'communications strategy': We should 'lead in Europe'; change the EU to be 'for the people', more accountable; modernise Europe, so more efficient and less wasteful; present our 'Vision'; use Presidency to spell out New Labour's way; reject Thatcher hostility; reject European corporatism and protectionism. We have a third way – 'flexible, competitive and socially cohesive'. Apply new Labour's domestic philosophy to Europe. Will only change British public's view if we change Europe. He concluded, as if still in the election campaign, 'New Labour, New Europe'.

Robin Cook looked askance, as if a crude election poster had been unveiled at his stately Cabinet committee. It was a bit self-consciously Saatchi and Saatchi, and I knew it was not my political world. But Mandelson did it well.

Afterwards, coming down the great staircase, I pointed out to Peter that among the busts of former Foreign Secretaries there was none of his grandfather Herbert Morrison. He said that Herbert wouldn't have wanted one, not liking the Foreign Office. Perhaps he has read the chapter in mine and George Jones' biography showing how badly they treated him. We walked up Whitehall together and he said he was getting copies of more letters from Jack than anyone else. I said that Jack was being very active and that although he had a reputation for being laid back, even idle, that was not true now. 'That was his reputation', he said, rather ominously, so I was glad I had put in a word on the right side. We also discussed the Agriculture Ministry and he was aware of the need for radical changes, but said that they (the PM and him) were not sure they wanted consumers on the MAFF advisory committees.

That's the private office network in Whitehall mobilising opposition to Jack's plans to have more consumers involved. I later told Jack and we decided to be even more insistent on doing it.

Mandelson's style is very prim, with measured words, offered with the authority of knowing he can get the PM's backing. His body language is balletic. But he is clearly shrewd, intelligent and very clear, so I respect him and can see why the PM uses him. But it's the new political world of PR, of image and presentation, with which I am out of touch and out of sympathy.

Back for an interesting meeting with the Northern Ireland politicians on BSE. David Trimble, Ian Paisley, John Hume, etc. They have been hit hardest since so much of their economy depends on farming. They 'want the beef ban lifted first for Northern Ireland, and not held up by the rest of the UK'. Jack handled that carefully, knowing the Scottish opposition in Cabinet to letting the Irish have first bite at their markets. But Ulster meat is cleaner, with less BSE and better animal records. It was the first time I'd met Trimble. Going into the conference room with him I said, 'I am a friend of David Montgomery', and his eyebrows shot up. I think he made the link. In the meeting, I lip-read him saying to his Ulster Unionist partner, 'That is David Montgomery's friend.'

Spoke to Jonathan Powell at No. 10 about our policy statement for Northern Ireland (I had done more amendments to the Trimble document and targeted it more on Blair's recent Belfast speech, which Trimble accepted without changing a word). I have now written about a third of the document! Agreed to deliver it to No. 10 late tomorrow, after Cabinet etc. so the PM can have it for his weekend box.

Thursday 5 June 1997

Disastrous start. Got up at 7.00 am to do my covering letter to Blair re. Ireland. Took hours to get it right. But when I tried to print it my computer crashed. Couldn't save it or print it, so finally switched off. Three hours' work lost and I still have to fit it in to today's heavy programme!

Then our regular front bench ministers meeting. Straight from there home to change for my Buckingham Palace audition to shake hands with the Queen. There were a couple of dozen other ministers, including the clown Tony Banks, trying to appear to disapprove of it all but unable to hide how much he enjoyed it. I chatted with Mark Fisher, Graham Allen and the Queen's Secretary Robert Fellowes, and waited at the back of the queue. This meant I had longer with HM, since there was no one else waiting to come forward.

She said how important she thought Agriculture was. We discussed racing and next Saturday's Derby, not knowing who could beat the favourite. Then she told me how pleased she was with a present 'from Arnold' (Weinstock): a TV set on which she can watch racing from France. She thought the French Derby winner looked very good – I told her how Henry Carnarvon (who she affectionately calls 'Porchy') and William Huntingdon had left our Sunday's lunch table to watch it. Also discussed the Irish election; she said Bruton was an 'above average Irish PM', clearly implying the average was pretty low. Her secretaries told me she had been impressed by Labour's efficient start in government. We had tea – us in very large cups, she in a small one – and then returned to the office.

Finished my Blair letter on an ancient office portable typewriter. I went over to No. 10 and handed it in 'for Jonathan Powell's eyes only'. Now we wait and see.

I cleared a huge pile of papers and finally went home to the country. Feeling very tired but now enjoying it much more.

Friday 6 June 1997

Heavy day, reading two huge red boxes, the second arriving mid-afternoon with Maggie before the first was finished. Most testing – but interesting – were three huge papers, one on BSE, one on sheep scrapie, one on reforming CAP. I learn a lot but am knackered by the final page.

Saturday 7 June 1997

Wonderful day at the Derby. In the big Derby suite just after noon. Chatted with loads of racing friends. A real celebration. Also chatted to Peter Savill, a welcome new broom at the British Horseracing Board. Also with us was ex Home Secretary Michael Howard. He is always friendly to me, and not the ogre our party sees.

Sunday 8 June 1997

Nice mass. Father Flanagan quoted his favourite Oscar Wilde: 'Every saint has a past and every sinner has a future – so there is hope for us all yet.' Read the papers and then bashed out this diary. Later George helped me save it on to a floppy disc. Am even more wary of these machines after Thursday's disaster with the Ulster letter to Blair. Am much more cheerful as I get on top of this agricultural stuff and enjoy the politics of it more each day.

Monday 9 June 1997

Maggie drove me up in the morning to a meeting of officials who briefed Jack and me on the problem of organophosphates (OPs) and sheep dips. Dreadful complacency. A lot of people have been ill, including the campaigning Countess of Mar in the Lords, but the officials seem quite unconcerned. Convinced their previous line was fine, even though various Tory ministers twisted in the wind on it. At the end I exploded and said it would not do. Jack was measured as always but severe. I have a debate in a week and want a more positive approach.

Barely had time for a sandwich at my desk before a briefing meeting with Professor Krebs, who is doing a study of the problem of badgers giving TB to cows. It went well, much better than this morning, when again you saw the problem with a department completely shell-shocked from its previous failures and concerned only with defensively trying to cover up the past.

Jack told me he is nearly convinced we must change our offices to another building and this week is doing a tour of Smith Square, where officials sit in splendour sending defensive briefs to ministers in our dreary offices.

My debate on the EU tobacco regime went very well. The tobacco regime is a scandal. The EU CAP pays more money subsidy per acre than for any other commodity, to produce dreadful tobacco, which nobody in Europe smokes. Just poisons the third world. When I raised with officials that we should oppose it on health grounds as smoking causes cancer, one said that would not wash since 'nobody smokes it anyway'. He meant no Europeans smoke it.

I had sent back my departmental briefing on organophosphates (OPs) as being hopeless: no numbers as usual and no attempt to respond to the Select Committee report (because they have contempt for parliament). This caused a fuss and I hope spoilt their lunches. I rewrote the speech and used less than half of the original. Later Cathy McGlynn, Jack's special adviser, told me this had impressed the parliamentary unit upstairs, who knew that the Lords debates are always of a high standard. My original departmental draft cannot have taken the official more than 10 minutes and was just a rehash of previous statements of the department's general position.

I felt elated afterwards from being told how well the debate went. Opened dozens of letters then bed.

Tuesday 10 June 1997

Really enjoying it now. Attended ministerial meeting on European agricultural policy reform, where we are not as optimistic in private as we pretend to be in public. On nearly every CAP issue, the Continentals have a different interest from ours, and only the odd Scandinavian shares our approach. It will be a long haul and only the external pressures of world trade negotiations will force the French and Germans to shift.

All our briefs and speeches say that the enlargement of the EU eastwards will also force a change. But, in the meeting, Permanent Secretary Packer simply dismisses that with contempt. Afterwards I dictate a note to him saying if he is right he must stop his officials from briefing us that enlargement will bring a change. Don't expect a reply. Have noticed that often there is no reply to questions I ask him.

Had lunch with my Tory predecessor, Tim Boswell. He is a fellow Northamptonian so is very helpful on a number of issues. Thinks I have the best of the private offices – and that Packer is too arrogant and contemptuous of all politicians. 'It's OK for civil servants to think that all ministers are idiots, but there is no need to push this view into their faces all the time.'

Worked in the office all afternoon and then went to the Racing and Bloodstock committee – want to keep my foot in the racing world.

Wednesday 11 June 1997

Early 8.00 am ministerial prayers meeting. Then Denis Carter dropped by for a political chatter. He is enjoying it, but wondering whether he should have rescued Andrew McIntosh and made him deputy whip after Blair dropped him. Finding Andrew full of posturing attitudes based on sixties *Guardian* leftism.

Took the train to Huntingdon for my first visit to an agricultural show, Cereals 97. Took three officials, toured the show and made a speech to the press afterwards. Slept a bit on the train back. Then straight into the back-bench Committee on Agriculture where Jack gave a superb performance. Very technical questions, which he answered with detailed knowledge and political skill.

Around the corner to a B SKY B party. Not that I support Murdoch, but it's nice to keep in touch with the media sector. Lots of politicos there. Chatted with Stephen Sherbourne, a political advisor to Major. We agree it's a mistake for Blair to abandon using the No. 10 study, which Wilson, Callaghan and Thatcher always used.

Thursday 12 June 1997

Walked down to the Treasury to see Helen Liddell on my proposals to raise more tax from gambling – and use a little of it to ease the burden on racing! Helen picked it up quickly, though she said she's beginning to feel very tired.

Actually Dawn Primarolo is responsible for tax, but I don't know her or trust her as an old Bennite. Helen says Dawn 'is sinking without trace. She needs a protector.' I would love Helen's Treasury job.

Dashed off to the Lords for a quick lunch with Tessa Blackstone. She asks if I will help her on her Education Bills. Tricky. It's a great honour and would help me at the next stage if I wanted to shift from Agriculture (especially if Tessa moves up to be leader). But it will add to my burden even more. I show interest but say her boss Blunkett must clear it with Jack – who may not be too keen.

In the grill bar I was interrupted by telephone to tell me that I have an emergency statement on BSE this afternoon so I dashed back to the office for an urgent briefing on the EU vets' rejection of our request to have herds which are certified free of BSE exempt from the export ban. It's a setback. Back in the Lords my statement went very well. Nice compliments from Mark Schreiber and David Stoddard. Each pointed out that the BSE epidemic never actually happened and that over £3 billion had been spent on the panic reaction. I was cautious in reply, pointing out that there have been 18 new CJD deaths this year. But I didn't say there are that many more deaths from diabetes every week and we spend only £10 million a year on research there.

But, above all, I really enjoyed it. Felt on top of the material and was again able to answer all the questions without referring to the briefs in my folder. Denis Carter smiled and whispered, 'I will find a question where you do have to refer to your damned folder.'

Dashed home to change for the great ball at Claridges for Zahra Aga Khan who gets married next weekend. This was given by her mother Sally. Her wedding will be given by her father K. He won't be here for tonight's ball and Sally won't be there for the wedding. Sasha is perhaps Zahra's closest friend and Sarah was a teenage friend of K and of his brother Amyn.

I was tired now the earlier adrenaline had subsided, but talked a lot with Max and Jane Rayne and ate lots of wonderful food. We toured the ballroom, barely able to talk for the big band, and met a lot of Sarah's old friends. I envy her that she regularly sees so many people she has known since she was a child. My only two adult friends who I knew from my childhood – brother Clem and Gerry Fowler – both died in their 50s. My friends go back only to my time at Oxford, and I don't see enough of them.

Had nice long chat with Lady Iveagh, Guinness billionairess, who told me she is just moving back from Ireland to here. So much for the Tory scares that people would emigrate under Labour. Dazzling Joan Collins was also there, looking remarkable for her uncertain age. Colin Ingleby-Mackenzie arrived late with Sarah's sister, Susan. She looked around for two minutes at the tables of glitterati and quickly concluded that it might not be the ideal place for her.

It was a remarkable occasion, really one of the parties of the year. But I didn't enjoy it all that much because too many minor celebrities were present for my taste. (Major celebrities would have been worse.)

We drove home to Shurlock Row in the early hours. Wanted to wake up in the country. Worth doing that however late one arrives. In the car remembered I had promised photographer Geoffrey Shackley to go and sit with Princess Margaret, who doesn't like being abandoned and yet does little to encourage her companions. I forgot. I'm sure she won't mind.

Friday 13 June 1997

An ominous date, but a very nice day. Andrew Parker Bowles (whose ex-wife, courtesan of the heir to the throne, had a car crash last night and is being hounded by the media) rang before I woke to invite me to Sandown. We have a horse – Prime Minister – having its first run there, so delighted to go.

Then home to work through my big red box till nearly 9.00 pm.

Saturday 14 June 1997

Read the dull newspapers in the morning, then caught up on this diary. More red box in the evening preparing for a tricky PQ on Monday.

Monday 16 June 1997

Up for morning briefing for this afternoon's question on BSE. Felt more at ease now I know the details. Kate came in to hear the question, then we dashed off to take a train to Brighton to see my new grandson, Rachel's Ben. Paid first class to get a comfy seat, but there was no first class carriage. That's privatisation for you. The carriage was filthy, the floor and seats covered with old newspapers and food wrappings. The English are a scruffy race.

Tuesday 17 June 1997

Started with a painful visit to the dentist. Then sped to meeting already taking place on fishing. We'll have a debate today or tomorrow on what's achieved at the Amsterdam summit. Blair and team are claiming a big triumph in our battle against Spanish quota hoppers. We're not so sure. It's not a change to the bad fishing policy, just an exchange of letters between President Santer and Blair. But it makes some progress to establish links between their and our fishing communities. Blair wants us to make a statement to Parliament. Jack is less sure, thinking we'll be accused of over-claiming and hyping what doesn't amount to much. Blair obviously wants every aspect of his first summit proclaimed as a triumph. He has done well, but not that well on fishing. Obviously the fishermen will be angry. Elliot Morley, who is specifically the fishing minister, started moaning and whinging. But Jack is relaxed. He accepts this department has no good news, so you just have to take it on the chin.

A meeting of ministers and officials to discuss genetically modified herbicide plants. I had arranged this because I don't understand this genetic modification. The Greens and environmental fanatics are distorting all the evidence as usual. Jeff Rooker was terrific, inserting some sharp politics into this issue.

Then decided to move our offices to the old ICI building in Smith Square for November. I'm pleased. At least we'll get a decent room in which to receive visitors. Part of refurbishing the whole image of the department.

Wednesday 18 June 1997

Time flying. Ministerial prayers. All minds on this afternoon's Statements – first Blair on the summit in general and then Jack and me on fishing. I had my Ascot topper and morning suit all laid out ready, but had to call it off.

I had sandwiches in my office working on long and complex briefs. Snatched a TV view of the first two Ascot races, which seemed to shock the civil servants. I invited Dr Grimley, my private secretary, in to watch, but it's clearly not his scene. He is very efficient and able, though being a scientist is not strong on politics. That doesn't matter. He has the science and I have the politics, so we are not a bad team. But he is overworked. His deputy is really only a diary secretary and it means we are understaffed on the policy side. Often streams of policy papers come through to me unsifted and without a steer. Peter doesn't have time. So we discussed changing the office. Instead of one policy man and two administrators (one diary and one typing), I need two policy people with just one combining typing and diary. MAFF is certainly not part of the Rolls-Royce machine I knew at the centre of Whitehall in the 1970s.

Our fishing statement had been greatly lengthened by No. 10 insisting on all kinds of guff claiming how great a triumph it was. Proved the principle that the longer the statement the less the substance. The Tories came straight in on the attack. Ralph Lucas, previously the Tory spokesman in government, went over the top. He called us 'vacuous and empty' and used very aggressive language. Sitting there with Cranborne, you could see the arrogant disbelief on their Etonian faces that the electorate had actually had the impertinence to throw them out of office. So they explode in bluster. I fielded a lot of questions, mainly from the other side, and tried to be as gentle as possible, not least because they often know more than me.

The most tricky moment was when they all produced copies of the old fishing licence and said the present deal is no improvement. The briefing had not alerted me. I sent back a rocket to officials. Their briefing lacks political nous. Gives answers to a million technical points, which won't come up, but misses the obvious flaws in our political case. I will need friends on the other side and have already drafted letters to their agricultural experts asking to meet regularly so they can feed in their views. If I tried to run agriculture in the Lords on a partisan Labour basis I would be slaughtered.

Several people came up to say I had done OK, which was nice. Felt good from the adrenaline. Back to the office where Peter said the officials were very pleased with my performance. Then suddenly drained. Back to bed and asleep by 9.30 pm. Haven't done that for years.

Thursday 19 June 1997

Cleared papers and saw my press officer. Told him I want no publicity. He said that was a relief after all the Tories who wanted him to get their photos in the papers all the time. I give him a very short list of the serious journalists I'm happy to see.

Quick lunch at the Lords. Had a briefing meeting with officials on next week's debate on organophosphates. Their briefs were hopelessly hard line, suggesting that the department is perfect and its scientific advisors infallible, and that the illnesses were all the victims' fault. I gave them a rocket and demanded different briefs. Somehow we have to make this department take into account the consumer and not just be in the pocket of the agrochemical producers and farmers. Peter is quite sympathetic on this.

Sprinted to the Commons to hear Jack open an agricultural debate. His predecessor Douglas Hogg was sitting there, slumped on the Tory bench opposite like a mutilé de la guerre. The Tories look a beaten lot. Returned to the Lords for a late tea with Denis Carter. Agree I shall need an advisory group on reforming CAP. I am pleased to have Denis at my elbow.

Drove to the Waterside Inn at Bray. Michael Stoute the trainer was taking us to dinner, with Peter Savill and his wife Ruth. We had a terrific evening. I forget my exhaustion and loved it. Peter and I had some useful exchanges on reforming English racing. He has the brains, energy and the money to change things.

Friday 20 June 1997

Slept right through till 9.00 am when the phone woke me. Feel deeply tired, so that mere sleep does not cure it.

Saturday 21 June 1997

To Paris and a hotel at Chantilly for the grand ball – for the marriage of Zahra Aga Khan – at the Aga Khan's lovely great chateau at Aiglemont. It was like a fairy castle, with torches burning up the long drive, and the château decorated beautifully. Everything was done exquisitely, especially the chandeliers made of flowers in the ballroom.

The crowd had some overlap with last week's Claridges affair, though the social quality was higher. Lots of European royalty and princes and princesses. We mixed with friends. The Aga came over and had a long chat. Much friendlier and more relaxed than ever in the 10 years I have known him a little. Very loving to Sarah. He was aware of my new ministerial job and pulled my leg about it.

At table I sat with Victoria Rothschild, wife of Evelyn. She is very shy, but I always like her. She remembered when my ex-wife Carol and I went for dinner with them over 20 years ago, and how George Weidenfeld originally introduced us. Like me, she doesn't see George any more.

It was an astonishing evening, perhaps the best party I have been to since Downing Street – and certainly grander. Must have cost £2 million, Sarah thinks. But that is not the point. Many rich people spend fortunes and end up with vulgarity. This was done with real class.

Sunday 22 June 1997

We had a delicious old-fashioned French lunch in Chantilly before the appalling British Midland plane again.

Monday 23 June 1997

Up early and off by train to Bristol to visit the southwest region. Grimley and my press officer already there.

Visited the Wessex regional headquarters and met the staff – some 200 and not over-staffed, given all the complex CAP payments they execute. Then drove through the Cheddar Gorge to a large farm that uses its milk to make cheese, and the whey waste to feed pigs, which end as bacon – and uses the pig muck to nourish the fields, which feed the cows, which give the milk for cheese, etc., etc., in profitable circles. Nice people. Also gave some media interviews. I like local journalists. Different breed from the London types.

Then to a much smaller farm, which makes specialist cheese from sheep and goats milk. Nice family operation. Back on the fast train to Twyford and sitting in the conservatory with Sarah before 6.00 pm.

Intrigued to read in the papers that the awful Greenwich Millennium Dome has been rescued by Blair and handed to Mandelson to manage. When I gave Peter a copy of my Morrison book a fortnight ago, I inscribed in it that his 'grandfather would be proud of you' – and drew attention to the pages on Morrison's rescue handling of the 1951 Festival Exhibition, saying he might do the same. He has!

Tuesday 24 June 1997

Able to take my time getting ready and then went to present the prize for the best British wine of the year at our local vineyard, just half a mile down the road. Maggie took me up to London in the scruffy Vauxhall, me clearing a red box on the way.

Spend the afternoon preparing for my speech on organophosphates. The Countess of Marr has campaigned on their dangers for years. The department has always done its usual stonewalling, basically saying there is no problem because nobody has proved that there is one, even though lots of people are ill from exposure – including Margaret Marr herself. Last week I sent my briefs back as too defensive and told officials not to bother to come to any meetings unless they can take a more constructive line. They and Grimley were quite shocked, but today's briefs and revised speech are much better.

I wrote in a lot more positive stuff in longhand in the chamber, so the rats couldn't get at it, and the speech went down well. I have committed the department to look again at many of its procedures. Margaret was pleased and took me for a drink after. One astonishing feature was the speech by the Tory spokesman Lucas. He was agricultural spokesman when they were in government. He stated bravely that he and they had been quite wrong in government to swallow the department line, for which he apologised, and he hoped I would not swallow it as well. Fortunately I don't, otherwise I would have been outflanked. Felt good after, and much more favourably of Lucas, though tired. Pleased to get to bed.

Wednesday 25 June 1997

Morning ministerial prayers, in Jeff Rooker's room because Jack in Luxembourg at an agricultural council. Good fun as always with Jeff. I raised the question of ministerial control of the Horse. At present it's all over the place in Whitehall, and mainly in the Home Office because of betting. It should be in Agriculture, as it is on the Continent. We ask for a paper and I will press it when we do the department reconstruction.

Went to the party for Labour peers, where Tony Blair gave a short good speech. Said, 'Government is much better than opposition.' He nodded hello to me, but no place to talk about Ireland – which has really bubbled up. He has made a fresh bid to get Sinn Fein on board again and a truce from the IRA. He kindly went over to speak to Mary Wilson, then to Jim Callaghan, so he was at last doing the Old Labour round.

I left early to collect Sarah and go to dinner with Camilla Panufnik. Fascinating evening. Labour peer and old friend Bob Gavron was there with his bright wife Kate. He told us about the *Guardian*, where he is on the Board, and the libel saga against Jonathan Aitken, and how they thought they would lose beforehand, and offered Aitken a last chance to settle, which he declined. How the judge initially (and understandably) showed he didn't like the *Guardian*. And they only got the key evidence that sank Aitken because: a) Aitken flew BA, which kept and revealed its records of Mrs Aitken's flights whereas Swissair would not; and b) because the hotel was in receivership and the British receivers gave them access to its records, which a management would not. I told him I still found the self-righteous sanctimoniousness of the *Guardian* insufferable. He agreed.

Thursday 26 June 1997

Went to see our prospective new offices in Smith Square. Totally different: a dignified building in nice surroundings with parking and above all some lovely listed rooms. I was cheered and met some of the staff happily.

Back to dismal Whitehall Place to talk with my oldest French friend Jacques Pomonti. He filled me in on the scene with the new French government. He knows Prime Minister Jospin and offers to help me with introductions on the agricultural side.

Had a meeting with the Permanent Secretary Packer on meat rendering. He was very helpful and not playing his East Ender wide boy role. Perhaps cheered by the great news that McDonald's has agreed to start using British beef again. Politically a boost and will cheer up the farmers.

Went over to the Lords to our front-bench meeting. The business in July is terrible with three-line whips two or three times a week. Some of my regional visits will be cancelled and maybe even the Prague Budapest visit. Sarah won't like me sitting in the chamber till nearly midnight every night.

Helen Liddell phoned me to say that Chancellor Brown was delighted with my paper on taxing gambling, that they saw great prospects in it for next year, and I am 'Gordon's blue-eyed boy this week'. Let's hope it lasts. It does give me satisfaction to be involved in wider matters than cows, such as taxation and Ireland.

In the evening went to a small party at the Tate. To give Vivien Duffield a Sutherland portrait of her father in thanks for all the help they receive from the Clore Foundation. Chatted with Bamber Gascoigne and Hayden Phillips. Also talked to Nick Serota, who is looking forward to Chris Smith defending free entrance to museums (he said the British Museum is crucial: 'If that goes we all go.'). And to Mary Allen, who is very buoyant about going to run Covent Garden. I hinted that Jack wanted me as Arts minister. And that I had a scheme to do a long term deal with the Opera House. Give them £15 million more money but in return they must sort out their Spanish practices, their poor management and also do more TV deals.

Finally I chatted with Douglas Hogg, our predecessor at MAFF. He was very pleased to be out of Agriculture. He said in his time, 'it was a boring department, which with BSE became nasty'.

Friday 27 June 1997

Long telephone conversations in the morning. With Joe Haines: we both agree we couldn't have succeeded at the centre in the modern political world. Because we were trying to get polices right, however inadequately. Today all the effort is to get them presented right. So the media covers them favourably on the first day. After that it doesn't matter; they move on to a new story. Our fishing story was a prime example. Jack and I, of the older generation, wanted to speak the truth and not claim too much for it. The new men had a different story – that Blair had succeeded on every issue at Amsterdam – and that required us to speak untruthfully. By now the media has forgotten and moved on to Ireland.

David Montgomery phoned about Northern Ireland. He'd had supper with Trimble and fellow Unionist David Burnside. I said Trimble should assert himself as the leader of the constitutional centre of the province, marginalising the extremists. David said he is too insecure, and a bit narrow because his main position is 'hating papists and having no affinity with people from south of the border, who he sees as wildly passionate'. That is disappointing, because we need someone broader to detach the constitutional republicans from the IRA. But at least Trimble is working constructively with Blair and ignoring his own extremists.

What is clear to me is that Blair is cleverly moving crabwise towards a position close to ours: based on Unionist consent and embracing the other parties, even including the Sinn Fein. David said there is 'no point in moving without Sinn Fein, because the train would be derailed within ten minutes'. He is very perceptive and realistic.

Monday 30 June 1997

Off early to the Royal Show at Stoneleigh, Warwicks. Astonishing display, like a small town, very interesting and I enjoyed every minute. All four ministers went – the first time that's ever happened – and Jack got a great reception for a very good punchy speech.

I visited various stands in a large four-wheel drive then had lunch in the main tent. Finished with hosting our party till 7.30 pm, by when very tired feet but in good spirits. Am really beginning to enjoy this.

While relaxing, Jack asked me to take on public appointments in the department. That should be interesting – Packer will resist that since civil servants love to control the patronage.

Tuesday 1 July 1997

In early for ministerial meeting on reforming dog quarantine. Jack is clearly beginning to share Jeff's caution, seeing it as a middle class minority concern. It's certainly one of my priorities. Jack made a humorous remark about me being 'the brains' of the department and I gathered that the BBC had said that on 'Farming Today', which they had all heard at 6.15 am while I was asleep. Must be careful about that. Commons politicians may laugh but they don't like these favourable references to Lords colleagues in the media – especially implying they don't have brains! So must repair that. Anyway much of my brain remains unused in MAFF. Here it is mainly a question of stamina and determination to overcome institutional inertia.

Across to the Home Office for George Howarth's group on the problems of alcopops and teenage drinking. Met Estelle Morris from Education, who promised me something on school milk. Tessa and I agreed there must be no Whitehall turf wars between Health and MAFF over the new Food Health Agency. But there will be. Officials fighting for power and jobs.

Walked to the Lords for a quick lunch with Jim Callaghan. He is following Jack and me very closely. Warned me against getting 'ministerialitis' and said, 'Never forget the politics.' He said I must not expect too much of MAFF officials since they had never been much good, and that I had been spoilt by working in No. 10. He said he had a great shock when he moved from the Treasury to the Home Office and found serious official deterioration. He pressed the farmers' case as suffering poor grain and meat prices. But conceded to me there was no reason they should be protected from market forces when miners and steelworkers were not protected. Again said Jack is lazy, but I said how well he is doing now. He likes Rooker; gave him his first front-bench job. Said he 'used to have a chip on his shoulder, but better now, though still a loner'.

Had drafted a note to my colleagues on 'Brains' and 'Farming Today'. Pointed out that Packer had removed all our brains as a BSE Specified Risk Material when we entered the department. Spent the rest of the day at the Lords under a three-line whip expecting a vote – which as usual never came.

Wednesday 2 July 1997

Hadn't noticed it's July already. And Gordon Brown's first budget day. Straight into our weekly ministerial meeting. Jack again referred to me as 'brains' and Jeff Rooker burst out laughing and said, 'I won't say another word till you have read his memo.' Packer, who is normally resilient and quite funny, looked dour, seeming not to have enjoyed my reference to his removing our brains.

After the formal meeting, Jack called us into his office. He told us that last night the Chancellor has sent him a letter warning him of the budget references to our department. In a large envelope saying 'From the Chancellor Only for the Minister', and within that another sealed confidential letter. Both had been opened by an official. Jack has asked the establishment officer to look into it. I told him to get in security. Somebody could sell that information to a tabloid for thousands. Jack said it's because the officials cannot bear not to control and know every single thing about the minister. This is why I now write to Jack separately and put it directly into his pocket. He mentioned my note to him on needing an internal enquiry into the BSE crisis and said he agreed. He has discovered that his new private secretary David North has already spent three years in the Cabinet Office writing a history of the BSE crisis, but we are not supposed to know because it happened under the previous administration. I may talk to Cabinet Secretary Robin Butler.

Had a nice meeting with the Australian Labour Agriculture spokesman Neil O'Keefe – they all want to know how to become 'Blairite'. Then to the Parliamentary Labour Party meeting addressed by Mo Mowlam on Northern

Ireland – very impressive. I spoke and praised her and also asked about her relations with the Unionists. Later the chairman, Clive Soley, correctly said it was better if ministers don't question other ministers. This meeting is for backbenchers. But not many of them wanted to speak and I wanted to get a word in for Mo. She was appreciative.

Had lunch with Melvyn Bragg. He wishes Jack and I were at Heritage.

Back to the office to watch on TV a confident Gordon Brown do a clever budget. Doesn't hurt anybody – he will leave the Bank of England to do that with interest rates.

Appalling paper in the office today on veal compensation for BSE. The previous ministers had received EU money to compensate both beef and veal farmers but decided to give it all to beef. The veal boys are now suing the Ministry and the lawyers say we don't have a cat in hell's chance because they had a right. I asked what the lawyers advised before and if they had been either wrong or ignored. Grimley immediately ran to Packer who instructed him that I could know nothing of the previous administration. This has all become a way to prevent any exposure of the earlier total balls up in the department on BSE. The officials are just as guilty and keen on a cover up as the Tory ex-ministers.

Thursday 3 July 1997

Our front bench was a sad tale of future three-line whips. Then I returned for Jack's meeting with 30 NFU representatives, orchestrated ably by David Naish. No doubt farmers are suffering, from BSE and the rising pound, but what astonishes me is their total assumption that they should be shielded from all the vagaries of the market. Any fall in prices and they must be compensated. They suffer from complete welfare dependency.

Some figures in my box showed that 25 farmers are receiving arable grants of over a half a million pounds a year; 325 get between £200,000 and £500,000; 1400 get £100,000 to £200,000; 4000 get £50,000 to £100,000; and 40,000 get up to £50,000 a year. That is arable subsidy alone. The beef compensation has been nearly £4 billion. But the poor family hill farmers get little. The taxpayer is being completely ripped off to maintain the richer part of the farming community.

Over to the Lords for another boring session waiting for a three-line whip vote. This time there were two – we lost one, which is stupid of the Tories since it will confirm our Commons colleagues that they must abolish our hereditaries. It's unacceptable that when a government, just elected by the biggest majority ever, brings in a measure from the manifesto approved by the electorate, the Tories turn out 100 hereditary peers to overthrow it. That cannot last.

I sat in our gloomy room in the Lords all afternoon and most of the evening. Pat Hollis, Helene Hayman and myself grinding silently through two red boxes each. I took a break to have a drink and a quick supper with Trevor West, over from Dublin, and we discussed the Irish situation. We have worked together on this for 20 years. He thinks Irish PM Bertie Ahern will be better on Ulster than the media says. Ahern was in the Irish parliamentary football team that I played against 20 years ago. Hope I didn't tackle him in my old traditional way and he still remembers it.

Very late I had a cigar with Ivor Richard and discussed our team. He is stunned by Blair's energy. He told me how he put Margaret Jay in as deputy leader in the Lords to stop Tessa Blackstone, who he finds difficult. There is no doubt Margaret is doing well at Health, commanding the House. Father Jim is openly proud. Ivor also described how the Scots ministers are being incredibly arrogant. They want devolved Scotland to have all the powers – and even wrote into the paper that the Scottish Office would lead for the whole UK in Brussels on questions such as agriculture. Jack stopped that very well. But at the next meeting it was all back in the paper and he had to stop it again.

Ivor is clearly enjoying it greatly. Especially as Lords leader he has the prestige of being in the Cabinet without the chore of having to run a department.

Friday 4 July 1997

Did some letters and drafted a memo to Jack on setting up machinery to advise on CAP reform – Denis Carter has been helpful on this. I said we must have outside advisers and he agreed. Today I drafted my suggestions; but will probably wait till next week to put it in his pocket. Certainly won't send it through the official machine, since they will be alerted and will set up a wholly official committee retrospectively to counter it.

Saturday 5 July 1997

Terrific but exhausting day. Went to Sandown for the Eclipse. Lunch in the Royal Box. We went back to the Royal Box to watch the race. I stood behind Arnold Weinstock who showed no sign of emotion as his horse won, just saying, 'He is quite a good horse.' Sarah and I then slipped away to drive home and head off for our evening's entertainment.

This was with Marcella and Francis Dashwood at their grand Italianate house near High Wycombe. Francis and I were both Henry Fellows to Harvard nearly 40 years ago. We had a superb dinner in the Florentine dining hall, with its beautiful painted ceiling, and then adjourned to listen to an opera concert floating across the lake. I chatted with Petronella Wyatt, who I had not seen since the election. She told me that the Tory journalists on the *Spectator* and the *Telegraph* preferred Blair to Hague – a better kind of conservatism.

Sunday 6 July 1997

The social whirl continues. After mass at Twyford, lunch with Jacob Rothschild at his country home at Waddeston. There was a group of us – Claus Moser, Eric and Mrs Anderson from Lincoln College and Harold Pinter and Antonia Fraser. Jacob showed us round the chateau, which he's restored. We also went to the new cellars and saw racks of old Moutons and Lafites.

We had lunch outside beside a small lake and I sat next to Serena Rothschild. We mainly discussed racing and the threats to hunting. There is a huge countryside rally in Hyde Park on Thursday in defence of hunting. Labour is being very foolish in appearing to be against the countryside. Blair had sent an emissary with good wishes to the homosexual rally in Battersea yesterday, it's terrible if he cannot do the same for the countryside. Not so politically correct of course.

Back home I phoned Robin Butler to discuss MAFF and Permanent Secretary Packer. I said I had come to appreciate him more lately, especially his directness, knowledge and humour. But we agreed he is still too arrogant and dismissive of everyone who questions the department. Robin said, 'He'll have to move. It's just a question of when.' Robin is retiring at the end of the year. He said he wasn't looking forward to going, but is pleased to have seen in the new government with a splendid transition, and to have left the civil service with no taint now of having become too political. We agreed to go walking next year when he is free – and I may be!

Monday 7 July 1997

Up to the Lords for another three-line whip on devolution – we have three whips this week, ruining social life. Cleared more papers and began to prepare for Wednesday's difficult meeting with the House of Lords Agriculture Select Committee. My knowledge is still too thin over a very wide field.

Also put in a sharp reminder to Grimley that nothing had happened over organophosphates. After the Marr debate, and again each week verbally, I have asked for a response to the questions asked and the promises of change I made. Not a word. The officials have gone back down their rabbit holes and hope I will forget about it and move on. Hope I won't. But it's a battle, having so many responsibilities, and a department which isn't behind me when I want change. It simply isn't possible for a minister to follow up all the detail. Of course they know that, which is why they hide and wait. *Yes Minister* again.

Tuesday 8 July 1997

Spent much of morning preparing for tomorrow's question on quarantine. Then drove to Hampton Court for the flower show. Scorching hot. Met Sarah there and we lunched with the President, Simon Hornby, an old friend of Sarah's. He asked me not to give the long speech I had brought along so I abandoned 90% of it and ad libbed a few generous words, which seemed to go down well. Everybody, especially me, wanted to get out of the sweaty tent. We did a quick tour of the stands and then returned to the Lords with Sarah just before the clouds opened.

Had a nice meeting with the brewers and then off to Spencer House for a party for Yorkshire TV and its chairman Ward Thomas. It was nostalgic for me since I worked at Spencer House 17 years ago for *The Economist* Intelligence Unit. Jacob Rothschild bought it after I showed him round and has done it up opulently, a bit like a trial run for Waddeston. Curious to think how all those now gilded rooms then contained secretaries and research assistants and are now quite grand.

I took Anji Hunter, Blair's long-time secretary, on a private tour and we had a good gossip. She said they'd been grateful for my memo on taking over No. 10 and had tried to follow it – though she said they hadn't managed to do it all. She particularly resented the huge space occupied by Honours and Church Appointments. I had warned them about this and advised them to move them; it's too late now. You have to make radical changes right at the beginning. We discussed Thursday's country sports rally and I urged her to get the PM to take it seriously and to send a message of goodwill – as he had to Saturday's gay rights rally. Anji was sympathetic since her brother is helping the rally. She promised to press Blair again to send a message.

Most striking at this top party was how it was full of Labour ministers with almost no Tories there – none of their old media and Heritage team. In politics you are soon forgotten when out of power.

Wednesday 9 July 1997

At our ministerial meeting at 8.30 am – Jack had to be at a Cabinet committee at 9.00 am. Elliot Morley was whining on about the hunt rally, saying they wouldn't have more than 20,000 there and that abolishing hunting wouldn't create any unemployed. I said the Department of Employment estimated 14,000 and Morley got heated.

Went off to the Lords for the Sub Committee grilling on my departmental work, under Hugh Reay. They were courteous and friendly, but the questions were very testing over the whole range of agriculture. I was able to give full answers and now feel on top of it. But on fishing I was less confident and they kindly didn't press too far there. Afterwards, I felt very pleased with how it had gone, but quite drained.

Straight off to speak at and open the Food From Britain exhibition at the Savoy. Only had time to snatch a few snacks, surrounded by people trying to shake hands and press their interests. Then dashed to the Lords for the quarantine PQ. It went exceptionally well. I was able to answer all the questions without referring to my folder – not that I can find anything in it anyway. Also managed to get a few laughs. Said that rodents were subject to rabies quarantine, but tabloid journalists were for some reason exempt.

Then out to dinner at Le Gavroche – never been there before – with Arnold and Netta Weinstock and Sarah. Across the way were Kenneth Clarke, enjoying being out of office; and Tessa Jowell, with husband and five children, enjoying being in office.

Arnold is very frail. I asked about his youth and he told me how he became a civil servant after the LSE and enjoyed it greatly. He most enjoyed working 'with people of such integrity' – implying that his colleagues in industry had not always been the same. He then went into property and was about to make millions in the 1950s, when his father-in-law, Michael Sobell, took him in to run the family electronics firm that Arnold built up to be GEC. He is very critical of his successor George Simpson. He sees modern managers as full of business-school-speak, always trying to impress the media with their artificial 'strategies', when all that is required is to increase value. I asked what he would have liked to have been. He said, 'A musician, but I lacked the talent. Failing that talent, a lawyer, because I like arguing. Also they earn so much money for doing so little.'

Thursday 10 July 1997

A new BSE disease scandal has emerged. The Tories didn't bother to introduce the necessary legislation to give statutory powers to enforce the EU beef ban. That is incredible. An enormous gamble – which has now gone wrong. The Commission has discovered British people exporting banned beef. And without new legislation we have no powers to stop and arrest them even if we catch them. This puts us in the soup trying to get the beef ban lifted. No wonder the civil servants don't want us to know anything about what happened before. But when it blows up we carry the can.

I exploded and demanded to know why ministers hadn't been alerted to this landmine when we took office. (It emerged that it was deliberately excluded from the huge file of pending issues put before us on taking office.) I demanded a meeting next week with relevant officials. This is a scandal. Clever official Richard Carden's paper said they had 'calculatedly under-implemented the EU rules' on the beef ban (good Sir Humphrey language). He also mentioned 'other ways' they had not implemented. I mean to get to the bottom of this.

I was full of this when I went to the Lords for a meeting with the family farmers and didn't give them the attention they deserved. It's hard having one's diary full of meetings with all of the 10,000 trade associations in farming and also trying to fit in the policy work.

Then take to lunch Liz Lloyd from the No. 10 Policy Unit. Am very interested to hear how my Unit 'baby' is developing. They have a dozen members, which is more than I ever had – on the top floor, away from the action and access to the Prime Minister, and in danger of losing central co-ordination, especially since David Miliband is seen as only a temporary head and has an office elsewhere. But Liz was on the ball on all the issues we discussed – especially the failure to legislate the EU beef ban and the phosphates poisoning issue. We agree to meet regularly. She is bright and could be very helpful to me, since I need policy back-up, which is trying to advance things and not just trying to stop and hide everything.

Back to the department for a meeting with Michael Meacher and Angela Eagle from the Environment Department about rural environment policy. Went very well and Meacher, who I usually think is a bit Bennite batty, expressed surprise that we're so interested in the rural environment and are not just supporting the farmers. Agree to move towards a joint white paper.

Being away, I missed the party meeting, where apparently Hugh Jenkins said our front bench is doing well and some of his visitors had said 'and the man with grey curly hair is nearly as good as the ladies'. Praise indeed. Have decided that the BSE beef crisis is like unpeeling an onion – each layer gives off a strong smell and causes tears.

Was stuck in the House till 10.00 pm on a three-line whip but again no vote. Went through two more boxes and felt square-eyed. Had a nice supper with fellow ministers Tessa Blackstone, Margaret Jay and John Sewell – with whom I began the process of improving our relations with the Scottish Office.

Incidentally, at the meeting with Meacher, Jack revealed that this morning he was summoned out of a Cabinet committee to No. 10 to discuss the country sports rally. There were 120,000 in Hyde Park, with Hague and Heseltine cultivating it for the Tories and no Labour presence except lovely Ann Mallalieu. They had panicked and realised they must send a message. They asked Jack if he wanted to go and he declined. Together Jack, Blair and Mandelson drafted a message, which they sent off. I would have been happy to take it but Jack felt it was best if we kept out. The rally was more impressive than anyone expected, huge, well behaved and emotional. That won't please animal rightist Elliot Morley who forecast that only 20,000 would attend.

Friday 11 July 1997

Up at dawn to catch the train to York. Met some farmers for breakfast. Then toured the MAFF York headquarters, which was interesting.

Went to York races. Delicious lunch sitting with Peter Savill and the Mantons (parents of Claire Hesketh) and watched with other racing people in a comfortable box. Several kindly said they wished I had got the Tote (now announced for Peter Jones). Peter Savill told me he is having terrible trouble with the old farts at the BHB [British Horseracing Board] – especially Wakeham. Thinks he will have to go.

Back on a hot, crowded train. But enjoyable talking to Chris Brasher, once a great athlete, who had just won a big race and had his trophy on the table among the tea cups and newspapers. He is suing the *Observer*. They had printed an 'exclusive' piece attacking him; the story was stolen from his own book but they still got it wrong!

Maggie picked me up at Kings Cross and we crawled through the Friday evening jams. I finished off another red box in the car, thus frustrating the office ambition to spoil my weekend. None of the papers had been sifted or contained advice. Just all dumped in for me to do the work.

Sunday 13 July 1997

Nasty attack on Jack in the *Mail* for moving to posh new offices. The writer, an ex-editor, worked for years in a palatial office earning nearly half a million a year, just to publish rubbish. But denounces ministers who work twice as hard, earn only a tenth of his salary and often work in a shoe box.

The story of Major's failure to implement the EU beef ban with backup legislative powers is slowly seeping out, but no journalist has seen the full significance. The Tories didn't bring in the necessary laws because they didn't want a Commons row with their anti-Europeans. Now we are stuck with the ban being extended because of their failures.

Monday 14 July 1997

Realise that one of the unsatisfactory aspects of being a minister at Agriculture is that one, in fact, has few discretionary decisions. Everything comes to me asking for a decision. On most of the big items, however, there is in fact no choice. If it's financial, then 80% is decided in Brussels, and we merely execute, risking legal action if we don't. And if it's an animal question, like BSE, then we have to take the scientists' advice; to ignore that and get it wrong would be political suicide and risk a judicial appeal and review. So I have little choice to exercise any political judgement.

Went in late morning to see Jeff Rooker. He was very agitated about the BSE beef ban business. The Brussels Commission is about to take action against two grubby British meat plants, which have been exporting British beef to Europe claiming it's French. So we have to move in first to demonstrate that we are in control and not just following the Europeans. But we don't have statutory powers so we have to get the criminals on hygiene grounds. Jeff said the department seemed unprepared and is in a shambles. We agree we need a beef crisis unit.

Lunch with Helen Liddell at the Commons on the terrace. She told me that my gambling ideas would be in the next budget. Gordon Brown is apparently getting tired. We also discussed my idea for introducing a state index-tracking fund to manage portable pensions. I am the only person in the government, or probably even in the whole of Whitehall, who has ever run an index-tracking fund.

Back for a series of meetings on milk, and especially restoring school milk, which the campaigners want for nutritional reasons and the farmers in order to offload their milk. The basic problem is the crazy milk quota system. The trading in quotas is now more active than the trade in milk.

Had a good presentation with Jeff on the new cattle traceability system. We are setting up a huge computer operation. I ask why it will work when every other computer system in Whitehall in the past 20 years, from the Inland Revenue onwards, has failed.

Had to cancel a horticultural meeting to meet with Jeff on closing the unhygienic beef plants. Chaos in the department. Our vet who inspects the bad plants has never found anything wrong, though clearly dirty and cupboards full of French labels to help them defraud.

Jeff showed me a paper – not copied to me – which states baldly that, 'The beef ban was implemented through administrative procedures not legislation.' Using administration meant simply withholding export health certificates. The paper conceded that it left officials with 'no authority to take enforcement action'. Port checks might 'inadvertently identify' illegal exports, but no sanctions were then possible. It admits that the administrative procedures didn't legally constitute implementation of the EU beef ban. That is political dynamite.

Dashed home and changed, then off to a great gala for Covent Garden Opera with Sarah. Dazzling turnout. Everybody there, with those notable aesthetes Prince Charles and Princess Margaret in the lead. What was wrong was that they were nearly all Tories – yesterday's men – and they occupied the best seats. Only Chris Smith, Tessa Blackstone and I were from the new government. Worst, Chris Smith, the new Arts secretary of state, was seated at the far end, whereas his Tory shadow, young Francis Maude, was in the centre. That will cost them several millions of grants. It was crass and politically insensitive. Not difficult to see why the Garden is always in trouble.

In front of me sat three people who never spoke to one another: Margaret Thatcher, William Hague and his fiancée. The body language of each was uncomfortable, not to say hostile. Also with me was Robin Butler and I alerted him about the chaos in MAFF. He said that, as Cabinet secretary, he was never told that the beef ban had not been legally implemented! I said I was coming round to the view that we needed big changes there.

I managed to corner some sandwiches in the crush bar, and got a couple for Michael Heseltine, but he was very hungry and invited us to join him afterwards at the Ivy Restaurant for dinner with Anne, and Jeremy Isaacs and his wife Gillian Widdicombe. Michael was in terrific form, doing a lovely skit on Thatcher and advising Jeremy (who is doing a TV series on the Cold War) on how to tempt her to give an interview, by appealing to 'her raving ego'. He said that, in his view, Thatcher 'is now barking mad'. He has clearly recovered from his heart attack and is enjoying his freedom. I never thought he would accept retirement, being addicted to politics. But he was more relaxed than I'd ever seen him and even shared jokes and stories with me, from the other side, something I've never seen before. Losing office and ambition is a great liberator.

I reminded him that he'd always said that the Tories would win the election with the recovery in the economy. He said, 'I was quite wrong. Everyone made up their minds years before and the whole election campaign was a complete waste of time.'

I mentioned that it was unwise of Covent Garden to put the Secretary of State for Arts on the outside with his Tory shadow in the centre. Widdicombe intervened to say, 'That will teach Smith a lesson for talking crap about Covent Garden being opera for the people.' I saw even more how this privileged gang who previously ran Covent Garden like a private club has actually ruined it.

Tuesday 15 July 1997

Seeing the Cabinet minutes reminds me how much concern there is for presentation. Much of what the PM says is about presenting ourselves better and in a more electorally friendly way. Twenty years ago it was all about policies not presentation – but this lot is certainly more electorally successful than we were.

Had very interesting meeting with Richard Carden, probably the brightest of our MAFF colonels. Told me all the background to not implementing the BSE ban – and promised that I would be on the copying list henceforth. Said the real reason for the Tories not bringing in implementation of the beef ban was their 'war on Europe'. Didn't want to be seen bowing down to EU directives at the same time as waging a war on Europe. And afraid of their Eurosceptics voting against. So a political decision. Also didn't want to make expenditures on monitoring and enforcing the ban.

I raised the problem of the department being always on the back foot, always reacting. I forced him to admit that it would have been better if ministers had been alerted to this problem and acted with initiative, instead of now guiltily and sheepishly moving to close down the beef plants just before the EU closes them. That is bad for the department and looks bad to Europe. Delays us getting the ban lifted.

Sat in on Jeff Rooker's meeting with the NFU. Heard nothing new.

The NFU is like a gramophone record, which has established the right to come to MAFF and be played and heard every other day. At least, unlike our Tory predecessors, we don't go kow-towing to their offices every week and phone them every weekend. Still, it's an efficient trade union, which has established primacy over the department and assumes it's running agricultural policy. That is why farmers have done so well. But the future is not so bright, both in terms of farmers' incomes and NFU access. The issue is simply whether we will be using them or, as in the past, they running us.

Jeff Rooker continues impressive. He is like a little Jack Russell in ferreting out information; and his political judgement is first class. Also a man of gritty integrity.

Fascinating lunch with Charles Anson, now public affairs director at a hotel group but for seven years the Queen's press secretary – and long ago in No. 10 with me. He views Princess Di as a basket case. Scarred by her childhood, feeling neglected by her parents and now always looking for rejection. So courts the media as a substitute for a human relationship but complains when they say anything unfriendly about her. Blames Charles, who rejected her, for everything that goes wrong in her life. Is obsessed with getting revenge on Charles. Next crisis is when she ceases to look good. Like me, he doesn't find her sexy at all. He says, 'She looks like an android.' Says Charles's disastrous revelation about his affair with Camilla was the fault of his then private secretary who thought it was the trendy thing to do and advised him, 'to let it all hang out and then the media would lose interest'. The Prince's office kept it 'all very close' and didn't tell the Palace anything.

When Anson found out he warned them that this would give the media the excuse to camp outside Camilla's house for ever, as they have since, because she was the confirmed mistress of the future king. 'But it was too late.'

He had interesting views that the arrival of Blair and Cherie and Euan etc. as a presidential family had side-lined our royals a bit and that is 'a good thing'. Less attention on the minor horrors in the younger royal family.

Followed up with a brief meeting with nice Anne Robinson of the retailers. I suggested that the big food supermarkets, instead of forcing the closure of village shops, should sponsor them to keep them open.

Then a very good meeting in the tea room with half a dozen Tory peers who are agricultural experts: Middleton, Soulsby, Monk Bretton, Selborne, Brookeborough etc. Kindly arranged by Elizabeth Carnegie. Went very well. I told them they had forgotten more about agriculture than I could ever learn and I wanted a dialogue, from which I would learn, and would give them a chance to feed in their informed views. No point in running a partisan Labour agriculture policy in the Lords or they will demolish us. Might soften them at Question Time too! Elizabeth told me afterwards that they were all pleased and keen to come to the next one, which I mean to focus on Fischler's CAP reforms in the autumn.

Sprinted home to change and go with Sarah to the British Museum for its annual dinner – always a grand affair. We were seated in the Great Hall surrounded by magnificent friezes, including the Elgin marbles, which Chris Smith is fortunately committed to retain despite Mark Fisher's *Guardian*-guilt instincts, but the dinner was a disaster. We sat down late at 9.30 pm and heard 55 minutes of speeches before we could eat. This was at the request of Princess Margaret – whose path we dog this week – since she doesn't like speeches after dinner.

The golden rule is that if you have a boring speech the least you can do is make it a brief boring speech.

Incidentally I asked Hayden Phillips why Graham Greene still had only a CBE despite his huge public work. He wrote me a reply on my name card that said: 'Because he hasn't done it for very long. We don't any longer give honours to offices (except to permanent secretaries of course!) but to people. But it will come!' The problem is what Hayden calls 'the total chaos' at the British Museum, with bad management and financial control. I hope it does come – before Graham's ex wife kills him off!

Wednesday 16 July 1997

Good ministerial meeting. Since enforcing the beef ban needs more vets, I proposed looking at vet training and opening it up – they keep the entry small in order to have a shortage and their fees high. Packer reacted positively to this and we agree to have a meeting with Blunkett's team.

Spoke at an arable farmers lunch in the Royal College of Physicians. Boring text so I tell officials to have one positive message in every speech or I won't bother to give them. Back at the ministry I had a quiet word with Packer about my need for better support in the office, needing two policy secretaries instead of one, and only one admin post instead of two. He promised action.

Then over to the Foreign Office for another task force preparing for the European Presidency. Very waffly discussion of our aims, all of which are of the variety 'improving the quality of life' and 'better government'. Mandelson was good again, pointing tartly to the 'lack of focus'.

Met Liz Lloyd of the No. 10 Policy Unit at the bottom of the back entrance to Downing Street and we went for a private walk in the park discussing the beef ban. She has some bright ideas, though is as always particularly keen on presentation. Agree we will continue to work together. I enjoy staying in touch with No. 10 and the Policy Unit, which I somehow still think of as partly mine. I remember how often in the 1970s I had secret meetings in the Park when I didn't want the office to know.

An idyllic dinner with Max and Jane Rayne and a hundred others at their lovely house in Hampstead. Hilariously, many of the friends we saw at Covent Garden and at the British Museum were again here. The same little group going around and around to the same parties. But I prefer my old friends to strangers so I don't mind that.

Thursday 17 July 1997

Not home again till 1.30 am so beginning to fray. Had a good early livener with the department's regional directors. Tried to give them a lift by saying how important the regions are and a sketch of how I want to run it differently from before. Will try to restore relations with the regional press. Discovered we don't issue press notices when we visit for fear of exposing us to criticism. Result is nobody knows we are there, except the NFU, who issue their own critical press notices anyway. Propose to change that.

Early lunch with the imminent president of the Country Landowners Association. Picked up some comments on the CAP reform which was helpful. Have to be like a magpie, storing away information in the great empty warehouse of my agricultural brain.

Front bench mainly concerned with pay for Lords ministers. The Commons people have pocketed their big pre-election rise and now feel it might incense the nation if we had one as well, so we are to be denied. The fact is that every Lords minister does more work than the Commons ministers, because they just work on a small departmental section whereas the Lords man must cover the lot. But they take home nearly treble in money, including their office expenses. My colleagues are incandescent. Derry Irvine stepped in smartly and has written a savage letter both to the PM and Gordon Brown.

Train to Plymouth for another official visit to the southwest. Stayed in an impressive Elizabethan hotel, but disappointed they didn't serve fine West Country beers or Devon food. They are missing some regional tricks down here.

Friday 18 July 1997

Had a working breakfast with local NFU, the Country Landowners and tenant farmers. Very useful. Then to a huge local bakery, which makes Cornish pasties. Then a lovely visit to the Tamar valley where we have put some money in to improve the water and the valley environment, teaching the farmers not to leak so much toxic fertiliser into the river and slowly getting the river fish life back. It was a lovely spot. The local journalists were very pleasant and I gave them as much help as I could.

Off to Tavistock for another cheese visit and another basket of cheeses. Pity I don't really eat cheese. More TV and then lunch with officials in a stuffy hotel. I began to learn about Environmental Special Areas (ESAs), which had hitherto passed me by. We then went off to one, at Roborough Common on the edge of Dartmoor. Lovely views and met some authentic Common Holders, who graze ponies and cattle there. More media and then off to a fine family farm in Devon. Straight out of the Archers. Farmer and his two strapping sons working hard with lovely Devon red cattle and a great Charolais bull, also some pretty black-faced hill sheep. His wife ran a B&B and told me all the problems, while the sister-in-law produced a delicious tea of cream and strawberry jam scones. Six hundred feet up and so cold and wet in winter that only certain strains of cattle thrive. He had to pay £3000 an acre for extra land – and there is no way he can get a return on that in the future. But he didn't complain too much and is obviously very resilient and deserves to survive.

Pretty shattered but a wonderful day. Liked those small Devon farms. A long way from the rich grain barons in East Anglia.

Saturday 19 July 1997

Woke at just after 6.00 am so I collected my red box from downstairs and went through it till 9.00 am. Nothing very exciting. But reminds me that nothing is happening on public appointments so I give a prod there. Dozens of letters to sign to MPs. It seems that many of the letters to my Commons ministerial colleagues come to me to sign – because I cover virtually everything and am seen by officials as a mug from the Lords.

Fell asleep in the late morning, but woken by David Montgomery about Northern Ireland, where the IRA have announced a tactical ceasefire. He wants me to phone No. 10 and tell them to make some concessions to the loyalists, but I may pass on that one. Must use that access carefully. Blair is seeing Trimble and will know he must nurture him or it will all fail.

Off in a sunny evening to Michael Heseltine's house near Banbury. Party for his daughter Annabel. It was beautifully laid out. Oriental white tents around the pool with lovely flowers on the table. The theme was 'White Mischief' and all the girls were dressed in 1940s style.

I chatted intriguingly with Ian Maxwell, who I had not seen since the horrors of my job with his father. He was ebullient and we made no reference to his monster father. Then I spent much of the drinks time – me on fruit juice – with journalist Tony Howard. I sense he will ghost Heseltine's memoirs. He has mellowed with the years and is now a wise commentator rather than his early manifestation as a snide gossip columnist. He is certain Ivor Richard will go soon and that Margaret Jay will replace. He has read Ken Morgan's biography of Jim and said it's, 'as you would expect, full of pious platitudes'. I prefer that to acid.

I sat in the top position next to Anne Heseltine and we had a good chat. She is incredibly open and frank with no attempt to dissemble. That must have been good for Michael over the years. Our main problem was the increasing cold, with everyone shivering. I put napkins around my neck as scarves and took Sarah to dance to warm us up . Michael has clearly recovered from his heart attack. Sarah sat at his table, with Sunny Marlborough on the other side, and said he was in fine form. Anne said that the great thing is that Michael is not tired the whole time, which he was as a minister. We slipped away, getting home by 2.30 am.

Sunday 20 July 1997

Quiet day reading the papers and writing up some of this. Slept beside Sarah on the grass after lunch and felt it's a nice life. Then a phone call from Joe Haines saying there is a nasty piece about me in the *Sunday Telegraph* Mandrake, saying I want a posh car as well as a posh office and have upset all the civil servants – clearly the source of this. And all about Maxwell. Usual shit from the usual shit-mongers. But they cannot spoil this.

Monday 21 July 1997

Went up early for meeting ahead of Jack's visit to the Agricultural Council. Maggie my driver was devastated to hear of the nasty piece in the *Telegraph*. She roared with laughter at the idea that I was seeking a 'top range' car, as a shabby Vauxhall Vectra without air conditioning hardly comes into that category. Apparently nearly all other ministers have air conditioning.

The meeting went through the Council agenda; how we would handle our threat to impose a sort of beef ban on them, and discussions of the Agenda 2000 CAP reform. Jack seemed on top of everything and the main official, Kate Timms, is one of our best.

Jack adjourned us into a ministerial meeting with Jeff and myself and we discussed the CAP advisory group, where we each suggested some names; I put forward Andrew Graham, my old No. 10 adviser. We discussed the new comprehensive spending review, which Chancellor Gordon Brown has announced for all departments; we have first to decide our departmental objectives and then the spending allocations will follow. I have done the text on objectives.

So it was a good ministerial team morning. That is what is good about Jack – much better than most other Cabinet ministers from what I hear. He includes us all in the general decision taking. Elsewhere the junior ministers complain of feeling cut-off. Later shook hands with Joe Walsh, the charming Irish agriculture minister, who I hope to see in future in Cork. Then back for the three-line whip. We lost one of the three divisions so I was stuck late and missed the opening of the Proms at Albert Hall.

In the voting lobby saw Jim Callaghan, who told me privately he had just been to No. 10. Blair wanted to talk to him about government in general. He said Blair 'wants to do everything', but he told him he had only another 12 months of honeymoon, perhaps less, and then it would all start to go wrong, as in 1964–66. He felt strongly that Blair's style was 'completely different' from his own – some understatement – and said he found going back into No. 10 felt 'familiar but not nostalgic'. Jim's time there was not all sunshine.

Blair also particularly wanted to talk to him about Ireland. Jim warned him that, 'It's impossible to get a rational solution to an irrational situation' and advised him to distance himself from the details: 'That is what you have ministers for.' But he sensed Blair's instincts were to take the lead and bravely take the flak.

Jim chatted to Anji Hunter in what was Marcia's old room. Told her the story of when Churchill took over in May 1940. Horace Wilson, an appease-ment adviser, had long occupied that room for Chamberlain. So Randolph Churchill and Brendan Bracken went in to his office at dawn on the first day and sat in his chairs. Wilson came in, took off his hat, but had nowhere to sit down. They didn't move. So without a word, he put his hat back on and left, never to return.

Tuesday 22 July 1997

Started with a meeting with the British Equine Trade Association, part of my campaign to get policy relating to the Horse into Agriculture. I advised them to organise into a single body and ask the Prime Minister to give the responsi-bility to a single department (Agriculture). I shall be pleased if this comes off.

Took my PQ on fishing still not using my unfathomable reference file. Went well. Afterwards 'Black Rod' came up to me and said people like this direct approach to answering questions, because it means I answer them direct, with particular reference to their specific question, and not just read out a general splurge of civil-service-speak.

Had quick chat with Billy Blease about Northern Ireland and then a drink with David Montgomery discussing the same subject. There are increasing difficulties with the Unionists, who are about to vote against the proposed new arrangements because they provide for no decommissioning of arms by the IRA. David talked to Blair yesterday (before Jim saw him) and encour-aged him to press on regardless and try to keep Trimble and the Unionists in the talks. Blair was still positive and wanting to be encouraged. We discussed how to steer Trimble back into a more positive position. He needs to regain the initiative, now appearing to be the only one against the peace talks. It's bizarre, but skilful, how the murderous IRA have manoeuvred themselves into the situation where they appear more devoted to peace than the Loyalists. Trimble needs to go to Washington and Dublin and return recommitted to the peace process. David will try to influence him. But Trimble, of course, has to watch his back and make sure his own extremists don't just cut him off. Paisley is already trying to do that.

Wednesday 23 July 1997

Jeff took the weekly ministerial meeting, but Jack walked in halfway through, just back from his triumph in Brussels where we won the vote to impose similar BSE controls on beef in Europe as on our own beef. Jack's most striking recollection was of the behaviour of the Germans, who behaved as if they owned the EU (perhaps they do, they certainly pay for much of it). The other nations defer to them as if it's still 1941.

Attended Jack's big meeting preparing for the Presidency, where he announced that I am to be the UK representative at the Agriculture Council and will attend all bilaterals. This is good for me and now I can get ahead with setting up the CAP working party. Jack and I are getting on very well. I would prefer to work with him, as a colleague, than any other member of the Cabinet. Of course would rather be at the Treasury or the FCO!

The party meeting with the Lib Dems apparently went very mildly. They are aware of Blair's new moves to get into bed with them, letting Paddy Ashdown on to a Cabinet committee and discussing proportional representation for the next election but one. Hope it won't happen, though.

In the evening went to dinner at the Four Seasons hotel. Was held up at the entrance by someone selfishly blocking the road chatting to someone in a car. Was about to admonish him when I saw it was the boxer Prince Naseem. Decided to tolerate it. My friend Jarvis Astaire, the boxing promoter, came up to introduce us and it all went off well, with the Prince giving Maggie his autograph.

Henry Carnarvon had been given a free dinner table in the smart hotel dining-room and asked some close friends – the Weinstocks, the Huntingdons and Sarah and me. Also his son Geordie, who has a dynamic new girlfriend, Miss Aitken, who has set up a new clothing business and floated it on the Offex exchange. Arnold was impressed by her and said she will go far. Henry provided some delicious 1976 claret from his own cellar – though not very much, just two glasses each. Geordie told me he gets over half a million in CAP farm subsidies. The Devon hill farmers sadly don't!

Arnold told me that his GEC successor Simpson will soon get a Labour peerage but has 'never supported Labour in his life'. I fear that the huge Blair peerage list next week will shock the party. Full of luvvies and business Tories.

Thursday 24 July 1997

Lunch with Margaret Jay and Helene Hayman, both worried that Blair's imminent peerages will go to people who won't work here and won't be here to vote. Sat in the Lords on a three-line whip waiting for an Education Bill, which never arrived, then gave up and went to the country. Try to get an early night to prepare for the social onslaught that lies ahead this weekend.

Friday 25 July 1997

Maggie arrived after 5.00 pm with a huge red box, which I ignored. Then back to London for the big Channon Ball at Kelveden, Essex. First to a nice dinner in Eaton Square with Patricia Rawlings, who has become a firm friend of mine. Patricia doesn't like her Tory leader Robert Cranborne, whom she describes in the unkindest terms. Not unkind enough in my view.

The Heseltines were there – my third dinner with them in 12 days. Michael still in cracking form. I asked him about the deprivations of leaving office and told him how for Herbert Morrison it was like a divorce or a bereavement. He completely agreed. Listed the things he missed: the power, the daily routine and excitements and, with commendable honesty, the media and public attention – 'People aren't very interested in one any more.' It was interesting that he was so open and reflective on this. The old Michael in office didn't seem interested in this kind of reflection.

The Marlboroughs were there, Sunny with a bad cold following our freeze-up at the Heseltines last Saturday, about which they were both severe and funny. The current (4th?) Marquess is quite sparky and an attractive Dane, I think named Rosita. I discussed with Victoria Reagh how the wife survived life with Sunny, who is pleasant but hardly a barrel of fun. Victoria, from her own experience, was very clear. 'For an upper class lady, it's a question of taking the whole package: enjoying the fruits of money, lovely houses like Blenheim, the plush social life and the children.' If the man is boring it's possible to arrange things so she does not have to spend too much time with him. 'There are plenty of interesting friends – and even discreet boyfriends.' I completely understood (even if Princess Diana was too fragile and naive to accept it).

Others there were the Lennox Gordons. He was a bright diplomat and came up to me and said from full Whitehall experience: 'You have the worst job in the worst department in Whitehall.'

We broke quite early, and set off at great speed for the Channon house in Essex. Kelveden is stunning, entered through vast arch gates and up a long torch-lit drive. Many guests were arriving in a procession of buses hired to leave from Belgrave Square every half hour. It was funny to see various barons, knights and ladies pouring out of these buses.

The party was in a huge marquee half the size of a football pitch, with hundreds of sparkling lights in the roof to make it seem like a night sky. Endless champagne, which I ignore. Danced a lot with Sarah. Paul was dancing with his children and Ingrid looked better than I have seen her for years – we first met 20-odd years ago at a George Weidenfeld dinner and then again at Harold Lever's.

Chatted mainly with Sarah's old friends; but managed to avoid Princess Margaret, though she was looking well and had a friendly chat with Sarah. Also talked with Mick Jagger, who seemed very respectable and was not with a lady – though was surrounded by several later when Sarah found him using the ladies lavatory. Some politicians there – Ken Baker, David Howell, plus Heseltines – but very few considering Paul is an ex-Cabinet minister.

And not a single journalist. Paul has always been clear about his standards. He once had concerns about inviting Sarah and me, though she is a life-long friend, because he thought I was still a journalist. The funny Earl of Onslow was there and was very nice about me to his wife, saying I as a minister had been more helpful to him than his own Tories during 18 years. We sat with them for an early hours breakfast, where he explained BSE to Sarah – something I have never so far risked.

Nice final thought of Paul Channon was that his great formal photo of him and the Thatcher Cabinet was tucked away in the kitchen loo. Incidentally, Michael Heseltine told me tonight that he had returned to his publishing empire, Haymarket, but they had moved on since 25 years ago and didn't have anything for him to do. Told it in a nice self-deprecatory way.

Saturday 26 July 1997

Set off for Ascot in torrential rain. Lunch in the BBC box with nice Will Wyatt, who is unlike the new BBC management army of grey accountants. Loves racing and we share a jumper with some friends. And Foreign

Secretary Robin Cook with his nice race-loving son Chris. Robin was in lively form; chatting and joking with the ladies around him. Told a story about how the FCO had finally persuaded him to go to his Foreign Office residence at Chevening and not Scotland 'for a quiet weekend'. But it was very noisy with some grand fête. Chevening is mainly run for the benefit of the trustees, who have sole rights to shoot there. He wanted to change some of the upper crust trustees but found the last Tory government had given the present club a long lease.

I went to the paddock with Robin to watch the horses parade. We discussed the Labour party at length. He is openly critical of Blair and New Labour. Admits they have 'put together an impressive coalition to win elections', but says they have no principles or objectives for which to use the majority. Fears they are trying to move to a US Democratic Party, winning elections on low turnouts. Says Blair actually hates the Labour Party and thinks we are in power only because of him, and despite the party. He attacked Gordon Brown: saw no point in trying to cut taxes when nobody thinks they are high any more. Better to help education and the Health Service. He clearly feels very Old Labour and out of line with the new regime. His problem is that he is a loner, not a team player, and I cannot see him lining up a team to launch a coup. I have been racing with him many times over the years but this was the first time he has been willing to talk at all, even about racing. He was much more open and witty. Office is obviously good for him. He told me that the FCO wasn't tiring and he had told them not to give him too many papers. Must try that with MAFF.

On reaching the car park to leave, I ran into ex-Tory minister David Mellor and his new lady Penny Cobham. He told me to enjoy Agriculture and said that it rounded off my career nicely since, 'You have done most other things.' He thought Hague was 'a disaster' as Tory leader, said the Tories will be out for a very long time, and that he is 'pleased to be out of it all'. His brushes with disaster have not left a scar.

Went to bed for a quick kip and then to another grand thrash – Peter Savill's 50th birthday party, at Danesfield House Hotel near Marlow. Another grand marquee, though not as big as the Channons'. Still must have been 250 people there. For supper I sat on a table with the outstanding young race trainer John Gosden, the Bottomleys, and the Governor of the Cayman Islands. Rachel Gosden was very lively and told me she and her friends didn't trust William Hague at all. Virginia Bottomley sat on my right and kept stroking my arm in a friendly fashion. She is still very partisan, criticising the Labour ministers, especially Tessa Jowell, and asking if 'it's true about Derry Irvine'. I could not elicit what 'it' was. But she shared my view of the current press. 'I hate them; but Peter is very keen on them, always phoning them to try to get himself in the newspapers', she said. He is a publicity addict.

Sarah and I had some nice dances and we went home after 2.00 am. I didn't feel too tired and am pleased to have come through such a social offensive relatively unharmed.

Reflecting on Robin Cook, I can see his intelligence, political judgement, craggy integrity and sharp humour, but I don't see him becoming Prime Minister. Something missing there. No sweep. No vision. Confined. All he says is very party based and confined to his own slightly narrow personality. Also, of course, he is very and proudly Old Labour (unlike me – I am Antique Labour). That is his constituency base, but it's a shrinking base. Blair is expelling the unions and marginalising the party, liking neither. So even if they all rally round Robin, he won't have a big base. And nowhere to attack from, since the National Executive Committee (NEC) and Conference no longer have power.

Today's *Sunday Times* has an article by a New Labour insider, describing how the new gang operate. Just like Clinton in America. All media focused, all the message and the image, and everything tightly controlled from the centre. Anything Old Labour, including its best principles, is seen as a threat and an enemy, since the New Labour message must monopolise the media. Compared to that panzer-like political machine, Robin looks very quaint, old-fashioned and touching.

Also reflecting on Virginia Bottomley, she may be suffering from the same destabilising effect of losing office that Michael Heseltine referred to. Sarah, who is still a Tory, said Virginia seemed 'a bit wild'. I still like her and sense a basic decency beneath the bossy veneer.

Sunday 27 July 1997

Newspapers, diary-writing and lunch outside in the sun, ignoring the large red box Maggie brought on Friday. Feel relaxed about all of that.

Monday 28 July 1997

Finished the offending red box just as Maggie arrived and dashed up for a meeting with Jack and the Permanent Secretary on Honours. The officials had been reluctant to provide this but Jack had insisted – and that I be there though it wasn't on my diary. They produced the New Years honours list. All the usuals. Jack quickly spotted there was no one from the North of England

and we tried to repair that. Everyone on it was prosperous from the South. Jack asked me to look further into the system.

Lunch at the Savoy Grill with Chris Bell from Ladbrokes. Discussed the racing scene. Says Wakeham not doing a good enough job at the Horseracing Board and ought to go early. He thinks the new government is doing astonishingly well. Tell him I hope to move out of politics into racing before too long. But in fact am really enjoying being a minister now. Great change from two months ago, when ready to quit. Helps to know a little more of what I am talking about. Also a good and happy team.

Back for a meeting with Barry Leathwood of the TGWU [Transport and General Workers Union] and his colleagues. Discuss health and safety, especially increasing accidents on farms. Still feel instinctively close to working trade unionists.

Bob Worcester of MORI came in to report on a survey he has done for the department on outside attitudes to MAFF. Not surprisingly, hostility from the media and the general public. But the farming community was favourable, especially to our local level officials. I propose to give them more support and local initiative. Then tough meeting with Lib Dem Matthew Taylor and two employees from Truro about our decision to close that office. Employees shattered, face either unemployment or moving home away from family etc. I felt awful. Packer bounced that through me on the first day to save £100,000 (allegedly; those savings often don't appear – really it's administrative tidiness). But cannot say that. I did refer it to other ministers and special advisers, but in the end it was my inexperienced decision.

To supper with Michael Bedford. We had a good gossip. He says Kleinworts is in a poor way, having just lost stars Simon Robertson and David Clementi – and today sacked my old friend Michael Short after 30 years in the firm. The City is a harsh place now, with no sentiment or sense of community. Glad I am not there.

One MAFF reflection. Officials again praised the press office to me, saying, it 'is the best in Whitehall at killing a story'. No sense that this is a purely negative attribute and they have no skill at handling the media positively. The result of years under the cosh. And Packer's view that the whole of the world outside 3 Whitehall Place is enemy.

Tuesday 29 July 1997

Best meeting yet: ministers and officials, covering the whole BSE and meat hygiene field. Very disturbing. Showed the department didn't really know who we are controlling, where they are, and what hygiene controls there are – and anyway too few staff to monitor the controls. Jack said it 'is a shambles'. He was very tough but fair with them. He decided to take a broad thrust forward to attack bad hygiene. Central purpose is to reassure the EU and get the beef ban lifted.

Officials were all over the place. Hadn't cleared matters with Brussels. Unclear on the legal situation. Didn't know how to make the pet food ban legally watertight. Jack exploded and said all this trouble arose because the Tories had not legally implemented the beef ban and we now had to bend over backwards to reassure the Europeans. He clinically demolished Packer. It was the best and most vigorous exchange between ministers and officials so far. Made me more optimistic we will get a grip on the department and turn it round.

Jack said, 'There is a culture and ethos here about not enforcing the hygiene rules, hoping we can get away with it. The department is too cosily close with the meat people. It has got to change.' It's clear that both the existing rules and enforcement are quite inadequate. Brussels is right on that at least. But the head of the Meat Hygiene Service from York was very impressive in defence of what they're doing to improve standards – and the problems they have with meat men intimidating their hygiene officers. Jack revealed that his strategy was to get No. 10 so committed to getting the meat ban lifted that the PM will press the Treasury to pay the costs of our enforcement measures on improving hygiene.

Afterwards Jack saw me alone and asked me to probe the whole public appointments field. I have been asking for papers on this for weeks but officials have stonewalled. Now he has extracted the key file and passed it on to me.

At midday had a great meeting with Tessa Jowell from Health and Estelle Morris from Education. On reintroducing free school milk in needy areas. They were both keen – though I know Health officials are against. Very positive, productive meeting, typical in its small way of the good spirit still prevailing between ministers in this government.

Terrific lunch at Buckingham Palace with excellent Queen's private secretary, Robert Fellowes. Also Stephen Lamport, Prince Charles's long-suffering private secretary, and press officer Mary Francis, who was at the Treasury and then worked for John Major in No. 10. They clearly see little hope of securing better coverage for the royals. Robert said that Wakeham as Head of the dodgy Press Complaints Commission is 'in the pockets of the press barons' and he hoped Labour would bring in a Privacy Bill.

The Blair/Queen relationship is going very well and they said, 'Cosy relations have been established with this government faster than ever with the previous administration.' I repeated Charles Anson's view that it's easier for the royals now we have a presidency in No. 10, diverting media attention from minor royal yobbos. I also recommended they cultivate Derry Irvine, who they didn't know, and invite him to see the royal paintings and even to Balmoral or Holyrood.

Much on Charles and Camilla. Robert thought marriage not on. Lamport less sure. Mary Francis, as a practical woman, thought they should get on with it and get married; that today people accepted remarriage but didn't like mistresses without marriage. I thought of me and Sarah, and afterwards Robert said the same thought crossed his mind. But I am not the future King! Thank God. I said play it slowly and public are coming round to Camilla, especially now they've realised that Diana is not so perfect.

Robert said on the way out to me that the Queen 'is a pushover' for him, doing everything right ('even Phillip in his cranky way'). But Charles is 'very difficult, not wanting to listen to advice he didn't want to hear'. I warned them not to try to be too trendy – that was how Charles made his catastrophic mistake admitting adultery on TV. (That was his previous private secretary's advice!) Robert said but they didn't want 'to be caught in an Edwardian time-warp'. Fair enough. I said they should aim to be timeless. Not try to be like ordinary people. Most of the Windsors, except the Queen, are actually very ordinary; but the Monarchy isn't.

On the way in I entered through the front side Privy Purse door and was taken along a lovely corridor the whole length of the palace, looking into the inner courtyard. Passed Prince Andrew on the way, who looked quizzically at me as if he might know me. Doesn't. Must be confusing me with a look-alike Irish golfer. The lunch room was very pretty, looking over St James's Park. Furnished in Chinese style. Food just a cold plate with fruit and cheese.

Robert kindly thanked me for the supper I arranged with some Labour politicians at Henry Carnarvon's a couple of years ago, which he said began their getting closer to the Labour side. Four of those, Ivor Richard, Gareth Williams, Robin Cook and myself, are now ministers.

I had put on my white lightweight suit when leaving home this morning, completely forgetting I was having lunch at the Palace. I was ready to dash home and change. But Sarah said nonsense. She phoned Robert's wife Jane (sister of Di), who also said nonsense and that, 'They are lucky to have you in a white suit.' She is a very good sort, with no side, and quite different from her sister.

A fascinating drinks meeting with Robin Butler in the Cabinet office. He still treats me like a young mate, as 23 years ago in No. 10. We discussed Packer. He said he wanted to move him, but the problem is where. Didn't want to sack him. I agreed, must not do that. Has so many virtues, is able and I'd discussed it with Jack this morning who said, 'Don't humiliate him. But he must go because he has this department in a deathly grip. They're all trapped in the past and dare not change because they're afraid of him.'

Also discussed restructuring the department and I suggested bringing in the Countryside Commission and Rural Development Agencies from Environment when we lose the Food Standards Agency function. That would make us a genuinely rural as well as just a farmers' department. He said he'd given it a lot of thought but hadn't decided. His own successor will be announced next week.

Good dinner with Colin Ingleby-Mackenzie and Susan and Sarah at the Lords. Good chat on cricket. He thinks our selectors hopeless – and he is President of cricket's governing body, the MCC!

Wednesday 30 July 1997

Routine ministerial meeting then a good meeting without officials. Jeff is magnificently resisting pressure to take our new cattle traceability unit to Guildford, which is convenient for officials, but doesn't need the jobs. He means to take it to Workington. Jack seemed very relaxed and feeling we are finishing the term well.

My Question on the Food Safety Agency went quite well. I answered all the follow-up questions comfortably and the Countess of Marr congratulated me and called me 'a breath of fresh air'. But I knew I had gone on too long, offering too much information – and Jim Callaghan said that afterwards. Will be snappier next time. But must watch out. Some people will think answering without notes is 'too clever'.

Thursday 31 July 1997

Last day of the first term; and a lovely visit to the local Berkshire region. First to Shiplake farm near Henley, seeing all the usual cows, hearing all the usual farmers' complaints. Then visit the regional headquarters in dreary Reading.

After to the highlight, which was visiting Brakspears Brewery in Henley. Lovely old fashioned building, with workers there for their fourth generation. Tasted some good beer – they supply the Bell at Waltham St Lawrence. These are the kind of people who should have honours, not just the big Beerage who finance the Tory party.

Home quite tired. Fell asleep reading *Wind in the Willows*. Jack is Badger, Jeff is Ratty and I am toad. Not sure about Elliot Morley.

Friday 1 August 1997

I spend most of the day slogging away clearing my desk. Brought this diary up to date. Wrote letters. Then Maggie arrived with the last red box horror and I had to flog through that. Want to clear everything before leaving for France tomorrow.

Curiously, Labour failed to win the Uxbridge by-election yesterday, with the Tories holding it with higher majority. Partly because Labour foolishly imposed outside candidate. But also sign that no majority is forever.

It has been an exciting term and I am lucky and proud to be included in it. All my early doubts and pessimisms have passed. I really enjoy the ministerial and parliamentary part of it. Jack's support has greatly helped. The department is a problem. My office is not quite right. We have to get the staffing right.

Grimley is a mix as private secretary. Very bright and knowledgeable. That helps enormously. Works hard and fast. All the usual virtues of the young mandarin, helped by a science background, essential in the Agriculture ministry. At times reflecting all the MAFF characteristics of negativeness. But he is improving and begins to suggest initiatives. Where he stonewalls, as over public appointments, I imagine that is Packer refusing to give. He will be better when we get a policy assistant and he can concentrate on the most important things. I have enjoyed most the parliamentary performances and the regional visits – will do more of those and encourage the local officers to take more initiative.

As for the government, it has had an exciting start. Impressive momentum and clear on what it wants to do. Blair has given a remarkable lead. He is obviously intent on being a kind of President, with all power in No. 10. That is OK while he wins but will be tough when things go wrong. They are trying to get all ministers to clear all media meetings and all speeches with No. 10. I don't see how they can avoid being snowed under. That will fall apart or fade. As for the Cabinet, I can see from the minutes that it deals only with broad issues in general. Little detail discussion. And fewer Cabinet committees to do the spade work on legislation.

Blair's main contribution is to talk about presentation – Mandelson style. But Uxbridge shows some of the problems. Electorally the general election landslide was the peak and it's going to be difficult to match that later once the government starts upsetting people, as all do. Also the desire to centralise everything, kicking out the local candidate and imposing a new Labour clone, does produce local resentment. The party problems will increase. Blair really dislikes his Labour Party and, like Jimmy Carter in the USA, would prefer to rule via the public and the media, ignoring Parliament and the Labour Party. Denis Carter said the whips had spotted that Blair knows little about Parliament and has little feel or affection for it. Hence his affinities with Thatcher and Clinton. None of the great Labour parliamentary leaders are heroes to him – if he actually knows who they were. His knowledge of Labour history is thin.

In the Cabinet, those who have done well are: Brown, Straw, Blunkett, Beckett, Dewar, Irvine and Jack Cunningham. Less good are Prescott (whose Department of the Environment is in shambles) and Harriet Harman. Gavin Strang is hopeless at Transport and Jack tells me David Clarke is weak at the Duchy of Lancaster. Anne Taylor is on hold. In the Lords, Margaret Jay and Liz Symons stand out. Tessa Blackstone is very knowledgeable and hard working; she has a tough task at Education and looks strained. She needs to relax and enjoy it more. Ivor Richard is a stately leader at the dispatch box and should hold on. Denis Carter is doing very well as chief whip and is terrific at helping me out on agriculture when I am out of London.

But how lucky I am. Great finish to my career to do the minister bit; something I have watched, written about, advised, but never done. There is nothing quite like it. Even so, I am the fourth oldest member of the administration, behind John Gilbert, Ivor Richard and Stanley Clinton-Davis. So cannot expect to last long and won't complain when it ends. Funny me being old. Most of my career I have been the promising young one – always 'Young Bernard' at the LSE, on the Sports Council, in No. 10, in the City, as a peer. Now suddenly a generation shift. Blair has put my generation on the scrap heap, with aggressive implications that the old, especially Old Labour, are redundant. No respect for wrinkly wisdom. So I am lucky to be still in there. And will enjoy it while I can.

Will be back from France on the 19th. Never had such a short holiday there. May be time to sell the beautiful house? Or keep the house and give up being a minister?

Saturday 2 August–Tuesday 19 August 1997 (Ceret, France)

Very good holiday, busier than usual, with visits from Rachel with grandson Ben, from Kate and husband, and from Graham Greene and new girlfriend Camilla Panufnik. Suited me since I was not feeling like a long silent read lasting five weeks as often in the past. Though I did greatly enjoy three Patrick O'Brian novels; a book on the first day of the Somme battle and Lorna Doone (which I had never read as a child and found wonderful story-telling).

The flawed swimming pool blighted a few days. It is threatening to slip down the hillside. One reason it's not insured by the builders is that they have never declared it for tax or insurance. That is life on the Mediterranean.

Bought *The Times* and *Telegraph* each day and followed British politics. The term ended badly for the government, with a series of minor scandals. A Scottish MP committed suicide complaining colleagues had hounded him to death. That West of Scotland Labour Party has always been dodgy, linked with corruption and lots of nasty political fixing.

Then the news broke of Robin Cook's marital separation after 29 years. Apparently No. 10 ruthlessly gave him only ten minutes at the airport to either deny the alleged affair with (inevitably) a Commons secretary, or announce he was separating from his wife. He did the latter. We would never have done that in 1974–79. Marriage was a politician's private business. This sleaze and moralistic obsession with sex, which obsesses Anglo Saxons and especially their media, is vomit-making. The French do it better by accepting the politicians are human, with human flaws, and their private lives are private. Politicians in Westminster with wives in the North living separate lives are always at risk. Funny, I saw Robin often at Westminster and had no clue of this.

Campbell and Mandelson tried to spin away this story in the modern fashion, by planting other diversionary stories that day. It worked at first but not for long. Mandelson attracted much criticism in the media and he seems a bit waspish when under pressure. Oddly he rarely appears or speaks in Parliament. Like Blair, he is not really interested in the Commons. Believes the media is all that matters and that is where he performs, impressively. It symbolises how Parliament has declined and the real politics now takes place in the TV studios.

Blair is on holiday in Italy and then moves to France. There are lots of references to him in the French media, so he has clearly made an international impact. But I feel the New Labour honeymoon is ending. Since taking over in 1992, Blair has had a soft ride against a divided Tory party. It will be interesting to see how he reacts when subject to the daily manure-throwing that poor John Major and previous Labour prime ministers suffered.

Saturday 9 August 1997

The English newspapers are full of trash about Princess Di's affair with Al Fayad's son, Dodi. Also attacks on Mandelson for losing his temper. Also because he foolishly boasted that Blair had left him 'in charge of the shop'.

Must realise that 'eminence grises' must stay grise. That is the source of strength for the man behind the scenes. Must be invisible, pulling the strings unseen. Once he takes the spotlight, he will become a target – and then just another one on front of stage. So bound to run into trouble – though I still have great respect for his clever ability.

Press also full of attacks on Robin Cook for leaving his wife. Typical humbug. A third of Britons divorce – even more among journalists. Still, Labour has asked for it, by so often taking the prissy high ground against the Tories. As Harold Wilson said to me: 'The higher the moral high ground you take, the further the inevitable fall.'

Sunday 10 August 1997

Our last evening with Rachel and Benedict. Pleased Rachel finally called him that and not Benjamin. Victory of Rome over Jerusalem.

Monday 11 August 1997

Delicious dinner with our neighbours, the Count and Countess Lecaillon de Chamblage. They have just sold their house – to Nick Glydon, who I employed at Kleinworts a decade ago. (He said he remembered me for being an early fan of quantitative analysis investment – I recruited the first 'quant' analyst in the City.)

Tuesday 12 August 1997

In the evening we sat on the terrace watching a beautiful sunset before going out to dinner. Glorious. Idyllic – yet have just spoken to an agent about possibly selling this beautiful house. Feel very divided. The hassles of maintaining a house abroad grow increasingly irritating to me. Yet can I really give this up after 24 years? So much of my pleasurable life – my reading, walking, the children growing up – is bound up with our summers here in Ceret. We will see.

Am reflecting on my being a minister. It seems of very small political consequence and does not impress me. We have cramped offices, modest level civil servants and grotty cars. The media says politicians are only interested in grabbing their 'big black limousines'. In fact, it's symptomatic of their reputational decline, as most ministers, certainly junior and middle rank ones, now have worse official cars than they own privately. Their civil servants are themselves diminished in professional stature and have much less respect for their ministers than was the case 20 years ago. The media is contemptuous and the public scornful.

So it's not very impressive to be a minister of the Crown in 1997. Not like it seemed 30 years ago. Blair has improved things temporarily, by bringing the buzz and panache of a fresh administration with a great skill in media manipulation. But basically it feels very mediocre in Whitehall. That is reinforced by the sense that we ministers have very little power – especially in Agriculture, where most of the decisions are taken in Brussels.

It does not bother me personally. I am content to be a diminished minor minister. And the sheer excitement at first of being a new minister in a new administration does give it a special feeling, so I should not complain too much.

Thursday 14 August 1997

My secretary Peter Grimley phoned from MAFF to raise various office issues, including the coming visit to Northern Ireland and my plans for promoting the export of British cheeses. Realise I have become very interested in MAFF. Helped by Grimley being much more positive and I think we can work successfully together. The private secretary is the key to any minister's success.

But the problem is that the department generally views ministers as marginal. Their view is that they run it all on a permanent basis and that ministers are mere transients who they have to fit in with as little disruption to their normal routines as possible. This view is reinforced because agricultural decisions are often taken in Brussels and so London MAFF ministers are seen actually as just rubber stamps – as for much of the time we indeed are.

Well, I will work on changing them and will encourage Jack to do the same. For a start, I am removing both of Grimley's assistants, who are really just administrative secretaries, and bringing in a young policy assistant, so we can spend more time on policy issues. Then I can make better use of Grimley's undoubted policy abilities. After that I can turn to the press officer – and then, more challenging – the Permanent Secretary!

Saturday 16 August 1997

Daughter Kate arrived in the evening, beeping her hooter as she drove along the Col de Bousseils. Terrific to have her. She has always loved it most among the children. Brings back a flood of memories to me.

Tuesday 19 August 1997

Drove to Montpelier and fly to Gatwick, then home to Shurlock Row. Sorry to leave Kate, but really nice to be home.

Wednesday 20 August 1997

To the office on a stifling day. Collect masses of post from home and then clear a pile of papers at the office. Grimley is positive and bright and I feel that's going to be OK.

In afternoon go to the proposed new office in Smith Square. Then home to the country via Kempton Park, where our syndicate horse Memorial ran impressively badly to finish 20th. The weather was so oppressive that I left after the third race, driving my own Toyota because, although 11 years old, at least it has air conditioning. Won't use the official car till the cool weather returns.

Saw Jeff Rooker in the office. Told me that Permanent Secretary Packer had intervened in his Accounting Officer role to stop his decision to send the new cattle traceability section of MAFF to Workington. The officials want it to be in comfortably convenient Surrey, despite the low unemployment levels there. The North is thought to be terrible. Intervening as Accounting Officer is thought to be the last resort in a Permanent Secretary's control over ministers. With Packer it seems to be a somewhat early resort!

Thursday 21 August–Friday 22 August 1997

Worked very hard. Cleared red boxes. Dealt with my huge personal mail accumulated over the holiday. Also spend a long time completing my analysis and recommendations on reforming the departmental system of public appointments and honours. Although ministers are held responsible, we have little say in the process, getting only the final list of recommendations, usually with the statement that it must be agreed immediately. Basically, officials, especially Packer, do it all. They love patronage. I suggest a menu of reforms to open it all up. Sent it by post to Jack's home in Durham. If it went through the department, the officials would intercept it. Curious when two ministerial colleagues have to use subterfuge to communicate. A previous memo I sent him was intercepted by them and hidden away in his file described as 'unimportant', which he never gets time to read. All *Yes Minister* stuff!

Late on Thursday evening, Mo Mowlam, Northern Ireland secretary, phoned me from Belfast to apologise that she won't be there when I visit. She has to fly back to visit Blair. We discussed Northern Ireland and she asked for my help in getting the Ulster Unionists around the negotiating table. Said Trimble is being undermined by his treacherous colleagues. But that the IRA is ensuring that the ceasefire holds. She sounded very tired. Hope she is not ill. She concluded, 'The real work hasn't yet begun.' So I hope they have a big new peace settlement in mind, as David Montgomery and I always did.

Sunday 24 August 1997

David Montgomery phones me from Italy and asks me to warn Mo Mowlam that the Unionists will be frightened out of the peace talks if Ahern and the Republic government are triumphalist about them meeting the IRA. Will pass that on to Trevor West in Dublin.

Monday 25 August 1997

Quiet bank holiday, raining steadily; just the two of us. I write a letter to Mandelson about the need for a new Media and Communications Act and the need to strengthen the Culture team with someone who understands communications – imply that he could do it well. Rang his private secretary for Peter's home address – but he said he didn't know it! Ludicrous lie. How do they contact him at home? How does his driver find him to drive him to the office? Typical of Whitehall's obsessive need to control everything in a minister's life. Cannot bear the idea that a minister might get a letter they do not see. He gave the game away by saying, 'Send it to the office and I will make sure he gets it.'

Tuesday 26 August 1997

Maggie came at 7.30 am to collect me for my first ever visit to darkest Northern Ireland. Met Grimley at the airport desk and took the grubby shuttle. Improved at Belfast when collected by Colette O'Connor, the Northern Ireland Office agricultural representative who was in charge of my visit. All smiles and curly hair, and clearly from the right side. She confided that she was delighted to see my letter to her minister Alf Dubbs talking of the 'Six Counties' – the Catholic nationalist code for Northern Ireland. In fact this was accidental, and not very clever politically. Would understandably have upset any Unionist. Just subconscious. She said, 'We call it that, but it's the first time I have known a British minister refer to that on paper.' Indeed. And ironic, since I have rarely had less sympathy for the nationalist cause, at least in its extreme forms. They nearly murdered Sarah! Won't ever forgive them for that.

Began with a visit to the Northern Ireland Agriculture Ministry offices in Dundonald House on the Stormont estate. Excellent briefing on the whole policy area – and also on cattle traceability, which is nominally my main reason for being here (my real reason is to see the political problem on the ground). Then into Belfast for lunch at the Stormont Hotel. Dominated as ever by the Farmers Union, banging on about how they will all go broke within six months unless given ever more grant welfare. The separate farmers union for smaller (mainly Catholic) farmers had problems getting a word in edgeways. The Permanent Secretary was very good at handling them. In fact he took the political issues and I stuck with the technical ones, which protected me from later misquotations.

Onto the BBC where I pressed my main political point: that we need to restore indigenous democratic government to Northern Ireland so that politicians can deal with the real issues that concern local people and not leave a political vacuum for the gunmen.

Then a meeting with a local trade unionist, Terry Carlin. He had been involved with 13 Secretaries of State for Northern Ireland, ever since the first, Whitelaw in 1972. Says Mo Mowlam is quite the best and everyone trusts her. He confirmed my view that the 1974 Protestant Workers' Strike could and should have been resisted – and he took part with Len Murray in making sure that the 1977 similar strike attempt was seen off: they made the Secretary of State, Roy Mason, face it head on, which, earlier, Merlin Rees would not do. He said his worst ministers were Francis Pym and my dear old friend Humphrey Atkins.

Colette helped me to fit in a private off-agenda meeting with a famous Catholic priest at 5.00 pm. His church stands in the small Catholic enclave of Short Strand, surrounded by massive Protestant estates. There used to be some mixed areas here, but the minorities have been driven out and there are firm sectarian housing lines. Father O'Brien told me that he had 3000 parishioners, of whom 1300 come to mass each week, giving £900 a week (at prosperous Wargrave we raise £500, and Sarah's Anglican church has trouble raising £50). His entire parish is lower class. Most are permanently unemployed, some into their fourth generation. He said that if they got a job offer from the Harland and Wolff shipyard, which we could see down the road, the men dare not go in case they are murdered walking through the Protestant area. (Republican areas offer the same hospitality to Prods.)

But he had an encouraging story to tell. He had persuaded the local authority to tear down the horrendous school blocks, from which almost nobody emerged with any qualifications, and build smaller schools, with better teachers. He had worked on the parents to take more interest and now people were proud of the qualifications their children were achieving. When he first arrived, there were nine drinking clubs – 'mainly raising funds for the Provisionals' gunmen' – whereas now there was only one. He had helped to restore a community, and to restore his lovely church. He said the Tory ministers Tom King and Brian Mawhinney had both given him great support. But he admitted his main purpose was to help the young people to climb out of the enclave: 'There is no future for anyone here.'

It was eerie driving to the church, with people watching us suspiciously from street corners or from behind net curtains. Our driver Des is a Protestant and he looked quite nervous; when he got lost he wouldn't get out to ask the way. Colette did that.

We drove down to Newcastle on the coast under the Mountains of Mourne. We covered over a hundred miles and got a good view of the countryside towards the border, including some of the bandit country. Interestingly, there was very little sign of our security forces. The recent ceasefire has definitely made a difference. My visit would have been different without it, if I made it at all.

Also interesting was the difference between Colette and Dave. She bubbly and very 'Irish', referring to 'Derry' not 'Londonderry'. He dourly 'Scottish', referring to 'Londonderry'.

Back to Hillsborough Castle by 7.30 pm and met by a young butler who is very suave and informal and does mischievous imitations of his famous previous guests. Cannot imagine Henry Carnarvon – or Lord Brookeborough for that matter – putting up with that. But he is clearly very bright and entertaining.

I was put in the great 'Queen's Suite': three rooms, a vast bedroom with a huge double bed under a canopy, where the Queen sleeps when she visits. A quick bath and then down to the drawing room for a reception with the selected top Ulstermen for the dinner. There were the three editors of the main Belfast newspapers. They fitted in with their sectarian images. The *Newsletter* man, Billy Kennedy, craggy and inflexibly dogmatic; the *Telegraph* man, heavy and formal; the *News* man, Tom Collins, ebullient. Alf Dubbs chaired it all with his usual relaxed humour. I realised with relief that Alf is older than me, so I am only the fifth, not the fourth oldest minister in the government.

Dinner in the smaller of the official dining rooms. We had a good run over the Irish situation. It's clear that the sectarian divides are as wide as ever and that the Protestants didn't expect the talks to produce anything and that they saw the IRA as being bound to return to violence. Also they don't think that Trimble will last in the Unionist leadership and perhaps

Taylor will oust him. In the end, we Brits were saying they 'must take a chance on peace'; and the local Protestants were saying, 'You cannot trust them and it will all end in tears.' The latter may be right but Mo and Blair must take a chance. However thin the chance may seem, the situation has never been better – or less bad.

At 11 o'clock, Alf was visibly getting tired and he thanked them for coming. They paused only momentarily to let him say that, and then launched off again. He finally got rid of them at midnight. Still, it was very lively and I learned a lot from seeing the sectarian sides in action together. They certainly need a permanent talking shop – which we can provide.

I slept deeply and was woken by the butler's call at 7.30 am. Watched the TV news coverage of Mo's peace talks, with Loyalist criticism of the lack of an effective vehicle for decommissioning IRA arms. I never expected anything on that since no revolutionary movement ever finally gives up all its arms before a final agreement.

At breakfast, Mo's able political adviser, Chris McCabe, gave me a terrific briefing on her talks. A very open and detached Protestant, he said that the Prods are the most paranoid, always questioning his loyalty, while the Nationalists don't seem to care what his religion is; they are accustomed to having the other side in power.

I asked him to describe the scenario over the next nine months and he was very clear. The Unionists will go for the maximum on the 'first strand' of devolution, probably wanting a legislative assembly, though I canvassed my moderate view of an administrative assembly as a first stage. The Nationalists will want the maximum on strand two – the cross-border institutions and cooperation: all-Ireland tourism, sports and arts, perhaps roads and even agriculture. Here the Unionists will be scared of the slippery slope into a united Ireland and will walk out if it goes too far. He said that Gerry Adams knows he cannot have a united Ireland all in one go and will accept a compromise. Strand three is amending the Anglo-Irish Treaty, where the Nationalists want it strengthened and the Unionists want it weakened, so they may not get very far.

He was overall mildly optimistic, though realistic from all his years of failed initiatives; and thinks Gerry Adams will be tempted to come on board, since he knows the Armalite rifle military option has failed against the British army. He said Mo is very good and people trust her.

It was a fascinating discussion and demonstrated again that I am more interested in Northern Ireland politics than in agriculture. Would like to be in Mo's team – but Sarah, with her Irish wounds from the Brighton bomb, would never stand that.

Drove off to a poultry factory in Antrim. The weather was sunny and breezy driving through a pretty cattle landscape. But the poultry plant was for me horrific, a nightmare. Dante's Inferno. Or like a Belsen for chickens. It was the cleanest and safest in Britain. But the process made me nearly physically sick. The chickens were queuing up in fluttering thousands to go in, perhaps looking forward to being fed. In a flash they were hanging upside down on lines of hooks, feathers torn off, heads and innards ripped out, some stripped of their legs and wings. Miles of them moving head high around this factory, skirting our heads and dripping blood. Horrific smell. Miles of hanging corpses, moving in endless rows. Soon they were spiked and workers in white uniforms and gloves tore off their breasts for freezing.

Afterwards we were taken straight to the factory canteen for a quick lunch – of various kinds of cooked chicken. I couldn't eat any of it and made an excuse to leave as soon as possible. I am not a vegetarian but this could make me one. It will be a long time before I can eat chicken again.

Sped to the north coast to see the Devil's Causeway. A very attractive coast-line with Scotland only 40 miles away. Perhaps they should build a tunnel so the Prods can escape should the Papists prevail at the talks.

Quick tour of the Bushmills distillery, which is the oldest distillery in the UK and makes fine whiskey – less oily than Scots because distilled three times instead of twice and also not peaty. I had a double, which washed away the chicken smells. They also gave me a fine bottle of their special aged whiskey – which I passed on to Dave the driver who had done a fine job for me. He commented that 'It's not often that a Catholic gives me a drink.'

Raced back through Antrim to Greenmount College of Agriculture from where I did a radio interview over the line. Like everyone here, their priority is to get the beef ban lifted for Northern Ireland alone – and bugger the rest of Britain. But I always silence them by asking them if they really want to be viewed by Britain as a separate place, not part of the Home country. The Prods then all back off, because, of course, that route leads to a United Ireland. They want to remain integrated in the Union.

Although exhausted, I was quite sorry to leave. It had been a fascinating trip, and, except for the extremists on both sides, they are a truly lovely people. I would love to go again, but it will be difficult to find another artificial excuse.

Thursday 28 August 1997

Lunch at the Gay Hussar for sentimental reasons with Graham Greene. We used to go there 20 years ago when it was the centre of radical eating in London. Now it's less used, old Fleet Street having moved down the river to

Canary Wharf. But today it still had sparks of yesteryear, with several familiar oldies. In my usual window seat were Labour left wing icon Michael Foot and former *Mirror* editor Bob Edwards – certainly averaging 80 years between them. We chatted with Bob, but Michael could not see us. He looks like Methusala with his grey locks, and his sight has gone. They go back together to the Beaverbrook Press over 50 years ago.

Friday 29 August 1997

Spent hours writing up the diary for which I had kept extensive notes. Did another red box and signed loads of letters for other ministers in my regular duty role.

Saturday 30 August–Friday 5 September 1997 (Ceret, France)

Off back to France again. Don't really want to go – first time in 24 years have felt like that. Have had enough holiday. Enjoying the ministerial work in London. But also a curious and ominous feeling, as if there is something bad going to happen in France. Maybe that the plane would crash. Never had such bad vibes and such a strong presentment before. Made me very nervous on the flight and didn't sleep well.

Sunday 31 August 1997

Had breakfast and switched on the French radio station to hear that Princess Diana had been killed in a horrific car crash in a Paris road tunnel, with her boyfriend Dodi killed as well. All my ominous apprehensions confirmed.

Am devastated. Dare not tell Sarah for half an hour, could not believe it, hoped my bad comprehension of French had somehow misled me. But then it was confirmed on the BBC World Service and Sarah burst into a flood of tears. She is distantly related by marriage, since Diana's aunt was the first wife of Sarah's late husband, Tony Berry. We were devastated and sat for hours on the terrace listening to the World Service, which cancelled all its other programmes to run this sad item all day. But the one thing they didn't say was that it was these fucking tabloid journalists who murdered her. Harassed her 24 hours a day and now the paparazzi had chased her car on their motorbikes until it crashed trying to escape them.

It isn't just the photographers, though they are vile, It's also the British tabloid editors, gossip columnists and proprietors who pay the paparazzi fortunes for their intrusive photos. The French radio stated this directly, quoting the huge fees paid by the British newspapers compared to the small offers from the French media. But they are all indirectly guilty and it would be some consolation if some were sent to jail. But they won't be – though Hell must, fortunately, await some. And, of course, the tasteless wider public that avidly consumed these intrusive photos must share the blame.

We walked together in the sunset and then had a quiet supper on the terrace. Still listening to the BBC – excellent coverage, but not a single journalist presenting the programmes said sorry on behalf of his low trade. Many journalists were paraded, all concerned only to argue that this must not lead to any constraints on their licence to continue to make huge money out of intruding into people's privacy.

Remembered that when I last met Princess Diana at Althorp – at Raine Spencer's great party – she was delightful and wickedly funny, saying she had come only so she could secretly tour the house and note which Spencer family heirlooms Raine had allegedly filched and sold off. (Though Raine recently told us the two of them had finally grown affectionately close together, which is nice since both, in their very different ways, are stars). Diana was certainly a global star, in her own celebrity way.

She was also, of course, a symbol of much in the modern world that I don't like: glamourised public sexuality; her media creation as a celebrity, dependent on the media, ever conscious of them, needing them and exploiting them, as well as being exploited and abused by them; but at the same time also hating and resenting them for their relentless intrusiveness.

Yet beneath all that glittery veneer, which I disliked, she was very special and millions of suffering people throughout the world felt they could identify with her vulnerability and that she somehow touched them from afar. We think of those poor boys, left now with Charles and that dysfunctional Windsor family. Charles himself is a casualty of them, unable to express proper emotions, except in his occasional adolescent foot stampings.

Perhaps Charles should now marry Camilla and enjoy his private life. If he gave up his claim to the throne, William would have a united nation behind him. Soon wounds will heal.

Monday 1 September 1996

A morning full of phone calls from England: Jane Rayne, Corinne, Susan, Charles, all saying how weird it is in London. Strangely quiet in the offices and in the streets. I try to resist this because I don't like mass hysteria, nor do I like the glitterati world into which Princess Diana had drifted. But regret not being in London to observe this extraordinary response.

A lovely morning, but rain blew in from the Pyrenees in the afternoon. Ceret very autumnal, quiet and damp, few tourists. I am keen to get back to England and the job.

My long French honeymoon is nearly over. Starting in 1949 working as a gardener at a château in Dijon and culminating in buying this house in 1973, and now coming to a close. Ceret began with the children young and a need for me to expand, broaden my context. Now children grown and flown. Local French friends gone, divorced or dead. One-time friends in the village old and I never see them there, never in the bars where we met for aperitifs when younger. Once Ceret was a village community of which I was a part. Now it's a tourist town where I know nobody. Anyway lots – too much – travel lies ahead with the job. Czech and Hungary Republics next week, Poland and Indonesia after that.

Tuesday 2 September 1997

Quiet day. Did little except read O'Brian. Continuous phone calls, mainly to Sarah, about the atmosphere of collective grief in London.

Wednesday 3 September 1997

French media still full of Diana. And English full of criticisms of monarchy for not allowing changes of protocol for Diana because she is not a royal. So no flags at half mast, no special funeral route. Public is very angry, blaming Charles, Camilla and royals for having driven her out and to this end. Clearly the Windsors have got it wrong, not realising that Diana had struck a unique chord with the public. I can hear Phillip saying, 'That removes one of our main problems', and Margaret saying, 'Diana would be enjoying all this media coverage.'

I am a strong monarchist who believes our present Queen is our greatest monarch and appreciate how hard their job is; but they seem to have got this wrong.

Thursday 4 September 1997

Read some of Patrick Leigh Fermor on his walk across Hungary prior to next week's ministerial visit there; still a great read but spot bits of pretentiousness. Prepare departure from Ceret. The usual sad ritual of clearing the terrace, putting away chairs, closing shutters, all the steps to bring summer to an end.

Friday 5 September 1997

Home to Shurlock Row for tea. Henrietta Knight phoned to say poor Peers Folly has bled again and cannot race, so must find a nice home for him. That is nearly 7 years I have had jumping horses and had the pleasure of only two completed races.

Saturday 6 September 1997

Worked on two red boxes here to remind me of the treadmill. Then watched the service for Diana from Westminster Abbey. The sisters very good. Blair a bit over dramatic. Outstanding was the address by young Charles Spencer. Conveyed his sisters character perfectly and the love he felt for her. Plus a savage and popular attack on the media. The congregation in the Abbey and in the roads and parks outside exploded into applause at the end.

We watched on TV as her cortege went through the Althorp gates and they shut behind. It was poignant for me watching it wind through those Northamptonshire villages where I often went in childhood, to play football or to stay with Gerry Fowler (another old friend gone).

Sunday 7 September 1997

Lunch outside. Chatted with Henrietta Knight, planning to give away Peers Folly to Rose Baring who lives near her. I would like to visit him sometimes. More dangerous is that Henrietta has another horse that I might lease. I had sworn I wouldn't do it again, but am weakening.

Nice little letter from Peter Mandelson, saying he likes my idea of him handling a new Media Bill, but there are 'sensitivities' which may stop it. Also my son Stephen told me a Northern Irish friend told him I am 'the main conduit for the Ulster Unionists.'

Monday 8 September 1997

My 63rd birthday. Don't feel older, except for my stiff shoulder. In fact younger than before taking office. The adrenaline softens age. Lots of lovely birthday cards – nine, the most I have ever had in my life. As a child never had more than two. As a teenager just one card from dad and one from my girlfriend Jill.

Spent the morning clearing papers and packing for my visit to Prague. Then to London for a pre-trip press conference. End of the afternoon I walked down the Mall to see the flowers outside St James's and Buckingham Palace for Princess Di. The road was closed, the crowds silent and the scent rich. Thousands of poems from small children. It's too much, over the top. It's in danger of becoming big celebrity show business. Then I will switch off.

Evening family birthday dinner. I am uncomfortable with both birthdays and Christmas because of bad childhood memories.

Tuesday 9 September 1997

Off to Prague on a glorious early September morning. Called in at Kensington Palace to see the acres of flowers glittering in their cellophane covers. The people have avoided the Palace, blaming the royals for her death, and have gone direct to her home. Streams of silent people, often crying. It was a very un-British sight.

Waited an hour for the luggage at Prague's bright new airport, so the liberated Czechs are obviously copying capitalist Heathrow habits.

Went straight to the city centre to walk around the old city. Pretty and well restored with stunning views from the Danube bridges. Has become a bit of a tourist theme park, but a five star one. Lots of German tourists. Some old enough to remember their occupation and when they burned the innocent town of Lidice after massacring the population. Not sure they do.

Returned to the Residence, a most impressive Austro-Hungarian imperial mansion with a lovely garden under the castle walls and stunning views from my room over the Danube; the old city, bridges, spires and rose-coloured roof tiles. I had the grand room, which Prince Charles would have occupied now had he not cancelled in apparent mourning. I look forward to living a few days in elegant Foreign Office style. Amused that my bags were carried up four flights by two hefty central European ladies. They reminded me of left-wing members of Labour's National Executive Committee long ago.

A quick briefing in the sitting room and then out to the nearby Palfry Gardens, which have been renovated, partly with Charles's help and money, and were being officially opened by the Czech President Havel. Very pretty, with tiers of wall and gardens scaling above to the high fortress castle overlooking the city. The President spoke, referring to Diana. Other local dignitaries gave endless speeches. I drifted off enjoying the wine and the gardens.

After the ceremony we had a buffet supper and a delightful chamber concert in the lower garden. Apparently there is a huge number of fine musicians here and the music education in the schools is superb and free, far superior to ours. Communism had a few pluses.

Incidentally in the gardens I met Diana Phipps, a friend from Downing Street days. I had lost track of her, like many fair-weather friends, when I lost power and headed for the wilderness. She was invited back by Havel to restore and run her family castle – no doubt very well, since she had fine decorating taste.

Wednesday 10 September 1997

Heavy work day, but fascinating. Opened with meeting in the Parliament building with the chairman of their agriculture committee. Very well informed, but serious and definitely no jokes. On his other side were two ladies who never said a word, bulky Stalin Grannies, probably with time in the KGB.

I learned a lot about Czech agriculture. The big issue for them is to prepare for admission to the CAP when they join the EU in about 2002. Their Communist background and training in fraud will prepare them well for it.

Then to a farm on the edge of a village 30 miles southwest of Prague, where new British management is helping them to improve the crop yields. As far as I can see, all it requires is teaching them to plough straight, a bit of spraying and a couple of new machines. The yield is up 30%. Many of their farms are very big; the hangover from large Communist collectives. This was over 2000 acres. Production dropped dramatically after Communism, because the new private owners often sold off the machinery and went to spend the proceeds on consumer living in Prague. Freedom meant drink and washing machines, but less food production.

The ambassador was classic 1960s Foreign Office: elegant, slim, smooth, able, reactionary, pro-Arab and anti-Israel. He said that Scottish devolution, a main plank of the government that employs him, 'is a total waste of time, just hot air, nobody wants it, not even the Scots'. It was reassuring to see the FCO mandarins as closely in touch with the pulse of British life as ever. But it was a lively dinner and he handled it all very well.

Thursday 11 September 1997

Had breakfast with Grimley (who is doing very well, good company and good advice) and then strolled in the garden. Impressive Henry Moore statue, which the Moore Foundation wants back, but so heavy nobody willing to pay the transport costs. Then fly to Budapest. By chaotic Hungarian airlines, in a dodgy Tupolev, with huge hand luggage piled on seats and in the aisle.

Relieved to arrive in one piece. Met by another very smooth FCO man who seemed to make everything glide.

Lunch in a restaurant on the hill above the Danube hosted by their minister, Dr Kis, who was very political but colourful and lively. Told us the Hungarians were naturally depressive and had the highest suicide rate in the world. Liked him.

Went down into Budapest to the impressive wedding cake Parliament building and then dropped in on our joint working group helping them to prepare for entry to the EU. Afterwards met Minister Nagy, who was first class, and we held a huge press conference together.

The embassy residence was another winner, smaller than Prague but the same kind of imperial 19th century elegance, like a small French chateau, with lovely large rooms and again a pretty garden. My room again grand with heavy central European furniture and superb views. Had a quick soak in a huge metal bath and then off to the ballet. Supper at a nearby restaurant where the waiters and waitresses sang between courses, all being students at the nearby opera school. I loved the feel of the old Austro-Hungarian empire everywhere, resisting all the efforts of the Communists to eliminate it. They are a very intelligent people.

Friday 12 September 1997

Lovely relaxed day full of beautiful horses. Opened with news of massive Yes victory on Scottish devolution. Tempted to phone the Prague ambassador but don't want to appear ungrateful for his hospitality. To lunch at a vast state farm, Babolna, half way towards Austria. 50,000 acres and 3000 workers – probably bigger than any working estate in England. There since set up by the 18th century Hapsburgs as their prime stud farm. Saw a parade of fabulous grey Arab stallions. Left reluctantly to drive to the stunning Pannonhalma Benedictine monastery where they gave us an organ recital; like Monte Cassino dominating the countryside from a high hill. Sixty monks and a fine school, the only monastery left open by the Communists.

Saturday 13 September 1997

Visited another stud farm, troupes of lovely foals. Reluctantly left for Vienna airport. Had good conversation with the Ambassador in the car and agree to try to press our food sales to central Europe. Our producers sell nothing here, but I shall try to push them, using Tesco's new supermarkets as the vehicle. Arrange to set up meetings back in London.

Flew home and early to bed feeling very tired.

Sunday 14 September 1997

Went to visit and say a tearful goodbye to Peers Folly. He is with Rose Baring at the big house in nearby Ardington and looked very happy. We had a sentimental farewell with polo mints. I felt quite emotional, quite apart from the £40,000 he has cost me for just a couple of completed runs.

Monday 15 September 1997

Ambled the morning away clearing papers. Up to London for a delightful reception at the French embassy. Chatted with the economic attaché, who on CAP reform said the French don't disagree with us as much as it appears, 'but we must go along with the Germans and not upset them'. The French have abandoned their patriotism and snuggled into the capacious German pockets.

John Wakeham came up to me to tell me what the Press Complaints Commission is doing about privacy post-Diana. He claimed to be bringing in big reforms but they didn't add up to much. His main concern is to stop a Privacy Bill. Is worried that the entrenchment of the European Convention of Human Rights will bring it in anyway, so wants an amendment to say it must not introduce any rules not currently in British law – so no privacy rules. That will please the press barons. Once Diana is forgotten they will all be back to Business as Usual.

Wednesday 17 September 1997

Had to cancel today's planned trip to the potato banquet in East Anglia (great relief) because of sudden meetings with Jack on the presidency and next week's Agricultural Council. Also problems with the French attaché, who phoned to fix lunch. Grimley says he and another official must be present. I cannot be trusted to talk alone to a French diplomat. I pointed out that I was doing that 25 years ago and Prime Ministers Wilson and Callaghan didn't mind. But their passion for control is insatiable. So I give way. They can come. But they will pay. And I will see the French privately anyway.

Despite these nonsenses, am getting on well with Grimley. He admitted on the phone that the first few months had been difficult for officials as well as for ministers and they had been 'feeling their way'. I told him to be more open with me if it was the department, and not him personally, that was blocking things, as with the appointments nonsense (on which, incidentally, Jack told me that he liked my July memo and had given instructions for me to be the designated minister on appointments). Peter is very intelligent. His problem, like with all officials, is finding it difficult to admit that not all ministers are complete fools. There is also, of course, the deeper problem in the minister–civil servant relationship. On the surface, officials have to be servile, carrying the bags, fixing the diary, saying 'Yes, Minister this' and 'Yes, Minister that'. They understandably resent this, often indeed being brighter than their ministers, sometimes having contempt for them. The mixture of servility, resentment and contempt emerges as a kind of superciliousness, which we captured well in *Yes, Prime Minister*. That was there in Grimley early on. But things have improved. They have grown to respect Jack's shrewd common sense. And I feel Grimley is much easier with me now. Of course, he has to reflect the department will. He told me that was his biggest difficulty, faithfully obeying the department but trying to achieve what I want. He said it wasn't such a problem under the Tories since their ministers 'were not so pro-active'. I also think Jack initially sacking his private secretary shook them. Grimley told me that would never have happened under the Tories.

Thursday 18 September 1997

Early start to a meeting with Jack and the NFU. Their leader David Naish is quite impressive. He attacks us, but Jack doesn't mind, saying that is his job, he has his own constituency. Certainly the farmers are now being squeezed from all directions. But many of them have had a cushy time, with enormous income growth in the past five years. And they are not top of Labour's priority for scarce funds. Naish is having to adjust to the fact that he is no longer running MAFF.

Cleared a lot of papers. Silly Elliot Morley has intervened to try to stop me going to a country sports conference, saying, 'This is my policy area', like a child. Not worth making a fuss about. But he's simply not one of the team. As Jeff Rooker says, 'He has his own agenda', and doesn't care if it puts Jack at risk and, 'He doesn't realise that being a minister is different from irresponsible opposition.'

Went to strange Cabinet committee in the lovely Treasury Board Room in the Cabinet Office, where 22 years ago we fought out the incomes policy. First item to try to stop streams of illegal refugees coming through the tunnel on Eurostar. Jack Straw was impressively tough – for me he is the surprise in the government, much better than I had ever expected. He has a sense of public opinion and none of that liberal woolliness that wants to open our doors to these people and let our working people pay for it and suffer the strain on the social services and competitive reductions in their pay levels. Alistair Darling, very impressive as chief secretary, very dashing with his young grey hair and black eyebrows. Another impressive Scot.

Most of the other ministers didn't speak. Tony Banks was sitting next to me, playing the clown as usual, and he left half way through. Prescott was strange in the chair, menacing, sometimes intervening, but often unintelligible, a stream of words at ever increasing speed. He must be uncomfortable for Blair.

Then walked to No. 10 for a meeting of junior ministers with the Prime Minister. I noted that since the IRA ceasefire they have removed the security barrier that Major had in the corridor. We sat around the Cabinet table, about a dozen of us. Blair opened by saying we must never lose sight of the 'Big Picture'. In all our speeches, broadcasts, etc. must keep referring to his four key themes: modernisation; justice for all not some; our party discipline; and the bad Tory inheritance. 'Modern. Fair. Strong.' I could see the strength of this. They are winning themes, which will hold the party together. But they are also a string of advertising soundbites, which he kept repeating like an automaton. Sounded a bit like Saatchi and Saatchi. But he does win. He looked very young and a bit hypy, but with puffy eyes, so he is obviously taking a pounding. His eyes really are curious, not quite looking in the same direction. But he is very open.

Ministers spoke in turn, mainly about their sense of isolation in their departments and the danger of losing sight of the politics. It was agreed they must find a structure to meet more often. Blair said he found his recent public question and answer meetings 'very salutary' and recommended them to ministers.

I intervened to say that it was important to have good ministerial teams and to recommend him to ask Cabinet ministers to be inclusive with their junior ministers, as we have in MAFF, or they could feel isolated. I saw some colleagues nodding in support but sensed that Blair wasn't taken with that. Really he was interested in his Commons colleagues and not in peers.

We filed out after an hour, meeting the TV businessman Alan Sugar coming in. Prime ministers have to do those things, as I realised with Harold and his clique of business supporters. Outside in Downing Street I chatted with Jeff Rooker. Came away feeling I like Jeff and his sort, but don't really get on with the new New Labour regime. Not in policy terms, since I have always been in their position, even before they were out of pushchairs. But simply because they have written us Old Labour off and there is no way we can get back in. Club membership is closed.

Walked back up Whitehall feeling a bit dissatisfied. To a meeting with John Burnett the Devon Lib Dem who is quite the nicest and most able of that southwestern group of MPs. None of the sanctimony of the average new Lib Dem. Sense he is really a Tory.

Then to Bond Street for a display of Allen Jones's latest wonderful paintings at Thomas Gibson's art gallery. Would have loved to buy two of them, but they were big and am not sure we have a wall for them. Chatted with our recent Lords Chief Clerk, who was very tickled by me being at Agriculture, since he heard me for years sounding off on the arts. Said that MAFF is 'a dreadful ministry'.

Friday 19 September 1997

Woke to hear we had scraped a yes in the Welsh referendum by a margin of 0.3% on a low turnout. Doesn't matter. At least we won. Our Welsh secretary, Ron Davies, is genuinely third rate.

Saturday 20 September 1997

Went to the Newbury agricultural show, which I enjoyed immensely. I like the country people and the animals. I finally learned the difference between sucklers, heifers and steers.

Sunday 21 September 1997

Joe Haines phoned to say heard from good source that Mandelson and Alastair Campbell have fallen out. Mandelson is blaming Campbell for recent press mishandlings, including the balls up over Cabinet ministers' salaries – and his own troubles in the summer. Campbell is obviously trying to shut Mandy out of press handling. So when the question of salaries for special advisers like Campbell came to be settled last week, Campbell, on Joe's advice, asked for the same salary as the principal private secretary. Mandy was on the ministerial group of three that settled it and tried to cut it back. He failed, getting the worst of all worlds, Campbell's enmity and failure.

Tomorrow start a heavy two weeks, at the office, then Cornwall, then party conference. Sarah complaining I won't see her and it's life with a politician all over again, which she swore she would never have again after her Tory husband Tony was killed, and that I wasn't really a politician when she met me etc. etc. See her point. And will organise my diary better in future.

Monday 22 September 1997

Terrible rail crash at Southall. Seems the safety equipment not working – consequence of privatisation where top management save on safety to get their profits and bonuses up.

Another lovely day and walked down Whitehall to the Cabinet Office for a Cabinet committee meeting on Freedom of Information in the Old Treasury Board room again, which I love. Nice olive green wall paper, gilt and white domed ceiling, fine 18th century portraits of Walpole, Harley, Spencer Churchill etc. and a throne for the monarch when he chaired the Cabinet there. Lord North, my Oxford doctoral thesis subject, was here as First Lord of the Treasury. A lovely view west across St James's Park, still full of flowers in the sunshine.

Lord Chancellor Derry Irvine chaired the discussion strongly and well. Jack Straw spoke well again – he does impress me more as a Cabinet minister than he did as a special adviser 20 years ago. He rightly argued for caution and pointed out the huge costs of full freedom of info. There were two ministers of state – John Reid (very good) and Mandelson (again didn't speak, just watching and looking pale, angry and unhappy). Straw argued well to exclude advice to ministers since that would make officials write nothing down but do it verbally.

Privacy came up because we could include a privacy clause in the Bill, but decided not to, since that is for the European Convention of Human Rights (ECHR). Irvine would clearly have liked to do it here but said that Blair is against. Afterwards Irvine took me back to the Lord Chancellor's lodgings and we discussed privacy. He would love to do a Privacy Bill because he hates the media. Says the PM is worried that the media will look to have a battle with him over this and he doesn't want to fight them. Irvine and the Law Lords think they can secure privacy through the back door of the Human Rights Convention. I warned him that Wakeham wants to block the privacy people by excluding from the ECHR everything that is not already in our law – and privacy isn't. He hopes that after the ECHR the judges will build up a good case law on privacy. We both agree that Blair has 'walked on water with the press' since 1994 and has no idea what it will be like when the rats turn and try to destroy him.

I admire Derry for his honesty and intellectual power. We agree on quite a lot of law matters. I think he will make a remarkable Lord Chancellor because of his mental and physical power. He arrives and starts work before 7.00 am each morning and is steering the three heaviest committees. The progress on devolution is mainly due to his drive.

Tuesday 23 September 1997

Unusually satisfying day of diverse meetings. Well organised by Grimley, who is now fitting in very well. Finished with very painful meeting with the unions and staff at Truro on the closure of our office there. This was bounced through me by Packer on day one; with claims of financial savings of over £100,000 a year. I checked with ministers and the special advisers and all said do it. But I wouldn't do it now. I don't believe in the savings. Think it's just a question of tidiness for the local office. And people lose their jobs with no prospect of getting another one down there. I thought the union case much better than ours. One of the Truro ladies could not speak her bit because she was in tears. I had to tell them there was no chance of reversal. But afterwards I let our people know that I think we are wrong. I would prefer to spend the small amount saved on keeping those good and loyal servants in work. But as minister must defend my wrong decision in public and carry the can for it.

Dinner with Monsanto, the giant US agrochemical producer. Don't know how I agreed to it. Don't usually do anything with the PR people. These agro-giants are interested only in money. They pushed the horrible OP pesticides. Afterwards, never felt more ill in my life and will never risk another oyster. Finally to bed and asleep at 5.00 am, but woke at 7.00 because due to go on my fruit visit to Kent. Felt very drained and wobbly with terrible sore throat. Sarah said I must not go and I agreed – until I watched the TV news and a lead item was my important visit to Kent. So dare not drop out and staggered off to Victoria. Had to sleep on the journey to recover. But a good visit. The fruit farmers had suffered terribly from the frost. They didn't whinge too much, even when I told them we had no money. And my positive press release, which the press office tried to stop, went down well. Problem of casual labour keeps coming up. Soft fruit people need it and cannot get English labour because our young people don't like hard physical work and the social security system is too inflexible. So they end up importing Poles and Albanians. Crazy when we have such rural unemployment. I will try to change it; but the bureaucrats will want a tidy system and bugger the unemployed.

Back for a hurried meeting with Estelle Morris and Tessa Jowell on school milk. The nutrition fascists oppose milk, meat, or anything but fruit and vegetables. Still I will get some progress in the end.

Thursday 25 September 1997

Wonderful visit to Cornwall. But bizarre start. Collapsed exhausted into bed last night and Sarah said not to worry about the alarm for my 7.42 am train since she always wakes at 5.00. She did, but she didn't tell me she sometimes falls off to sleep again at 7.00. Which she did. I was deep down the well when she screamed at me that it was 7.30 am. Just 12 minutes to dress, shower, shave and get to Twyford station two miles away. Aged 65, I was running over the bridge and down the stairs as the train pulled into the station and I just got it. These early mornings are killing me.

Bodmin at midday and a nice lunch with locals. Walked around Padstow harbour in the sunny afternoon, hearing about a new lobster project. On to Port Isaac – memories of those lovely lobsters and my great cliff-top walk from Port Quinn – to talk with the fishermen about their problems with the Common Fishing policy. How did Thatcher ever sign up for it? Opens our rich fishing grounds to the continentals, especially the greedy Spanish, who have completely denuded their own.

Friday 26 September 1997

My visit on local TV and in local papers. BBC did an interview over the phone. Am stressing the export potential of the local food industry and job creation projects there. Grimley good company and intelligent advice despite his bad cold. We get on well together now. He says he has finally realised and accepted that we are quite different from the Tories: 'more proactive'.

Visited two breweries, one tiny and one big. And a wonderful vineyard in the Camel Valley run by two Labour councillors. Stunning site and good wine, including a rare red. Lunch at Lanhydrock National Trust, beautiful house and site, with a group of locals to discuss their problems. The media hung around and I gave several interviews to sensible local journalists. Then at the smoked fish factory at St Austell, where the unions and Truro workers waited in a trap to nobble me and chant for their office to be reopened. I knew I could not duck them so I arranged to see one sweet lady and the union man in a garden overlooking the harbour. I knew they were doing their job and much was at stake for them, though I could not change the decision. But afterwards again told the officials that we were wrong and that jobs mattered more than administrative tidiness. Slow train back and staggered to bed feeling signs of a cold.

Sunday 28 September 1997

Supposed to go to Brighton for the Labour conference race day. But woke feeling off. Stayed home and read and rested. In the evening did the red box and very relieved didn't go to Brighton.

Monday 29 September 1997

Papers and diary in morning. Arrange to go to Brighton by train at teatime. Am looking forward to it. First went there in 1962 for party conference. Some terrible conferences in the 1970s and 1980s. But now the lunatic left have been demolished by Blair. This will be a jolly celebration. First time for me there as a minister. Hope to see lots of old friends. And of course Ben and Rachel who live there.

Joe Haines phoned. Alastair Campbell yesterday sent him the draft of Blair's conference speech. Thirty-two pages, too long, with too much detail and too little real vision – just sentiment. Speeches should never be written by committees.

In Brighton it took me an hour to get into the hotel. The Oak is right behind the conference centre and that central part was entirely cut off from the street by a fortress of railings and policemen. I had to drag my suitcase for half a mile, around the block and under tunnels, through a security apparatus like at an airport.

I showered and went off to the Friends of Israel meeting. Only person I recognised was Gordon Brown on stage. So I moved on to the Metropole, met up with Clive Hollick and Michael White, a good old pro from the *Guardian*, and we dined there. William Keegan of the *Observer* joined us. Robin Cook came up for a chat – interested in the journalists not me. I asked him how I should handle my visit to Indonesia, falling apart in civil war. He said, 'Two options: 1) don't go; 2) head down and don't say a word.' Robin was with a small group, presumably from the left, and I didn't recognise any of them. Although topping the NEC elections, he does seem a bit side-lined and friendless. Gordon Brown came up smiling and clearly pleased with his today's announcement on 'job opportunities for all' – a modern soundbite for old fashioned 'full employment', and clever since it doesn't actually commit us to a figure. Tessa Jowell was looking happy; office suits her and I feel close to her again. Chatted with Margaret Beckett and her husband Leo – old lefty and adversary of mine in CND [Campaign for Nuclear Disarmament] days, but a very good sort. Clearly the Metropole is now the conference centre, not the Grand, since the NEC moved there because the Grand won't recognise trade unions. The Metropole does – and the room service is accordingly slow and awful! We all have to suffer for our principles!

Going back to my hotel, I saw Peter Mandelson surrounded by journalists, quizzing him on his defeat in the National Executive Committee elections. In fact he did quite well with a respectable first time vote. Informed him that his grandfather, the great political manager Herbert Morrison, failed at his first attempt. Peter will succeed in due course, having Herbert's genes (not that it will matter since the NEC is being downgraded by the New Labour reforms that Mandy has himself advocated). But the party activists want to rap him over the wrist and tell him not to assume he can get everything he wants easily. He accepted defeat very well, saying it 'will make me more humble'. On that we will wait and see.

Tuesday 30 September 1997

I rose slowly and walked to the Grand where I chatted with Mark Fisher. He complained that Chris Smith is completely under the control of his cunning permanent secretary at the Department of Culture, Hayden Phillips. This is a familiar cry from junior ministers who don't know how to work the machine and get isolated in their departments.

Went into the conference centre at the last moment for Blair's speech. Was refused entry at most doors because it was packed but finally with Geoffrey Robinson we talked our way in and found seats in the ministerial ranks. I sat behind Mandelson and next to the empty seat marked Michael Foot. Jim Callaghan wasn't there either. In the Metropole last night he told me that he had received only the standard computer letter saying he was invited but had to get there early and they could not guarantee a seat. At 82, and the last Labour prime minister to attend conference, he wasn't too keen on that. So he didn't come. I warned Anji Hunter this morning that they should get on to him quick and make him comfortable, but they clearly failed. The old bugger can be obstinate.

Incidentally, with Anji outside the Grand this morning was Irving Alka Selzser, the Murdoch economist who wrote a creepy letter to Blair after the Tote lunch last year saying I was opposed to Murdoch and to free markets in broadcasting (re. the Broadcasting Bill) and should be sacked. (Leading to my vitriolic response to him.) We made it up, as he seems to have a nice sense of humour.

Blair's speech was better than last year, shorter, tighter and a better balance between the hard policy nuggets and the general uplift guff. Clearly speaking to the nation beyond the faithful in the hall. Very impressive and had everyone captivated. But I still find a touch of Lady Di schmaltz in it, tinges of Nuremberg mass populism, and too much moralistic preaching. In this self-righteousness, he is too close to the sanctimonious Lib Dems – and even to the Labour old Left, which he has bravely and rightly eliminated – for my taste.

What really worries me is that there are a lot of hostages to fortune in the speech. Not just in specific policy promises we can't meet. But in the visionary uplift. Always talking about a future greater Britain, with no one on the streets, no illiterate children, everyone in happy families at work and looking after the old. All apple pie and everything getting better. People love it, especially after the dreary visionless time of Major. But what when in three years we still have a million and a half unemployed, still have people homeless on the streets and vandalism and poor education and queues for the health service? There will be a sense of disappointment. He may be raising unattainable expectations, which will later lead people to feel that he has let them down. Wilson, Callaghan and Major never risked that.

But for the moment it's nice to have hope and young politicians with hope. And to see the press cynics so unhappy because people are happy. There were two overflow meetings for the speech today: one cinema was crowded with party people giving a standing ovation to Blair on the screen. The other cinema had media people loudly giggling and sneering, and desperately trying to demonstrate that they were cynically unimpressed and were superior to the rank and file and clearly miserable that people were having a happy and constructive conference.

I walked out of the back of the conference with Jack Cunningham. We ran straight into Blair and Cherie and stopped and had a chat. I told him that the speech was good and tight. 'You should have seen it 24 hours ago', he said. Jack told him about tomorrow's dog rabies quarantine enquiry announcement. Blair said, 'Give it to the *Daily Mail*. Vere Rothermere will love it.' I said, 'And the diplomatic service.' He said, 'The whole diplomatic service', and they waltzed away on a wave of adrenaline. Cherie looks on high, clinging on to him by hand as if in danger of losing him in a high wind of hype.

Tea at the Grand. Long talk with the Irish Ambassador, Ted Barrington. Tell him to curb the Republic's triumphalism and work to keep Trimble in the talks. Also met David Irvine, the new Ulster Loyalist who Trevor West recommends. Saw Pat Hollis; we had a laugh about civil service tricks. Apparently David Clarke at the Duchy of Lancaster took in his special adviser on his first day and asked to have him in the office next to him. Officials said that would be very difficult since that office had to be decorated. The decoration took several months while they tried to steer the poor advisor into a distant office.

In the evening, I went to the 1000 Club fund-raising dinner in a huge hall at the Metropole, which Jack hosted. I was stuck on a table paid for by some curious Russian company with the Russian ambassador. Managed to push idea of MAFF doing consultancies to improve efficiency of Russian agriculture, as I saw near Prague. Finished the evening at the ITV party, full of politicians and media. Had good long chat with David Montgomery. He is seeing David Trimble to discuss how to handle Trimble's meeting with Blair next week. The Unionists are still split about participating in the talks and some are still trying to get rid of Trimble.

Afterwards, walked back along the front. Am unusually enjoying conference, where the atmosphere is friendly and constructive. Incidentally, I was sitting behind Mandy at Blair's speech and said to him that he had done well for a first try. He said, 'But they never see that. The media judge me by different standards.' I agree – but he is responsible for that, being inextricably wedded to them.

Wednesday 1 October 1997

Spoke to Robin Butler, who is arranging a big retirement thrash as Cabinet secretary, wants me and Joe Haines to go – in recognition of our saving him when Harold Wilson's political secretary Marcia Falkender angrily demanded Harold sack him. That should be good.

Conference today, mainly on education and charging fees. Expected to go through; Blair is currently unbeatable. The opinion polls give him 93% support; Wilson was lucky to get 43% and Major lucky to get 23%.

I sat in a deck chair on the beach and read *The Times*. Afterwards, walked back to Jack's room in the Metropole and spent the afternoon there – much of it waiting for a plate of sandwiches from the notorious Transport and General Workers Union room-service. Jack dealt with his speech for tomorrow, including the announcement of the enquiry into quarantine and rabies. Clearly he has come down for reform and he said cannot imagine the proposed report will support the status quo of stopping dogs from travelling into Britain. Sends for David English of the *Mail* to give them the advance scoop. English was delighted, knowing it would please his proprietor because it will let him bring his dogs over from Paris.

Then a nasty little spat with our London press office. We want a press release for my visit to the Downs tomorrow and Jack's excellent special adviser, Cathy, phoned the press officer to offer to help. He told her to bugger off, that he didn't think there should be a press release and he didn't want her interfering. This was with her standing beside Jack and me, and she was upset. Jack immediately phoned his office and said to tell the press office that if they wouldn't co-operate with his political adviser he would replace them with somebody who would. I phoned Grimley and said I had two brief points: one, that I wanted a press release for every visit – if it wasn't worth a release it wasn't worth me going; and two, that I would decide and wouldn't tolerate this man always deciding that there was no need for a release. These officials would see success as when neither MAFF nor its ministers appeared in the media at all. Then they could stay in bed all day. Jack, Cathy and I then discussed the press office and decided we had to make changes. Interesting times ahead.

Leaving the Metropole, I ran into David Trimble with David Montgomery so we had a chat. I congratulated Trimble on his courage in taking the Unionists into the peace talks with the IRA present. He was very pleasant and said he was taking a 'calculated risk'. He knows some of his troops are against him. Mo Mowlam also came up to talk to him, looking exhausted and not her usual jolly self.

To the *Mirror* party and met David Montgomery and we agreed to go off to English's restaurant for dinner. Mo Mowlam was already in the restaurant with ex tabloid editor Kelvin MacKenzie, who does TV stuff for the *Mirror*. Monty told me that, on *The Sun*, Murdoch had ruthlessly exploited MacKenzie, driving and hectoring him, till he started having nervous breakdowns and had to leave. Said Murdoch 'pays them off well but cannot sack them face to face'. MacKenzie was very loud, occasionally funny, more often just vulgar. Like a Tory Tony Banks. He admitted that Blair has put Tories like him in a dilemma, having stolen all their policy clothes.

Mo and David had a private chat about Ireland and then she came to talk to me. She was, perhaps for some medical reasons, wearing a curious turban. But she is brave.

Also had a long talk there with David Miliband, running the No. 10 Policy Unit on a very long rein. Press my views about the need to establish government policy priorities for the second and third years – and how awful the press office is in MAFF. He said how awful the Permanent Secretary is. I defended Packer, saying he is able, but needs a new department. David is friendly as ever; but not sure he is in the mainstream of No. 10 action.

In bed by 2.30 am. Am enjoying conference greatly. Providing I can take my own time, attend selectively at the debates and at fringe meetings and don't any longer have to sit up all night helping to write the PM's speech.

Tessa Blackstone returned from Italy on Monday. She told me she was bumped off the overbooked plane. They picked the wrong victim. When they said they were full she asked to fly with the pilot. They capitulated and she did.

Thursday 2 October 1997

Up early to pack and book out. Virginia Sylvester, our Southern Region Director, took me on a lovely visit to an Environmentally Special Area on the South Downs above Brighton and Ditchling. Wonderful views across the Sussex Weald. Then she drove me home to Berkshire; she lives nearby. We had a fairly open talk about the department. She thinks Packer has been there too long and that our press office is hopeless. She likes Grimley and I told her so did I – that I intended changes but he was safe. She will pass that on.

Friday 3 October 1997

Watch conference end on TV. Great final rabble-rouser from Prescott, whose words completely run ahead of any meaning. But morale clearly great. This government can now do whatever it wants – providing it knows what it wants.

Will try to recharge the batteries so ready for Poland on Monday. Have had enough travel.

Saturday 4 October 1997

Worked on the boxes in the afternoon. Main interest a terrible paper by the senior information officer suggesting spending another £400,000 on loads more press officers. I write a reply saying we don't need any more, just better.

Sunday 5 October 1997

Finished my boxes with a lot of letters to sign. A copy of a memo from Packer to Jack, ticking him off for saying something at conference critical of the department. That will shorten his reign even sooner.

Monday 6 October 1997

Met at Warsaw airport by Ambassador Christopher Hum (are all ambassadors called Christopher?). Straight to the residence for meetings. Whole embassy building clearly Ministry of Works 1960s Stalinist-municipal, with touches of modest art deco. The Ambassador is nice, elegant (why are all top FCO people so slim and slightly effete?) and academically bright; cannot imagine any of them playing rugger or drinking pints.

Went on long walking tour of old Warsaw. Remarkable how they have restored such a huge area to its exact old style, after the Germans, with characteristic efficiency, systematically dynamited the whole beautiful mediaeval centre in 1944. At least the Communists were good at restoring. Shown round by a lively Polish lady, who was aware of the ruthless ethnic cleansing that had gone on in central Europe, after the war as well as during it. So Warsaw, like Prague, is now almost wholly Polish, having successively got rid of the Jews, the gypsies, the Ukrainians, then the Germans and recently the Russians. She bravely said it was now 'more boring and less cultural'. Must apply to the rest of central Europe.

Tuesday 7 October 1997

Very early meeting at round table with the deputy minister; in charge of preparing for their entry into CAP. They are desperately keen to join CAP, which they see as an open tap of money for their farmers, most of whom have no more than 10 acres of land and do subsistence farming. It would be crazy to apply the rigid CAP regime to these million gardeners.

From there, hair-raising 45 km drive west to a farm – 30 acres, big by their standards but small by ours. Just one long strip of land on which was mainly grown fodder for the 27 cows and two bulls chained up in a scruffy shed. The roads were busy and the overtaking suicidal – I was driven by the Minister of Agricultural Production himself; clearly the speed limits don't apply to ministers. It was pretty flat and I recalled the old newsreels of the Nazis driving through Poland and setting fire to everything. Farmer very nice with classic, cheerful wife. Between them they do everything. A pity if the bureaucratic CAP eliminates such good people.

A troop of ministers came to the airport to say goodbye and continued to press me that Poland must get all the subsidies under CAP. Clearly they believe they are applying for free access to the Agricultural Central Bank in Heaven. But they view UK as a friend – and know the Germans and Spaniards are not. We must try to help them. They have suffered terribly in the past 60 years. Amazing they have survived at all.

So have completed my visits to central Europe. Has been quite an education for me, since didn't know this part of the world. They desperately want to join the Western club. I like them. Feel a strong sense of history there. All my wartime memories focus there, with them the victims, screwed between the tyrants of Nazi Germany and Communist Russia. Ethnic cleansing has left both Czechs and Poles more mono-cultural and less interestingly cosmopolitan, but less socially and politically volatile. Like Germany, they are all culturally and economically poorer without the Jews. Britain gained from that exodus. Hitler's only blessing and gift to us was the brilliant 1930s Jewish exiles.

Home to change and beginning to sneeze. Aeroplanes, the underground railway and doctors' surgeries are the biggest spreaders of germs in Britain.

Dinner at Admiralty House, where Jack was hosting Fischler, the EU Agriculture Commissioner. They got on famously. Jack has cultivated him cleverly, entertaining him at home in the North. After the meal Jack launched a round table discussion. Fischler was very good and close to our CAP approach, though he warned we wouldn't achieve a great deal very fast. He also mentioned 'the German problem', assuming we all understood what that was.

Chatted with Jack after and he told me he agreed with my paper on our information office and that he was fed up with it. Yesterday he had a great meeting with Fischler in Newcastle, probably the most important single event of his office, and the press officers hadn't prepared any coverage. MAFF's ideal would be no coverage of the department at all. I remember when my man explained that he hadn't issued press releases on my regional visits because 'it would draw attention to them'.

Wednesday 8 October 1997

Nose totally bunged up. In for first ministerial team meeting of new session. Decided to support a memorial to women's land army. I asked why we didn't have an opportunity to submit a brief for Blair's visit to Russia. Packer admitted it was 'a total failure on the private secretaries' side'. He promised to produce a note on providing agricultural knowhow to Russia. But I suspect nothing will happen. They are interested in their in-trays, not new initiatives that might help our private sector earn some exports.

I then sat in on a meeting with the Countryside Commission, where an impressive young man expressed their justified worries about Labour losing touch with the countryside. All agreed central problem was that Environment is the lead ministry and is a shambles. The Commission would like to come under us, but Prescott has resisted and Blair supports him – without really knowing the issues.

Lunch at the Lords with Denis Carter. He has had a long meeting with Blair on Lords reform. Says Blair doesn't really know much about the Lords or how to reform it. Denis also told me that out of Labour's 31 new peers, only seven were members of the Labour Party when nominated! He said his box is full of belated application forms for party membership hurriedly filled in by the new celebrity peers. We won't be able to rely on them voting late at night too often.

Thursday 9 October 1997

Began clearing huge backlog of personal letters. Also looked at my tomorrow's speech. Appalling. Originally nine pages, I cut it to three. Still nothing in it. I faxed my cuts to poor Grimley and instructed him in future to accept no speaking engagements unless we have something to say.

I persuaded Jacob Rothschild to let Tony Blair use his Spencer House for a reception – for free. So Anji Hunter is pleased with me and will invite me to the party. Some small pleasures.

Friday 10 October 1997

Woke with my cold feeling a bit better, until ruined by visit to London. Just to give a speech at the Dorchester to lunch of the Cake, Biscuit, and Chocolate manufacturers. Just the name conveys how far from my normal interests that is. Certainly a threat to the health of the nation – especially diabetics like me. The speech was still 20 minutes – 19 too long. I felt quite wobbly, with husky voice as I ploughed through and left immediately after. By the time I was back to Shurlock Row I had a temperature and my chest felt bronchially. Finished my second red box of the day but then went to bed.

Saturday 11 October 1997

In bed all day, woozy and dozing, nose prickly, eyes streaming.

Sunday 12 October 1997

Felt a little better. Still stayed in all day as must be fit for Indonesia next week.

Great excitements in the arts world. Gowrie has resigned from the Arts Council, following the departure of the Chief Executive. Chris Smith should take the opportunity to cut it down to size, getting rid of the politically correct clap-trappers who dominate its panels and officers. And Covent Garden is in a financial mess, having totally ballsed up its rebuilding. Wish I was minister there to help sort them out.

Monday 13 October 1997

Still feeling rotten with ugly cold sore, but up for a delightful lunch with the Equestrian Awards at the Hilton. Sat at top table as chief guest instead of Princess Royal. Next to Andrew Higgins, excellent President, who in his speech praised my support for horses.

Back to MAFF for briefing meeting on Indonesia visit, with Industry and FCO present. Planned how to push agricultural exports. It was freezing in my room. MAFF has still not put on the central heating to save money. Then when I went afterwards into the private secretaries' room, it was warm as toast. They had arranged for an electric heater for them – but the minister of course was left to freeze. That is MAFF in a nutshell.

Tuesday 14 October 1997

Lunch with George Parker from the *Financial Times*. I tried to talk to him about agricultural exports but he glazed over. Came alive at the end to ask three questions. What kind of expensive car did I drive? (Disappointed when I said my Toyota is 11 years old and worth only £2000 if lucky.) Were Jack's special advisers 'at one another's throats'? And would I be 'Mr Horse in Whitehall'? He said he might use the latter for the diary.

From there to pick up Graham Greene and go to see our old friend David Sainsbury about boosting cheese exports. David very helpful; he never looks as if he is worth £4 billion. He is coming into the Lords next week to take the Labour whip. Soon I will know more people in there than out.

Sprinted back for a three-line whip vote; just squeezed in. Chatted with Tom Chandos and we agree that the Arts Council should be slashed in its bureaucracy. But Tom says that Chris Smith does not have the balls to do it.

Back to the office and had a long chat with Jack. He complained about the civil servants still being secretive and not open with him. He had to go personally to get a copy of our comprehensive spending review for me. This sets out the departmental spending for the next two years, and so it's our policy strategy reflected in its relative financial allocations. All the decisions on my policy sectors were being taken and set in concrete without even consulting me. Worse, the provision for supporting our food exports, one of my pet subjects, was halved! It has to go off to the Treasury tomorrow and I still haven't seen it, and Jack only just has. The officials are hoping to bounce it through with minimal ministerial comment. I told him about my ideas for food exports and he said to give him a note and he would get more resources.

Wednesday 15 October 1997

Had a good morning at home reading papers, especially on the Spending Review, where I phoned in and insisted on a ministerial meeting to discuss it this afternoon.

Had to be on the front bench to support Helene Hayman doing a debate on the countryside. I should really be doing this. But Prescott at Environment won't release any territory to MAFF. So the minister for urban roads ends up talking about CAP and the countryside. Actually I had to abandon her and rush back to the department for the spending meeting. Jack was supportive, and arranged for another half day meeting to make our final policy allocations.

Nice evening reception at the Turf Club to celebrate Jean Trumpington's 75th. Kind of her to invite me – the only Labour person there. Carrington told me that the Tory conference 'made me feel sick' and he thought the U-turns by Hague and Portillo were 'disgusting'.

Thursday 16 October 1997

Embarrassing start. Due out at 7.45 am to visit new Covent Garden vegetable market. But alarm didn't work. Woke at ten to eight. Shaved and dressed in four minutes and in the car with my breakfast of apple and banana on the back seat in a plastic bag. Still fuddled when greeted at the vegetable market and taken on a tour. The flowers were lovely and I took some back for Sarah. But not a very professional start to the day. Grimley, who I like more and more, was there at 7.45 – while I was still asleep. I was never an early morning man.

Took Jack's special adviser, Cathy, to lunch at the Lords. She has been with Jack for five years. She will move back into the horse world after the Presidency. We discussed the press office. The recalcitrant press officer has disappeared since our Brighton tiff. But she says he continues to do – or not do – my work below stairs, just that the deputy chief comes to me instead for meetings. I will sort that out. More important is that Jack sorts out the whole press office mess. More difficult now that half the Cabinet have sacked their information officers, it's all on the front pages, and every move becomes a headline about Labour spin doctors. In fact in MAFF we don't want any political spinning; just some competent people who don't spend all their time in the pub.

Friday 17 October 1997

Melvyn Bragg phoned, just off to America. About the Arts Council. Still interested in running it under us, but depends on its shape. I advise him to cut it down to size without all those panels of luvvies giving money to one another. Can rely on him, a good Cumbrian.

Saturday 18 October 1997

Off to Heathrow for Jakarta and Indonesia for the first time. Very brown and dry after a long drought. Hazy sunset because of the forest fires causing smog all over the region.

After booking in at glitzy Shangri La Hotel went to the Residence for supper with the ambassador: Robin Christopher – always a Christopher in these FCO names – blonde, slim, good looking and ably smooth as they all are. Why do none of them get middle-aged spread like the rest of us? Drinks on the lawn and supper with 20 British businessmen preparing for Spotlight UK week. Only one from agro-business, which is par for the course for MAFF. Our people leave it to DTI – who of course look after their own.

Monday 20 October 1997

Woke at 6.00 am on a hazy morning. Remarkable views from my 28th floor across a townscape of dramatic sculpted skyscrapers with acres of shanty huts in between. Started with meeting of the Indonesia British Business Council, where Stanley Clinton-Davis did the business as our minister of trade. He is very busy for 69 and made a good speech. Indonesian made a good local joke: 'Britain taught us how to rule the waves; now we will teach you how to waive the rules.' Apt given their intense corruption.

Then drove 40 km to see a huge state fruit farm with all kinds of tropical fruits. Back to the city for a nice lunch at a military museum, where we were joined by a fascinating horse owner and farmer, Mr Siggitt. Elegant, sophisticated, with a ponytail and shoelace tie. We went with him to his stud with a huge police escort and policemen saluting on every corner. His mother is the boss and she showed us her stallions and mares. Remarkably they have in four generations bred from the local Subaru pony, tiny and spirited, to handsome thoroughbreds. Mr Siggit's a friend of the president, who had ordered the police and masses of press to cover our visit. Tea and cakes and cigars from his own tobacco farm. He is a clever and charming man – as most of them are.

Back to a grand reception to launch Spotlight UK. Stanley was already in the line up shaking hands with hundreds of them. I helped out a bit but it was really his show and he did magnificently. After the buffet, Stanley and I went upstairs for a private gossip. He said Margaret Beckett is a difficult secretary of state, 'cold and totally inaccessible to her six ministers'. Told me that in 1981 Jim Callaghan, as leader of the Labour Party, advised him to 'leave and join the SDP', adding, 'You can always come back later.' Prescient. Many others did leave – and have returned. Stanley doesn't like the bad manners of New Labour – 'They never thank you for anything.' (We have all suffered from that.) Says Blair and the clique around him are very arrogant. Gordon Brown the worst of all for arrogance.

Tuesday 21 October 1997

Wonderful drive (with Grimley and an embassy man) up to a tea plantation in the hills. Pretty villas and stalls of bananas on the road up. Had formal meeting with agricultural minister. Emerged that great opportunities for British fish and food processors if we would take them.

After seeing the tea processing plant, drove back discussing with my civil servants how we can export more here. Needs new focus and resources in the department.

Wednesday 22 October 1997

Lunch at the British Council, much more commercially aware than when I first knew them as the social welfare for modest poets.

Thursday 23 October 1997

Woke with a sore throat, worsened by the smog. Made my big speech in croaky voice to 150 businessmen. Then press and TV conference. Flew to Bandung, and hosted the local notables for dinner, first drinking round a log fire especially for the British – which raised the temperature from just below to just above 100 degrees.

Friday 24 October 1997

Completely lost day. Very ill and high temperature.

Saturday 25 October 1997

Day passed in a haze. Back to Jakarta on a nice train, through steamy mountain country and then paddy fields waiting for the monsoon. Then onto the jumbo and slept across the world till arriving at London at 4.50 am. Pleased to see Maggie, then Sarah.

Don't want to travel again for years. But a fascinating trip. The ambassador and Grimley – who served me brilliantly – said all the feedback was good and we had made inroads. Did my telephone round to the children. Then to Joe. He had had a phone call from Blair to thank him for his help on the conference speech. Perhaps they are learning manners.

Monday 27 October 1997

Went to London early feeling groggy to a terrific meeting on the MAFF comprehensive spending review at a hotel in Buckingham Gate (so not disturbed). All four ministers plus Packer and half a dozen officials. Good papers and a slide show on the department's spending allocations. Packer opened by saying stiffly, 'These were decisions previously taken by officials.' (So no interference then from Tory ministers in their own central policies.) Yet these are the key decisions for the next two years, deciding the policy priorities. When I later talked to Tessa Blackstone she said that in Education she has already had about ten meetings with officials on their spending priorities, right from the beginning of the process. Shows that MAFF under the Tories was totally run by officials.

Packer and the papers also made it clear that there was no scope for altering spending from how it had been under the Tories. But we wouldn't have that. Jack had done his homework and we began to grill them on relative priorities. Jack wants more for organics and pressed them on property sales. I want more for exports, where they are halving the allocation. I pointed out that much of the R&D, which assists the agro-business, should be paid for by that business. We went on right through a sandwich lunch. I felt it was the first time I had really understood how the department worked.

Tuesday 28 October 1997

To the Lords in the afternoon for my regular tea with the Tory agricultural peers. Nice atmosphere and I learned quite a lot. They said they liked the opportunity to feed in and we will fix another.

Wednesday 29 October 1997

I dashed off to Millbank for a launch of the gambling charity Gamcare, where I was due to be the first President until government intervened. Good attendance, including many racing friends and son Stephen. I had, suddenly, to give a speech which went OK, as usual when spontaneous. I shamed Ladbrokes and the Tote into giving a donation.

Lunch with Robin Butler. Our last meal together while he is Cabinet secretary. Robin finds Blair very easy and open to deal with, willing to admit mistakes and quick to praise. Said he doesn't go for the detail, so doesn't know what individual ministers are up to. Means he often has to pull them back when half way along a course – especially Robin Cook. Said MAFF doing particularly well, but is still critical of Packer; says he treats the rest of Whitehall how he treats ministers. All as enemies to his MAFF.

Robin is very worried about our proposed enquiry into BSE. Doesn't want another Scott Report, which he looks back on with personal horror, or a lawyers' bonanza. Says he has written to Jack from the PM saying have a limited nine-month enquiry. I suppose all officials in the past regime are opposed to exposing the awful mess they took part in. We discussed the Whitehall information service. He admits it's hopeless.

Agreed basic Labour problem is that Gordon Brown is trying to run the Treasury as if it's not part of the government. Currently Blair does not control Brown, and hasn't found how to do so without falling out with him. He may have to.

In the evening took Sarah to beautiful Spencer House in St James's for a terrific party given by Blair to thank his election donors. I qualified for having persuaded Jacob Rothschild to let them have it for nothing. Jacob was there with Serena, who is in love with Mandelson; understandable since both have a touch of delicious acid. Peter came over to chat and charm.

Blair toured the room with Cherie and chatted briefly with me twice. I told him that in 1974 no special advisers from any department could talk to the press without the permission of Joe Haines in No. 10. 'We will readopt that system immediately', he said. I said they had finally got into the right position on European Monetary Union. 'Yes, right position, but a balls up', he said.

Went upstairs with Anji Hunter to show round some entertainment people including Mick Hucknell and Eddie Izzard, the latter with thick make-up. David Miliband said, 'Your Packer is a real special', implying he had to go, adding, 'Don't fancy him taking on two old pros like you and Jack.' Actually Packer hasn't taken us on. Simply hasn't joined up with us.

Thursday 30 October 1997

Lunch with Tessa Blackstone, who is feeling very sore from constant press attacks. As Education spokesman, her war against Oxbridge privilege has left her exposed, since journalists see her as having the jealousy of an LSE 'chip on the shoulder'.

Had a briefing meeting for next week's Question on dog quarantine, which should not be too bad. Maggie drove me down to Shurlock Row late.

Friday 31 October 1997

Read through two red boxes and a lot of newspapers.

Sunday 2 November 1997

Drove to Eton for birthday lunch for Sarah's friend Clemency Ames (60). Chatted with Michael Portillo, who is still sore from his election defeat. Will come to dinner with us but not at the Palace of Westminster, cannot bear to go there.

I am putting on weight dangerously, partly big lunches but mainly lack of exercise. Still feel low from the bronchials and the endless antibiotics – and the diabetes delays me getting better.

David Montgomery phoned when I was in my bath. Had seen Mo Mowlam, who finds Trimble very difficult. Trimble won't reflect on strategy, won't take advice. David is also going to see Bertie Ahern in Dublin, which could be helpful. David has broadened immensely in his approach since we first met. He would make a good politician in Ulster, since he is almost unique in being able to rise above his sectarian background.

Monday 3 November 1997

Cleared some papers but mainly finished wonderful Waugh *Men at Arms*.

Tuesday 4 November 1997

Up from the country to work on the briefing for my PQ on quarantine. Lunch with Joyce Anelay, the new Tory spokesman on agriculture. We agree to be open about our intentions on PQs, continuing my tradition with William Astor, Jean Trump and Richard Inglewood. Like me, she starts knowing nothing of the subject, but is bright, works hard and will soon catch up.

The PQ on rabies quarantine went very well, with soft queries and a lot of support for our reform proposals. Now we must make sure the risk assessment doesn't take too long. Next summer time will be tricky if fellow peers – and we – still cannot take the dogs on holiday abroad.

Went to National Gallery exhibition of wonderful Holbeins. Saw Allen Jones and admitted still haven't paid for his lovely painting of a jazz singer I recently bought. Took Sarah to supper with conductor Michael Tilson Thomas. Lots of chat about Chris Smith's new scheme to merge the ENO and Covent Garden Opera into the one building, with the ballet. We don't think it will work. Surely London, the world's greatest arts centre, can support two opera companies.

Michael was doing his homework for tomorrow's great LSO concert on the Mahler 7. I decide to go if I can.

Wednesday 5 November 1997

Early meeting of ministers. Discussed my PQ on organophosphates. Then animals, where poor Elliot Morley will now have to support the culling of the badgers he loves (they spread TB), and also cull minks. I suggest he shoots them all personally. Might take his mind off foxes. Also discussed the Covent Garden shambles – now clear the Opera House is bankrupt and will go into receivership within a fortnight. Wish we were in that department sorting it out.

Good meeting on the MAFF budget. Good papers. Jack put the pressure on them and got the organic provision trebled. My export expenditure increased. We flushed out lots of small items. Clear officials in MAFF never before subject to this kind of scrutiny on priorities.

Worked hectically on my briefing for today's much feared PQ on organophosphates. Then a crisis when No. 10 vetoes my intention to announce we have set up a co-ordinating inter-departmental committee of officials on OPs. Jack had done this to help me since we need more co-ordination if we are to avoid scandals like the Gulf War soldiers ill from their tent sprays.

I was furious and suspicious of who had set up No. 10 to veto it. Jack's private secretary said, 'The Prime Minister personally intervened to stop it.' I said, 'Balls, the PM does not get involved in that kind of minor issue. One of his officials is speaking in his name.' They said, 'Well, that is that.' I said, 'No, it bloody isn't. I am going to talk to No. 10.' So I phoned Liz Lloyd in the Policy Unit, who sounded shifty but promised to talk to Jonathan Powell and then came back to say OK. But then our officials wouldn't go ahead until they heard from the No. 10 Principal Private Secretary. Clearly turf wars. Officials trying to snub No. 10 politicos.

So I said I would go ahead anyway. But it gave an odd picture of No. 10. Clearly the private office there is fighting battles with Jonathan Powell and the Policy Unit – refusing to accept their decisions and insisting they have a right of veto also.

Denis Carter later confirmed that Downing Street is often like this now. It's not like the old vertical clearly-structured Prime Minister's office. It's very presidential, with all the aides competing for Blair's ear, and each claiming to speak for him, with others dissenting, when in fact the PM knows nothing of it. I recalled what Robin Butler said about Blair not having a taste for detail – that allows all the aides to move in and handle the detail on his behalf. The clear areas of overlap and conflict are between Jonathan Powell and the Principal Private Secretary, as they are both doing the same job.

So I was able to announce the new committee and got a very warm reception from Lady Marr and some others. My officials – who are now very much in 'positive mode' – were pleased. Thank God I fought that battle. But that is the advantage of having been inside No. 10. I suppose most other junior ministers would be reluctant to argue with the top, and would believe it actually was the PM who had vetoed it.

At 6.15 pm Alastair Campbell came in with some official to discuss the Government Information Service. Following all the complaints, they are going round to each department to discuss the situation with ministers. Jack was very severe, pointing out their lack of creativity or forward thinking, making clear we don't want politicisation of information, nor spin, just able people who can project the department in its new image. He was savage at times. So was I. When I finished, Alastair said, 'Bernard must have made some enemies 20 years ago.' (Certainly Marcia.) It was useful and left us convinced we needed a different information set up. Jack as good as said he would bring in an outsider.

Thursday 6 November 1997

Went in to interview a prospective press officer, who seemed suitably alive. Off to the old National Liberal Club to give a speech to the Meat and Livestock people. Went well. Peter had written an excellent text. Went to the Barbican with Corinne Laurie to hear Michael Tilson Thomas conduct a stunning Mahler show, though my brain was so tired I often lost the thread. Saw a lot of old friends from the orchestra and discussed Covent Garden shambles with brilliant LSO boss Clive Gillinson. Then home, wanting only sleep.

Friday 7 November 1997

Home till collected for a lunch speech at the Aubergine restaurant in favour of eating fruit and veg. Fun, with rugby player Jeremy Guscott, broadcasters Jill Dando and Des Lynam, and other stars. I made a serious speech full of support to the cause and they appreciated that. Afterwards Maggie took me to the country where I launched at red boxes.

Sunday 9 November 1997

Papers full of so-called sleaze about Tessa Jowell and her husband in relation to her allegedly excluding car racing from the ban on tobacco advertising. David is a solicitor acting for the racing companies. In fact ludicrous to suggest she would change her anti-smoking policy because of him. In fact, Blair vetoed it – because of Labour getting money from the industry.

Monday 10 November 1997

There was a pathetic letter from No. 10 about last week's Lady Marr PQ on OPs. From the Principal Private Secretary still bruised from me turning him over. Clearly things are in a bit of a mess there and the regulars are fighting turf battles with the politicos – so when Jonathan Powell and Liz Lloyd said I could go ahead, the PPS went into a sulk, declined to confirm it till the last moment, and now is trying to change it. Jack's private secretary said the Downing Street PPS, Angus Lapsley, is 'a bruised and wounded animal'.

The scandal of the motor racing industry's donations to Labour and Blair's U-turn on our cigarette advertising policy rumbles on. Being badly handled. Always having the information dragged out of us. Too inexperienced. The tactics of Opposition don't work in government. Also bizarre that the PM was allowed to meet dodgy donors – without minutes taken so no record to prove what he did and didn't say. I watch amused. But sorry for Tessa Jowell who is dragged into this as the Health Minister who announced that motor racing is exempt from the smoking advert ban – though she opposed the exemption and was overruled by Blair. But her husband David is involved by association with the racing people. The millions on offer as political gifts are breath-taking. Harold and Marcia used to do a lot for £5000 for the party – or for someone.

Tuesday 11 November 1997

Started with meeting with the bacon and cheese traders. Try to get them involved in cheese exports. Lunch with the Royal Horticultural society. Friendly but they are not very on the ball. Walked back to the Lords for three-line whip. On the way called in on my new room in Noble House, Smith Square. Looked very smart.

Came home around 6.00 pm and dropped in at a reception in the Irish Club in Eaton Square. To launch a book on Roger Casement's diaries. Don't know why I was invited. Knew nobody there except the Duke of Norfolk. He told me about his time as an army officer in Kenya. He loathed the white settlers for their racism. A decent – Catholic – man.

Wednesday 12 November 1997

Started morning with super meeting with my new press lady, Natalie, with Cathy McGlynn and Peter Grimley. Planned our future speech programme and media coverage. These are all working positively together and I am happy with the whole team now. But had to get rid of three out of four. They are doing an excellent job. Makes me look forward to staying on more in the job.

Afterwards I kept Cathy, Jack's political adviser, behind. She has been looking sad lately, because of being cut out by the department. I said I would continue to use her. She is very fond of Jack and they have worked together five years. But she is aware that, like most of us, he doesn't always like grasping nettles so he delays difficult issues till the last moment.

Quick lunch at the Lords. Chatted with Joyce Anelay, my Tory opposite. We agree on how to handle the PQs in the weeks ahead. Back to the office to work on the evening's talk – to the Agricultural Forum of the top people in farming and food. The talk went quite well, for two hours with questions. Peter Grimley said it was my best presentation so far, as I seemed more relaxed.

Dash home to change for dinner with Angus Ogilvy and Princess Alexandra at their St James's Palace flat. Angus told Sarah that he spends most of his time there, having been ill and with a bad back, while Alexandra is usually at home in Richmond.

It was a lovely occasion. I sat on Princess Alexandra's right and told her all about Father Flanagan; she is quite spiritual. Marcus Kimball was on her left and charmed her magnificently throughout. Patricia Rawlings was there looking very tired and almost grey from the heavy Opposition burden she has taken on. I asked her why she did it when there is no chance of being in power for 10 years. She sensibly said it kept her busy and interested and in the mainstream. I hope her cancer doesn't return.

After the ladies adjourned, Angus raised the issue of the Communist spy Anthony Blunt and who knew his treachery. Robert Armstrong said he did an enquiry as Cabinet secretary in 1980. He concluded that the Queen's private secretary knew (did the Queen?); but that Alec Douglas-Home as PM didn't. Robert also said that Marcia Falkender's friend Lord Kagan had regular meetings with a spy at the Russian embassy, a Lithuanian he thought. Robert was in good form and much more open about past secrecies than he usually is. He was very amused that I was a minister for agriculture, since he knew how little background I had for it. Lovely evening and dinner – nicely given for me.

Thursday 13 November 1997

Early meeting on next week's Agricultural Council. Brief chat with Jack before he went to Cabinet and agree he must make one last approach to Treasury for more money for poor hill farmers. Jeff was very critical of the Health ministers saying they were dithering on the Food Agency and might delay the White Paper and lose the Bill from the next session. That Frank Dobson and Tessa Jowell were 'incapable of taking more than one decision at a time and are paralysed by the tobacco issue'.

Met Jack back from Cabinet and he said nothing of importance now happens there, quite different from 20 years ago. All policy decisions are now taken by Blair and Brown outside of Cabinet. Did briefly discuss the still rum-bling tobacco scandal. He laughingly said, 'There is, of course, no connection whatsoever between our change of policy on the tobacco advertising and the £1 million pound donation.' There are rumours that racing tycoon Bernie Ecclestone also gave millions to the Tories and William Hague put him up for a knighthood.

I went to the Presidency Task Force Cabinet Committee. All pretty general and waffly. Robin Cook relaxed in the chair.

Quick lunch at the Lords then another boring front-bench meeting. Patricia Hollis and I decide to press Ivor to at least give us a report from the morning's Cabinet. Dash back for a good meeting on how we can link with Jacob Rothschild's lottery money to clean up our river system. Want to get lottery plus EU money and us (not useless Environment!) to co-ordinate it. I phone Jacob to say all looks good.

Had drinks with Denis Carter and Margaret Jay. All criticise Blair's handling of the tobacco advertising scandal. Denis said because of the presidential system. Too many comparisons with Clinton. Cannot imagine getting Jim Callaghan to meet dodgy donors for half an hour without a record. Margaret said her dad put it all down to inexperience. Denis said that he had to stop Michael (Lord) Levy using his Lords desk and phone for party fund-raising!

Then Ivor Richard came in. Said will report to us on the Cabinet but it didn't do anything worth reporting. Just useful for ministers to gossip and settle bilateral matters on the side. Ivor also told a story of David Owen in 1977, just after David had succeeded the late Anthony Crosland as foreign secretary. Ivor came over from the Brussels Commission to attend the memorial service of his friend and late colleague. Owen said, 'Who gave you permission to come to London? When I want you here I will tell you.'

Friday 14 November 1997

Set off for Cheltenham's country sports race meeting before 10.00 am and there by midday. Lovely displays of hunt beagles and a funny terrier race. Big lunch to raise money for country sports, with an auction that fetched over £80,000. It was a bit of a political risk for me to be there just ahead of the anti-hunting bill, but I don't care. No other politician from any side was present.

Lots of racing friends there and lots of decent country folk. It was their first autumn day out in tweeds, heavy hats and strong boots. That class is inde-structible. I admire them for dressing like their caricatures in the *Guardian* or

Tottering Gently in *Country Life*. They don't give a bugger what the politically correct phoneys think, and quite right.

In the evening to Terry Wogan for supper. Exhausted after Cheltenham with less than an hour to recover in between. But, as always, his food was superb and Terry in great amusing form.

Business lady Jennifer d'Abo told me a lovely story about the Duke of Marlborough (she has a cottage on his estate). Sunny is a bit unworldly and has been disabled by his classic under-privileged upbringing – great estate, distant mother, hateful father, brought up by nanny, boarding school and army; all meaning cannot handle ordinary people and especially women. But in fact I always enjoy meeting him and find him kind and modest. But a little out of touch for reasons given above, which are not his fault.

Anyway, one day he told Jennifer that he wanted to go to Covent Garden market. He is a horticulturist and had heard of Covent Garden and wanted to visit it. She said, 'Don't be silly, you wouldn't know how to dress for it.' He insisted and she said, 'Wear old trousers and jacket and a flat cap.' So they went. He told her he had problems getting old trousers and had to borrow some too big and showed her the safety pins holding them up. All went well. Then at the last stall he saw some garden produce he wanted and he ordered it. Of course, like the Royals, he didn't carry any money so she had to pay, but that was OK. The Cockney man asked where to send it. Sunny went pink and spluttered but then said, 'Blenheim Palace nurseries'. That was OK and the man said, 'I know them. Very nice. Often go in the morning. Have a fag and a cup of tea there. Often think "I wonder what that Dick the Duke is doing up in the great Palace. Port for breakfast, I suppose"' ... then, slowly looking up very worried, 'Oh bleedin' 'ell, it's 'im!' At that point, Sunny's safety pins gave way and his trousers fell down.

Sunday 16 November 1997

Newspapers still full of Formula One sleaze and now saying everyone, including David Sainsbury, whoever gave 4p to the Labour Party is guilty of getting policy decisions changed. Can see the press happy again. For six months they have been miserable, while the public enjoyed having a government they liked and respected, and journalists had to write facts, jokes or nothing. Now they are off the leash again; can insinuate that everybody in politics is as corrupt and sleazy as they are. I shall be afraid to tip a taxi driver 50p in case a journalist sees it and accuses me of bribing him.

Watched Blair on TV interviewed about the tobacco scandal by John Humphreys. I thought the PM was a bit like a hurt boy accused of stealing the biscuits. Too boy-scouty for my taste. I think the experience will be good for the New Labour boys and girls. They have walked on water for two years and came to believe in their own publicity. I always disliked the sanctimonious style in which they attacked the Tories.

Monday 17 November 1997

Wrote a little of this. Then read Waugh *Officers and Gentlemen*. Find it's crucial for my well-being that I do not spend all the time on policy documents. Literature and music still essential. There is a lovely piece in *Men at Arms* describing the relationship between the platoon commander and the sergeant in the Halberdiers Regiment:

'The normal relationship between platoon commander and sergeant was that of a child and nanny. The sergeant should keep his officer out of mischief. The officer's job was to sign things, to take the blame and quite simply to walk ahead and get shot first.'

For sergeant, read private secretary; and, for officer, read minister. Or Sir Humphrey and Jim Hacker in *Yes Minister*.

On to a fascinating Cabinet committee in Commons conference room. About Welsh devolution. Perpetual battle between Ron Davies, slippery Welsh secretary trying to steal more power for the inevitably corrupt Welsh Assembly, and Jack Straw, who ably opposes most of the nonsense. Brilliantly chaired by Derry Irvine, who really is of high calibre. Jack does his homework better than anyone else other than Derry in the Cabinet (the chief advantage of lawyers in politics!), is clinical in argument, and won most of the points. Derry managed to count the majorities for Jack, who I supported on every count. Kim Howell broke Welsh tribal ranks and supported Jack, saying all Welsh government was 'bound to be crooked'.

Walked out with Jack Straw.

Tuesday 18 November 1997

Meeting on complex Brussels working time directive issues. Momentarily understood them with guidance from a bright official, but the moment she left, the blank returned. By then I had signed an impressive letter on it to Margaret Beckett.

David North, Jack's private secretary, tells me we have another Formula One style problem, this time on the proposed Food Standards Agency. No. 10 has intervened to tell Tessa the new Agency must not cover nutrition. This is in response to pressures from the food industry – though in our national consultation everyone said it must include nutrition and we had said we agreed. (I am not upset on the issue, since I don't like the food fascists in the Department of Health telling everybody what they must or must not eat or smoke.) But politically it would be a disaster if once again poor Tessa had to do a U turn at the behest of Blair and the party contributors.

Wednesday 19 November 1997

Big speech in the morning on relations between agriculture and the environment to a seminar at the Dorchester with the King of Sweden present (talked to him several times but he seemed shy and distant).

Lords Questions didn't go too well. I felt tired and weak from missing lunch. Worst of all, I failed to answer Joyce Anelay's question from the Opposition front bench, despite the fact that she had told me beforehand what it would be. Felt dissatisfied with myself and low. Wrote Joyce a letter of apology.

Back to the office for a meeting with Andrew Higgins and the chief of the vets. Made progress towards persuading them to allow introduction of a lower layer of para-vets, to help us with the BSE and meat hygiene service work, where we are understaffed. They need to revise the whole education system for vets, which is out of date.

Jack grabbed me in the corridor to accompany him to a bilateral with Molterer the Austrian farm minister. The Austrian was small and sharp with a deep knowledge of the whole subject. They will have the Presidency after us and we planned how to co-ordinate overlaps.

Thursday 20 November 1997

Worked with Sarah's old friend Della, acting as my private secretary, on my private correspondence. Then to Whitehall Place office for the last time – move into Smith Square on Monday. Good meeting with Jeff and his officials on vitamin B6 ban. Taught me a lot I didn't know (not difficult). Afterwards, Jeff told me about his breakfast meeting with Jack, Tessa Jowell and Frank Dobson. To thrash out whether new Food Agency had a remit for nutrition. Intended all along and in previous statements. Now Mandelson has intervened on behalf of the food interests to say leave out nutrition – the food industry afraid of anything to do with health. This is Formula One all over again, with the industry that contributes money to the party appealing over ministers' heads to No. 10 to get policies reversed. And Tessa in the U turn role again, which would have really destroyed her credibility. Apparently Jack and Jeff won, saying don't change in response to the pressures; we are having a consultation anyway, so if you want to change, change after that. But it's all a bit worrying. Presidential government with the centre as a court of appeal for party contributors against ministers.

Then a good meeting with the pig association. Chivvy them for allowing huge Danish and Dutch bacon imports, when English bacon tastes better. The usual deficiency in marketing, as with apples. Then off to Hanslope, Bucks, near my birthplace in Ashton, to visit a farm with the Austrian farming minister Wilhelm Molterer. The usual cows and sheep and milking plant. Good opportunity for a photo but the department had characteristically forgotten to tell the press – probably the first time in history an EU farming minister was in Bucks, and the local press not told.

Friday 21 November 1997

Talked to the office where they are clearing out for the move to Smith Square later this afternoon. Feel no regrets at leaving 3 Whitehall Place, even though it's my first ministry. A drab concrete building, with an entrance like a sentry box, dirty walls and off-colour paint. Everywhere scruffy. Because no pride in the place, everyone demoralised.

Sunday 23 November 1997

Read more Waugh – clearly mocking poor Cyril Connolly, Auden and all the brave wartime literati who either abandoned England for the safe USA or escaped into the Army Education Service. After fighting in Crete, he had a right to feel like that.

Monday 24 November 1997

In my new room in Nobel House. Totally different atmosphere. Lifts my spirits when I go in.

Quick lunch at Lords and then PQ on vitamin B6, where we have limited the dose to 10 mg a day. Quite right in light of evidence of nerve damage. But the questioner, the Countess of Marr, understandably asks why we don't exercise the same caution on organophosphates. I said that I had conducted job from beginning on assumption she might be right on OPs – and said didn't wish to discourage her from pursuing questions. I am sure she is right. Peers came up after to congratulate me on my detailed knowledge of vitamins. Not until this morning! A lot of homework went into that, but it paid off.

Stuck in Lords rest of day and evening with a three-line whip that never happened as a vote. Had supper with Tessa Blackstone in Lords restaurant. She is a bit down because of the vindictive pieces about her in the press. Said she wept when she read vicious attacks in the *Standard* and the *Mail* on Sunday. She began to wonder if they were true about her. I reassured her; they tell you much about the journalists, nothing about her.

Talking of that, John Wakeham today moved an amendment to the Civil Rights Bill, trying to remove the right to privacy to please his newspaper proprietors. Derry Irvine was very good at handling him.

Chatted to Patricia Hollis, who is having a tough time at Pensions with the dire Harriet Harman as secretary of state. Harman has decided to cut pensions to the disabled to please her friend and sponsor Gordon Brown. Patricia has opposed this cut but has been overruled. Pat now hears that Harman's spin doctors are briefing the media that it's Patricia who has been proposing the cuts, so she gets the blame.

Tuesday 25 November 1997

Early to doctor for check-up on my debilitating diabetes (which perpetuates all infections). Rest of morning in my lovely new office, moving furniture etc. Total chaos in secretaries' office, computers not working, still clearing away the paint cans.

At 5.00 pm, gathered in the grand new conference room for an emergency meeting on BSE. Professor Patterson was there, the key man from the SEAC committee that advises us on BSE. Disaster. Fresh spread of the disease. Now found in the dorsal gangliform, the nervous system spreading out from the cow's spine into the meat. Means our existing measures to remove the spine not enough, must go wider. Very expensive and will ruin local butchers as huge extra costs.

Only affects the 4% of meat sold on the bone – T-bones, sirloins etc. Will have to be completely de-boned. And with the supervision of trained officers – which we don't have. But bigger worry is that if BSE is in this nerve then can spread throughout whole nervous system – and that casts doubt on safety of all beef. Decided to rule all beef must be de-boned for sale. Will kill lovely John King our village butcher.

At 6.00 pm, Jack organised a nice party for all the people who had worked on restoring the beautiful listed rooms in Nobel House – not just our rooms, but also several conference rooms. Very nice occasion. Jack made a gracious speech and they were all very pleased. One said to me that he had never 'felt so appreciated in the ministry'.

I made two suggestions to Jack: one that he should invite Jocelyn Stevens in to see the rooms so English Heritage might give us an award for restoring the Heritage (this will help head off Commons criticisms of the expense); and that we should let out the rooms for commercial events to raise money. He was enthusiastic.

Evening, excellent supper with Carnarvons. He has been to Melbourne as manager of the Queen's racehorse and is leading the cross-benchers on Lords reform. Arrange for him to meet Denis Carter and me to discuss it.

Wednesday 26 November 1997

Very full day. In early to the ministers' meeting. Jack mentioned my two suggestions on the refurbishment with approval. Packer said he 'didn't think much of them'. Also emerged that in the EU the Germans and others are reneging on the July decision to apply the same meat controls to them as to us. So Jack will put down ministerial orders before Xmas to ban the import of their beef.

We adjourned to Jack's room for a private ministerial meeting. Depressed by BSE developments. Also that the White Paper on the Food Standards Agency is still stuck; not only problems with Health, but also the Treasury now insisting the industry pays for all of it. But general morale good.

Back to my room for excellent meeting on future press and publicity. In the middle, my wonderful new Allen Jones painting arrived, brilliant reds and blues, of a jazz singer, head facing both ways, six feet high and fitting perfectly in the central panel. Pop art and classical Wedgwood background, a bit odd but it works, and the colours light up the room against the quiet blue and white. Staff were a bit shocked and nice Gerald, who camply serves my tea, looked quite nervous.

The Food From Britain people came in to discuss exports. Excellent. I set out my plans for boosting exports and they were enthusiastic. They are the key. A minister can do nothing except talk and exhort. Only works if there is a vehicle like them with funds and staff. By the end I felt things were beginning to move.

Off to annual *Spectator* lunch at the Savoy. Sat next to a new Tory MP, John Bercow from Buckingham, who is different, not a typical smooth Tory, more like a taxi driver and a strong Portillo supporter. Like him. The peers awards went to the Countess of Marr, to my delight, as suggested her to Frank Johnson last year. Frank was very funny, but most funny was the Labour backbencher award winner, a barrister in his fifties with a double-barrel name. Hilarious. His name was apparently on Mandelson's list of 41 'dangerous' backbenchers.

He said he knew of colleagues who were near suicidal, phoning up Mandelson, quoting implausible dubious backgrounds such as Fabian membership, and begging to be on the list of Mandy's dangerous backbenchers, saying their careers would be ruined in the party and the constituency unless they could claim to be on the 'unsound' list.

But Tory right-winger Redwood was dreadful and ungracious as the 'Questioner' winner. Arrogant and unpleasant to his opponents. Virtually no applause – and no future on that performance. Jim Callaghan was superb as 'Statesman of the Year'. Said he knew how to win it. 'Just shut up, say nothing, and people will think you are wise.' He felt 'young Ted Heath' was finally beginning to qualify.

Had to rush back to meet the Lithuanian agriculture minister – bright and lively – but annoyed they are left out of the first wave for accession to the EU; the Estonians are given a better chance. Asked me to visit. May do, but not in freezing January.

Then a stunning meeting on dog quarantine and rabies. Jack yesterday announced the advisory committee of independent experts to advise us on change. He had just received a fax from a trusted vet friend pointing out that the only vet on the committee drawn up by our officials is an 'implacable' enemy of change and defender of the status quo. We had been 'set up', as Jack said. The department had sent a list of recommended names with this man, with no comment on his having known views; just said he was a distinguished vet and a former president of some great veterinary body. Ministers cannot be expected to know who all these vets are. I had met few vets in my life until a few months ago. We ministers stood around discussing this, aghast, as the chairman of the committee, Professor Kennedy, filed in to discuss how his committee worked. I pressed Jack to get rid of the rogue vet, otherwise the committee would be written off by reformers as having been set up to protect the status quo.

Jack brought it to a quick end and then had a face-to-face meeting with Kennedy, which he told me about shortly after. They agreed they had been 'set up' and that, in principle, they would try to get the vet off the committee, though the alternative was to put two independents on to counter him. Jack was furious and the department officials were scuttling around trying to cover up. The atmosphere was electric. This was the old MAFF – straight *Yes Minister*. No change of building can alter that.

I saw Jack at 6.30 pm and we had a glass of whisky together. Agreed Packer must go. Jack reluctant on that previously, but now convinced by this disaster. The department will never change its devious ways while he is at the top.

Ironically I was due to attend the annual party of the Royal College of Vets. On the way in I met my only old vet friend, Andrew Higgins, and he immediately said, 'In there they all say you have been stitched up.' I asked him for a list of better names. Then into the party where Lawson Soulsby, top Lords vet, shouted, 'You have been stitched up.' Another said, 'This is so blatant, it must have been done to humiliate you.' Packer lurked in the background, watching nervously as I talked to them.

Afterwards I went home to prepare for the Michael Portillo dinner, but first wrote a note to Jack and sent it 'For his eyes only' with my driver to the Commons reporting this reaction. Maggie also told me that Prescott's driver has resigned – the second such departure since May – because 'He is a lunatic'.

Portillo dinner was terrific. First we met at Michael's house in Victoria. With Clemency Ames, who was his and Sarah's late husband Tony Berry's secretary (Michael replaced Tony in Enfield) and whose 60th birthday it was; also Michael's wife. Dinner at the Goring. Michael sat me opposite him and we talked politics. He thought Redwood was appalling today at the *Spectator* lunch. He obviously thinks Hague is nice but hopeless politically. I like and respect Michael very much. Told him he shifted too far to the left in his conference speech; as a Tory, he must not abandon basic Tory values, which are majority values. The last government wasn't defeated as a rejection of those values, but because they had abandoned those values and Blair had hijacked them. Told him about the vets saga and he said, 'Join the club. I had experiences at Defence where officials lied through their teeth to me.'

Thursday 27 November 1997

Started badly. Doctor phoned to say my medical findings were bad – diabetes ratings doubled. He said I would have to go on drugs. I said, 'Let's have one more go and I will try to give up alcohol and sweet desserts.' Chocolate will be more difficult.

After front bench, had a chat with Jack about vets. His private secretary came in and argued for keeping the man on the committee. I argued against and Jack instructed him to take my view, saying, 'It's tough, but the cleanest way.' Not a question of the MAFF conspiracy, but restoring the credibility of the committee. May have to appoint new vets.

Then off to our first visit in six months to the NFU headquarters in Shaftesbury Avenue. I was late, stuck in traffic, and Jeff Rooker decided not to come as a gesture of political independence from them. Very serious and helpful dinner. Obviously the farmers are close to rebellion. This is a time of massive change for them. Huge structural adjustments in the industry. Huge adjustments in food safety. Both hostile to farmers but no alternative. Plus tight budget constraints and difficult EU background. Question is how to ease the pain. But why ease pain of change for farmers and not for miners, dockers, steelworkers etc. But we did realise we must help manage that change together and must work closer with NFU than so far on presentation. Jack quickly spotted that and promised to spend more time with them next year. Went on very late.

Friday 28 November 1997

Started gently and then sat down to write this. Took nearly three hours. So much is happening now. At least a lot which interests me.

Huge majority for banning hunting in the Commons today. But so there is for hanging. Doesn't mean we should do it.

Saturday 29 November 1997

I read the papers and had a good walk. Nasty piece in *The Times* attacking Helen Liddell as a lickspittle in Maxwell's crimes. In fact she opposed and irritated him to the point where he was on the point of sacking her when he went down. But that is a fact so of no interest to the journalist. I noticed a recommendation by Anthony Howard of Patricia Hollis's fine biog of Jennie Lee. My heart rose until he gave his reason: that it 'reduced the reputation of a Labour hero to tatters'. That is the optimum ambition of our journalists: to show that all successful people who have achieved something have feet of clay.

Sunday 30 November 1997

Complete red boxes and fax Jack and Jeff on need for tough action on quarantine – a terrible mealy mouthed paper from officials defending their vet recommendation.

Monday 1 December 1997

Wake up thinking that there are two approaches to running a government. One is to try to establish what are the appropriate policies and then see how best to implement them. The other is to find a policy that won't offend the big financial interests and then sell that to the party. The first is Old Labour;

the second current Downing Street. The present compromise is to allow departments to go well down the path of establishing, even announcing, the right policy. Then No. 10 is used as a court of final appeal by the big interests and it intervenes to reverse ministerial policy.

Arrived only just in time for a first meeting of our advisory group – with Andrew Graham, John Eatwell, Green fanatic Jonathon Porritt, a farmer and a couple of academic agricultural specialists. Jack was in good form in the chair. I brought Denis Carter, the only farmer in our government, along although the department had not invited him despite my request. The terms of reference were typically narrow, looking at only the agricultural aspects of CAP. Andrew intervened to broaden them to include the wider economy and the environment. It might do some good.

Tuesday 2 December 1997

Off at dawn to Kings Cross and then deep into East Anglia with snow on the ground to give a speech on arable farming. Good reception, but signs of an imminent farming revolt over declining incomes and prices and the whole farming squeeze. Back for lunch in the Lords then sat in on PQs. Stuck there by a three-line whip then back to MAFF for a meeting of ministers and officials on BSE. We have to ban meat on the bone because the BSE disease is in the ganglia and the marrow. In fact the risk is slight and affects only 5% of meat sold. But being advised of the danger we have to take action. Won't be popular. Jack to make statement tomorrow.

Jeff came to my room and discussed appointments to the veterinary products committee. He is trying to get new kinds of people but it's difficult to change the department's mind set. One bit of progress is that, under pressure from us, Packer has suggested we ask the advisory committees to be open to the public – to head off my suggestion to allow Lady Marr to be personally involved. They don't like her. I do. Jeff liked my Allen Jones painting.

To the Scottish Office to a whisky reception. Long chat with Adam Ingram from the Northern Ireland office. He sees my memos about Northern Ireland to No. 10, so obviously Jonathan Powell passes them on – part of the new policy of not leaving Mo Mowlam unaware.

The Turner prize dinner at the Tate was great fun. Sat with Candia McWilliam, novelist, previously married to various earls and famous people, and now a close friend of Mark Fisher. She said she'd been a girlfriend of Graham Greene, hoping to marry him, but it didn't work. Surprise, surprise, the relationship was destroyed by the intervention of ex-wife Sally. Interesting recurring pattern of behaviour here.

Next to Candia was a nice old mate, Peter Patterson, with whom I was now extremely angry. A year ago he wrote a rave review of the dreadful Bower TV programme on Maxwell, concluding it was time I told all I knew of his crimes. So I cut him dead at the table and declined his hand. He told Sarah he always admired me and was upset I cut him, with no idea why. She told me this, so I sought him out and gave him a rocket. He apologised, said he had no recollection of it, and we had a good gossip. Sarah is right it's best to get these resentments out of the way. I tend to let them fester, which is worse for me than the guilty party.

Good chat with Culture minister Chris Smith and his very engaging young friend Dorian. He is nervous of the Kaufman Report savaging the Royal Opera House, due out tomorrow. Chris and Dorian have been together in a lovely relationship for 10 years. It was shrewd to make it all public, otherwise the media would be mercilessly hounding them.

Wednesday 3 December 1997

The Greeks came in for a pretty low level CAP bilateral. I stayed because ministers were thin on the ground with only Jack and two officers. After 45 minutes of oranges and olive oil I passed Jack a note suggesting that he say he 'must' telephone the Prime Minister, if he wanted to escape to deal with BSE. He rose immediately, said he had to phone the PM and left. I have never had advice taken so fast. So I was left for another hour going through their tobacco and cotton regimes etc.

Their minister was quite open about the huge fraud in the Greek olive oil regime, and annoyed that the Spaniards are worse and won't agree to do anything about it.

Back to the department for a lively meeting with the Young Farmers. Pleased I today announced some quota changes that will help young farmers. These are the future, with no welfare mentality, and I enjoy helping them. Then dashed to the Commons to sit alone in the Lords gallery and support Jack's statement on the BSE beef ban. Hogg was good and generous in offering support. The Tories are basically stymied because we inherited this mess from them. But the media will attack us for having taken the hard choice.

Thursday 4 December 1997

Sat in quiet PQs and then home for Della to arrive to clear the correspondence I prepared this morning.

Evening to the annual Arco dinner at Claridges. This is the annual gathering of the London power elite, to hear a top American. Previously have heard Reagan and Colin Powell, very good. Tonight was Newt Gingrich, the Republican Speaker of the House. Very impressive, sharp, quick, funny, with a boastful vision of the future, in which America will lead the world alone because she will have weapons and information technology of such sophistication that no ally will keep up with her. Also strong defence of Anglo-American culture as leadership culture, rejecting the multicultural crap. Thatcher and Ken Clarke and other Tories were there and must have been made to think. I sat with Jean Trumpington and my old friend and ex-Washington ambassador Peter Jay. We had a good chat. Peter characteristically suggested we close down all farming.

Was a bit nervous using the official car to this non official dinner but then I noticed that all the permanent secretaries were using theirs. The biggest car was occupied by Charles Powell, who has clearly done well since leaving Mrs Thatcher.

Friday 5 December 1997

Home in the morning clearing another box, second in 24 hours and did another this afternoon, and another in the evening. Late to bed.

The *Evening Standard* today carried a story that a professor from Edinburgh had written to MAFF protesting that the vet on our quarantine committee is biased. So it's out. I phone Peter and tell him to get officials moving on getting the independent vet on board. Angry. Knew this would happen. They should have done this days ago instead of writing endless memos justifying their mistake.

Saturday 6 December 1997

Collected Stephen from the railway station and then early to Sandown for a full day's racing. Lunch at table with Robin Cook and his new lady. Also sat with Douglas Wass, now chairman at Nomura UK. We gossiped about the old days when he ran the Treasury 20 years ago.

Sunday 7 December 1997

Main story in the newspapers is Geoffrey Robinson and all his offshore trusts, working as Treasury minister when Gordon Brown has said we will stop the offshore tax avoidance. Looks a bit uncomfortable for Geoffrey; though both

Blair and Brown have enjoyed his Italian hospitality, so they will find it difficult to abandon him.

Actually much worse is the new savings policy he announced – Labour's
ISA personal savings plan. Complete botch. Low ceiling and giving the
new small plans to all the same crooks in the insurance sales industry who
mis-sold pensions. A great opportunity missed. We could have offered cheap
and simple savings, through the post offices and the supermarkets, just simple
cash, fixed interest or index-linked equity schemes.

Nice pre-lunch party in Sonning, where the local Tory MP, Theresa May,
was jubilant at Labour's troubles. I told her that there are no troubles worse
than just being in Opposition.

Monday 8 December 1997

After lunch dashed to London for a good meeting on OPs with Lady Marr
and some others. Jack was good and reassuring; and fortunate to be well
positioned by the work Jeff and I had done to reposition MAFF on this
issue. The group were wary and suspicious but had to admit there had been
a big change with the new government. It emerged there are 20,000 farmers
dipping sheep with OPs; only 13,000 have certificates of competence. The
basic problem is that the farmers refuse to use them safely. But Jeff and
I agree that is not the point; we should not license these poisons unless they
are easily used; it's not enough to say that they are safe providing you use
them wearing a space suit.

Home and dashed out again to dinner with Michael Bedford and Deborah
at Marks Club, where Sarah is a life member; very elegant and delicious food.
On to Annabel's, Sarah also a life member, and we had a lovely dance.

Tuesday 9 December 1997

Heavy but interesting day. Big and good meeting on genetically modified
crops. I asked for the meeting with Jeff to sort out our general approach on
this. Becomes clear that the Green opposition is mainly based on emotive
exaggerations and even lies. No scientific basis. Next a meeting with
the Horticultural Export Bureau. Nice lot. But our horticultural exports
terrible – only 5%. So I told them to have a target of double that; or we might
question their grant.

Lunch with young *Telegraph* journalist, Rachel Sylvester. Interested in
serious issues and I will help her. Dashed back for a pre-Presidency bilateral
with Agricultural Commissioner Fischler in Jack's room. Very interesting.

Fischler is a basically good man, though always under pressure from the Germans and a weak President in Santer. Became clear that the latter two and the French are trying to undermine our presidency. Are putting all our proposed CAP reforms into one basket and saying discuss none until all are ready. This is a way to delay it all and means we cannot get to work from the beginning on the most promising. We won't now have even the earliest and easiest measures until half way through the Presidency. Will have to start with all the Mediterranean measures – oranges, olive oil, tobacco – none of which is central to our interests. Jack spotted this immediately but there is little Fischler can do to help.

Discussed the delays in implementing beef controls throughout Europe. They are passionate to impose these on us in the UK but refuse to do it in their own countries. Jack insists they must and he will lay orders in the New Year to ban them if they don't. Fischler admits that the EU vets committee is 'in a mess', still delaying on allowing our clean certified herds after nine months, always raising new questions when we answer the old ones. Come to understand some of the impatience of the Eurosceptics.

Depressed about whether we can make any progress at all in the EU Presidency. The working groups will bog it down. So we have to get our seven agricultural reform issues into the higher levels above the Agricultural Council.

Hung around in the Lords waiting for the vote, which as usual didn't come. Thought of Woodrow Wyatt who died yesterday. An old rogue, but we always had fun together at the races and in the Lords and I shall miss him. First met him in 1965 in Bill Rodgers's or George Brown's office when Woodrow was a rebel against Labour's then foolish plans for steel nationalisation.

Saw Tessa Blackstone, very angry with Gerald Kaufman. His select committee report on Covent Garden is characteristically waspish, full of spite and good tabloid headlines, which is Gerald's true metier. She says it's also full of lies, and they would sue but for parliamentary privilege. But I still think the old Covent Garden gang were an incompetent bunch who ran it as their own private club, with the poor taxpayer subsidising their pleasures.

Annual BBC Christmas drinks party at Broadcasting House. All the usual suspects were there, but more Labour and fewer Tories than hitherto. Heseltine was there and we had a good laugh about me being at Agriculture and his gardening magazines writing about me – the old lion looked sad at being deprived from office and said, 'There is nothing like being a minister.' Chatted with Mary Allen of the Opera House who looked very battered by the crisis and the recent Commons report on them and said if Gerald Kaufman arrived she would throw her drink over him (he prudently stayed away, or the BBC with unusual taste, didn't invite him).

Had longer chat with Alastair Campbell. Told him about quarantine, and that Packer should be moved (he said, 'I thought he had been.'). On tobacco advertising on racing cars, he said he had written a paper for Blair saying that once the Ecclestone donation had emerged, they should have revealed everything and had one very bad newspaper day, instead of having it dragged out over seven bad days. BBC Chairman Christopher Bland came up to say hello with a nervous smile (an executive from the old Maxwell Corporation has apparently successfully sued the BBC over that same Bower Maxwell programme). Wasn't there very long but did a lot of useful networking.

Wednesday 10 December 1997

Exciting ministerial meeting. Jack just returned from the Treasury where he (plus the other territorial ministers) had just won £100 million to help the riotous farmers who are under the cosh from all directions and blocking the ports. I'm worried that it looks like giving in to violence and especially as it comes on the day we have a huge Commons revolt because the Treasury is taking £100 million from lone mothers. Put together, taking from poor mothers to give to the cosseted farmers will not look good. But Jack is pleased to have screwed the Treasury at last. He hopes to make a statement quickly, which means I will have to repeat it in the Lords.

Adjourning to his room without officials he says this must be the last one-off bail-out for farmers. Must restructure the agricultural industry. Now too many people living at the margin, so the moment there is an economic squeeze they are unviable and expect to be rescued. They should leave the business, as would happen in any other industry. That is our long term strategy. But in the short term we have to ease the pressure and help those, like the decent hill farmers, who work hard and are really suffering. Labour should always support them.

Liz Lloyd was there from the Downing Street Policy Unit and we raise with her the future of the department after we lose food safety, which is about a quarter of our staff. Press the case for us taking the countryside aspects from Environment. She came to my room after and said we must put up a strategy paper on this and she will give support. We must move quickly or they may close dear old MAFF and wrap up its remnants in incompetent Environment.

Lunch at the Lords with my old friend Professor George Jones from the LSE. Good gossip. He told me his Welsh farmer in laws had been instructed by the NFU to take part in the ports blockade. They are instructed on their computers by e-mail, taking it in turn. This at the same time as the NFU is publicly and officially denouncing the blockades!

Back for a meeting with Tesco, who are central to my food export schemes and regional foods. Made some good progress. Followed by a meeting with UKASTA (never did discover what it stands for). Decide must force these hundreds of trade associations to merge, since it takes all of a minister's time seeing them individually.

Thursday 11 December 1997

Briefing at home with official who has given me a huge awful file for today's question on banning beef on the bone. Then went to the office and Jeff Rooker dropped in to discuss appointments to advisory committees. He is fighting a long battle to break up the existing cosy establishment networks. Some are now threatening to resign if he puts on an Indian. Also officials are trying to subvert our schemes to put consumers on by having them described as mere 'observers'. I really like him; totally authentic. We work well together. He reminds me a bit of Joe Haines, but Birmingham instead of Bermondsey.

On quarantine, I saw another official's memo to Jack, describing those who had questioned the rogue vet's credentials as 'contemptible'. But they are slowly conceding my position and will appoint another balancing vet – hopefully my distinguished vet friend Andrew Higgins on my suggestion.

No lunch as I worked on my briefs for the BSE PQ. Fifty pages of it but nothing on lamb, which is bound to come up now the EU is threatening to ban that as well, which would cripple our industry. The question went really well, and Tories came up after and said it was 'polished'. Funnily, the department has now accepted that I don't use their file of questions at the despatch box, and today they didn't even include it in the file – just the single page of the formal first answer. In other words, they are saying, 'If that is how you want to play it, get on with it.' Fair enough. I prefer to do it without notes, so I can hone my answer to the actual question. Lamb, of course, dominated the questions.

Sarah and I went to the Racehorse Owners dinner and dance at the Hilton. We were on Peter Savill's table, with some nice people. Everyone is talking about and supporting Sheikh Mohammed's Gimcrack speech threatening to withdraw his horses from England and attacking Wakeham as unsuited to be BHB chairman. Peter Savill has a great strategy plan, but he says it's no use trying unless they can first get rid of 'the deadbeats like Wakeham'. Lovely racing politics!

Blair had the IRA into No. 10 today, Adams and McGuinness and various other unsavoury characters. But it's right. If it keeps them in the peace process – and splits the IRA. The Unionists don't seem to understand this. Not surprised if, like Michael Collins in the 1920s, Adams will one day get shot by his own nutters. They like doing murder more than anything else.

Friday 12 December 1997

Read the papers, had a good long walk and wrote this. Preparing for Monday in Brussels. Office now wants me to go early so I can host the UK official reception. Jack coming from the North and not there till just before the Council. A nuisance since it puts me in the rush hour traffic, but I shall enjoy going.

Sunday 14 December 1997

Spent all afternoon writing a memo to Gordon Brown about revising our proposal for an ISA savings account. What Geoffrey Robinson has produced misses a great opportunity to produce a cheap equity state savings scheme.

Monday 15 December 1997

Off to Brussels for my first Agricultural Council. Nearly missed the plane because of gridlock on the M4. Virgin plane scruffy and disgusting breakfast. Air travel is becoming a nightmare.

The Council started late and droned endlessly on. No one was listening. Just droning on reading prepared statements. Jack only intervened twice. Fischler was very good. The Austrians sitting next to me were very nice. The Germans not so nice. And the Spanish Appassionata was very frightening. Aggressive and all in black, like widow's weeds.

Sat there five hours till nearly 9.00 pm and then had pleasant supper at the hotel with Grimley. Jack had a formal dinner with other ministers and told them of his beef ban on their imports, which shocked them. Beef safety controls, apparently, are for only the British. The USA has just imposed a ban on all European beef. The EU will have to learn it stands, or falls, together on beef safety, they cannot load it all on the UK.

Waited in hotel bar for Jack till nearly midnight. David North, Jack's secretary, arrived first and was very open and brave, saying Packer 'must go'. Because he is responsible for MAFF's 'bunker mentality'. Also said some Tory ministers – especially Gummer – are very vulnerable in our BSE enquiry. Said Hogg was totally controlled by Packer. When they went to No. 10 about the beef crisis, Hogg would read out the brief Packer had given him, but once questions started, Packer would elbow him aside. North was there from the Cabinet Office. Said Major didn't respect Hogg and set up Tony Newton at the Duchy of Lancaster as an alternative minister of agriculture.

Jack is preparing his package of subsidies to hill farmers. Darling, chief secretary, agreed it last week, Brown tried to reverse it. With No. 10 wobbling in between.

One thing North did reveal was that Packer misled us when he said we could not target and cap our aid package, so hoping only poor farmers could get it. Packer said under EU rules everyone must get the same. North said that wasn't true, but department didn't want us to cap it to help poor farmers because officials are ideologically against so-called 'modulation'. So Jack and I said go ahead and cap it.

Tuesday 16 December 1997

In to the Council meeting. Late and desultory start but soon became interesting when discussing better conditions for transporting animals. North–South divide. North Europe supports better animal welfare, but broadly the South does not. The *Guardian* had a front piece on Jeff Rooker and me. Presumably from Geoff. Spelt my name wrongly as usual.

Back on midday plane. Bought a sandwich in Westminster and ate in my room. Cleared a lot of paper.

Our ministerial Christmas party was very nice with a lot of friends – Joe Haines got on well with Rooker (who he resembles, both being completely genuine), my sons, Jim Callaghan and several from the Lords. I pressed Liz Lloyd from No. 10 to insist on capping our aid package to the most needy farmers. Took her to David North to confirm we could do it. 'Yes; but it's undesirable', he said, repeating the department's official view. Ministers being ignored as usual. The farmers are behaving badly, jamming our phones and faxes, so bugger them.

Wednesday 17 December 1997

Morning ministers meeting. Press awful. Everyone attacking our beef bone ban, without acknowledging that without it the EU would never lift their beef export ban. Also the *Financial Times* said that Jack 'stormed out of the Agriculture Council'. Total balls.

Nice meeting with Denis Carter on exporting agricultural expertise. Problem is how to take it forward in MAFF. It has taken them three months to fix this first meeting; and the department has contributed nothing. I simply cannot do it all myself.

Then a good meeting on school milk with Tessa Jowell and Estelle Morris. Health is opposed and had tried to call the meeting off saying Tessa was not available. But I went ahead and of course her diary was free. Had a private talk with Tessa and Estelle before officials arrived and got it on course. I will bid for some money – for fruit as well as milk. Must get something for the kids. Though the food fascists in Health are opposed to milk because it contains fat, as if there is a problem of these kids getting too much cholesterol!

Took my staff off for Xmas lunch at the dear old Gay Hussar. Not like the old days. Nobody there I knew; no politicos or journalists – since the latter have moved to Canary Wharf and had their expenses cut. And us upstairs – never been there before. But still the same old waiters remembering and chatting to me, the same decor, same Hungarian bean soup, goose and summer fruit pudding. So I enjoyed it and think the staff did.

Meeting on promoting cheese, then another party, this time the official department one. Full of farming clients. A few friends – Mike Buswell from Towcester. Spent my time buzzing around finding about our financial aid package helping farmers, still maybe tomorrow, Friday or Monday. Officials have persuaded Jack not to cap the aid to devote it to poorer farmers. A mistake. He gives in to them too often; but it's exhausting always fighting them to try to get some politics into it. But when it goes wrong politically it will be we ministers who take the blame.

On BSE, Mike Adams of UKASTA told us that four years ago he went to the Tory minister and said that the cattle food was dangerous and should be banned, but he was shown the door. Mike Buswell did the same. Now it's suspected of being the source of devastating BSE.

The BSE enquiry will be announced with our package. Looks as if Whitehall has ensured the officials are protected, ministers not.

Maggie told me a nice story. Each year there are masses of Christmas presents for ministers and officials at our Brussels offices. There were huge cases for me there on Tuesday, though officials get most. The Whitehall problem is how to get them back to London. Hitherto they have sent a MAFF driver and car to collect. Last year Packer discovered and stamped on it – he is certainly not corrupt. So this year they have arranged to send Elliot Morley to tomorrow's Fishing Council by car across the channel, instead of flying as usual.

He doesn't know why. Then they can bring back their presents in the minister's car boot! They are certainly ingenious at solving the administrative problems that they consider to be the most important. This one could have gone into one of our *Yes Prime Minister* scripts.

Thursday 18 December 1997

Off to Northumberland. Jammed on M4 and almost missed the plane again; arrived sweating and irritable. Swirling wind and driving rain for the whole visit. Drove to Hexham market for a farming meeting and sandwich lunch. Couldn't see anything of the wild moors and hills. After to dreary Carlisle to visit the regional headquarters and give out prizes to some nice staff.

Back to a lovely hotel at Farmley. A working dinner with the industry went very well and the regional officer was pleased.

Friday 19 December 1997

Off to see Farmers Union leader charming Don Curry's lovely hillside farm. Visited the heifers and steers, had coffee in his wonderful farm kitchen and interviewed by pleasant local press people. Then to Hexham racecourse. Always wanted to visit. Lovely site, simple like Towcester. But sadly the meeting cancelled: waterlogged. So I won't ever race there. After a nice lunch Don took us to Hadrian's Wall. Muddy and bleak but still worth it. Can see why the Romans went no further. Nor did I and drove back to Newcastle airport.

Saturday 20 December 1997

All my children plus my nieces, Tania and Nadia, and Sarah's Sasha and George, came for Xmas lunch at the Royal Oak in the village.

Exhausted afterwards. Still to do a huge red box and the Christmas cards, and revise the ISA memo to Gordon Brown.

Sunday 21 December 1997

Nice mass. Brief sermon. Father Flanagan revealed that his purpose in his sermons is 'not to make saints of you, but to keep you out of jail'.

Back to work more on my Brown memo on encouraging ISA savings. Had to redo it because Helen Liddell told me that, because of his bad eyesight, anything to him must be in capitals. She also didn't know his address. She says Treasury has great difficulty finding him sometimes.

Monday 22 December 1997

Worked more refining savings memo to Gordon Brown. Then up to London for lunch with David Montgomery. David in good form. Finding it difficult to expand the *Mirror*, a mature business with good cash flow but no growth. Needs to be taken over. He said the editor Andrew Marr is demoralised. Also his two Sundays are slipping, especially the *People*, and he will change the editors. The *Mirror* is doing better against the *Sun* – 'but Rupert won't allow that to go on for long'.

Discussed Ireland. (Blair told a friend that he has spent 40% of his time on Ireland since being PM.) My pre-election memo to Blair warned him that Ireland would dominate more than he realised – and that he would have to slay the Welfare dragon, which he has now bravely taken on. Welfare now costs more than schools, hospitals and police put together.

Back to the Commons to hear Jack's 3.30 pm statement on the compensation to beef farmers and the BSE Enquiry. But it didn't happen. He looked embarrassed and told the House that due to computer failure it was not ready. The Speaker suspended the House for 15 minutes and then moved on to the Education Bill. I went to Jack's room with Jeff. He was angry. The MAFF computers had broken down – probably especially designed for MAFF experience. But that wasn't the only reason. The Treasury had been arguing till after lunch refusing to give permission for the £109 million expenditure. It was a bad start.

Resumed again at 5.00 pm. Jack is commanding at the box, measured and severe without ever losing his cool. But we have had a bad week on beef; with the announcement delayed for days, and even our best friends unconvinced why we have to ban boned beef when the chances of CJD from it are billions to one. The answer is that it's the only way to convince the Europeans that our beef is totally safe. They have a gun to our head.

I was due to go to the Hollicks's for a party but failed to get there. Instead was pursuing Gordon Brown to give him my savings memo – didn't want to trust the officials who would have torpedoed it. Made lots of phone calls and finally talked to his efficient Commons secretary. She immediately invited me to his Xmas party in No. 11 at 7.30 pm and said, 'Give it to him then.' I went over and talked to him and gave him the memo. He said the only thing wrong with the proposed ISAs was 'the presentation'. I told him no. Hope he reads it. Have delayed sending copies to No. 10 so they won't contact him before he has time to read it. Also discussed welfare reform with him. Suggested limit child benefit to two children. He said he would think about that. Will have to come in the end. But may take a decade. We agree the Welfare debate is going wrong because it's emerging as a succession of cuts, to lone parents or disabled, when needs to be put in coherent intellectual framework, with the cuts following logically. I praised him on sticking to the Tory spending targets and thus saving big expenditures for pre-election.

Long chat with Frank Field and Kate Hoey; about No. 10. Told Frank that I know what it's like to have a woman in the office always trying to knife you (he's under constant attack from Harriet Harman and knew what I was saying). Sarah Macaulay, Gordon's nice PR girlfriend, who I knew back in my Kentish Town days, came over to talk. She must be valuable to Gordon, keeping him in touch with normal humanity.

Walked through to No. 12, the whips' office, which has lovely big rooms and walls covered with fine paintings. Talked with Murdoch Macleod about chief whips' secretaries – there have been only three: himself, Freddie Warren and Percy Harris. Went with Murdo and Treasury Chief Secretary, Alistair Darling, into the little office where in 1978 I last saw Freddie Warren, asleep like a bird at a desk surrounded with half-empty whisky bottles, and Freddie's girlfriend Dot came in (as described in my Callaghan Diaries). Didn't discuss farming with Alistair, who must have had enough of that with Jack.

Left for home, walking down Downing Street in the rain, as so often 20 years ago. Still gives me a kick.

Tuesday 23 December 1997

Woke in the middle of the night realising I must send a copy of my Gordon ISA memo to Geoffrey Robinson, since he's in charge and will rightly object to being bypassed. Also did scores of Xmas cards between 3.00 and 4.00 am. The new diabetic pills certainly make me less soggy. Spent morning with Della clearing letters and many more Xmas cards. Then to the Cafe Royal for lunch with Michael Bedford. Missed going to the Gay Hussar this Xmas, first time for decades, and decide to go in the New Year.

Michael came back to my office to see how lovely it is. I was the only department minister in at this late stage, as the officials pointed out, accusingly. I promised to go soon, but was the last to leave, the building empty like a morgue when I slipped away at 7.00 pm.

Did more Xmas cards and went to the Commons to catch the last reliable post in Britain before Christmas. Drove down to the country and gave Maggie the driver a present. Sarah took me out to the White Hart in the village for supper, the pub all decorated and with a blazing log fire and carols over the music system. So I finally realised Christmas has come, even though no sign of snow.

Wednesday 24 December 1997

Rose slowly. Talked on phone to Celia and Tom Read about arrangements for our Madeira holiday on Saturday.

Am very aware how for the first time I feel happy at Christmas. Previously I always had waves of sadness about my childhood, often got sick, and sometimes felt almost clinically depressed. This time very happy, the past finally buried. Mainly because very happy with Sarah and also loving the job.

Nasty anonymous piece in the *Mail* saying the DTI must publish the Maxwell Report as soon as possible because Helen Liddell and I are now in the government and are the main people denounced in it. Possibly by the obsessive and inaccurate Bower. Pathetic. Helen was not really involved in the Inquiry and I have already read the draft small reference to me, which is fairly harmless (and I was not even called as a witness in the Maxwell sons' trial). But I feel untouched by it. My personal happiness is a protective coat.

Lovely midnight mass at Twyford.

Christmas Day, 25 December 1997

Woke at 9.00 am and opened the lovely Christmas stocking beside my bed, with lots of practical presents from Sarah. Spent afternoon reading travel books on Madeira for my coming holiday there. Sounds fascinating. Really a lovely day, everybody in great form and some beautiful music on the radio. All my children phoned in turn from Norfolk in the morning; they had better weather there. Nice they go to keep their mother Carol company. In bed at midnight.

Friday 26 December 1997

Quiet Boxing Day. Walked in the morning. Read in afternoon.

Saturday 27 December 1997–Saturday 3 January 1998 (Madeira)

Not a bad flight to Madeira, though the food was the most disgusting in my 40 years flying. My expectations of Madeira not too high, since I think of it as an old person's home. In fact beautiful island and Funchal a pretty town, like in Italy, with terrific cheap restaurants and wonderful grilled fish. Our hotel was superb and my room had lovely view over the sea.

Most days at first went walking in morning and came back to barbecued fish by the pool for late lunch, then slept and read till evening dinner with friends: Tom and Celia, who I have known 25 years since they lived nearby in Parliament Hill, and Margaret Callaghan/Jay and her attractive new husband Mike Adler, a top consultant on AIDS, whose Jewish parents were Jungians who escaped from Nazi Berlin just before the war. He got on with Celia who is a Freudian analyst. Lots of good gossip. Margaret told me many stories about Blair and about life at Ministry of Health.

On Monday we took a taxi up into the mountains and walked 13 kilometres beside the levadas, the water gulleys which cross the island. Wonderful views. Margaret told me how Jonathan Powell was responsible for the tobacco advertising farce and had treated Tessa Jowell badly, leaving her to carry the can. He tried to get Margaret involved with various drugs businessmen who were offering money to the party. She said there were other beetles in the woodwork but they hoped to cover them up.

Margaret says she has no political ambitions and doesn't expect to rise further – and will retire at the end of this Parliament to spend more time with Mike. She contrasted herself with Tessa Jowell, who is very ambitious and spends half her life cultivating the media. I agreed that we gang of peer ministers – Tessa Blackstone, Patricia Hollis, us – are in our last political jobs, so it's best to recognise that, don't take it too seriously, and enjoy it. Nowhere to go except out – and, in Margaret's case, run a quango, in mine, go to the races. She says Alan Milburn is brilliant at Health and would make a good secretary of state. Sadly Blair will be influenced by the press view; at least Harold wasn't, and, commendably, often enjoyed promoting people the press didn't like.

Margaret told me two nice red box stories. How Quintin Hailsham refused to read his boxes because he said it was 'better to be fresh than briefed' (I might agree and follow that). And that when they sent five boxes to Ken Clarke, he said to his driver, 'I will read one of them. You choose.'

Wednesday was cataclysmic. The most terrifying day of my life. Went on a frightening walk. Taxied high up and then followed a high levada. Fine at first, but we got lost, took wrong turns and, not knowing where or when it would end, I finished up, from my own foolish bad decisions, separated from the others and following a path a foot wide for miles above a precipice. I suffer from vertigo and became totally terrified. Had to get to the end so I marched for hours in the freezing levada water gully – at least there I didn't fall down the precipice. But, at times, had to get out and clamber over little bridges and under waterfalls, high in space.

The others had turned back in terror but I didn't know that. Gritted my teeth to get to the end. Finally, in early afternoon, after a couple of horrible hours, I reached a steep path down to a village below and arrived there, soaking wet, boots full of water, freezing and exhausted. And didn't know where the others were. Went to a cafe and had several coffees and whiskies, but they didn't have a phone. Finally found a lone lost taxi, which took me back to the hotel. There they told me Celia had phoned from the mountains. They thought I had fallen and had called in the mountain police, ropes, helicopters, the lot. I had to pay for that.

When Celia got through she was understandably angry and shocked with fear, having not known how to tell Sarah and my children that I was dead. I nearly was. Margaret was preparing to phone Blair. Never in my life had I been in so much danger, crawling like a fly, aged 63, along narrow ledges thousands of feet up. Hated it and will never go high again. I felt strange and shocked and angry with my foolishness for the rest of the day, hands trembling and legs like jelly. The rest were subdued.

After that I stayed the next two days at the hotel. My incipient sinus cold much worse after those hours with my feet in the cold water. No desire to risk the outside world, which seemed to me a most dangerous place. Sat on my balcony and read excellent John Keegan's book on naval battles.

New Year's eve was nicely done in the hotel restaurant, with superb food and dancing. But I was still stiff and tired and I went to bed early, falling asleep exactly at midnight. Realise I was lucky to be alive to see 1998. What will it hold? Will I still be a minister this time next year? Am enjoying it, but I won't mind if it comes to an end.

The plane back was inevitably hours late. Terrible gales. And then at Gatwick, 10.00 at night and freezing cold, I couldn't find my car keys. So I abandoned it and took a taxi. Welcomed by Sarah, Charles and Sasha and felt I was back in civilisation, watching *Match of the Day* and catching up on the newspapers till the early hours. Sasha made me a lovely hot toddy and Sarah found my car keys in my bag in their usual place. Will have to collect the Toyota next week. Rather feel I won't be taking any more dangerous expeditions without Sarah. Too old for all this nonsense.

Sunday 4 January 1998

Didn't go to mass, though I should have gone to give thanks for being alive. Just nice to be at home. Read the papers, though nothing in them, and slowly unpacked.

Main story all week about Jack Straw's son drug dealing. In fact, entrapped by a seedy *Mirror* journalist. Then they were all desperate to name him, even though that is against the law since he is only 17. They did in the end.

Against the PCC Code. Shows that is a farce. Self-regulation will never work because they won't let it get in the way of a nasty story.

Monday 5 January 1998

Chaos from gales throughout the country: floods and trees down, electricity cut. Yet it's good to be back in a warm house with Sarah and the children on the end of the telephone line. Also have to admit the pleasure of the sport on TV. Watched soccer and rugby all afternoon.

With the New Year launched, it's worth reflecting on how the government is doing. Certainly the happy post election euphoria of seven months ago has evaporated. Not just because a few small things have gone wrong. But there were several signs of things not being well handled. The lack of experience is really showing at the centre. The emphasis on presentation looks artificial: it works in opposition, but when in government people expect substance. The media is rightly resenting being spin-doctored and so is consequently sceptical.

Blair remains Teflon, untouched by anything that goes wrong, but the flaws in his style and character show through. His presidential style, insisting all decisions go through him, means he is isolated from his Cabinet, who feel excluded. That is fine while all goes well. But will become a liability when things go wrong. Then he will not have the collective support of his team. The liability will lie with him. Ministers will not rally to defend controversial policies in which they were not consulted or involved. This is particularly dangerous when the alternative sources of advice used are all so young and inexperienced.

No. 10 has become like the White House but without its experience. A presidential court, where lots of advisers compete for the king's ear, where decisions are taken on the hoof without the knowledge of relevant Cabinet colleagues, and which is used as a final court of appeal by vested interests who don't like the direction of departmental policy. It was clear from my organo-phosphates experience that the regular civil servants and the auxiliaries in No. 10 overlap and compete, squabbling in a way we never did in Downing Street in 1974–79.

They try to ignore Parliament, which is just possible with such a huge majority. But treating the Cabinet as a formal and dignified adjunct, like the modern Privy Council, without power and not involved in the serious policy decisions, is a political mistake. As is the abandonment of most Cabinet committees except those for specific big policy legislation, as with the con-stitutional issues. Those committees were useful ways of spotting land-mines early in our proposals, and getting Whitehall on side.

So it's the COLLECTIVITY of government that has been abandoned by Blair, in favour of a personalised, presidential system. At the top is the president who takes advice narrowly but not in a Whitehall structured way, which risks bad implementation. He also looks increasingly like a boy scout leader deeply resenting accusations that he is breaching the Scouts Code; saying too often, 'I am an honest man and you must believe me that I didn't touch the bottoms of any cubs.'

For myself, I am happy to go on at Agriculture, though my main pleasure is from being a MINISTER, wherever. I hope to continue for a while, though perhaps not right to the end of this year, Blair and God permitting. But if it comes to an end I have lots of books to read and racing to watch and Sarah and family to be with.

It would just be nice to observe more of this government from the inside and have another diary volume. My self interest is increasingly more as a diarist than as a politician. My first priority each weekend is to get all this written down from my voluminous daily notes; before I touch the red boxes. Whether they can be published does not interest me too much.

The presidency in the EU will be very interesting in the New Year, especially attending the Agricultural Council as minister. I hope to make some good Continental contacts and grasp how they think. Certainly they are very different from us. Although I am always a cultural 'European', I cannot believe that full membership of a closer integrated political and financial EU, which Brussels seeks, will ever have less downside than upside for us, especially financially. Yet to me, the UK doesn't have an alternative option to Europe as its closest partner. It is a no win situation, where we have no clear better option. We should make the best of it.

Later on this first Monday of January 1998, the skies brightened as the wind swept away the clouds and gave us some wintry sun.

Should be an interesting year facing me. After my horrific experience in Madeira, I am lucky to be here to enjoy life – and even to write a diary about it.

Index

Bernard Donoughue is referred to as BD throughout. Tony Blair is TB; Rupert Murdoch is RM and Jack Cunningham is JC.

Also by Bernard Donoughue

British Politics and the American Revolution: The Path to War, 1773–75

The People into Parliament: An Illustrated History of the Labour Party (with W. T. Rodgers)

Herbert Morrison: Portrait of a Politician (with G. W. Jones)

Prime Minister: Conduct of Policy under Harold Wilson and James Callaghan, 1974–79

The Heat of the Kitchen

Downing Street Diary Volume 1: With Harold Wilson in No. 10

Downing Street Diary Volume 2: With James Callaghan in No. 10